THE LEGEND OF THE MIDDLE AGES

THE LEGEND OF
THE MIDDLE AGES

Philosophical Explorations of
Medieval Christianity, Judaism, and Islam

RÉMI BRAGUE

Translated by Lydia G. Cochrane

The University of Chicago Press
Chicago & London

RÉMI BRAGUE is professor of philosophy at the Université Panthéon-Sorbonne (Paris I) and at the University of Munich. He is the author of several books, including *The Law of God: The Philosophical History of an Idea* (2007) and *The Wisdom of the World* (2003), both published by the University of Chicago Press.

LYDIA G. COCHRANE has translated a number of books for the Press, most recently Rémi Brague's *The Law of God: The Philosophical History of an Idea* (2007).

The University of Chicago Press, Chicago 60637
The University of Chicago Press, Ltd., London
© 2009 by The University of Chicago
All rights reserved. Published 2009
Printed in the United States of America

18 17 16 15 14 13 12 11 10 09   1 2 3 4 5

Originally published as *Au moyen du Moyen Âge: Philosophies médiévales en chrétienté, judaïsme et islam.* © Les Éditions de La Transparence 2006.

Published with the support of the National Center for the Book—French Ministry of Culture.
Ouvrage publiè avec le soutien du Centre national du livre—ministère français chargé de la culture.

ISBN-13: 978-0-226-07080-3 (cloth)
ISBN-10: 0-226-07080-8 (cloth)

Brague, Rémi, 1947–
    [Au moyen du Moyen Âge. English]
    The legend of the Middle Ages: philosophical explorations of medieval Christianity, Judaism, and Islam / Rémi Brague; translated by Lydia G. Cochrane.
        p.   cm.
    Includes bibliographical references (p.   ) and index.
    ISBN-13: 978-0-226-07080-3 (cloth: alk. paper)
    ISBN-10: 0-226-07080-8 (cloth: alk. paper) 1. Philosophy, Medieval. 2. Philosophy and religion—History—To 1500. I. Title.
    B721.B7213   2009
    189–dc22

                                                                            2008028720

♾ The paper used in this publication meets the minimum requirements of the American National Standard for Information Sciences—Permanence of Paper for Printed Library Materials, ANSI Z39.48-1992.

Contents ｝⧜˙˙

Preface

Most of the texts that make up this book have already been published in collective works or journals, as noted at the end of the volume. For the most part, they are recent in date, even though two or three were written in the early 1990s.

All of these texts have been reworked. The most recent available translations have been used, and I have revised my own translations. I have attempted to impose consistency among the references and eliminate repetitions or pare them down when they were unavoidable.

These articles start in the early years at the Université Panthéon-Sorbonne (Paris I), where, after the departure of M. Pierre Thillet in 1990, I was charged with teaching "Philosophy in the Arabic Language." I have taken that mandate in a broad sense, to include not only Muslim philosophers, but all who philosophized in the Arabic language—Jews such as Jehuda Halevi or Maimonides, and even such freethinkers as Razi. Moreover, I have emphasized a comparatist perspective: even if the authors to whom I introduce my students wrote in Arabic, I try never to lose sight of their Greek sources, nor what had been thought, was being thought, or was later going to be thought in Latin and Hebrew.

The same is true of this book. I have focused less on Christian, Jewish, or Muslim philosophers, taken separately, and more on the interactions between philosophical worlds. Those different worlds were faced with the same problems, and the solutions they gave to those problems are at times astonishingly similar, although often modulated on the basis of their authors' religion. At times they cast a furtive glance at one another. Finally, as a body, they transmit to each other both their common inheritance from the Greeks and their own philosophical acquisitions.

❖

I have chosen to begin with an interview. The false oral style proper to that literary genre may perhaps help the reader get a better grasp of the person who is speaking. The contents serve as a sort of overture, announcing themes that will be developed in the texts that follow.

After that I examine the common traits in medieval thought, then some of the themes running through that thought. Next I consider how certain central themes in the philosophical worlds of the Middle Ages differ from one another, and, finally, how those themes arose, the one from the others, as texts, problems, and concepts were exchanged.

❖

The title of this volume can be explained by a desire not to take the Middle Ages simply as an object, but rather to listen to it as a period of history that has something to teach us about ourselves. That stance is all the more necessary because we take ourselves to be "modern." Since the beginning of the period that adopted that title, the adjective has taken on an essentially negative connotation. "We are modern" in fact states, "We are no longer of the Middle Ages." The Middle Ages are thus the mirror in which we see ourselves.

In the age of the "Enlightenment" and of Positivism, that mirror was intended to remind us that we were handsome—or in any event less ugly than the grimacing caricature we were proud to have left behind us. With the early nineteenth century and in a parallel and equally subterranean fashion, that same mirror began to reflect the gilded image of a unified "Christianity" and an "organic society." It has now become the screen on which we project our dream of a future of "dialogue" and "conviviality."

It is hardly surprising, then, that legends abound about the Middle Ages. I have done my utmost to destroy that teeming vermin. The latter part of the present volume takes on that task. I have no illusions about the success of my venture: any fast-talking media star can do a thousand times more in one minute to perpetuate falsity than we library rats can do in ten lifetimes to unmask it. That said, you do not have to have hope to take on a challenge. And if what the "intellectual" has to sell is a "fine-talk" version of the dominant opinion, the duty of the university professor is above all to reestablish what he or she believes to be the truth, whether it is agreeable or not.

Whether anyone is listening no longer depends on him.

Paris, April 2006

Note: I have systematically chosen to use less pretentious, more common forms of names and terms, even if these are not the most rigorous versions of them. Thus we have: Muhammad, al-Kindi, Farabi, Avicenna, Averroes, Ibn Khaldūn, as well as *fatwa, jihād, sharia,* and so on.

Translator's Note

First and foremost, my deepest thanks to Rémi Brague for his invaluable assistance. He has corrected many errors in my translation and given me unfailing encouragement. If infelicities remain, they are mine, but there would have been many more of them without his help.

Quotations that are not credited in the notes as taken from an English-language publication are my translations from the French edition.

Any reader with a command of Arabic or Hebrew will smile at the Gallic lilt of the transliterations presented in the text, as they have been lifted shamelessly from the French edition.

Interview]℘··

With Christophe Cervellon and Kristell Trego

As a historian of medieval Christian, Jewish, and Muslim thought, how do you view the relationship between the three religions of the book and philosophical activity?[1] In particular, do you think there is a difference between theology and philosophy in Christianity, and between Kalām and falsafa *in Islam?*

There are many differences, but they are interconnected. On the one hand, there is a tension within each of those two religions between a theological pole and a philosophical pole. But there is also a vast gap between theology in Christianity and Kalām in Islam, and between philosophy in Christianity and in Islam, where it is called *falsafa*. Consequently, the tensions between those two poles are by no means produced or negotiated in the same way.

Institutionalized *Philosofia* and Private *Falsafa*

The major difference between philosophy and *falsafa* is perhaps social in nature; it resides in the word "institutionalization." In Islamic lands, *falsafa* remains a private affair, a matter for individuals in fairly restricted numbers. The great philosophers of Islam were amateurs, and they pursued philosophy during their leisure hours: Farabi was a musician, Avicenna a physician and a vizier, Averroes a judge. Avicenna did philosophy at night, surrounded by his disciples, after a normal workday. And he did not refuse a glass of wine to invigorate him a bit and keep him on his toes.[2] Similarly, among the Jews, Maimonides was a physician and a rabbinic judge, Gersonides was an astronomer (and astrologer), and so on. The great Jewish or Muslim philosophers attained the same summits as the great Christian Scholastics, but they were isolated and had little influence on society.

In medieval Europe, philosophy became a university course of studies and a pursuit that could provide a living. It also supported a mass of untenured, garden-variety "philosophy profs," few of whom have left their names in the manuals, even though we can exhume their courses, which we discover to be full of surprises. But these were the men who made it possible for philosophy to make a profound impact on the minds of the jurists, physicians, and others they taught, hence for it to become a factor in society.

This had an important effect on the relationship between philosophy and theology. You can be a perfectly competent rabbi or imam without ever having studied philosophy. In contrast, a philosophical background is a necessary part of the basic equipment of the Christian theologian. It has even been obligatory since the Lateran Council of 1215. In Christianity, the tension between philosophy and theology can be said to be vertical, setting apart people who had followed the same course of studies, given that all theologians began by studying philosophy. The two disciplines spoke the same language. In Islam, the tension between Kalām and *falsafa* was horizontal, distinguishing between specialists in different disciplines, all of whom contested the legitimacy of the other camp's methods.

Theology is a Christian specialty. To be sure, several religions developed stores of knowledge, at times of an extremely high degree of technicality and subtlety, concerning the adventures of the gods, regulating the cult due to them, and explaining their commandments, when such had been emitted. But "theology" as a rational exploration of the divine (according to Anselm's program) exists only in Christianity.

The Word and the Book

In the final analysis, this is true because of what permits a theology to exist—that is, because of the *logos* and its status in the various religions. Here I have to correct an expression in your question. You speak of the "three religions of the book." The expression has become current, but it is deceptive. First, because people often imagine that it translates the Arabic for "people of the book" (*ahl al-kitāb*), which is a technical term designating the religions that preceded Islam and whose adherents, because they possessed a holy book, had the right to a "protected" (*ahl al-dhimma*) juridical status that was recognized by the Muslim community. In that sense, the term excludes Islam itself. If, on the other hand, we take the term in the broader, non-technical, sense, it includes Islam.

But at that point we see that the expression conceals a second trap, symmetrical to the first: it implies that in these three religions, which do, in fact, have a book—as do other religions[3]—the contents of revelation would be that book. As it happens, however, in Judaism that content is the history of God with his people, whom he liberates and guides by giving them his Teaching (torah); In Christianity, it is the person of Christ, who, for Christians, is a concentrate of the previous experience of Israel. The written texts record that history, or, in the case of the Talmud, gather together the discussions of the scholars regarding the interpretation and application of the divine commandments. But in no way do those books constitute the actual message of God to humankind. It is only in Islam that the revealed object is the Book. In the final analysis, the only religion of the book is Islam!

Why does this matter? Because the very way in which the god speaks, the very style of his *logos*, decides how that *logos* can be elaborated. If the divine word is a law, it has to be explicated and applied with maximum precision. But that law says nothing about its source. If that divine word is a person—and, inversely, if that person is a word stating *who is* its emitter—that is one step toward a certain knowledge of God.

In your opinion, to what extent is Christianity indebted to Islam for its philosophical thought, and for its theological thought?

Let me begin by drawing an elementary distinction, without which we will bog down in endless misunderstandings. In French we can distinguish between "*islam*," a common noun written with a lowercase "i," which is the religion of an integral placing oneself (the meaning of the Arabic word) in the hands of God, and "Islam," a proper noun written with a capital "I," which denotes the civilization that is marked by "*islam*," the religion, but which has a long history and vast geography that include phenomena having little to do with religion. Similarly, English can distinguish between "Christianity" and "Christendom," and French between le *christianisme* (the religion) and la *chrétienté* (the area of civilization).

Debts?

What is the debt of le *christianisme* toward *islam*, the religion? Properly speaking, there is none, because Christian dogma had already crystallized well before the birth of Islam as a religion in the seventh century, and for even greater reason, well before that religion began to philosophize in the ninth century. That crystallization was the work of the series of great ecumenical councils, and it was from Greek philosophy that the Church Fathers borrowed their conceptual tools, while making profound changes in it. But that is another story.

What about the debt of la chrétienté—Christianity as an area of civilization—to Islam as a civilization? Here the debt is a real one, but unfortunately the topic has been overloaded with ideology. Moreover, legends abound. For example, is it true that the role of the Arabic heritage was ever forgotten?[4] Repeating it endlessly seems to echo publicity techniques for pushing a product that claims to refresh the memory of the West. We need to state who (scholars or "intellectuals") denied the importance of that heritage, when that occurred, and in what contexts. There has been a broad range of opinion on the topic. For example, in the eighteenth century Condillac minimized the role of Islam: "I don't know that we have any great obligation to the Arabs." A marginal insert in the same text is even more categorical: "They have hindered the progress of the human mind." In contrast, a generation later, Condorcet recognized that at least the Arabs had the merit of safeguarding and transmitting the heritage of the ancient world. Having made this admission, however, he adds a teleological representation that was later to flourish among such writers as Ernest Renan: "The work done by the Arabs would have been lost to the human race for ever if they had not done something to prepare the way for the more lasting revival which was brought about in the West."[5]

After the translations of the twelfth century, Scholasticism owed an enormous debt to Arabic thought. That debt primarily concerned Muslim authors such as Avicenna and Averroes, given that Farabi, the first true and perhaps the greatest Muslim philosopher (and whom the other two used constantly), was translated much less frequently. It also concerned Jewish authors such as Maimonides. Razi (Rhazes), whose radical criticism of prophecy situated him outside of Islam as a religion and outside of all revealed religion, was largely known only as a great physician (which indeed he was). The Scholastics had no trouble separating the philosophical contribution of a Muslim author from his religious affiliation. Duns Scotus, for example, states that Avicenna "mixed his religion, which was that of Muhammad, with the things of philosophy, and he said certain things as philosophical and proven by reason, and others as in conformity with his religion."[6]

Lack of Knowledge about Islam as a Religion

Islam as a religion remained poorly known in the Latin West. The Byzantine East knew it earlier and better. The Qur'an was translated into Latin only in the mid-twelfth century, at the urging of Peter the Venerable, the abbot of Cluny, but the translation had only a limited circulation. The prophetic traditions of the hadiths were almost unknown, except for the story of the Prophet's "night flight" to paradise, known as "Muhammad's Ladder" (in Latin, *Liber scale Machometi*), a work that had an enormous influence as late as Dante, but that represented only an extremely partial aspect of the entire corpus of the Hadith.[7]

As for Muslim "theology," it left little trace in Christian lands. Kalām was known, above all, through Maimonides' refutation of it in the first part of his *Guide for the Perplexed*. Its atomism and its occasionalism exerted an influence that was more philosophical than theological, in counterpoint to Aristotelian continuism. Those intent on demolishing it sought inspiration in Maimonides or in Ghazali, whom they recycled by adapting their ideas. Traces of the occasionalism of the Kalām can be found even in Malebranche and Berkeley.[8]

As for Averroes, his famous—perhaps too famous—*Fasl al-maqāl* was not printed until the nineteenth century, by a German Orientalist. The "theological" works of Averroes were known by such fifteenth-century Jews as Simon ben Zemah Duran and Elijah ben Moses Abba Delmedigo.[9] Still, if Duran's *Unveiling of Methods of Demonstration Regarding the Principles of Religion (Examen religionis)* was translated from Hebrew into Latin in the fifteenth century, no translation of the *Fasl al-maqāl* seems to have appeared.

Need of the Other

What seems to me to be essential, in any event, is to have done with a stupidly hydraulic representation of "influences" in which knowledge supposedly flows naturally from the summits to the plains. In reality, demand precedes offer. Translations are made because someone feels that a text contains things that people *need*. And it is that need that we have to explain. In this connection, the real intellectual revolution of Europe began well before the wave of translations in Toledo and elsewhere. This has been shown by the American jurist Harold J. Berman in his important book, *Law and Revolution: The Formation of the Western Legal Tradition*.[10] This work has finally—after twenty years—been translated into French, but unfortunately the major publishing houses (to their shame) have once again failed to rise to the occasion, leaving the book to a university publishing house that is courageous but with insufficient distribution resources and media support. The intellectual revolution this work describes dates from the rediscovery (better, the invention) of Roman law with the so-called "papal revolution" at the time of the investitures controversy in the late eleventh century. Reducing law to system required more refined tools, which meant that the West turned to the East, seeking out Aristotle's works on logic, along with which they received the rest of the Greek and Arabic heritage.

How do you imagine a harmonious coexistence among the three religions of the book, and is such a coexistence even possible, given that Christianity has never stopped presenting itself as the verus Israel, *and that Islam, as a religion, presented Muhammad as the key to the prophets? Should the latter notion be modified in the light of the works of Christoph Luxenberg, who claims that the Qur'an was not intended to replace the Bible, but rather to furnish a version of it intelligible to Arabs of the time?*

Let me begin by rectifying a small lapse or two, which seem interesting to me. First, the formula that states that the Church is *verus Israel* ("the true race of Israel") does not appear in the New Testament, but only in the Fathers of the Church, beginning with Justin.[11]

Judaism, Christianity, Islam

And after then, if the idea is accepted, how was it understood? Did it mean that the Church was to be *the* true Israel, which supposes that the Jewish people would no longer be so? Or did it mean that the Church is *one* true Israel, truly Israel, and that it is truly attached to the experience of the God of Israel, because it sees itself, so to speak, as the resuscitated body of a Jew?

Next, the Qur'an does not speak of Muhammad as the *key* to the prophets, but rather as their *seal* (33:40). In context, the meaning of that expression is not totally clear, but it was interpreted as signifying that the message of Muhammad sealed the preceding messages, both because it confirms their content and because it brings prophecy to a close. If there is a key, it does not open anything (even in the sense of a hermeneutic key—such as a "key to dreams"); it closes. Behind this thought there is a claim to return to the series of the prophetic revelations of the past and to end it—

a claim that Manes (or Mani, from whom we get the term "Manichaeism") had perhaps already made in the early third century.[12]

Christoph Luxenberg is just beginning to publish works to which I have tried to call the attention of a non-German-speaking public.[13] For the time being, they remain dryly philological. He attempts to show that certain obscure passages of the Qur'an can be explained by the Syriac and involve Christian hymns. According to him, the Qur'an is, at least in part, what its title means in Syriac—a "lectionary," or collection of biblical texts translated and adapted for liturgical use. I am not a specialist in this field, but this hypothesis seems extremely plausible, and its fertility speaks for it: many a mysterious passage becomes transparent. But we will have to wait for the true connoisseurs to give their opinions.

As for the problem of the basis for coexistence, you have put your finger on a fundamental difficulty. It contains a paradox: what is troublesome is not that any one religion finds another strange, but rather a certain manner of interpreting a real proximity. What exasperates Jews is that Christians claim to understand "their" book better than they do themselves. In similar fashion, what perplexes Christians—and why they often refuse to recognize Islam—is that Islam sees itself as a post-Christianity destined to replace that religion.

Recognizing or Refusing Filiation

For Islam, the survival of the Christian religion is an anachronism. Islam presents itself even as the true Christianity, given that, according to Islamic thought, Christians have disfigured the authentic Gospel, just as the Jews, for their part, have sold out the authentic Torah.[14] Thus it is out of the question to appeal to common Scripture. This means that, from the Muslim point of view, the "Islamo-Christian dialogue" is a dialogue between true Christians (that is, the Muslims themselves) and people who imagine themselves to be true Christians but are not. This is why dialogue interests Christians more than it does Muslims.

In order to improve awareness of religious and philosophical traditions other than Christianity, but also in order to increase knowledge of Christianity itself—all caricature aside—would it not be desirable for young teachers of philosophy, who today face a variety of publics, to have an opportunity in their course of studies to be initiated into medieval philosophy and into the complexity of intellectual and human relations among Jews, Christians, and Muslims? Is it normal, for example, that works such as Abelard's Dialogue between a

Philosopher, a Jew, and a Christian *or Jehuda Halevi's* Kuzari *be left out of the philosophical curriculum?*

You will not be surprised if I answer "yes" to your first question. I am simply pleading *pro domo* by doing so, because that is precisely what I have been trying to do with the students preparing their *maîtrise* for the fifteen years I have been at the Sorbonne. The examples you give of great medieval works are well chosen, but we might speak more generally about all of the thought of that age. It is a sad French specialty to have excluded the Middle Ages from its philosophical teaching, when the period is an integral part of the curriculum everywhere else, even in the United States, a creation of the modern age. In France both the *prof* and the average *potache* often jump right over eight hundred years in the history of thought, pausing for Plato (Aristotle, as the inspiration for Scholasticism, and Plotinus, as a "mystic," remaining somewhat suspect) and begin again at Descartes. I appreciate your mention of Abelard in this context. He is one of the greatest French philosophers, to be placed beside Descartes or Bergson.

The Middle Ages as Part of the Academic Program?

From another point of view, the works that you cite—two dialogues by authors who were contemporaries and could have known one another—are religious just as much as they are philosophical. Thus it is excusable not to put them on the program of studies. By contrast, there are treatises of Avicenna's (his *Psychology*, for example) or Abelard's (the *Ethics*) that are almost purely philosophical. And an out-and-out theologian like St. Thomas Aquinas includes in his *Summa theologica* treatises on the virtues, the passions, laws, and more, which are admirable for their philosophical depth and would make marvelous teaching texts.

Averroes has just been placed on the list of authors one of whose works may be presented at the oral examination for the *baccalauréat*. That fills me with a joy that is not unmixed. For one thing, I fear that Averroes might become the intellectual equivalent of the "nice, serviceable Arab" named by decree and supposed to be representative. But also, for very simple reasons, the text that will be studied can hardly be anything other than the *Fasl al-maqāl* (in French translation, *Discours décisif*), a work that is not overly technical and is available in paperback. The problem is that it represents only an infinitely small part of the vast production of Averroes, who wrote, among other things, a commentary on every one of Aristotle's works, and often two, at times three, commentaries. Paradoxically, it is in those commentaries that Averroes says what he would consider to be the truth. For him, in fact, Aristotle represented the summit of humanity— after Muhammad, of course. What Aristotle said was thus true, period, next paragraph. The *Decisive Discourse* is a work of circumstance in which Averroes defends the official doctrine of the Almohad sovereigns whom he served. Hence what is going to be taught as a "brief for tolerance" ended up being a call for the repression of his adversaries.[15]

Generally speaking, in your opinion to what extent do religious representations dictate how we interpret the world, and, more fundamentally, how we view the relations between humankind and the world? This is a theme that runs through-out your works, from Aristote et la question du monde *(1988) to* La Sagesse du monde *(1999) (*The Wisdom of the World, *2003)? In particular, do you think that the pagan representation of the world was fundamentally modified by monotheist revelations?*

If what we understand by a "representation of the world" is cosmography, a description of the way in which the stars, the earth and its parts, et cetera are made, those revelations did not change much. That was not their purpose. The sacred books return to the vision of the world commonly accepted at their time. Well before Giordano Bruno and—last but not least—Spinoza, John Philoponus had already remarked, in the mid-sixth century, that the Bible's only aim was to lead men to a knowledge of God and to a life that corresponded with that knowledge, not to discourse on physics.[16]

Polytheism?

Those revelations were not even exclusive to what we call "monotheism." Aristotle gives an astronomical and noetic version of them in book lambda of his *Metaphysics*. When you come down to it, has there ever been a genuine polytheism? Even Homer supposes a sort of fundamental unity of the divine that permits the gods to identify themselves as gods, even when they dwell far from one another (*Odyssey* 5.79ff.). What the revelations bring is, rather, the end of a "cosmotheism" that makes no radical distinction between the divine and the physical.[17]

What changes with the monotheisms is not the description of the physical universe and its articulations, but rather the way in which man expresses his sense of his own presence within that universe. In my *Wisdom of the World*, I began with four ideal-typical models: the "Timaeus" model (broadly speaking, the main current of ancient philosophy from Plato to Proclus, including the Stoics), Epicurus, "Abraham," and Gnosticism. Building on generally similar descriptions of the world, each of these proposes a different response to the question "What we are doing on this earth?" Are we imitating the beautiful order of the heavenly bodies; comfortably settling in on an island of humanity within an indifferent universe; drawing ourselves closer to the creator of a good world, but obeying his law or following his Son; or, finally, fleeing, not, as Mallarmé invites us, *là-bas*, but to on high, toward an alien God, escaping an imperfect or prison-like world? The ancient and medieval model, which held firm for a good millennium and a half, emerged out of a compromise between "Timaeus" and "Abraham." What interests me is not so much its description (even if I have had to pursue a description in some detail), but rather the problem posed by its disappearance with the modern age. It left us alone. Nothing in the physical world responds to man's ethical demands.

Cosmology as a Postulate

To be sure, for premodern man, the presence of the world, which he felt as a *kosmos*, was not a model to be imitated in any literal sense. Pretending to believe this to be the case is unfair, as it might be amusing to explain by the use of Kant's concepts. The role of the cosmic order is analogous to that of the postulates of practical reason. Those postulates—liberty, the existence of a just God, and the immortality of the soul—are of no use as a basis for moral law, which is sufficient unto itself and draws its obligation from an intrinsic authority that it has no need to borrow from elsewhere. Such postulates serve to guarantee the possibility of the supreme Good— that is, the agreement between what the Law demands and the order of the real world. One might say that the *kosmos* was less a model demanding conformity than an example that shows, from the simple fact that it exists, that ethical conduct is possible. The major difference between the premodern vision of the world and Kant's morality is that realization of the good is for Kant only postulated. It remains, so to speak, in the domain of faith and hope. For men of ancient and medieval times, on the other hand, the sovereignty of the good was already given in the cosmic harmony. One only need acknowledge it.

If it is true that monotheisms modified the "pagan" vision of the world, is it not also true that, in the final analysis, believing in God is, in a sense, refusing the world as it is and as it appears to an unprejudiced eye, with the result that ac-

cording to a logic of "communicating vases" (found, for example, in Nietzsche),
all that we take from God would be that much gained for the world?

It is true that I have had occasion to note in Nietzsche a fairly unso-
phisticated representation of the relationship between the divine and
the human according to which the one gains what the other loses. To be
sure, Nietzsche said many powerful things. But his writings contain a fully
worked-out version of the hydraulic image: "There is a lake which one
day refused to flow off and erected a dam where it had hitherto flowed
off: ever since, this lake has been rising higher and higher. Perhaps that
very renunciation will also lend us the strength to bear the renunciation
itself; perhaps man will rise ever higher when he once ceases to *flow out*
into a god."[18] This image already appears, discreetly, in the young Hegel,
and emphatically in Feuerbach. Today even more mediocre minds wallow
in the idea: man must demand his good, supposedly projected in God, and
so on. I would love to have someone explain to me the verb "to project,"
which everyone seems to understand.

The World, God, and Man

If the relationship between the world and God were of this sort, Prometheus (in the Romantic interpretation of that figure) would be right.
But how much naïveté does that imply! To begin with, man and God exchange homogeneous goods, in finite quantities, within the same system.
One of the first rules of theology, however, is that it is not in the same
sense that we attribute properties (justice, power, knowledge, etc.) to God
and to man. A bit of Neoplatonic therapy is called for: ideas do not *possess* the qualities that they confer. As well as a small dose of theology—I
mean, theologians' theology, not the variety knocked together by the *profs
de philo*. Let me offer you two phrases of Thomas Aquinas for your meditation: "To detract from the creature's perfection is to detract from the
perfection of the divine power"; "We do not wrong God unless we wrong
our own good."[19]

*To read your works, it seems that Kant's ultimate distinction between heter-
onomy and autonomy is fugitive, to say the least, given that your past works,
including* The Law of God, *seem to support the idea (or have we misunder-
stood you?) that man, if he renounces the law of God, seems necessarily to have
to admit the law of the world.*

The line of thought that you attribute to me is basically quite traditional: one can never escape from a law. The question is to know what

law. In abandoning a superior law, one falls under an inferior law. If you don't respect the laws of figure skating, you fall—if you will forgive the expression—under the strictures of the law of gravity. Similarly, renouncing the law of reason leads to submission to the laws of nature, and whether that nature reflects statics, biology, or psychology makes little difference. Kant places himself within that same tradition: he would say that if we renounce moral law, we must necessarily admit the law of penchants, which is the pathological. That concept is the Kantian version of the law of "my body's members" mentioned by St. Paul (Romans 7:23), which became, in the Middle Ages, the *fomes*, which we might amuse ourselves by translating etymologically as "that which foments." One is either subject or subjected.

As for the distinction between autonomy and heteronomy, Kant himself is much more nuanced than his followers. There is a tendency to read Kant's idea of autonomy in the light of the modern project of the emancipation of man and the domination of nature. Kant himself flirted with that tendency, for example, in the text of one of his admirers, which he reproduces in *The Conflict of the Faculties*.[20] It is even amusing that Kant, for whom the law is pure repression of the pathological, should be enrolled in the band of the emancipators!

The Law of God

Kant belongs within a tradition of the reduction of the law to an imperative that begins with Duns Scotus and William of Ockham, occurs in Marsilius of Padua, then in Suárez and Hobbes. The law of God was understood as an external commandment, not as the internal logic of created things. Andrew Ramsay, a student of Fénelon's, formulates the concept of law underlying the medieval vision of things thus: "The law in general is nothing else than the Rule which each Being ought to follow, in order to act according to his Nature."[21]

Can the wisdom of the world that the Greeks knew be opposed to the wisdom of God, given that the world and the revealed book—as claimed by medieval men (for example, the "Platonic" Alain de Lille or the Augustinian tradition that finds a cosmoclast representative in Bonaventure)—have one and the same author?

The image of the two books that must be reconciled is an old one and a good one. The wisdom of the world that I try to get at, which is, in fact, Greek, shares only a name with the "wisdom of this world" that St. Paul declares God has "turned into folly" (1 Corinthians 1:20). In the first case, we are speaking of the fine order of the physical universe; in the second, of human existence, when it wants to be cut off from God and claims to act according to its own logic.

One way to render intelligible the content of the medieval image of the books would be to take the idea of providence seriously. Not as it is too often imagined these days, as God putting himself in our place in order to grasp us by the suspenders. But rather as it was conceived by people of the Middle Ages. Someday I hope to write a book on the subject, for which I already have at least a title: À chacun selon ses besoins (To each according to his needs). The medieval conception of providence supposes a God who gives. And without expecting anything in return, for what would God need? He does not give something supplementary to things that are already made. His gift coincides with the very nature of each created thing, the nature that is granted to it.

Rethinking the Idea of Providence

God gives to every creature, according to its own nature, what it needs in order to attain the good. He does not take the place of the creature in making its good. And the higher on the scale from the mineral to the vegetal, the animal, and the human, the more God delegates; the more he grants the creature care of itself. When his providence is granted to man, it becomes, in a conscious play on words, prudence; not the simple fact of watching out for what lies ahead, but all of the practical wisdom that Aristotle called *phronesis*. This is where the wisdom of God and the wisdom of man come together.

We would like to put a somewhat provocative and outdated question to you: To what extent can an atheist be a good citizen, given the very strong connection between religion and politics (thinking, for example, of the gods of the City or Petrarch's reflections on the Crusade in the middle of the fourteenth century)?[22] *In order to think of the independence of the political from the religious, do we have to return—as Leo Strauss did, for example—to some sort of classical political philosophy?*

Outdated questions are always good ones if they are dated precisely. That is one of the lessons that we can draw from reading Strauss. What he writes about classical political thought, what is more, is a good deal more nuanced, not to say artificious, than what certain binary minds have made of it. In any event, one cannot reduce a work as subtle as *Natural Right and*

History to a brief for a return to antiquity. Without speaking of the rest of his oeuvre.

In *A Letter Concerning Toleration* (1689), John Locke preached in favor of a gentlemen's agreement among the English Protestant churches. He excluded the Catholics as agents of a foreign prince, the pope. He also excluded atheists. His reason might seem odd, but it is profound: atheists are incapable of swearing an oath, for *on what* could they swear? "Promises, covenants, and oaths, which are the bonds of human society, can have no hold upon an atheist. The taking away of God, although but even in thought, dissolves all."[23] We may smile at this, but when we do, we are like the "unbelievers" who laugh when Nietzsche's Madman announces the death of God to "those who do not believe in God."[24] In fact, though, behind the somewhat anecdotic question of oaths there lies the entire question of meaning.

A "City" of Atheists?

Let me recall that the Constitution of the French Republic (the fifth of that name, the one in vigor since 1958) cites the whole of the *Déclaration des droits de l'homme* of 1789, which states that the French people do all sorts of things "in presence of and under the auspices of the Supreme Being." The expression is not restricted to the anemic clock-maker God of the Enlightenment, but also designates the Christian God, as in Fénelon, for example. And no one finds that mention of God unacceptable. This means that the rights that are asserted are not fabricated, but acknowledged. The problem that arises for modern democracies is that what someone does can also be undone. What is merely conceded by men—"rights," a "dignity," and so on—can one day be taken back by those same men.

Bayle brilliantly transposed and reformulated an old paradox of Plutarch's: it is better to be atheist than superstitious. But he shifts Plutarch's psychological question to the political domain: the atheist is a more peaceful citizen than the superstitious man. If we accept Hobbes's thesis that the city of men is founded on the fear of death, religion is intrinsically dangerous. Nothing can stop the superstitious, who fear hell more than death. This is because, at base, the eighteenth century accepted Hobbes's premise that superstition invented "fanaticism" as a scarecrow. And it is as "fanatics" that inoffensive nuns were guillotined under the Revolution.

The problem remains pertinent today: on the one hand, just *what* can a suicide bomber be threatened with? On the other hand, if our most basic virtue, our "tolerance," can prevent us from killing, it remains to be proven that it suffices to give us a desire to live. I offer for your meditation a passage from Rousseau: "[The] principles [of the allegedly wise man] do not cause men to be killed, but *they prevent them from being born* by destroying the morals which cause them to multiply, by detaching them from their species, by reducing all their affections to a secret egoism as deadly to population as to virtue. Philosophic indifference resembles the tranquility of the state under despotism. It is the tranquility of death. It is more destructive than war itself."[25]

Is "Tolerance" Enough?

If the problem is to assure the peaceful coexistence of the members of a given society, or even to make sure that they enjoy the most equitable division of available resources, all we need to do is to negotiate a formula that will allow the maximization of advantages. And in order to do that, we have no need for any sort of transcendence. But this is true only for what we have become accustomed to calling (quite symptomatically) "society," a term that originated in economics. That society is, at base, the club of the persons present, who dispose of the ability to call in new members or to blackball them. The hitch is that humanity as an animal species is constantly losing individuals, and therefore cannot persist without replacing them by others who can be drawn only from within itself. Man is not only mortal but, as Hannah Arendt put it, "native." If we know what we are doing, why bring children into the world who clearly did not ask to be born? If life is an affair not worth the cost, as Schopenhauer insisted, all parents are outright criminals. If we bring children into the world so they will support us in our old age, it is even worse: it would be impossible to push the utilization of another as a means to a more radical level. If it is in order to permit others to make a "delightful excursion through reality," bravo.[26] But it remains to be shown that life—all life—is a good so incommensurable that it can balance the suffering it involves. Suffering that, by definition, cannot be known by someone who has not been born. The only way out of all of this is through a metaphysics.

Is the theologico-political problem posed in comparable terms in the three religions of the book?
    The theologico-political problem is only a particular aspect of a broader problem that I have called, not without pedantry, "theio-practical." The first formulation, even if it has become classic, in fact has three drawbacks. It supposes that one can find oneself in a religion in which theology, in the

sense stated above, is possible. It also supposes that one is in a religion in which the divine (in the neutral in Greek: *theion*) has taken the form of a personal or more than personal being (in the masculine or feminine in Greek: *theos*). Finally, it restricts the genre of practical philosophy to only one of its species, the government of the city, leaving aside that of the isolated individual (ethics) and that of the "household" (which is economic: the relationship between spouses, between parents and children, between superiors and subordinates).

The narrow question of the relation of the political to the religious is not the most pressing one. A de facto separation exists just about everywhere, in different styles.

The Church as a Force for Secularization

Christianity has never ceased negotiating a concrete modus vivendi between these two dimensions. How this has occurred is a paradox: the Church secularized the medieval state by assigning to it a domain of its own, keeping the peace. Which the state was not eager to do, given that, for its part, it dreamed only of sacrality. "Paradoxical as it may be . . . it is the action of the popes that tended, beginning in the 11th century, to 'laicize' the political power by taking away from it all initiative in spiritual matters."[27] This happened because Christianity, from the beginning, had declared itself independent of the Roman state, which not only already existed, but was persecuting Christians. In Judaism, what political power there was came to be formed by drawing closer around the Torah, erecting a barrier around it to protect the one principle of identity that remained after the disappearance of the Jewish state. This means that the absence of a political dimension is what constitutes Judaism. In the religion of Islam, the birth of a state at Medina and of an empire with the Arab conquest came two full centuries before the Islamic religion became clearly distinct from the other monotheisms. And before the *sharia* became a counterpower opposed to the political power of the caliphs.

The question that I call "theio-practical" remains unanswered, however. It asks, "Are there commandments coming from God that impose more on us—or something different from—what practical reason commands of all humankind?"

What is your view of how the historian's knowledge articulates with philosophical and theological discourse today?

History is prominent among the good dozen major disciplines that I regret not having studied. Gaston Bachelard famously responded to someone who told him that all scholars had their philosophy that philosophers, too, have their own field of knowledge. One might say the same thing of history. It is too often taken for granted that all that is required in order to pursue the history of philosophy is to be a philosopher, and that historical method is something automatic that can be learned on the job. As for the average professor of philosophy's vision of medieval history, it is almost as much of a caricature as that of the man in the street.

Can one believe in reason, when today, paradoxically, it is reason that seems to have been in crisis since the early twentieth century, whereas many religious faiths seem to be thriving? In this connection, you have spoken of "the anguish of reason." What do you mean by that?

Where Is Irrationalism?

I have indeed used the expression *l'angoisse de la raison* as the title of an article.[28] People talk incessantly of the rise of irrationalism. Giving readers a fine case of goose bumps is the stock in trade of many a pen pusher. Such people, what is more, take pains not to ask themselves just why the "rationalism" they defend is so unattractive. In any event, supposing that irrationalism is indeed on the rise, it does not bother me overly much. Let me note that the connection between rationalism and irrationalism is extremely complex, and that the historical representation of a gradual ascension toward the light is simply the result of forgetting the shadows that such a light necessarily projects. Two examples: the high point of magic is not situated in the Middle Ages, but just before and just after. The first high point was late Neoplatonism: Proclus (d. 485) placed magic (or "theurgy") higher than all human knowledge;[29] the second came in Renaissance Florence of the fifteenth century. Nor should we forget the contents of Newton's famous trunk. That great thinker was just as interested in an exegesis of the Book of Revelation as he was in celestial mechanics. Magic and science are twin sisters, but one prospered while the other declined.

The real danger lies in the paradox of your formula: "believe in reason." For the ideology of the Enlightenment, which is still widespread among the intellectual proletariat, it is one thing or the other: either one believes, or one is rational. Reason is expected to destroy belief and replace it with knowledge. That reason itself is the object of a belief is a bit hard to swallow. Still,

Nietzsche had already identified in the belief in the truth a final echo of a belief that was first Platonic, then Christian ("Platonism for the people").[30]

Where Is True Rationalism?

Many of those who think themselves rationalists and even write highly useless screeds against people whom they call irrationalists (who do not read their writings) are, in the final analysis, just as irrational as their targets. They think that reason is simply an epiphenomenon of the irrational—for example, the result of natural selection among a given living species. That species—called *Homo sapiens*—and life itself being the result of a series of chance happenings during the course of evolution. Let me give the last word on the subject to Father Brown, the priest-detective of Gilbert Chesterton's novels: "I know that people charge the Church with lowering reason, but it is just the other way. Alone on earth, the Church makes reason really supreme. Alone on earth, the Church affirms that God Himself is bound by reason."[31]

The "crisis" of reason, as we have said, goes along with the excellent health of certain religious movements. Yet we can see in Europe growing disbelief and the banalization of atheism. Can a connection be drawn between the dedivinization of the world and the "distancing" of the Christian God, given that, as you write in connection with John of the Cross, "the divine has not come closer, but grown more distant" with the New Alliance?

That phrase referring to John of the Cross is part of a commentary on one of his strongest passages and should be taken in context.[32] I started with a passage in which St. John explains that God has nothing more to give us, not because he wants to refuse us anything, but, precisely, because he has already given us everything, all at once, in giving his Son.

The pagan divine is present everywhere. It is part of the furniture. The Greek gods are "the gods of Greece" (as Schiller says); they are a part of the landscape. For this reason, it is not necessary to "believe" in them. The God of the Bible concentrates all sacrality in himself, which can lead to the impression of a desacralization or a disenchantment of the world, as Max Weber has taught us to say, creating an impression that can very well produce a sort of nostalgia. That said, sacrality pertains to things, not to a liberty. No liberty can be sacred. In contrast, it can be *holy*. When the God of the Bible is presented as a personification, what occurs is not simply a desacralization of the world. It is also a transformation of sacrality into holiness.

A Sacred Liberty?

However, a God who manifests himself in a personal form solicits liberty. This is why he gives himself only within faith. Faith is, so to speak, the appropriate organ for perceiving the divine, just as the eye registers colors or the mind registers concepts. The question is then to know whether to accept taking that step toward the holy or remain with the sacred. In the latter case, one must either accommodate to a disenchanted world or (something that I find even more dangerous) attempt to reintroduce, forcibly, an artificial sacredness into that same disenchanted world.

*There is much talk today of the place that should (or should not) be reserved for the Christian heritage within the future European Constitution. You, who have written a well-received book on European identity (*Europe, la voie romaine*),*[33] *how do you see the relationship of Christianity with a Europe that is increasingly de-Christianized?*

I am by no means persuaded of the need, at any cost, to provide a European Constitution with a preamble that includes a recall of past history. That said, if a mention of history is deemed necessary, it would be simply stupid to be content with some vague mention of Europe's religious and humanist (to use the British euphemism for "atheist") heritage. Why not call a spade a spade and name the two religions that have marked the cultural space known as "European": Judaism and Christianity? The problem is, on either side people often confound acknowledgment of a fact with a demand for a right, and memory of the past with an option concerning the future. Anyone is free to want to see Europe continue to drift away from Christianity, but deliberately ignoring the past simply demonstrates an obeisance to the logic of ideology. Joseph H. Weiler, a practicing Jew and a professor of European law at New York University, has written a highly interesting book in which he defends the Christian identity of Europe with arguments that are, for the most part, juridical.[34] I hope that someday it will appear in French translation.

The (very relative) success of my book on Europe, with its translations, continues to amaze me. But I sometimes wonder, when my morale is low, if I might not have done better to use the time I spent writing it to learn Egyptian or Akkadian. The civilizations that used those languages offer the advantage of being thoroughly dead. But are Europeans really living? Do they want to continue to live? Or are they zombies frantically agitating their limbs so as to pass for being truly alive?

One last and perhaps more personal question: What place can someone who believes in one religion make for other religions?

A place where? In his library: in his quality as a cultivated man, he will give their documents shelf space, and he will strive to know something about them in order to keep himself from saying really stupid things about religions that are not his own. He may eventually discover fine expressions of religious sentiment in authors who profess other religions than his own and piously make them his own.

Do Religions Deserve Respect?

Can he respect those religions? Properly speaking, no. Not because he is or is not a believer, and not because he adheres to religion A rather than to religion B, but quite simply because he values the meaning of words. Religions are only *things*, and one can only respect *persons*. One can no more respect a thing than listen to a painting. I respect no religion, not even my own. I respect those who believe in all religions, not because they are believers, but inasmuch as they are human beings.

More specifically, I have no esteem for belief in and of itself. I detest the recent habit of considering the act of belief as having a value in itself, independent of its content. And I mistrust those who attempt to discover connections between "believers," even to lump them together, without asking themselves *what* they believe in. One can believe in flying saucers, after all! There were sincere Nazis and convinced Leninites. And the Carthaginian fathers who had their sons burned alive as a sacrifice to the god Moloch (the scene is narrated by Flaubert, but the facts are true) must have "believed in it" strongly.[35] For me, a belief is as good as its object, neither more nor less.

Can One Hate a Religion?

Since I'm somewhat immoderately fond of provocation, I would go so far as to demand the right to *hate* a religion. I am thinking of Yeshayahu Leibowitz, an Israeli of universal interests and erudition who died a few years ago. He declared in an interview, *"Je hais le christianisme* [I hate Christianity]." The French translator, who is among my friends and to whom I owe the anecdote, told me that when he suggested the verb *détester*, Leibowitz, who spoke an impeccable French redolent of the eighteenth century, responded, articulating clearly, *"Non, ani soneh, je hais."* I hasten to add that

Leibowitz was, in practical life, the most inoffensive man imaginable. In politics he was a sort of hyper-dove who demanded the immediate evacuation of occupied territories and compared the government of his own land to that of Nazi Germany! And he bears Christians no hate. Christian as I am, that phrase in no way pleases me. I deplore it; I regret it. I think it based on an error. But I prefer it to the instantaneous fervor of certain professional participants in interreligious "dialogues."

I'll give you another example: Ignaz Goldziher, a Hungarian Jew of the early twentieth century (d. 1921), perhaps the greatest student of Islam who has ever lived, and whose articles I have just finished having republished in French. There was a man who was literally disgusted by Christianity, especially Catholic Christianity.[36] If I had had a chance to meet him, I would not have said to him, "How nasty it is to hate!" Even less would I have called him a dirty Christianophobe who wasn't politically correct. I would have asked him, "What are your reasons? Precisely what do you not like about Christianity?" And I would have tried to point out to him that the things to which he objected do not strike the center of the target or touch the essence of the Christian phenomenon, but are only accidental accretions.

One further question: Why do we remain Christians?

The "remain" in your question suggests that Christians are a rearguard made up of people who haven't caught on yet. Religious sentiment, including its most varied (even its wildest) expressions, does not seem to change much. But it is true, as you have said, that in Europe the major Christian churches are losing momentum. Let me hastily recall that Europe itself is doing the same. And that Christians are, in general, disappearing more slowly than Europeans in general.

Your question can be taken as a question of fact, in the sense of Benedetto Croce's famous article, "Why We Cannot Not Call Ourselves 'Christians'"(1944).[37] At that point, one might wonder what, in our civilization, is still marked by Christianity. Croce had no intention of writing a historical apology of Christianity. Quite to the contrary, he claimed that modern secularism is the legitimate heir of Christianity, all of whose positive aspects it has assumed.

Christians vs. Christianists

To speak of the Christian heritage of Europe bothers me. And for even greater reason, speaking of "Christian civilization." Christianity was founded by people who could not have cared less about "Christian civilization."

What interested them was Christ, and the reverberations of his coming on the whole of human existence. Christians believed in Christ, not in Christianity itself; they were Christians, not "Christianists."

It took centuries to translate Christian reality into institutions. Think of the time it took for the Church to reverse inveterate habits and impose the consent of the engaged couple as the sole indispensable condition for marriage. The famous monogamous marriage that we now call "traditional" was in fact a hard-won innovation. What is really traditional is the contract between two families for an exchange of spouses, whose opinion was seldom asked. Until quite late, so-called "Christian" society regarded with a jaundiced eye those who married—before a priest, to be sure—without consulting father, mother, or the social conventions. In one telling example: when the silk-worker Gonzalo de Yepes married Catalina Alvarez, a poor weaver, for love, his family disowned him. Moreover, when Catalina became a widow, she had to make her way alone to raise her son, later known under the name of St. John of the Cross.

Who can say that Christianity has had the time to translate the totality of its contents into institutions? I have the impression that instead we are still at the beginning stages of Christianity.

PART I

Generalities

I

The Lessons of the Middle Ages

In an earlier collection of texts, I had occasion to cite a dialogue of Plato's in which Socrates remarks sarcastically that it is always easy to praise Athens when speaking before an audience of Athenians.[1] Praising the study of medieval philosophy before a public of specialists who study medieval philosophy would be both easy and useless. One might in fact presume them to be already won over to the interest or interests of their field of specialization.

Demonstrating that interest to both specialists and non-specialists is a totally different affair. We are citizens of modern states, not medieval ones, and our cultural references do not derive exclusively, or even mainly, from the Middle Ages. As it happens, I count myself, paradoxically, fairly well positioned for the defense of medieval studies, which is why I offer a rapid presentation of myself.[2]

Self-Portrait of a Turncoat

I am a university professor, trained in philosophy. My thesis discussed the most famous thinkers of classical Greece, Plato and Aristotle. Hebrew and then Arabic were at first hobbies for me, a "secret garden," as the lovely expression goes. I ended up occupying a chair of medieval philosophy—more precisely, Arabic medieval philosophy—in complicated circumstances having much to do with the somewhat absurd structure of the French university system. In the domain of medieval philosophical studies, I was thus, and basically I have remained, a newcomer, a beginner, an outsider.

That outsider status has one obvious drawback, which is, of course, the need to learn about what I was already teaching as quickly as possible. But, from my point of view now, it had an enormous advantage, which was a certain impartiality. In fact, a university specialization is also a profession, something that can be learned. One can acquire a certain familiarity with the tools and the methods, a certain habit. Moreover, a university specialization also offers a recognizable social status and a way to make a living.

A dual cause for suspicion arises: a suspicion of an intellectual or psychological sort, and another more sordid one. As for the first, when someone speaks in favor of his trade, is he (or she) doing so because he is truly interested in it, or because, having launched his career at a young age, he is used to it? Does a medievalist truly take an interest in the Middle Ages and its thinkers? At base, is his passion simply laziness? As for the second, more material, suspicion, it is clear that to praise one's profession is also to exhibit its social legitimacy. In cruder terms, it is to show that it is right to be paid for exercising it. Thus is the medievalist who praises medieval studies simply pleading *pro domo*?

I represent the case of someone who already had a profession—ancient philosophy, a specialization well established in the French university system—and who changed fields, with all the risks that comports. I might well have continued to live on Plato and Aristotle. But here's the rub: the Middle Ages seduced me. And because it is an interesting time. It deserves our interest in and of itself. One might even say that it deserves a disinterested interest. I speak of my own personal case, but it is not unique. Even within the French university, I am not the only one to have effected, or to be about to effect, a turnaround of the sort. For example, I know someone whose thesis was on the aesthetics of contemporary American painting and who is now publishing translations of John Duns Scotus, a philosopher of the late twelfth century who never said a word about aesthetics. As it happens, Duns Scotus's thoughts about the singular help us to grasp the essential singularity of the work of art.[3] There are also a number of logicians who have turned to investigate William of Ockham. Examples such as these show that an interest in medieval thought can exist outside of all institutional interests and all career-connected constraints.

Why, then, is medieval philosophy so interesting? I shall try to show why, and from the point of view of a non-specialist.

Two Contrary Legends

The history of philosophy, like history in general, aims at replacing a naive relation with the past with one that is more thoughtful. It implies an intention to strangle legends. As it happens, the Middle Ages abounds in legends. Perhaps we would even have to say that the Middle Ages is itself a legend.

The Legend of the Middle Ages

The term appears in the fifteenth century, probably in 1464, in Latin, as *media tempestas*. The author is the Italian humanist Giovanni Andrea, the text, a letter included in his edition of Apuleius. There is also Nicholas of Cusa, whose expertise covered the literature of classical antiquity and the modern age, but also that of "the middle period."[4] More than two centuries later, in 1685, a certain Christian Keller (Cellarius) used a similar three-part schema to classify the epochs of world history. According to him, the Middle Ages began with Constantine.

The concept was forged in view of a certain vision of the intellectual history of Europe, and only of that vision. Its non-critical usage was enough to foment a degree of "Eurocentrism." This is all the more irritating because the epoch so-named was bereft of any such quality, and, in fact, at the time Europe considered itself to be the ends of the world and to lie far from the main centers. It is only after the great voyages of discovery that Europe could think itself at the center of the world.[5]

In any event, the schema cannot be applied to non-European cultural worlds. Neither to Byzantium, which thought of itself in terms of dynasties. Nor to Islam, which thinks of itself and dates its history from the Hegira (622), the schisms, and the Umayyad (661) and Abbasid (750) dynasties, and whose apogee as a civilization in the ninth to the eleventh centuries was an obscure age for Europe. Nor to Jewish history, which defined itself in relation to the destruction of the second temple (70), the redaction of the Talmud (ca. 500), and other events. It was only in the beginning of the modern era that defining events in Jewish history coincided—to its misfortune—with those of non-Jewish history: 1492, the date of the expulsion of Jews from Spain, is one of the dates that has been chosen as the beginning of the modern age; 1648, the Peace of Westphalia and the massacres of Jews in the Ukraine (which was Polish at the time); 1789, the French Revolution and emancipation; 1942–45, World War II and the Shoah, or Holocaust.

The schema is ternary: a hollow between two summits. A time of latency, perhaps created as a phantasm on the model of psychoanalysis, as, for example, in Michelet.[6] It may perhaps have emerged out of a secularization of the idea of the three ages in Joachim of Fiore. It any event, it is hardly "medieval," given that in the Middle Ages periods were defined by the history of reigns, as with the prophet Daniel or in the Book of Revelation, or of six epochs corresponding to the six days of creation.

The representation of a Middle Ages supposes a time of obscurity and shadows, a "dark ages,"[7] interrupted by a brilliant period, a new age striving to reestablish connections with an earlier clarity. Thus history is thought to have leaped over an age that remained empty and could be defined by its intermediate position as a "Middle Age" or "Ages." In this view, the Renaissance defines the end of medieval obscurity.

The Black . . .

The legend of the Middle Ages as a time of shadows and darkness is a legacy from the Renaissance, then the Enlightenment, and carried on by a certain variety of positivism. It is not the only period in history that has been called obscure—after the fact, of course. I am thinking, for example, of official Czech historiography, which calls the "age of the shadows" (*temno*) the very same epoch that in Spain is known as the *siglo de oro* and that even in Bohemia was a time of the full flowering of the baroque. But what is exceptional is that even the term "Middle Ages" reinforces that viewpoint. It is in fact highly paradoxical that a period of history should be defined as intermediate, as a sort of empty passage or a hollow of the wave between two peaks.

The underlying schema comes from Petrarch (1304–1374).[8] He promoted a new literary school that was supposed to have put an end to the obscure times. The humanists followed a like rhetoric, describing what had preceded them by means of negative terms. The word "barbarian" came back into service. In antiquity it designated peoples whose language was incomprehensible and who seemed to emit sounds lacking sense; in like manner, Slavs called themselves "speaking" and the Germans "mute." The term "barbarian" now included the Germanic peoples ("Goths," "Cimmerians"), and even monks and Turks.[9] Rabelais has Gargantua's father say in a letter to his son, "The time was still dark, and smacking of the infidelity and calamity of the Goths, who had brought all good literature to destruction."[10] Oppositions of sleep and waking, light and obscurity, receive a historical dimension: ripped from their cyclical context, they are lined up and divided into successive periods. Mixing historical epochs, the philosophers called Scholastics were known as "Sophists."

The schema was picked up by self-styled innovative movements. Some Protestant authors charged the Church of Rome, identified with the Antichrist, not only with the theological shortcomings of past centuries (a common practice), but also with their cultural weaknesses.[11] Later the ideologists of the "Enlightenment" (Turgot, Condorcet) took up the same schema but shifted it. It conflicted with the representation that the Enlightenment forged for itself of the progress of civilization.[12] That representation demanded an explanation for why such a long low period had interrupted what should have been a continuous and irresistible momentum. What was needed was thus a plot and some "villains." For the humanists, these would be ignorant monks. But while the humanists, far from dreaming of attacking faith, dreamed, quite to the contrary, of purifying it, the radicals of the Enlightenment were set on stamping out superstition (Voltaire's *écraser l'Infâme*) and crushing "fanaticism." They held Christianity in general responsible. Gibbon famously ends his *History of the Decline and Fall of the Roman Empire* with a paragraph dated 1787 summing up the themes of his book, which include "the rise, establishment, and sects of Christianity" and "the triumph of Barbarism and religion." The relationship between the elements that he enumerates is left artistically vague.[13] In his *Esquisse d'un tableau historique des progrès de l'esprit humain* (October 1793), Condorcet broadens the perspective by forging the anthropological category of the "priest," who has a store of knowledge but is guilty of keeping it to himself when he ought to share it.[14]

An analogous schema can be found in the positivism of Auguste Comte, in whose works the second, metaphysical age recalls Scholasticism (or its caricature). The official and *républicain* ideology of the Third Republic is imbued with his ideas, which continue in our own day among "secularists." As a Frenchman and as a university professor, I am especially sensitive to that particular legend. It is thanks to it, in fact, that we owe the exclusion of medieval philosophy from the curriculum of the French university.[15] People in the Middle Ages could be admitted to have lived, struggled for power, sung, and painted, but that they thought rather than simply believing was downright insupportable. I have just referred to some of my colleagues who have turned to the study of medieval thought. They are autodidacts, as I am. What is more, any French man or woman who studies medieval philosophy is an autodidact. Or, if they have the luck to encounter a teacher, it is not in the university, properly speaking, but in such institutions as the Collège de France or the École Pratique des Hautes Études and their like.

These days the Middle Ages ends up as a commonplace for mass media ever ready to recall that "finally, we are no longer in the Middle Ages!" or to decry the resurgence, "well into the twenty-first century, of an utterly medieval barbarity."

. . . And the Gilded

An opposed legend sees the Middle Ages as a golden age. It constitutes a response to the first legend and a reaction to it. This idealized counter-image took shape roughly beginning with German Romanticism, and it reached its peak with the Restoration. Novalis (Friedrich von Harden-berg)—in an essay written in 1799 but not published until 1826, when it was read within the context of the Restoration—identifies Europe with the Christian religion.[16] The various European Romanticisms followed and launched a veritable craze for things medieval. It had its effects in litera-ture with Sir Walter Scott's *Ivanhoe* (1819) and Victor Hugo's *Notre-Dame de Paris* (1831), in painting with Caspar David Friedrich, the English Pre-Raphaelites, and the German Nazarenes; in architecture, with the entire neo-Gothic movement and the neo-Byzantine, in France with the restora-tions of Viollet-le-Duc, and in Germany with the completion of the Gothic cathedrals that the Middle Ages had left without a steeple; finally, in music with Wagner's *Parsifal* (1882).

A nostalgia for a medieval society believed to have been "organic" and without conflict, harmoniously divided into corporations, arose in opposition to a secularized state. Social ties, wholly situated in the do-main of interhuman relations, were supposed to have escaped the desic-cating character of our modern world. The Middle Ages were not only the framework for Romanesque intrigues, but also became the object of an often-aesthetisizing nostalgia, as in *La Cathédrale* by Joris-Karl Huys-mans (1898) or in a passage of *La Femme pauvre* by Léon Bloy (1897). What may well be the masterpiece of this sort of literature, *Mont Saint Michel and Chartres* (1904), came from the pen of a citizen of a land that had not experienced the Middle Ages, the historian and autobiographer Henry Ad-ams.[17] In this book in the form of a travel account and a guide for a seem-ing initiate's progress from one masterwork of architecture to another, Adams attempts to approach the mystery of the Virgin, who symbolizes the medieval world, just as the dynamo symbolizes the nineteenth cen-tury.[18] The female is the principle of medieval society, where love is law and even rules beyond the law.[19] Adams looks back on that society with nostalgia, as a lost childhood.[20] He stands before the Virgin like a foreigner and a heretic:[21] he does not regard her as pertaining to religion, but to art.[22] Unless religion itself is merely sentiment with him.[23]

The history of philosophy includes the dream of a golden age. That dream is not absent from neo-Thomism, which sailed before the wind during the nineteenth century, more than ever after the publication of the encyclical *Aeterni Patris* (1879). In the Middle Ages, according to that current, thought miraculously coincided with its object and with St. Thomas Aquinas attained the truth, if not in the totality of its content, at least concerning the best method for reaching the truth. But that apogee did not last for long. Thought in fact underwent a fall, an "original sin," the responsibility for which was attributed to the school of Duns Scotus, then to "nominalism." It declined after then, the same school of thought tells us, going from decadence to decadence in an accelerating decline, from idealism to subjectivism, then to nihilism, and so on.

Pricking Balloons

To study medieval philosophy is also to prick a good many balloons and reestablish a number of forgotten verities.

First, against the legend of a dark ages, it will be shown that people never stopped thinking, that in fact medieval people did a lot of thinking, and that many highly refined concepts were shaped during those years. Philosophy, it was said, was then inseparable from theology. But did that mean that it was theology's servant? A closer study shows that the relationship between the two disciplines was a good deal more nuanced. I cite only one example, but it is a massive one: Thomas Aquinas, at the beginning of his *Summa theologica*, does not ask himself whether it is legitimate to pursue philosophy. Quite to the contrary, he raises the question of whether there is any need of a science to be added to philosophy—and that science is, of course, theology. He supposes philosophy to be indispensable. What is more, it is before the tribunal of philosophy that theology is called to appear and before which it must justify itself.[24]

Next, against the second legend—that of a golden age, and of the decadence supposed to have followed it—I intend to show that medieval thought does not escape the phenomena typical of thought in general. Its passage from one thinker to another arises from a dynamics internal to works and to problems. The movement animating the history of philosophy is neither a progress nor a fall, but rather a constant search for a solution to problems, methodically taken up and resolved, constantly reformulated and sharpened.

Still, it is not enough to recall that a discipline permits the correction of common errors to prove that it is worthy of interest, hence to legitimate its exercise. In the final analysis, we can live with errors. Certain of them are even inevitable, such as the error that, centuries after Copernicus, makes us think we see the sun rising and setting. And in any event, those errors, like their correction, affect only specialists and the tight circle around them.

Medieval Thought and Its Pertinence for Europe

Thus it has to be shown that the study of medieval philosophy can help us to do a better job of posing certain problems today. And not only philosophical problems, something that we can all accept without too much difficulty, but very concrete problems.

I would like to offer only one example here of the interest in studying medieval philosophy, which is what it teaches us about ourselves, in the "hour of Europe." I shall choose three aspects of this question, taking them up one after the other. I shall show that the first two can also give rise to legends, and I shall conclude with the third, which seems to me to furnish an even more current example of a healthy relationship between the culture and the self.

A Europe without Linguistic Frontiers?

The first argument for the European pertinence of the Middle Ages is well known: it is the existence of a linguistic community made possible by the use of Latin.[25] The fact that the use of the Latin language made it possible for thoughts and persons to circulate from one end of Latin Christianity to the other has been described ad nauseam. The career of Anselm, who was born in the Val d'Aosta and died as archbishop of Canterbury, has been narrated again and again. As have the careers of the thinkers who came to teach in Paris from Naples, like Thomas Aquinas, or from Thuringia, like Meister Eckhart. The dream of reinstating a similar linguistic community in a Europe without frontiers is a legitimate one.

It is a good thing to recall the past. It is good to dream, for that dream is generous. But it is also good to draw distinctions: the Europe of today does not have a common language that is no one's native tongue, hence that stands, grosso modo, at an equal distance from all. Besides, in the Middle Ages Latin was spoken only by a small minority of educated people, and only a small minority within that minority were able to circulate. Taking that situation as a model for contemporary Europe is perhaps well intentioned but inadequate. This is all the more true because, as I have not yet had occasion to stress, that linguistic community concerned only one of the medieval worlds, leaving out Byzantium, which spoke Greek; Islam, which spoke Arabic; and the Jewish communities, in which the language of culture was either Arabic or Hebrew. This leads me to my second point, which concerns the idea that the medieval world was the theater of a constant exchange among cultures.

A Dialogue between Cultures?

Is there a medieval model for the "dialogue" among civilizations that we find so praiseworthy today? The answer to that question, as we shall see, is both "yes" and "no."

First, an emphatic "yes." That "yes" is all the more firm because what is in question is, precisely, philosophy. We have examples of discussions on philosophical topics among thinkers belonging to different religions. In Christian lands, that occurred between Christians and Jews, with Muslims accepted as participants only exceptionally, as, for instance, in Toledo immediately after the reconquest by Alfonso the Learned. Similarly, Isaac Albalag, a Catalan Jew of the latter half of the thirteenth century, reproduces a discussion with a cleric (kumār) on the interpretation of the central thesis of the ontology of Avicenna: existence is accidental to quiddity.[26] Somewhat later, in the fourteenth century, Moses of Narbonne narrates a disputatio (wikkuah) with a "remarkable (nifla) sage among the sages of the Romans" (whose name he unfortunately neglects to mention) and tells how he himself bested the man's logical cavils.[27] Much earlier in Islamic lands, however—in the ninth and tenth centuries—Christians, Jews, and Muslims had exchanged both arguments and students in Baghdad. These exchanges were facilitated by a unique phenomenon: the presence of Arabic as a common language of culture for the three religions. Farabi was the student of a Christian, and some have gone so far as to state that he studied for a time in Greece.[28] One of his own students, Yahyā ibn ʿAdī, was a Christian. In the later period of Muslim Aristotelianism, one might cite the famous responses of Ibn Saʿbīn of Murcia to philosophical questions put to him by Emperor Frederick II in Sicily.[29]

In more general terms, literary influences among thinkers who could not have known one another, given the gap in time separating them, were not stopped by confessional barriers. Thus such Christian thinkers as John Philoponus, and later John Damascene, played a key role in the formation of the apologetic theology of Islam, then of Judaism.[30] There were many Christians among the translators who transmitted the Greek heritage to Islam. Later the influence of Muslim thinkers on Jewish thought was massive: Maimonides is to some extent incomprehensible without Farabi, and his successors, without Averroes. Beginning in the twelfth century, Muslim philosophy and Jewish philosophy exerted an enormous influence on Christian thinkers, a situation that is too well known to require going into detail here.

Influence traveled in the other direction as well. This was true for the Jewish domain, in any event. If the thinkers of Islam seem not to have undergone influences come from Europe, the Jews entered into the Christian intellectual sphere, at a date still disputed, but that recent research tends to place earlier and earlier—perhaps in the early thirteenth century, given that (according to such specialists as Gershom Scholem and Alexander Altmann) it cannot be excluded that John Scotus Erigena was influenced by the Kabbalah, and not just any Kabbalah, but, precisely, that of the school of Gerona.[31] Concerning philosophy, a revolutionary article of Shlomo Pines sought traces of Scotism and nominalism in Gersonides and Crescas.[32] It is even possible that we would have to go back as far as Nissim, who was Crescas's teacher.[33] All scholars agree, in any event, in acknowledging that influence at a later date. It is manifest, what is more, among such authors as Joseph Albo, and especially in Hillel ben Samuel of Verona, who translated entire passages of Thomas Aquinas. Analogous phenomena can be found even within the Christian world, where the Greek East underwent the influence of the Latin West: Thomas Aquinas was also translated in fourteenth-century Byzantium.[34]

Here, too, however, we need to take a closer look and after a first "yes," risk a more sober "no." Indeed, on the one hand, authentic dialogue remains exceptional when it concerns persons who not only belong to different religions, but also represent them. When that does occur, it unfolds in a context of unpleasant polemics, for example, that of the *wikkuah* that Christians imposed on the Jews. Genuine efforts to understand the other religion remain rare. On the other hand, Christianity and, to an even greater extent, Islam before it "tolerate" (though the word is anachronistic) a good many heterogeneous communities on their territories. But it remains forbidden to preach another religion than the one that holds political power. For even greater reason, conversion from the religion that holds power to another one is prohibited. Thus we would do well not to project on to the Middle Ages the dream—admittedly a noble one—of a coexistence without conflicts. We should also avoid making too swift an analogy with our own secular Western societies. Two cities in Spain can serve to give a title to symmetrical dreams, and what we might call "the Cordova dream" seems to me just as mythical a "the Compostela dream."

The Intellectual Emergence of Europe: A Medieval Event

In contrast, there is a third point on which the experience of medieval Europe can present us with a stunning timeliness. I shall thus devote more space to it.

This is the nature of what might be called the European experiment—that is, Europe as an experiment, an attempt, a dynamism. I have no intention of narrating facts or events situated within European history, even though they are extremely interesting and instructive, like the two points that I have just treated. More radically, I want to ask just what is Europe. And to stress being aware that Europe is not to be taken for granted and to recall Europe to the particularity—even the bizarre nature—of its history. My thesis is that medieval studies can help us to understand the very essence of Europe.

Today we label "European" political phenomena (or cultural phenomena, in the broad sense of the term) that are present all over the surface of the globe and that are present there because Europe extended its reach by the power of arms. But at first the domination of the Latin West was an intellectual domination, perceived as early as the thirteenth century, for instance by Jews, disinterested observers well placed on the frontier between the Muslim and Christian worlds, such as Samuel Ibn Tibbon (d. 1232), the translator of Maimonides' *Guide for the Perplexed*. He writes: "I have noticed that the true sciences are very widespread among the nations under the domination of which and in the lands of which we live, much more than they are widespread in the lands of Ishmaël."[35]

A half-century later, in 1287, a Syriac-speaking Nestorian monk, Rabban Sāwmā, visited Paris as ambassador of the Mongols. He reports on what he found most striking:

> There were in [Paris] thirty thousand scholars [i.e., pupils] who were engaged in the study of ecclesiastical books of instruction, that is to say of commentaries and exegesis of all the Holy Scriptures, and also of profane learning; and they studied wisdom, that is to say philosophy, and [the art of] speaking, and [the art of] healing, geometry, arithmetic, and the science of the planets and the stars, and they engaged constantly in writing [theses], and all these pupils received money for subsistence from the king. And they also saw one Great Church wherein were the funerary coffers of dead kings; and statues of them in gold and silver were upon their tombs. And five hundred monks were engaged in performing commemoration services in the burial-place [i.e., mausoleum] of the kings, and they all ate and drank at the expense of

the king. And they fasted and prayed continually in the burial-place of those
kings. . . . In short, Rabban Sāwmā and his companions saw everything which
was splendid and renowned.[36]

For this author, everything worth seeing in Paris came down to two
things: the university and Saint-Denis. Those two institutions had in common that in them people who carried out non-practical activities were
supported out of public funds, in one case, to study, in the other, to pray.
Sāwmā notes that university studies also included profane disciplines, and
he enumerates most of the liberal arts, plus medicine. In a few summary
lines, this perspicacious observer saw the essential, which was a society
capable of freeing up a part of its social capital in order to finance the
acquisition of a store of knowledge not exclusively aimed at supporting or
lending legitimacy to the structure in place.

Still later a Muslim of the fourteenth century, Ibn Khaldūn, after painting a pessimistic picture of the situation of the intellectual sciences in Islamic lands (the Maghreb, in particular), states: "We further hear now that
the philosophical sciences are greatly cultivated in the land of Rome and
along the adjacent northern shore of the country of the European Christians. They are said to be studied there again and to be taught in numerous
classes. Existing systematic expositions of them are said to be comprehen-
sive, the people who know them numerous, and the students of them very
many."[37]

The Jews of the age were suffering from a genuine inferiority complex,[38]
but the same was true of such Byzantine scholars of the fourteenth century as Georgios Scholarios or the Cydones brothers.[39] A century later
Isaac Abravanel would shame those of his fellow Jews who doubted the
creation of the world and miracles by offering them the example of Christians, whose learning surpassed that of the sons of the East, and who still
believed in the literal meaning of Scripture:

> See the sons of Edom [read Rome]: one cannot imagine "the wisdom of their
> sages, and the intelligence of their intelligent men surpasses all" (Isaiah 29:12),
> for it is unfathomable; there are born to them "men who are wise, discerning,
> and experienced" (Deuteronomy 1:13), able to "give advice, offer counsel,"
> and serve as "a ruler devoted to justice and zealous for equity" (Isaiah 16:3, 5)
> in the wisdom of the discourse [logic], the wisdom of nature [physics],
> within divine things [metaphysics], and in all the wisdom of studies [math-
> ematics]. They were wiser than "all the Kedemites and all the wisdom of
> Egypt" (1 Kings 5:10), and there is no end to the works they composed.[40]

The tone of these texts is surprising, even—I would have to admit—a bit disturbing. One might think this was a Westerner of good conscience legitimating Western practices, but these texts come from non-Europeans or non-Christians, some of whom, what is more, were not accustomed to self-congratulation for their symbiosis with Christians: Abravanel was expelled from Spain. We should thus be astonished and ask ourselves where the progress achieved could have come from.

Learning How to Borrow

That progress was unexpected: Europe had come a long way, and come up considerably. I have already mentioned Samuel Ibn Tibbon, the translator of Maimonides, and his surprise. What did the Master himself say? The exact contrary. Just like all others who lived on the southern shores of the Mediterranean, he perceived the regions north of his own land as barbarian, and even dirty, lands. He justifies the biblical prohibition on eating the flesh of pigs in these terms: "Now if swine were used for food, market places and even houses would have been dirtier than *latrines*, as may be seen at present in the country of the Franks."[41] We smile at the passage. Change just who is being called a "barbarian" and it echoes a "Western" cliché that is, unfortunately, all too current.

Things are of course more complicated than this: Europe of the twelfth century was no longer an intellectual desert. Far from it. But Europe of the ninth century did not stand up to comparison with Iraq. In any event, it is salutary for us to recall Europe's humble origins. Not to gloat over the distance we have come, but to know to what we owe having made such progress. There is a duty of remembrance. It is also good to recall from where Europe drew the nourishing juices on which it grew fat. The answer is simple: they came from the outside. Europe borrowed its nourishment, first from the Greco-Roman world that preceded it, then from the world of Arabic culture that developed in parallel with it, and, finally, from the Byzantine world. It is from the Arabic world, in particular, that Europe gained the texts of Aristotle, Galen, and many others that, once translated from Arabic into Latin, fed the twelfth-century renaissance. The Byzantine world provided the original versions of those same texts, which permitted closer study and alimented the flowering of Scholasticism in the thirteenth century. What would Thomas Aquinas have been if he had not found a worthy adversary in Averroes? What would Duns Scotus have contributed if he had not taken Avicenna as a point of departure (to repeat Étienne Gilson's formula)? What is more, many texts consumed by

European intellectual culture had Jewish translators. Thus Europe would do well to be aware of the immensity of its cultural debt to these intermediaries (the French word for which, *truchements*, is even of Arabic origin), to the Jews, both inside and outside of Europe, and to the world of Arab culture, which includes both Christians and Muslims.

I am not suggesting that we seek some ultimate origin. Each people received contributions from other peoples in an unending exchange and circulation. A passage from the early ninth-century Arab encyclopedia of the "Brethren of Purity" (also known as the "Sincere Brothers") recalls this in a charming way. A Greek who found himself among representatives of a number of different peoples was boasting of the conquests of his nation in the realm of knowledge. He was reminded that the Greeks borrowed their sciences from the Persians and many others. He agreed cheerfully, responding with the generalization that no people has ever invented everything, but each always both gives and receives.[42]

In Praise of the Inferiority Complex

In order to borrow, however, two conditions must be fulfilled. First, we have to realize what we lack. Next, we need to accept the idea of going to look elsewhere for what others have invented. We have to accept feeling inferior. That demands a degree of courage. It would be easier to refuse to recognize our inferiority and refuse to admit our need. It would even be more comfortable to clothe ourselves in the dream of a primitive purity, eventually making an ideology of that poverty and seeing in it a hidden wealth that others have lost, thinking themselves "advanced" when they are in fact retrograde.

The attitude of accepting secondary status in relation to earlier and exterior sources and drawing from those sources with little hope of a total assimilation seems to me to characterize the Middle Ages as a whole. Not only Byzantine, Jewish, or Muslim thinkers suffered from an inferiority complex; it was also part of our own Western, Latin, and European Middle Ages. Thus when Greek works arrived in Europe in the twelfth century via the Arab world, Europe was already well acquainted with its inferiority complex regarding the ancient world. Basically, it had suffered from such a complex from the start—that is, from its Roman origins. Virgil states it magnificently when the shade of Anchises speaks to his son Aeneas in Hades: others than the Romans will be better sculptors, better orators, and better astronomers; Rome will have to content itself with the profession of arms and with politics.[43]

In the Middle Ages, that inferiority complex was not simply one attitude among others. In my view, the Middle Ages owed its existence to just that attitude. It is what made the age what it was. The Middle Ages is the period in which, to return to the famous image, people became aware that they were no more than dwarfs perched on the shoulders of giants.[44] The dwarf has every right to be proud of seeing farther than the giant, but he knows, deep within himself, that he owes his long sight not to his own stature, but to a situation that came to him by pure luck. A fragile and vacillating situation. A situation that combines—paradoxically—pride and humility: pride at being at the top, and the humility of being small.

That humility was needed in order to accept going elsewhere to draw from the sources, and that was what the Middle Ages never stopped doing. Historians have rid us of the image of an obscure Middle Ages, substituting one of an uninterrupted series of renaissances. One might even go so far as to say that the Middle Ages may have been the only historical epoch that never accepted being a "middle age." From the outset, it always strove to be a renaissance. And it never hesitated to go elsewhere to seek what it lacked: "authenticity" was never so important that it won out over a primordial desire for what is true, beautiful, useful, and interesting. When, in Baghdad of the ninth century, the caliphs encouraged the translation of Greek works of philosophy, mathematics, and medicine, they did not ask whether Aristotle, Galen, or Euclid were going to trouble the purity of their own identity. When Benedictines copied Ovid's *Art of Love*, did they seriously believe that they were reading an allegory to which Christianity delivered the key?

If I may be permitted a rapid philosophical generalization: What is "mine" is not necessarily what is good, let alone what is the Good. Europe was lucky enough to have a concrete experience of this difference, thanks to the geographical distance between its cultural sources. What made European culture—Hellenism and Israel—was not European, and the two cities that symbolize the two, Athens and Jerusalem, are not in Europe. For a European, studying them is not a means for appropriating one's own past, but of getting out of oneself. The sources from which Europe drew sustenance are outside of it. Therefore they might not have been sources; they became sources, for anyone who wanted to go draw from them.

In Conclusion: An Example to Follow

There is an example in all this for Europe today. Not only for what is enclosed within its geographical boundaries (which are, moreover, fairly poorly defined), but also for everything and everyone, in the five continents, claiming a relation to Europe. Men of the Middle Ages were capable of going outside of their own confines and outside of their own tradition to seek cultural goods in the Arab world. They worked over these acquisitions, developed them, and prolonged them. But they never forgot that what they were borrowing came from the outside, and that its source *remained* outside. This meant that they could always go back and find more to borrow. They could correct a received text thanks to more recently received original, thus permitting a new and more faithful reception of the sources. Thus Europe became engaged in an endless dialectic. It found its motive force in the very foreignness of what it needed to assimilate and what—since it remained outside—continued to arouse its desire. If I may be permitted an image that is somewhat baroque in the circumstances, Europe was a donkey induced to advance thanks to the carrot on a stick dangling before it that it could see but never attain.

May we never give in to the satisfaction of the possessor. May we never nod off, satisfied by our material wealth. What is perhaps worse, because the profanation involves something more worthy, may we never justify our sleep by our cultural wealth. That wealth is not ours. It comes from elsewhere. Moreover, it is not for us alone. This is what the thinkers of the Middle Ages understood. Studying them shows this more and more clearly. Men of the Middle Ages had the courage to act consequently. May we be capable of imitating them.

2

The Meaning and Value of Philosophy in the Three Medieval Cultures

The title of this chapter seems to promise a pompous style and a literary genre akin to the eulogy, even the panegyric. In reality, however, I am taking the words "meaning" and "value" in the closely defined acceptation given them in the linguistic terminology of Ferdinand de Saussure. De Saussure drew a distinction between the *sens* (signification) of a word and the *valeur* (value) that the word has in relation to other surrounding words, within the concomitant distinction between signifiers and the signified. Thus, to repeat de Saussure's own example, the French *mouton* and the English "sheep" have the same signification, but they don't have the same value, because *mouton* would be translated, in some contexts, not by "sheep" but by "mutton."[1]

My overall thesis is this: In order to comprehend the role of philosophy in medieval Christianity, Judaism, and Islam, it is not enough to study meanings; we also need to consider values. In other words, it is not enough to take "Christian" philosophy, "Jewish" philosophy, and "Islamic" philosophy in isolation and compare them term by term. Ideally, we should also consider the entire edifice of learning within a given culture—what one might call its *episteme*[2]—and see what place philosophy occupies in relation to neighboring disciplines. These might include what we know about nature, theology, law, and ethics, the mystical experience, and more. It should be understood that these terms are intended to serve here simply as labels, open to revision and adaptation in one culture or another, since the domains in question receive unequal emphasis and are understood differently. We can begin to see overall configurations in which philosophy, while maintaining the same "meaning," takes on a different "value."

The reader will have already grasped that the best we can do here is lay out a program. The discipline that could satisfy that program would be that of compared medieval philosophy, but it exists only as a dream. As for my own relationship with that branch of knowledge, I will permit myself to define it by adapting the old joke that if you don't know something, you teach it, and enlarge it to state, "If you don't know a number of things, compare them."

Within the limits of this essay, I shall begin with some remarks about meaning. Then, shifting to the perspective of value, I shall present three theses on the nature of the three medieval *epistemai* in which philosophy developed. Finally, I shall suggest two theses, one regarding the meaning, the other the value, of philosophy in medieval cultures.

Meaning

The problem of the meaning of the word "philosophy" was posed, for the Latin world, in a fundamental article by Marie-Dominique Chenu, published sixty years ago, in 1937.[3] It is in invoking his name and in celebration of that anniversary that I would like to place the present essay. Ideally, his contribution should be completed by a consideration of the destiny of both the word and the thing beyond the Latin world to which Chenu limited his investigation. There is an interesting imbalance between the various cultural areas in this respect.

On one point, all the cultural worlds of the Middle Ages shared roughly the same attitude; on another, the Islamic world differed in interesting ways.

A Foreign Word

The point in common is that the Greek word for "philosophy" was perceived as Greek, hence, as of foreign origin. This was the case in all of the medieval worlds, with the exception, of course, of Byzantium, which had always retained the Greek language and prolonged its ancient usage.

Latin Christianity was aware of the Greek etymology of the Latin word, which it simply transcribed.[4]

From the outset, Islam perceived *falsafa* as a Greek word, and it continued to do so. Al-Kindi decomposes and explains the word, then proposes several definitions of it, parallel to the ones we encounter in the Greek commentators of Aristotle. He also defends the right to borrow knowledge from a non-Muslim source.[5] It seems to have been Farabi, however, who insists, in his treatise on philosophy, on the fact that "philosophy" is a Greek word:

> The name of philosophy is Greek and [is] of foreign origin (*dahil*) in Arabic. According to the ways of proceeding of their language, it is *filsofa*, and its meaning is "predilection (*ītār*) for wisdom." In their language it is composed of *fila* and of *sofia*: *fila* is predilection, and *sofia*, wisdom. *Faylasuf* is derived from *falsafa*. According to the ways of proceeding of their language, it is *filsofos*. That [phonetic] mutation is frequent in their derivations. Its meaning is "he who has a predilection for wisdom." The one who has a predilection for wisdom, according to them, is the one who makes wisdom the pole (*wakd*) of his life and the goal of his existence.[6]

Farabi's statement was echoed several centuries later by Shahrastani, at the beginning of his presentation of philosophy.[7] Similarly, a "Refutation of Philosophy" figures in the *Muqaddima* of Ibn Khaldūn,[8] and a number of later authors, such as al-Amiri in the sixteenth century, treated the topic.[9] The foreign origin of the word reflects the imported status of the thing that it stands for: philosophy came into the Arab world from Greece.[10]

Quite similar ideas can be found in Jewish authors, who were just as aware of the existence of philosophy as the Muslims and the Christians.[11] Moses ben Ezra declares, "All of philosophy has become one of the names of Greece."[12] An awareness of the Greek origin of philosophy remained strong, and at times it served as an argument to contest the originality of studying philosophy or simply to decrease its authority. Thus a rabbi portrayed by Jehuda Halevi declares: "There is an excuse for the Philosophers. Being Grecians, science and religion did not come to them as inheritances. They belong to the descendants of Japheth, who inhabited the north, whilst that knowledge coming from Adam, and supported by the divine influence, is only found among the progeny of Shem, who represented the successors of Noah and constituted, as it were, his essence."[13]

In other languages, then, the Greek word was transcribed rather than translated or replaced. I might also remark that, with one exception, this remains true of the languages of modern Europe: Dutch has forged *wijsbegeerte*, a word modeled on the etymology of *philosophia*. In the early nineteenth century, Fichte could still remark that *Philosophie* continued to be taken as a foreign word, since no real German translation had found acceptance.[14]

Semantic Variety

The point on which it seems to me that the Islamic world departs from the other two is in the semantic variety of the word. At the end of classical antiquity, "philosopher" and "philosophy" had different meanings. In particular, *philosophia* described the monastic life.[15] This meaning is not so much in direct line with a pagan acceptation as it is with a pagan *practice*: that of philosophy as a "spiritual exercise," to borrow a term from Pierre Hadot, who did much to illuminate this aspect of ancient philosophy.[16]

Byzantium

It seems that the word had the widest variety of meanings in the Christianity known as Byzantine. There, too, the word indeed designates philosophy in the technical sense, as expressed in definitions that repeat those of the Neoplatonic commentators of Aristotle.[17] The word *philosophos* also designated the monk, however, as it did in the West.[18] In Syriac, the dictionaries tell us (and my competence in that language stops there), "philosophy" also referred to the "ascetic life." In Greek, it seems that the range of significations was even broader. Thus we have a stupefying text of Michael Psellus, who, probably with reason, defines philosophy in nearly the opposite way from ancient philosophy: "I call philosophers not those who explore the substances of beings (*ousiai tōn ontōn*), nor those who, while seeking the principles of the world (*arkhai tou kosmou*), neglect the principles of their own salvation, but those who scorn the world and then live with things beyond the world."[19]

The word *philosophos* eventually merged with *sophos* to designate someone who possessed a competence in any given domain, even to designate a cultivated man in general. But *philosophos* had a social connotation of belonging to the dominant class of functionaries who pursued studies, and for that reason were looked on with little sympathy by the common people. In popular poetry the *philosophos* was a character who thought himself clever, but of course was not. In animal tales it was the least sympathetic figure: the fox was the *philosophos*. It was not his wiliness that was stressed, as was true in the West, but the vanity with which he displayed his learning.[20]

The Latin West

In Western Christianity, that meaning of "philosophy" survived in the patristic period and can be found up to the twelfth century. One example is in a rare occurrence of the syntagm *philosophia christiana* in Bernard of Clairvaux, who writes: "Even if it can be established, in Christian philosophy at least, that nothing is suitable unless it is lawful, and that nothing is advantageous unless it is suitable and lawful, nevertheless it does not necessarily follow that all that is lawful will be suitable or advantageous."[21]

What we see here is something like a logic of Christian existence. Bernard's reflections derive from a phrase of St. Paul's, which I cite here from the Vulgate, the Bible that the abbot of Clairvaux would have read: *"Omnia mihi licent, sed non omnia expediunt"* (All things are lawful to me: but all things are not expedient; 1 Corinthians 6:12 and 10:23). This notion is totally unrelated to the *philosophie chrétienne* that caused so much debate in France in the early 1930s; rather, it refers to the highest principles of morality, the purest form of which appears in the monastic life. It seems, however, that Bernard was amused to state these principles in the form of a logical proposition, stressing the connection by using such technical terms as *continuo* and *consequens*. What we have is thus a syllogism *in Barbara*: All that is expedient is acceptable; all that is acceptable is permitted; therefore all that is expedient is also permitted. Or perhaps a syllogism *in Baroco*: All that is expedient is acceptable; all that is permitted is not acceptable (some things that are permitted are not acceptable); therefore all that is permitted is not expedient (some permitted things are not expedient).

Judaism: The Silences of Ibn Tibbon

The broader meaning of the word "philosophy" is not exclusive to Christianity. In this connection, there is a highly interesting passage in the glossary of foreign words that Samuel Ibn Tibbon adds to his Hebrew translation of Maimonides' *Guide for the Perplexed*. He states in the entry for *pilosofia*: "*Pilosofia*. Greek word. Its meaning is: love of wisdom. It is from it that *pilosof* derives. One also finds in the Talmud: *pilosof*. Perhaps [the word] was current in their vocabulary [lit., mouth]. The translators and the authors (*mehabberim*) among the sons of our nation transported it from its [original] language to our books. The philosophers built 'verbal' forms on it in the Arabic language, as we did."[22]

This text, in appearance simple, is already interesting in that it reconstitutes an (admittedly schematic) history of the word up to the time of its use by Samuel himself. It becomes even more interesting by what it does not say. Samuel was probably drawing his information on the Greek origin of the word from some Arabic source—in all probability Farabi, as we have seen. But his remark about the presence of the word in the Talmud is highly revealing. He is obliged to note that presence because his strategy, like that of his master, Maimonides, is to suppose that the redactors of the Talmud had access to a profound store of philosophic knowledge.[23] Moreover, he admits the rupture of the tradition, also following Maimonides' example.[24] It is as a result of that rupture that we have to content ourselves with weighing the usage of the Sages, in the absence of certain evidence. Finally, Ibn Tibbon takes care not to tell us in what precise sense the word "philosopher" is used in the Talmud. That sense is in fact surprising: the word designates the freethinkers who attempt to catch the Sages off guard by asking questions, for example, about the prime matter of creation.[25] Philosophers can even be non-Jews: Marcus Jastrow's dictionary offers this definition: "Philosopher, one living a life of speculation and self-denial, monk."[26] Later Ibn Tibbon mentions Jewish translators and authors, and then the philosophers. That order of mention is a bit surprising as it leaves their chronological order unclear. He seems to take it for granted that the philosophers speak Arabic: they integrate the Greek word into Arabic, not just as a borrowed term, but one completely absorbed into the language. They draw from it a verbal root with four consonants (F, L, S, F), *falsafa* and *tafalsafa*, on which one can in fact construct verbs. If translators and authors preceded the philosophers, as the order in which Ibn Tibbon mentions the three seems to suggest, it is hard to say what he meant. Finally, Ibn Tibbon seems to place himself among the "we" who have acted in similar fashion, but he does not specify precisely who he means by "we." Does he mean Jews in general? Or Provençal Jews, for whom Hebrew was the language of culture? Or perhaps philosophers in general? Or are "we" the "translators and authors," a group within which Ibn Tibbon might easily have placed himself? Nor does he specify what sort of activities "we" engage in. Is it simply linguistic creativity? Or if more is implied, what is it? Thanks to all of this vagueness, Ibn Tibbon recuperates the Talmudic legitimacy of the term and the Jewish legitimacy of the activity that it refers to, while giving both of these a new and more properly "philosophic" meaning.

Islam

In Islamic lands, on the other hand, it seems that from the beginning the word *faylasuf*, which also transcribes the Greek, had the meaning that we know today. To be sure, Arabic adjectives designating wisdom and learning do not apply only to the philosopher, but can also qualify those whom we call "mystics." This is true of *hakīm* (wise man) and of *'arīf* (gnostic, initiate). But the word for "philosopher" itself refers only to those for whom we would still use that term. Thus when a mystic such as the Egyptian Dhu Nun (d. 953) is called a "philosopher," he is not being called an ascetic, but rather he is being accused of being no more than an adept of a foreign science.[27]

The two are probably connected: distance from the language of origin is inversely proportional to semantic mixing. It is because the word *philosophos* is Greek that it remains subjected to the natural evolution of the language, following normal processes of diversification and semantic specialization.

That said, we need to investigate just what the word "philosophy" refers to. My only question will regard what is or is not philosophy in a given culture. We need to answer that question before considering, at a second stage, how the medieval *episteme* should be subdivided. The problem is particularly acute regarding Islamic philosophy, which used to be seen as beginning with al-Kindi, hence around the ninth century, and ending with Averroes, at the end of the twelfth century. As is known, Henry Corbin contested those limits in both directions. This means that we need to examine Corbin's theses.[28]

What is at stake is no less than the very existence of an object that can legitimately be called "Islamic philosophy." For Corbin, we have no right to separate such an entity from Sufism, Shiism, or any group combating for "spiritual Islam."[29] Semantic enlargement brings with it chronological extension: it is because Corbin stretches the chronological limits of the acceptation of the term "philosophy" that he can also note the presence of what that term stands for beyond the period usually recognized for it, both to an earlier period and, especially, a later one. Concerning the earlier period, he includes in philosophy what he calls the "prophetic philosophy" of Shiism, which (as he recalls on several occasions) concerns questions that are not Greek in origin.[30] But it is in extending the reach of philosophy that Corbin makes his most important contribution. He sets himself the task of showing that, even admitting the idea of an end point of philosophy with Averroes, that end concerns only a small canton of the Islamic world, which has continued to think down to our own day in other areas such as the Iranian sphere, where it followed the traces of Avicenna, then of Suhrawardi and Ibn Arabi, in particular.

The question remains, however. No one contests the fact that Muslims continued to think after Averroes, but what remains to be seen is to what extent that thought can be called philosophy. There are in the history of humanity highly respectable works that one would never call philosophical, but for which vaguer terms such as "wisdom literature" or "thoughts" would be more appropriate. Thus Heidegger—whom Corbin was among the first, if not the first, to introduce into France—does not hesitate to place thought on a higher plane than philosophy. Corbin himself is quite aware of the problem, and he announces his intention to "cut short all ambiguity over the word 'philosophy.'"[31] He avoids the problem through the use of several strategies, first among them, distinguishing between philosophy and metaphysics.[32]

Corbin's fundamental argument seems to me to lie within the ambit of a larger critical sensitivity regarding "Eurocentrism." His work, or at least certain aspects of his work, should perhaps be seen within the third-world atmosphere of the 1960s. Corbin does not grant himself the right to apply our definition of philosophy to what was written in Islam, hence to define its domain by external criteria.[33] Thus *falsafa* becomes the shadow that rationalistic Western philosophy casts on Islamic thought. He proposes reversing that image, rereading Western thought by privileging what is present in it that is in harmony with the tendencies he discerns in Islamic thought and focusing on all that is "traditional," as, for example, in Jacob Boehme and Swedenborg.[34]

A response to Corbin's theses requires consideration of the dimension of value.

Value

The Religious Restructuring of the Range of the Medieval Episteme

Concerning what I have called the "value" of philosophy, I have posited that it becomes comprehensible only within the *episteme* as a whole. However, the entire field of the medieval *episteme* includes a phenomenon that is not to be found in the ancient *episteme*, which is the emergence of revealed religions. The presence of religions based on authoritative texts within the three medieval cultural realms forced them into a thoroughgoing restructuring. Certain medieval authors attempted to distinguish between a given thinker's philosophical acquisitions and his religion, which might be considered false: this is what Duns Scotus does in relation to Avicenna, from whom he borrowed copiously.[35] Others suggested a comparison with the situation of philosophy in the ancient world. In a famous passage, Maimonides, for example, adds a fourth source of error to the three mentioned by Alexander of Aphrodisias, which is the opinion that the revealed books can be taken as authoritative.[36] Well before Maimonides, his master Farabi noted the same phenomenon, although he speaks of it with discretion: the "opinions generally admitted" (*mashhūrāt; endoxa*) within a given community constitute for all philosophies the base on which they can build. As it happens, those opinions are historically conditioned, and they come, in the final analysis, from the legislator of the community.[37]

Philosophers of the Middle Ages felt that presence as a pressure. In a famous and often-commented text, Thomas Aquinas speaks of the *angustia* of the Greek philosophical geniuses before the question of the ultimate beatitude.[38] In contrast, certain Jewish philosophers used the same image to express the weight of the Torah. Thus Gersonides writes about Maimonides' doctrine of knowledge through God: "It seems to us that Maimonides' position on this question of divine cognition is not implied by any philosophical principles: indeed, reason denies this view, as I will show. It seems rather that theological considerations have forced him to this view (*lahasato hat-Torah be-zeh ha-inyan lahas rav*)."[39] The expression is extremely strong: the verb that Gersonides uses is the one used in the Bible for the oppression to which the Egyptians subjected the Sons of Israel (Exodus 3:9).

All medieval philosophical worlds were affected by this phenomenon, but we need to see it in relation to the way in which revelation is presented in the various religions and how men received it. Muslim and Jewish revelations, which are presented as laws, do not pose the same problems as Christian revelation. Since the latter is the revelation of a person, hence of "mysteries," it is understood primarily as requiring faith.[40] Reconciling religion and philosophy is an epistemological problem in Christianity, and even a psychological one; in Islam and in Judaism, it is primarily a political problem. What is more, the philosopher who lives according to one of these religions has a responsibility of a political nature. To cite a concise but brilliant formula of Warren Z. Harvey's: "Socrates was judged; Averroes and Maimonides were judges."[41]

The Institutionalization of Philosophy

Nor was the range of each of the three medieval *epistemai* structured in the same manner. Unlike Islam and Judaism, Christianity includes the magisterium of the Church, an instance charged with discernment of minds, hence granted authority in the intellectual domain.

There is one massive phenomenon that it seems to me that specialists in Western medieval thought tend to take for granted, which is the institutionalization of philosophy. This took place—precisely—under the tutelage of the Church. To be sure, the medieval university has been extensively studied, but what is important is that it is exclusively European. There was indeed something like higher education in all three of the Mediterranean worlds, but the teaching of philosophy at the university level existed in neither the Muslim world nor the Jewish communities. Jewish philosophy and Muslim philosophy were private activities, which concerned individuals. The usual procedure is to compare the "great" philosophers of each tradition, for example, Averroes, Maimonides, and Thomas Aquinas.

This attitude is totally justifiable, but it masks the fact that the philosophers who are considered important in the Christian context stand out from a mass of persons of secondary or even less importance, all of whom were engaged in some sort of intellectual activity. These are obscure figures, common soldiers. To pursue the military image (if I may be forgiven a bit of irreverence), Muslim philosophy and Jewish philosophy are comparable to a comic-strip South American army of 3,487 colonels and 49 corporals.[42] The consequences of this imbalance are many. For example, there is no corpus of canonical texts that lent themselves to being studied in such educational contexts as the regular practice of the *disputatio*.

One author who has reflected on the consequences of the presence or absence of an institutionalized philosophy is Leo Strauss. According to him, there is a fundamental difference between the status of philosophy in Christianity, on the one hand, and in Islam and Judaism, on the other. For Strauss, the institutionalization of philosophy is a double-edged sword:

> The status of philosophy was, as a matter of principle, much more precarious in Judaism and in Islam than in Christianity: in Christianity philosophy became an integral part of the officially recognized and even required training of the student of the sacred doctrine. This difference explains partly the eventual collapse of philosophical inquiry in the Islamic and in the Jewish world, a collapse which had no parallel in the Western Christian world. The precarious status of philosophy in Judaism as well as in Islam was not in every respect a misfortune for philosophy. The official recognition of philosophy in the Christian world made philosophy subject to ecclesiastical supervision. The precarious position of philosophy in the Islamic-Jewish world guaranteed its private character and therewith its inner freedom from supervision.[43]

Also according to Leo Strauss, the tense relations between *falsafa* and Kalām at least prevented philosophy from suffering the same fate in Islamic lands and the Jewish communities that it did in the Christian West, where it played a secondary role to theology. Supposing this declaration to represent Strauss's real thoughts, I shall have occasion to contest it.

Modes of Appropriation

Thus far I have spoken only about the definition of the field of the medieval *episteme* in its religious restructuring and about the place accorded to philosophy within it. All of this concerns the internal geography of that field. What I would like to do now is offer a remark on its relationship with what lay outside of it.

It is well known that medieval philosophies took nourishment from ancient sources—Aristotle for the better part, to a lesser degree Neoplatonism, with some traces of influences from other Greek schools. That said (and it is obvious), one might note some interesting nuances in the relationship between the various medieval philosophical worlds and their Greek sources. I will not outline the various ways in which the Greek inheritance was interpreted. Indeed, that interpretation must be made in the function of already-constituted philosophical tendencies and, to a certain extent, it is the very history of medieval philosophy. Rather, I would like to situate myself face-to-face with the philosophical work itself, on the level where the possibilities that will be imparted to it are decided and where the choices it will have to make are lined up.

We tend to confuse the reception of a philosophic work with the fact of reading it and commenting on it. What is more, we spontaneously identify the commentary with one of its species. To simplify things, I shall distinguish between two of those species. A commentary can reproduce the lemmas of the text to be explicated, or it can present the text as an integral whole by paraphrasing it. In the first case, the letter of the source is maintained, surrounded by elements that enhance it; in the second, the source loses its independence and the difference between the commented text and the commenting text is erased. I see in these two styles of commentary particular instances of two more general models of the appropriation of a cultural heritage.[44] I propose to call them "inclusion" and "digestion." What I call "inclusion" is an appropriation in which the foreign body is maintained in its full alterity but is enveloped by procedures of appropriation, the presence of which highlights that alterity; what I call "digestion" is an appropriation in which the foreign body is assimilated to the point of losing its independence.

If we look at the different ways in which earlier philosophical texts—Aristotle, for the most part—were commented on, localizing them by cultures and placing them back in their time periods, we note that the Greek commentators of classical antiquity practiced both commentary and paraphrase. Themistius numbers among the latter. In contrast, the great Neoplatonic commentators, Simplicius, for example, had a predilection for commentary.

In Islam we have commentaries of Farabi's, for example, the *Treatise on Aristotle's De Interpretatione* as well as shorter texts that return to some of the treatises of Aristotle's *Organon*, adapting the contents of that work and even adopting its title. Avicenna represents an important step: unlike the Christian Aristotelians of Baghdad, Avicenna—a Muslim—is the first to prefer completely rewriting the Aristotelian corpus. He does so in his great encyclopedia, which, as a good physician, he titles *The Book of Health* (*Kitāb al-Shifā'*), but he also simply annotates certain texts of Aristotle, or thought to be by Aristotle, such as *De anima*, the *Metaphysics* (lambda), and the so-called *Theology of Aristotle*. He absorbs Aristotelianism to such a point that, after him, *"falsafa"* meant "Avicennism" much more than it did "Aristotelianism." Averroes, in something like a return to the method of Farabi, follows both procedures, according to the type of commentary that he is writing. He follows the "digestion" method in his abridgments (*jawami'*) and his "middle" (*sharh*) commentaries, and the inclusion method in his "great" commentaries (*tafsīr*).

Among the Christians, Albertus Magnus operated in much the same way as Avicenna. Thomas Aquinas wrote no abridgments, but rather great commentaries that all returned to the method of Averroes' commentaries.

Where Averroes' exegetical works are concerned, we can see a highly interesting difference between Jewish and Christian philosophers: Jews utilized the abridgments, not the great commentaries; right from the start, Christians used the great commentaries and had little acquaintance with abridgments until the Renaissance. Moreover, it is in the wake of Christian Scholasticism that the Jews came to be interested in the great commentaries of Averroes, hence, in the actual text of Aristotle.

The place of Averroes is decisive in this connection. With him, an era is considered to come to an end, even if that end was not the end of everything. In any event, Averroes is the last Muslim author to have written commentaries on Aristotle. Corbin notes all sorts of things regarding the authors whom he rediscovered, but their works do not include a single commentary on the works of Aristotle. The only exception is that of Qadi Sa'id Qummi, an Iranian of the seventeenth century, who wrote a commentary—or, one might say, a "counter-commentary" in response to Avicenna—on a work of Aristotelian pseudepigraphy, the famous *Theology*.

It is possible that the latter work represents a line of demarcation. The presence of Aristotle where he is not known simply as a name, easily transformable into a tutelary figure, but where the actual text of his oeuvre is conserved and commented on hinders the total digestion of Greek philosophy.

Against Involuntary Baptisms

I would like to follow what I have just said with two remarks, one regarding the name of philosophy, the other its status in the Middle Ages.

On the question of knowing what is philosophical in Islamic culture, I need to respond to Corbin. He argues that we have no right to apply our Western concept of philosophy to Islamic thought and exclude from it what does not enter into that concept. That argument can be turned the other way around, however: If we must refuse to take the Western concept of philosophy as a criterion of exclusion, why should we keep it as a criterion of admission? What right have we to call "philosophy" something that preferred other terms for itself? Those terms abound: "wisdom" (*hikma*), "gnosis" (*'irfān*), "divine science," or (as Corbin suggests) "theosophy" (*hikma ilāhīyah*), and more. My strongest argument can be drawn from a remark made by Corbin himself that seems to me of capital importance: "It is difficult to trace the exact boundaries between the use of the terms *falsafah* (philosophy) and *hikmat ilāhīyah* (*theosophia*). But it appears that after al-Suhrawardi the latter term has been used more and more to designate the doctrine of the complete sage, who is both philosopher and mystic."[45]

Thought after Suhrawardi is thus less and less called "*falsafa*" and more and more called by another name, for which Corbin cannot find a French equivalent, and hence feels obliged to forge a Latin term. It seems to me that we have here more than a question of simple terminology. In reality, the refusal to share the same term indicates a determination to establish a certain distance. Moreover, *falsafa* is a transcribed Greek word and, as we have seen, it was perceived as foreign. In contrast, *hikma* is an Arabic word that emerges from a root taken from the old Semitic base of that language. This shift from one word to another is a sign of the integration of a discipline that was first perceived as of foreign origin into the edifice of the Islamic *episteme*. This leads me to my second point.

Regarding the status of philosophy and the contradictory consequences of its institutionalization in Latin Christianity, I also feel the need to debate with Leo Strauss, or at least with what I have understood of his thought.[46] To put the matter succinctly and express it in my own terms, it seems to me that Strauss has not done enough to distinguish between inclusion and digestion. Thus I would like to risk the thesis that in Christianity philosophy was included more than it was digested.

The institutionalization of philosophy is a social reality. But it is parallel to an epistemological reality, which is what I shall call its installation within the field of learning in a place defined in relation to other disciplines. Here philosophy is defined above all in relation to theology. Conflicts are conflicts of borderlines. In Islam, on the other hand, *falsafa*, Kalām, Sufism, and even Shiite "prophetic philosophy" struggle not so much for a place in the sun as for a total reorganization, to their advantage, of the area of knowledge. Farabi's attempt to do this (which failed) perhaps consisted in reformulating all of Islamic learning around *falsafa*; Ghazali's operation of the revival of religious sciences (an operation that succeeded well) was an effort to put into place a similar reorganization of Sufism. Within Judaism, one can perhaps say that Maimonides had a project that paralleled that of Farabi, while the authors of the Kabbalah had the same objective as Ghazali. In a word, Christianity faced the problem of situating itself in relation to an authority that already existed, that of the Church; in Islam and in Judaism, it was a question of *becoming* the authority. This is what explains a fact on which Leo Strauss had the merit of throwing light: in the Islamic domain and in the Jewish domain, as long as it remained within the orbit of Islam, philosophy—by which I mean *falsafa*—had to become, in essence, political philosophy.

In fact, the institutionalization of philosophy in Christianity is the contrary of a digestion: if philosophy was absorbed within the larger edifice of a culture (that is, if it was digested), it is rather in Islamic lands that the phenomenon took place. It would be erroneous to say that grafting philosophy on to Muslim culture failed. We might even say, ironically, that the graft succeeded all too well. Philosophy was not so much expelled as it was phagocytized. It has been said that something analogous occurred in the domain of the natural sciences, where Greek thought was all too easily instrumentalized by Muslim culture.[47] In Latin Europe, whether or not the place of philosophy was subordinate—or ancillary, if one insists—it retained a relative autonomy. One of the signs of that autonomy is the continued presence, within the Christian intellectual sphere, of the text— that is, of the letter of what the pagan philosophers had said. Once again, we cannot comprehend medieval Latin philosophy, or perhaps the modern European philosophy that followed it, uniquely on the basis of its content. We also need to take into account what I have called its "value"—here, the fact that it runs parallel to another domain of knowledge and the relationship of comparison with the letter of the philosophical texts—whether that domain is dubbed philology, history, or something else.

Conclusion

In conclusion, may I be permitted several remarks related to the diachronic. The cultural areas that I have called *epistemai* are not immutable realities. They have nuclei and moments of rupture and redistribution. The end of the twelfth century was a moment of that sort. This is a well-accepted notion, and it is usually applied to Latin philosophy. Regarding the Islamicized world, Henry Corbin saw the nearly simultaneous death dates of Averroes (1198) and Suhrawardi (1191) as an important sign of a similar end.[48] All I would like to add here is a few more prosaic facts, seen in a comparative perspective.

A curious two-way exchange takes place during the evolution of the word "philosophy." If the Latin word *philosophus* has taken on the meaning that it has today, it was under the influence of the model of the philosopher imported from the Islamic world. Hence (and I might say incidentally) the definition of philosophy with which Orientalists are blamed for labeling Islamic thought is by no means Western; quite to the contrary, it too came from Islam. I attach the greatest importance to a fact that Jean Jolivet has stressed: the "philosopher" (*philosophus*) who debates with a Jew and a Christian in Abelard's dialogue is a Muslim. That personage, who is circumcised and claims descent from Ishmael, attempts to set up an ethics independent of revelation. It is possible that his portrait was inspired by real person, even if only through gossip passed on by someone like Ibn Bājja.[49] What is important is that this human type—one that some find a temptation and others, a type to be exorcised—continued to haunt Latin Christianity. As it happens, that model was by then exclusive to Andalusia, which stood out as different from the Islamic East; in its land of origin, it was already petering out.

This means that it was precisely at the time when the Latin *philosophus*—when it did not designate Aristotle—came to signify *faylasuf* that, in the Islamic world, the use of the Arabic word *faylasuf* began to give way to other terms. Call that development what you will. The fact remains that, in the East, the word for "philosophy" declined in favor of other words. In parallel fashion, in the same period the relationship with the Philosopher par excellence—Aristotle—ceased to have a textual dimension in that world. The twelfth century is the age in which Islamic thought fully digested Greek philosophy, the same Greek philosophy that Europe, somewhat later and perhaps to our own times, was to find hard to digest.

3

Just How Is Islamic Philosophy Islamic?

For fifteen years now I have been teaching a discipline whose name I do not know. Several have been proposed, and I maneuver among them as best I can. It seems to me that this perplexity and this hesitation contains more than a simple quarrel over words, and that it expresses a basic difficulty, about which it is important to be clear.

Names

We often hear talk of "Arabic philosophy." That supposes that we renounce the ethnic aspect to concentrate on language, because the only ethnic Arab to have indulged in philosophy is al-Kindi, "the philosopher of the Arabs."

Another expression that can be heard, "Islamic philosophy," supposes that we distinguish between Islam as a religion and Islam as a cultural space, given that there are Jews, Christians, and even freethinkers who also belong to the Islamic cultural world. Some scholars have forged neologisms, using "Islamic" or other similar terms to show that one should focus exclusively on the civilization. This is an attitude for which the late Lawrence Berman invented the adjective "islamicate."[1]

The oddest expression is perhaps the official description of my current post: I teach "Arabic-language philosophy" (*philosophie de langue arabe*). Admittedly, it is true that the authors whom I study wrote their works in Arabic. The fact remains, though, that certain authors who wrote in Arabic also published works in Persian, as did Avicenna, Ghazali, and Suhrawardi. Moreover, no one would think

of speaking of "Greek-language philosophy" or "German-language philosophy," preferring simply "Greek philosophy" or "German philosophy"
even if the language does not coincide with the author's ethnic origin,
and even less with the modern notion of nationality. Greek was used by
Macedonians like Aristotle, and even by Phoenicians like Zeno, the Stoic,
or Porphyry. There was a German philosophy well before 1871, which even
reached its apogee at a time in which hardly anyone was dreaming of German unity.

Can a Philosophy Be Named for a Religion?

Here I would like to consider the expression "Islamic philosophy." To designate a philosophy on the basis of a religious confession is perhaps an
even riskier enterprise than naming it on the basis of a language. What
is most astonishing is that we no longer find this astonishing: a particular
branch of philosophy's family tree is accepted as being "Islamic philosophy," just as if this were the most natural thing in the world.

As a thought experiment, one might try associating other periods in
the history of philosophy with religions. Plato, Aristotle, and Plotinus
pass for being the principal figures in Greek philosophy. Where religion is
concerned, they were—to use a Jewish and Christian concept—"pagans,"
but only very exceptionally are they called "pagan philosophers." To tell
the truth, I can think of only one example of this term, which appears in
the imposing work of Alexandre Kojève (d. 1968), the author of a three-
volume "reasoned history of pagan philosophy" extracted from the considerable mass of his posthumous papers and published in the 1960s and
1970s.[2] According to the somewhat eccentric interpretation of that Franco-
Russian government official and thinker, there are three sorts of philosophy: pagan philosophy, Christian philosophy (which reaches its height
with Kant), and atheist philosophy (which begins with Hegel and under-
goes a renaissance with Kojève himself).

The philosophy of German idealism retains clear traces of its origin
in the Protestant Reformation: it is not for nothing that Fichte, Hegel,
and Schelling started out as theology students. Nietzsche, himself the son
of a pastor, lampooned theology for the same reason.[3] And yet no one
would think of speaking about a "Protestant philosophy." Oddly enough,
the term "Catholic philosophy" is accepted, as witnessed by the existence
of a voluminous history of Catholic philosophy.[4]

In spite of all this, the expression "Islamic philosophy" is used without
hesitation. In collective works dedicated to it, we find chapters dedicated

to Razi, a freethinker and a pitiless critic of the idea of prophecy, as well as to Jewish and Christian thinkers. We also find—and this is even more suspect—mystics and jurists who never claimed to be philosophers, or who even accused the philosophers of being heretics. Speaking for myself, I would opt for a closer definition of philosophy, and have already argued in that sense.[5] What I would like to examine here is not the substantive in the expression "Islamic philosophy," but the adjective.

It should be mentioned in passing that a similar clarification would be welcome in the case of the expression "Jewish philosophy," not to mention "Jewish thought." Shlomo Pines, a man with a profound knowledge of that discipline, which he taught at the Hebrew University of Jerusalem, denied the existence of a specifically Jewish philosophy: the Jews, he claimed, did indeed immerse themselves in philosophy and even made advances in it, but they did not necessarily practice a *Jewish* philosophy.[6]

Debate

In France in the 1930s, a lengthy polemic took place around the term "Christian philosophy." Such highly eminent minds and members of the university establishment of the time as Étienne Gilson and Émile Bréhier, among the historians, participated in it. The focus of this debate was not the value, or lack of value, of one or another philosophical position, but rather the Christian nature of what was called "Christian philosophy," as well as the possibility of associating oneself, as a philosopher, with a religious position or, contrariwise, of pursuing philosophy if one was a believing Christian. No such debate took place about the appropriateness of the expression "Islamic philosophy." Perhaps the moment has come to make up for lost time.

Let me begin by turning the topic around: Why has the same question not been asked in an equally shattering way about Islam? I shall propose several reasons, all of which are pure hypotheses.

First, when the "Christian" character of a particular philosophy was under discussion, the question of Christian philosophy as a part of the Christian cultural domain—what was known as Christendom—never came up. It was simply taken as understood. In the case of Islam, however, it is not an easy matter to separate Islamic civilization and religious Islam. No difference in vocabulary allows us to distinguish between Islam as a civilization and Islam as a religious attitude, although French permits the useful convention of writing the first with a capital letter and the second with a lowercase.

Second, Islam, as a religion, accentuates the concept of faith less than Christianity does. In the latter, faith is the fundamental attitude where religion is concerned. The object of that faith is the existence of God and his action in the history of salvation. In Islam, the existence of God is almost taken as obvious: what one must believe is rather the oneness of God. The enemy is not so much atheism as it is what is called *shirk*, which associates other entities with the one God. Hence the difference between adhering to a faith and belonging to a culture is less clear in Islam than in the Christian religion.

Third and last, no theology developed within Islam that aimed at a rational knowledge of divine things, as was true in Christianity, beginning with St. Anselm: Kalām is purely apologetic. Within the Christian world, one can draw a line separating philosophy and theology. Philosophy's only instrument is natural reason, while theology requires revelation. Thus Thomas Aquinas devotes the first three sections of his *Summa contra Gentiles* to philosophical problems, but with the fourth, which treats problems founded on revealed truths, all possibility of dialogue with the pagan philosophers ceases. Still, some philosophers within Christianity also examine theological questions. Thus Descartes attempted to formulate a physical explication of the Eucharist in his correspondence with Père Mesland, S.J.[7] The fact remains that, roughly speaking, Christianity distinguishes more clearly between theology, a specifically Christian science, and a philosophy that is, in principle, neutral regarding faith. Islam, on the other hand, is forced to introduce a religious determination even into philosophy.

The Pertinence of Religion

First, however, we need to pose the general question of the pertinence of religious affiliation regarding the philosophers of the Middle Ages. I consider this question to be a program for further research. I am hardly able to offer a definitive answer to it, and I await the aid of my colleagues. What follows is thus little more than a questionnaire addressed to those more competent in this matter than I.

Let us begin with questions: Would the philosophers of one religious group consider the religious affiliation of their colleagues of another religion to be an important criterion? Very concretely: Does it happen that a medieval philosopher mentions the religion of a colleague when it differs from his own? If that happens only rarely, one might think that if he is silent on this point, it is because religious affiliation represents something obvious indicated by the very name of the thinker. And when religion is mentioned, in spite of all, we might well wonder whether the thinkers of the Middle Ages saw a relationship between the philosophical theses and the religious belief of those who argued in support of those theses.

For example, do writers try to show that their adversary's philosophical orientation derives from his religious affiliation? Can we read such phrases as "X argues for philosophical thesis T, which is hardly surprising, given that he belongs to religion R"? A declaration of the sort could be read in two ways. First, in a weaker version, it could signify that a certain vision of the world (taking "the world" in a very broad sense) could be expressed in the religious register just as well as in the philosophical register; second, in a stronger version, it could be a precursor of a latter-day "critique of ideologies" in which a philosopher would be capable of downplaying his true philosophical convictions so as to assure an advantage to his religion, in which case his confession of faith would be only lip service.

What follows is simply a few examples.

Ad extra: 1. Seen from Islam

One consequence of the Islamic elite's appropriation of the intellectual inheritance of the Greeks was the view that Islam was the unique legitimate heir to Greek culture, while Christians—and in particular the people of the Byzantine Empire, the political enemies of the caliphs—were decadent and unworthy.[8] Within such a context, an attack on the part of Islamic philosophers against Christians is to be expected.

Farabi tells of his years of philosophical training, and, in doing so, he seeks to present himself as the last descendant of a certain tradition of strict Aristotelianism. He mentions his masters and his fellow philosophy students. He says of his Christian comrades that they drifted away from the profession of philosophy because they became occupied with things of their religion—to put it bluntly, they became bishops.[9] One cannot help but note the pejorative nuance. Still, we have the right to wonder to what extent his remarks were aimed at a particular religion—here, Christianity—or religion in general. It seems to me that his target here is rather Kalām in general, his sworn enemy and a discipline that exists in Christian and Jewish versions as well as Islamic ones.

In his "Book of Equitable Judgment," a work of which we have only fragments, Avicenna attacks the Aristotelians of Baghdad, arguing his own "Oriental philosophy" against them. In a letter to his disciple Kiyā, he speaks of "those silly Christians of Baghdad (al-bulhu al-nasārā min ahl Ma-

dinati s-Salām)."[10] But is he taking into account the fact that they are Christians? Did he consider his adversaries silly because they were Christians or because they were incompetent philosophers?

The philosophers based in Islamic civilization were aware of the possibility that certain Christian philosophers would have argued some theses precisely because they were Christians. John Philoponus, mindful of Socrates' fate, may have defended the creation of the world in order to escape persecution. In any event, Farabi and Avicenna both expressed suspicions of this sort.[11] Maimonides did the same, suggesting that the real ancestor of the people of the Kalām was Philoponus, who attempted to use philosophical proofs to support a conviction derived from elsewhere than philosophy.[12]

Ad extra: 2. Seen from Judaism

Maimonides ends his response to a letter (which has disappeared) from his translator Samuel Ibn Tibbon with opinions on the value (positive and negative) of certain philosophers, probably commenting on a list of philosophical works that Ibn Tibbon had submitted to him.[13] For the most part, Maimonides mentions classical and Muslim philosophers. The place of honor, after Aristotle, the patron saint of the philosophical corporation, is reserved for Farabi, a Muslim. Avicenna, also a Muslim, is listed among the second-tier thinkers. Maimonides briefly mentions the commentaries on Aristotle of three Baghdad Christians, al-Tayyib, Yahyā ibn 'Adī, and al-Bitriq, pronouncing the rather severe judgment that reading them would be a waste of time. Maimonides does not say much about his own co-religionists, but the few words he does devote to them display a genuine scorn: the writings of Isaac Israeli are worthless, since he was merely a physician (Maimonides says the same of Razi); Joseph ha-Saddiq was indeed a scholar, but he was of the tendency of the "Brethren of Purity" of Basra, which was enough to discredit him.[14]

Maimonides never explicitly mentions the religion of the thinkers he discusses. We know that the three commentators whose commentaries he so brutally rejects were Christians, but did Ibn Tibbon know it? If he did, it was not from Maimonides.

Ad extra: 3. Seen from Christianity

The Christian Scholastics were well aware that Avicenna and other philosophers were Muslims. When they spoke of them, they did so using terms in use at the time, such as *Arabi*, *Mauri*, or *Saraceni*, all of which refer to their language more than their ethnic origin.[15] Still, the difference of religion was clear. It was just as clear to them that Maimonides was Jewish, in fact, a rabbi, "Rabbi Moses." From time to time, Thomas Aquinas explicitly refers to him as *Moses judaeus*.[16] On the other hand, the Scholastics were not as clear regarding the religious affiliation of Avicebron, and the same was true of later scholars until as late as 1846, when Salomon Munk recognized him as the poet Ibn Gabirol, who was, incidentally, famous among the Jews.

The Scholastics alternated between praise and criticism of these thinkers. Like all Christians, they were extremely critical of Islam as a religion.[17] But did they accord any importance to the religious affiliation of the philosophers as something that might affect their philosophy? When they were critical of a thinker's philosophical position, was their negative attitude connected with his rejection of Islam? I am not questioning the presence of the two elements, only a possible relation of causality between them.

Here, then, are a few examples, given in chronological order:

The philosopher who participates in Abelard's dialogue is without any doubt a Muslim: he is circumcised and a descendant of Ishmael. But Abelard never claims that the philosophical position of his interlocutor has anything to do with Islam as a religion. What is more, that philosopher is not a very orthodox Muslim, given that he defends the possibility of a purely philosophical ethics. It is possible, moreover, that he represents an attitude analogous to that of Ibn Bājja.[18]

Albertus Magnus states that in matters of doctrine regarding the intellect, he prefers the Arab philosophers to the Christian ones, whose views he scorns.[19]

When Thomas Aquinas attacks *loquentes in lege Maurorum*, as he does, for example, in the *Summa contra Gentiles*, he does so in the wake of the only authority he cites, Maimonides.[20] It is probable that the Mutakallimun attempted to use atomism to provide a doctrinal transposition of the worldview of the Qur'an. If so, Thomas was unaware of it. Whatever the case, he does not stress the religious affiliation of those whom he attacks.

Meister Eckhart often uses the expression "a pagan master" when he cites Aristotle,[21] Seneca,[22] Macrobius,[23] or others. Themistius is for him "a Greek master."[24] In similar fashion, the anonymous author of the *Liber de causis* is for him a pagan.[25] But he also calls the Muslim Avicenna "a pagan master,"[26] as he does the Jew Maimonides,[27] or, in an even more flagrant error, Boethius, a Christian.[28] Yet the value of what these authors say does not depend on their religion.

In the prologue to his *Ordinatio*, Duns Scotus distinguishes between what Avicenna teaches as a philosopher and what he was obliged to say as a Muslim: "He mixed his religion (*secta*), which was that of Muhammad, with philosophical elements (*philosophica*), and he said certain things as philosophical and proven by reason and others as in accord with his religion."[29] To my knowledge, this passage is more of an exception than the rule. It is amusing to note that Duns Scotus is repeating here a suspicion that had already arisen within Islam: according to Averroes, Avicenna diluted the wine of philosophy with the water of Kalām in an attempt to curry favor with influential persons of his day.[30]

Ad intra: Islam's Self-Image

Was affiliation with Islam, the religion, important for the self-image of the philosophers of Islam, the culture? In other words: Was there any point in remarking that a particular colleague was or was not a Muslim?

Farabi reconstructs the birth of philosophy among the peoples who inherited it from an earlier people. It is not hard to see that he was thinking above all of Greek philosophy as it was received by peoples of Arab culture.[31] Farabi speaks often about the Arabs and their language. He recalls that both the transmitters and the receivers had a religion, to which he avoids giving a name.

On occasion Averroes mentions thinkers whom he calls the "philosophers of Islam," by which he means Farabi and Avicenna,[32] whom he calls "the moderns among the philosophers" (*falāsifa*) or "among the sages" (*hukamā*)" of Islam,[33] and, even more simply, "the moderns."[34] He also remarks that a certain theory—in this case, the one according to which forms derive from a *dator formarum* (*wāhib as-suwar*)—is not to be found among the ancient philosophers, but only among certain of the philosophers of Islam, and he follows this remark with an explicit reference to Avicenna.[35] Averroes portrays the history of philosophy as being constituted by two parties: the ancient philosophers and, after them, the Muslims. Among the ancients, there was above all Aristotle and his master Plato, but Averroes is also aware of the existence of earlier thinkers, in later times known as "pre-Socratics," whom he calls "those who came before Plato" or "before Aristotle," or even "the first of the ancients" (*man salafa min al-qudamā*).[36] To my knowledge, he never uses the expression by which Islam often designates the period that preceded it: the "ignorance" (*jāhiliyya*). It was unthinkable to accuse someone like Aristotle, "the Sage" (*al-Hakīm*) par excellence, of being ignorant! Thus it seems that, for Averroes, "Islam" had, above all, a chronological signification. The word designated the second apogee of philosophy, after the Greeks. As for the possibility that he could have dreamed that philosophy might take hold among Christians or Jews, it seems highly unlikely.

In his refutation of Ghazali, Averroes speaks of "Avicenna and others as being among those who are attached to Islam"; once again he distinguishes between their doctrines and those of the ancients. Averroes claims that Ghazali, his adversary, had acquired a great reputation for himself "in the nation of Islam."[37]

In one highly instructive passage of his *Abridgment of the Physics*, Averroes speaks of the religious affiliation of certain thinkers. He speaks, in this context, of the "Mutakallimun among the people of our religious community (*milla*) and among the religious community of the Christians." Later in the same text, he mentions "those who philosophize (*mutafalsifūn*) among the people of our religious community,"[38] an expression in which the participle *mutafalsif* bears, as is often the case, a pejorative nuance, indicating something like an "amateur in philosophy" or even an "amateur philosopher." The word *milla*, unlike the word "Islam," which is the name of a historical period, designates a religious community in its religious aspect. We have the impression that it is only the sworn enemies of philosophy or incompetent, hobbyist philosophers who are designated in terms of their religious affiliation.

To date I have found only one text in which a philosopher's confession of Islamic faith is explicitly emphasized, and it comes in a relatively late work. In his treatise on ethics, Nasīr ad-Dīn Tūsī (d. 1274) cites a number of philosophers. Among the ancients, there is Aristotle, of course, but also Plato, even though the declarations he attributes to them often have little to do with the works that we now have available of those thinkers. For his treatment of economics (that is, the management of the household), Tūsī uses generous fragments of the work of a Hellenistic author of a treatise on "economy" (household management) known as "Bryson." Among the moderns, he appropriates the ideas of Farabi and Miskawayh. What is striking here is that he also cites al-Kindi, who, as is known, is not mentioned even once by the corporation of the *falāsifa* of strict Aristotelian observance—that is, Farabi, Avicenna, Ibn Bājja, Ibn Tufayl, and Averroes.

Tūsī discusses al-Kindi's brief work on the means for chasing away sadness, and he introduces the author thus: "Ya'qūb al-Kindi, who was one of the philosophers of Islam (*az hukamā-yi islām*)." That formula attracted the attention of the translator, who notes in his annotations: "The appellation given him by Tūsī . . . raises all sorts of problems turning on (a) the ambiguity of the Arabic term for 'wise man, philosopher,' . . . and, (b) the question whether 'of Islam' means 'writing within the Islamic era, as opposed to ancient times' or 'as a Muslim concerned to harmonize philosophy with the Islamic faith.'"[39] The same expression does not occur when Tūsī speaks of other philosophers from the Islamic world such as Farabi and Avicenna, who are named only once, what is more.[40] The same holds true for Miskawayh, his principal source and the author of the most famous of the treatises on the refinement of customs, whose name appears in Tūsī even sooner than that of al-Kindi, either as Miskawayh or as his *kunya*, Abū Alī.[41]

Contents

Are the principal themes of the Islamic philosophers closely connected to the religion of Islam? An excellent list of the five principal themes can be found in a recent and highly dependable introduction to Islamic philosophy by Massimo Campanini. These are: the *tawhīd* (the declaration that Allah is One); the structure of the cosmos; the human intellect; necessity or liberty in the actions of God (which amounts in fact to the question of the eternity or the adventitious character of the world); and the ethical and political domains.[42] These themes are quite evidently present everywhere in Islamic thought. But have we a right to neglect the question of the extent to which Islamic thinkers were thinking in Islamic terms?

A distinction seems opportune at this point. There are ideas that can of course be found in Islam, as a religion, but that belong to the common store of revealed religions, such as the oneness of God (the basis of monotheism), the creation of the world, and the survival of souls after death, as associated with eternal reward or punishment in paradise or hell. These correspond, roughly, to the first half of the Muslim confession of faith, "There is no other God than Allah." Others are found only in Islam and provide its distinctive criteria. They correspond to the second half of the Muslim confession of faith, which concerns the mission of Muhammad and all that depends on it. When that mission—hence the authenticity of the Qur'an—is acknowledged, certain details can be added to the common store of monotheism. Among these, for example, is a rejection of the Christian dogmas of the Trinity and the Incarnation, a more detailed presentation of the process of the creation of the world, and a more highly colored description of the voluptuous pleasures of paradise and the torments of hell, not to mention the dispositions of Islamic Law.

I would propose characterizing the first series of articles of faith, the ones that lie beyond the frontiers separating confessions, as "monotheistic" rather than specifically "Islamic." In that case, to what extent can we speak of a specifically Islamic content of philosophy? In order to respond to that question, we need a brief review of the five domains distinguished by Campanini.

1. The Tawḥīd

The use of the term *tawḥīd* gives an Islamic cast to the concept of the oneness of God and confers a sort of local color on it. But what is understood by the term is the reception of the intellectual inheritance of Neoplatonism.[43] That reception was massive. But what connection does it have with the Qurʾanic *tawḥīd*? If the fact that this reception is obvious, so is the simplification that Neoplatonism underwent in it. Plotinus had indeed defended a strict distinction between the One and the Intellect. Arabic Neoplatonism gave up that distinction, perhaps influenced by late Greek Neoplatonism, which was less rigorous on this point than Plotinus. Merging the One and the Intellect had the effect of creating an entity that was unique, knew everything, and had created everything, thus producing a philosophically acceptable equivalent of the God of the monotheisms, among them, the Allah of the Qurʾan.

But what does the One of Neoplatonism have to do with Allah? In the Qurʾan, polytheism is constantly gibed at: there is but one God. This is stated with particular clarity in the often-cited surah known under the title "Purity of Faith" (*al-Ikhlās*), which uses a formula with a Neoplatonic ring to it: "He begets not, neither is He begotten."[44] Relating such declarations to the Neoplatonic heritage depends, however, on a reinterpretation of the concept of "one." The Qurʾan maintains the *oneness* of God. The question to which it responds is that of the *number* of divine beings. This can be seen, for example, in the way in which it refutes a certain conception of the Trinity: God is not "one of three in a Trinity" (5:73). Neoplatonism, to the contrary, accentuates the *unity* of the supreme principle. It does so, what is more, by situating the supreme principle beyond the distinction between subject and object, a distinction that every act of cognition brings with it. This is true above all in the case of the self-knowledge of the Aristotelian God in book lambda of the *Metaphysics*, a conception against which Plotinus openly polemicizes.[45] For even greater reason, this insistence on the strict unity of the One excludes all possibility of attributing to it any knowledge of what is situated beneath it.

The philosophers speak of the "First" (*al-Awwal*). Does this entity coincide with the Allah of Islam? Not really. In his work on the opinions of the inhabitants of the virtuous city, Farabi, to pick one example, begins with a detailed description of the "First" in which the name of Allah does not appear. It appears for the first time late in the text, in the context of a doctrine of prophecy put into operation by the imagination. Among the objects of that faculty, there are Allah and the angels.[46]

2. The Structure of the Universe

When the philosophers describe the structure of the physical world, they discreetly leave to one side what the Qur'an says on the subject. They find *nine* celestial spheres nestled within one another, following the scientific astronomy of their age, rather than the seven heavens of the Qur'an (2:29 and elsewhere).

In his *Decisive Discourse* (*Fasl al-maqāl*), Averroes attempts to justify the practice of philosophy by citing certain passages of the Qur'an that recommend reflection on creation. When it is for the purpose of proving the existence of God, meditation on creation is supposed to be exactly what the philosophical enterprise means.[47] We can leave aside the rigor of these arguments and also the value of the definition of philosophy that Averroes furnishes. It was in fact forged ad hoc and does not coincide with any of the five or six classically recognized definitions of that discipline.

As for Averroes' use of the Qur'an, it depends on a shift of accent. The Qur'an does not aim at proving the existence or the identity of the Creator. Both of these were already admitted by those to whom the work was addressed (see Qur'an 29:6, 31:2, 43:87). What remained to be demonstrated was the all-powerfulness of God and, more exactly, his intervention into "nature." In such "natural" processes of development as the generation of animals or the growth of plants, the Qur'an is interested in sudden developments like the germination of grass (6:95) or the birth of an animal. The point was to make more plausible the brusque event of the resurrection of the dead and the last judgment that necessarily follows.

Philosophers have a totally different agenda. They take events occurring by natural processes as an illustration of the regularity of nature. The event becomes something that repeats itself again and again. For this reason, the historical dimension of occurrences, properly speaking, is left aside.

3. The Human Intellect

All of the philosophers' discussion of the soul and the intellect—whether they speak of God, the celestial spheres, or man—is rooted in the noetics of Aristotle and such Greek commentators on his treatise on the soul (*De anima*) as Alexander of Aphrodisias, Themistius, and others. The only point of contact is an interpretation of the famous "verse of light" (Qur'an 24:35), which has been commented on in every imaginable way.[48] It is quite clear that the philosophers cite formulas from the Qur'an only as illustrations, to support a point that they have already demonstrated on the basis of purely philosophical arguments.

4. The Eternity or the Adventitiousness of the World

It is interesting to remark that Campanini combines debate on the eternity versus the creation of the world under the heading "*Necessità o libertà nell'agire divino*" (Necessity or liberty in divine action).[49] But does discussion center on that question, for example, in the polemic between Ghazali and Averroes? There is no entry for the word "liberty" in the index to Simon van den Bergh's translation of Averroes' *Tahāfut*.[50] Use of the term refers to the problem of predestination, which did indeed preoccupy the people of the Kalām. But what was of central concern to the Mutakallimun was the problem of *human* action and liberty, not that of the action of God the creator.

In fact, the debate on the eternity of the world or its creation is at least as old as the debate between John Philoponus and Simplicius.[51] The thinkers of Islam were quite aware that they were taking up the point exactly where the Greeks had left off. This was already the case with Farabi, who reopened this debate in the Islamic world.[52]

5. Ethics and Politics

The distinction between ethics and politics has become banal to us, but we may not have any right to see it as quite so obvious. Some writers have tried to show, and have argued their point well, that Aristotle did not draw any such distinction. According to Aristotle himself, his treatise on ethics was a part of his political investigations.[53] Others have suggested the existence of an independent ethics within the universe of Islamic thought.[54] Still others have insisted that some conception of political guidance (Imamate) is essential to medieval Islam.

Farabi and Avicenna take care not to be too quick to identify their exemplary city, be it the "virtuous city" of the first or the "just city" of the second, with the Islamic "city." In his commentary on Plato's *Republic*, Averroes is even more daring when he leaves open the question of whether the founder of the ideal city has to be a prophet.[55] To be sure, the philosophers never stop flirting with such technical terms of the political doctrine of Islam as "Imam," to offer one example. But they avoid giving those terms an overly strict Islamic interpretation. What is more, they mix elements drawn from Islamic Law (*sharia*) with other elements that betray a Greek—for example, Platonic—origin. Thus Avicenna seems to deduce certain typically Islamic rules of comportment (up to and including the veil for women!) purely philosophically, and he divides his city into three classes that correspond to the three Platonic castes of guardians, soldiers, and workers.[56]

Conclusion

As a result of the preceding investigation—which, I repeat, is nothing more than a program for further study—I would like to submit to the judgment of my colleagues a provisory thesis: There is no "Islamic philosophy" any more than there is or has been a "Jewish philosophy" or a "Christian philosophy." What there has been, incontestably, is a use of philosophical thought on the part of Muslims, Christians, and Jews. Philosophy was practiced in a highly competent and innovative way by people affiliated with all three religions, and by thinkers whose sincerity and sense of belonging to those religious groups we have no right to doubt. Equally incontestably, philosophy passed through cultural domains marked by those three religions. It is thus acceptable to speak of an "Islamic philosophy," on the condition that we understand "Islamic" to refer to a civilization, not a religion.

PART II

Common Themes

4

Is Physics Interesting?

Some Responses from Late Antiquity and the Middle Ages

Introduction

Let me begin by explaining the two elements of the question that serves as the title of this chapter, that is, the subject and the attribute of the interrogative phrase that constitutes it.

First, I intend to take the word "physics" in its broadest sense, which includes the study of natural realities to their fullest extent. This is not exactly physics as the ancient and medieval world conceived of it. According to Aristotle and the medieval philosophers who followed in his tradition (the majority), physics, or "natural philosophy" (*physikē philosophia*), is one of the sciences that *do* nothing in the city, unlike the "practical" forms of knowledge. Neither do they *make* any object, which distinguishes them from "poietic" arts like the activities of the blacksmith or the potter. Physics is part of the "theoretical" sciences, those that are content to look at things and note how they are.[1] Among those theoretical sciences, physics often occupies a secondary place, after mathematics but before first philosophy (also called "divine science" or "metaphysics"). Physics is exclusively concerned with the lower world of generation and corruption. For medieval thinkers, astronomy was not part of physics, but of mathematics, as was the case with other disciplines that we would place among the branches of physics such as optics or statics.[2] Astronomy is a particularly interesting case: it was placed among the mathematical sciences because of its purely hypothetical nature, a situation that reflects what might be called a schizophrenia that lasted throughout late antiquity and the Middle Ages in which it proved impossible to reconcile the mathematical models of the movements of heavenly bodies, which permitted "saving the phenomena," on the one hand, and the principles of the science of nature, which permitted rendering an account of their movements, on the other. Thus when I speak of "physics," the term will include the whole of the study of nature, as in the German term *Naturwissenschaft*.

Second, we need to distinguish between three meanings of the adjective "interesting."

(1) First there is egoistic, even mercenary, interest. This is the sense of "interest" we use to indicate an interest in the rewards of a commercial society; it is the contrary of "disinterested." To designate things in which we have an interest of this sort—an interest in "what pays"—I will use the adjective "gratifying." The reward implied is not limited to a monetary reward or to social climbing: our very survival and our health can be involved as well.

(2) I shall concentrate here on intellectual interest, an interest in knowledge for its own sake. Any sort of knowledge can be qualified as "interesting" to the extent that it unveils something beautiful, and we know that nature is rich in this sort of reality, which can range from the delicate structure of a flower to the majesty of a sky constellated with stars. This sort of knowledge can provide a pleasure much like the one we get from a work of art. The comparison is banal. Aesthetic pleasure can absorb us. We forget ourselves when we are lost in contemplation of the beautiful. There is something charming, something that captivates us, in this experience. This is why common parlance borrows a word from the vocabulary of magic and calls the object of that experience "fascinating."

(3) Finally, I shall call "interesting"—in the strict sense, once again remaining faithful to the Latin etymology of the word—what makes a difference for us, what counts. More precisely, what is interesting is what is found between us and ourselves—what *inter-est*—so that we must pass through it in order to get at ourselves. In this sense, the interesting is a necessary stage in the process by which we come to know ourselves. It constrains us to reflect on the experience that we have of it, because the reference back to ourselves is already contained in the object in which we are interested. In French, the reflexive form of the verb *s'intéresser à* already indicates the reflexive structure of this interest.

Consequently, I need to refine my initial question and ask to what extent the science of nature was, for the ancient and medieval world, something that was interesting. I shall refrain from consideration of the social or intellectual factors that may have either inhibited or encouraged the development of physics, a question on which a number of fine works have already been written.[3] Rather, I shall concentrate on the intellectual aspect of things.

The Negation of All Interest

To what extent is the study of nature interesting? The question lost its thrust with the modern age. Ibn Khaldūn flatly denies that physics has the slightest interest. The context is a total refutation of philosophy, of which physics was at the time a part: "The problems of physics are of no importance for us in our religious affairs (*dīn*) or our livelihoods (*ma'āsh*). Therefore, we must leave them alone."[4] His response is brutal: physics must not bother us (*tahummu* or *tuhimmu*) because it cannot be applied to the two domains that are truly important to us, this life and the life to come.

As is clear with hindsight, this sort of total rejection of physics, founded on a denial of its interest for daily life, received a bitter refutation with modern times. If what is interesting is what affects our daily life, and even our survival, physics is to the highest degree that sort of reality. We do not ask a physician to justify his profession as such; we demand that he account for a particular treatment if it fails to heal the patient or even makes the condition worse. Thanks to the triumph of modern technology, the position of the physicist has become analogous to that of the physician: we know that modern physics is the necessary condition of what a familiar slogan calls the "conquest of nature." Similarly, the usefulness of modern physics seems obvious. To return to the famous image with which Descartes opens his *Principles of Philosophy*, in the tree of knowledge, physics is the trunk that produces the three major branches of medicine, mechanics, and—in prospect at least—morality.[5]

The thinkers of antiquity would have agreed, up to a certain point. They never asked why we weave clothing, sow wheat, or make furniture because the answer is obvious: we *need* those things. But before the advances of modern technology, people of the ancient and medieval worlds had little need to encumber their minds with physics. The paradox thus becomes: How does it happen that we study things that we have no real and urgent need to know? To put the question more pointedly: Why do we study things—the stars, the winds, and so on—that we can make no use of? One might give a number of responses to these questions, and a number were in fact given.

The Irrelevance of Physics

To begin with, some answered that question negatively: taking an interest in such things is superfluous. Socrates, if we may begin with him and if we can believe Xenophon, condemned the very idea of studying natural phenomena that we cannot change.[6] Several of the philosophic schools that claimed to represent a part of the Socratic heritage offered the same answer.[7]

The most interesting example, however, lies outside of the Socratic current, in Epicurus, whose response was negative but nuanced. To return to the distinction that I proposed earlier, he states that the study of nature is not intrinsically interesting, even though it can be and effectively is fascinating, and that it is a pleasure to give oneself over to it. Epicurus emphasizes the pleasure that physics brings: "In the study of philosophy, pleasure (*to terpnon*) keeps pace with growing knowledge; for pleasure (*apolausis*) does not follow learning, rather, learning and pleasure advance side by side."[8]

Fundamentally, however, we pursue physics only to rid ourselves of fear and acquire peace of soul.[9] It matters little that such an aim can be attained by more than one explanation of a given phenomenon. This leads Epicurus to a very detached attitude concerning physics, an unlimited "nonchalance," as Karl Marx states in his doctoral dissertation.[10] Physics demonstrates the extent to which nature is nothing to us. We study nature, not to imitate it, but rather to set it at a distance. Normally, we should be able to do without physics. If we meddle with it, it is because we are constrained to compensate for the bad effects of contemplation. As Epicurus puts it: "If our suspicions (*hupopsia*) about heavenly phenomena (*meteōra*) and about death did not trouble (*enokhlein*) us at all and were never anything to us (*einai pros ti* + acc.), and, moreover, if not knowing the limits of pains and desires did not trouble us, then we would have no need (*prosdeisthai*) of natural science (*physiologia*)."[11] This passage from Epicurus relies on ways of thinking that can be found elsewhere in the same philosophic school, to the point that it might serve as a basic schema for the Epicurean method, or, in any event, for what one might call the Epicurean turn of mind. Porphyry has transmitted to us a long fragment of a little-known Epicurean philosopher named Hermarcus, who states: "If everyone alike could see advantage and keep it in mind, they would not need (*prosdeisthai*) laws as well, but would of their own accord respect what is forbidden and act upon what is enjoined."[12]

Lucretius goes even further. He recognizes that nature can be fascinating, but he has a negative view of the results of its contemplation. Far from bringing the soul peace, contemplating the sky awakens anguish (*cura*) in us.[13] This occurs when contemplation is not accompanied by its remedy, philosophy. Physics is interesting because—and only because—it shows us that nature does not necessarily have to be fascinating.

Simplicius on the Interest of Physics

On the other hand, that same question aroused a very positive response from the majority of thinkers—or, rather, it prompted a broad range of positive responses, which were repeated over and over from the beginning to the end of the period ranging from classical antiquity to the Middle Ages. The principal types of positive response are furnished in a text of Simplicius that appears in the preface to his commentary on Aristotle's *Physics*. In conformity with the rules of this genre of literature, Simplicius first responds to a certain number of questions regarding the work he is studying. As a commentator he feels he must state what is the interest of the science contained in the work that he intends to explicate and teach. Thus Simplicius explicitly raises the question of whether physics (*physiologia*) is useful (*khresimos*). This is his answer:

Physics (*physiologia*) is useful

(1) not only in the affairs of daily life, by furnishing the principles of medicine and the art of military engineering and by aiding the other arts (for each of these requires a preliminary study of nature and of the natural differences of the materials with which it deals);

(2) not because it leads to its perfection that aspect of the soul within us that corresponds to the knowledge of natural beings, just as theology does for its intellectual and supreme part;

(3) but because it contributes to the highest degree to the other perfections of the soul. In fact, it cooperates with the practical virtues:

(a) with justice, to the extent that it shows that the elements and parts of the All cede to one another, are content with their rank, and observe geometrical equality, by that fact avoiding cupidity;

(b) with temperance, by showing the nature of pleasure: it is not a good that precedes, but a sort of accompaniment that seems intense and worthy of being chosen only as long as it is mixed with a great portion of what is not natural. As it happens, the leisure that comes from contemplating nature easily transfers the soul of the corporeal pleasures and of the excitement that pertains to external things; all things from which there flow temperance, justice, and the propensity to accept reaching agreement in contracts.

(c) Moreover, who could be as courageous as one who knows, from the study of nature, that the animal that we are is not even a perceptible part of the universe, nor is the measure of our life-span [a perceptible part] of time in its totality, that it is necessary that all that comes into being be followed by a disappearance that is a dissolution into simple [elements], a restitution of the parts to their corresponding wholes, a rejuvenation of what had grown old and a return to health of what had been ailing? To rot now or several years from now is negligible for anyone who has thought about time in its infinity. Moreover, if we become aware of the superiority of the soul in its separated state, compared with the derangements that come to it from the body, we will be enamored of death. But, among the other things purported to be terrible, which could frighten a person thus disposed toward death?

(d) It [physics] spontaneously produces wisdom, which has a very close affinity with the knowing [part] of the soul.

(e) It makes [us] magnanimous and generous by persuading us to consider nothing of what is human to be great.

(f) It makes [us] content with little, and at the same time ready to let others have a part in what we possess, without asking anything of them—hence, liberal.

(4) The greatest good that it procures is that it is the best path leading to the knowledge of the substance similar to the soul and to the contemplation of separate and divine ideas. This is demonstrated by Plato, who took natural movements as his point of departure to discover the substance that moves of its own accord, as well as intellectual and divine existence, and by Aristotle, who, in the present treatise, enquires as to the immobile cause of all movement, beginning from the eternity of circular movement.

(5) What is more, it kindles to the highest point our respect for divine transcendence by awakening [that respect] as is appropriate, beginning from the precise consideration of its effects to arrive at awe and praise of the Creator. That awe is followed by a stable communion of sentiment with God through confidence and hope.

Such are the principal reasons for studying nature.[14]

The same ideas can also be found in Averroes.[15] The reason for this may be very simple: the two texts probably had a common ancestor, the lost commentary of Alexander of Aphrodisias on the same Aristotelian text, a work to which Averroes refers explicitly when he explains the utility of physics, while Simplicius simply mentions Alexander's name elsewhere than in his preface.

Simplicius offers five arguments: (1) Physics is useful to daily life, through medicine and the mechanical arts (four lines); (2) it leads a part of the soul to its perfection (two lines); (3) it cooperates with the moral virtues (twenty-five lines); (4) it leads upward, toward the Ideas (six lines); (5) it awakens our sentiments of awe and gratitude toward God (four lines). He gives these reasons in a specific order, but we cannot be sure that it reflects their respective importance. They seem to advance from the lowest to the highest, but Simplicius explicitly emphasizes that the fourth reason is the greatest good that physics can provide. On the other hand, he gives half again as much space to the third argument as he does to the other four together (twenty-five lines; sixteen lines).

Simplicius's first argument is the utility of physics for the preservation of human life, both individual life and that of the city, thanks to medicine and the art of the military engineer. This argument reappears in medieval works as well. Neither their authors nor their predecessors in antiquity disapproved of the idea of applied physics, even though its practical consequences remained marginal.[16] An allusion to the same idea can be found in the works of Albertus Magnus, who was himself one of the medieval philosophers who displayed the most interest in the sciences of nature: "Knowing (*scire*) is not only agreeable (*delectabile*) for whoever tries to familiarize himself with (*cognoscere*) the nature of things, but useful (*utile*) for life and for the continuation of the existence of cities (*civitatum permanentia*)."[17]

Still, this argument is not totally convincing because, to return to the distinction that I made above, it shows that physics is *gratifying*, not that it is *interesting*.

The second argument is the value of science as something that leads a specific capacity of the soul to its highest point. On the one hand, it is obvious that exercise reinforces our capacities. But we can engage in all sorts of activities, including some that are utterly without interest, are simply agreeable, or are even downright criminal. In this case as well, therefore, the intrinsic interest of the object is presupposed. Or else we have to suppose that exercising one's mind has a general value. To quote Albertus Magnus again: "Training (*exercitium*) in any field of knowledge, whatever it may be, helps us to choose what is worth being chosen (*eligibile*). Training awakens a capacity, not only concerning its object, but of another object as well. A person who is capable of seeing the truth in one thing is disposed to see it in another. Hence astronomy, geometry, and other sorts of knowledge profit from (*proficere ad*) prudence, not of course because of the object itself, but because of the training acquired regarding that object."[18]

This argument supposes that the part of the soul that is involved with physics is the same as the part that takes decisions regarding moral questions, something that is quite far from being obvious. The price to pay for confusing the two consists in neglecting the fundamental distinction that Aristotle made between *sophia* and *phronesis*.[19]

Physics as a Path to Theology

Simplicius's fourth and fifth arguments met with particular success, to the point that one might say they became hackneyed in the period under consideration here. Physics can be the instrument of a higher kind of knowledge. To know the nature that surrounds us can lead us upward and allow us to reach a higher step on the scale of beings. The visible permits us to glimpse the invisible, in the spirit of Anaxagoras' formula: "Manifest things are a vision of hidden things (*opsis adēlōn ta phainomena*)."[20] That hidden dimension can be the Platonic ideas, the intelligible structure of reality. But it can also be the Creator. When that is the case, physics has something to do with knowledge of God, which is obviously interesting in itself. God's wisdom and power are manifested in the orderly structure of the world. The idea is an extremely old one, at least as old as the second part of the book of the prophet Isaiah or the Psalms. It returns in the New Testament.[21] It is also found, however, in such pagan authors as Galen.[22]

There is even a technical term to describe the attitude underlying this notion: in Greek it is *theōria physikē*; in Arabic, *i'tibār*.[23] It is described, for example, in the *Duties of the Heart* of Bahya ibn Paquda, who devotes an entire chapter to consideration of creatures:

> What is the nature of this meditation? It consists of trying to understand the traces of God's wisdom as manifested in creation and in appreciating them in proportion to the observer's power of discrimination. This wisdom, although it is variously manifested in creation, is but one in source and origin, like the sun, which is one in essence, although the colors of its rays vary when passed through glass discs of different colors—white, green, black, and red. . . . The meditation upon creation consists of the study of the construction and use of every compound thing and the traces of wisdom manifested in its creation— its form and shape, its usage, and the final purpose for which it has been created.[24]

In similar fashion, almost two centuries after that Jewish spiritual author, a Christian Scholastic, Bonaventure (d. 1274), explains:

> The whole world is a shadow, a way, and a trace; a book *with writing front and back* (Ezekiel 2:9). Indeed, in every creature there is a refulgence of the

divine exemplar, but mixed with darkness: hence it resembles some kind of opacity combined with light. Also, it is a way leading to the exemplar. As you notice that a ray of light coming through a window is colored according to the shades of the different panes, so the divine ray (*radius divinus*) shines differently in each creature and in the various properties. Hence, in Wisdom: *She . . . appears to them in the ways* (Wisdom 6:17). . . . When the soul sees these things, it seems to it that it should go through them from shadow to light, from the way to the end, from the trace to the truth, from the book to veritable knowledge which is in God. To read this book is the privilege of the highest contemplatives, not of natural philosophers; for the former alone know the essence of things, and do not consider them only as traces.[25]

I have chosen this passage because it contains two interesting parallels with texts already quoted. For one thing, we see in it the same image that Bahya uses of light taking on a particular color as it shines through a glass window. But it also includes the idea that nature is a collection of roads to God, a notion borrowed from the Greek Bible, Book of Wisdom (6:16), where Wisdom "graciously appears to them in the ways." This is an idea that Maimonides develops at length, but of course he draws it from another source, Moses' request to God: "Show me now Thy ways, that I may know Thee" (Exodus 33:13).[26]

The idea was part of a strategy aimed at rendering the study of nature acceptable to religious Law. In order to attain that goal, the philosophers who lived in an Islamic society had several strings to their bow. They could focus on drawing a connection between the content of philosophical truth with the prophetic message. This was al-Kindi's solution.[27] Or they could claim that the Qur'an itself made the study of the science of nature obligatory for believers. As is known, the holy book of Islam encourages man to reflect on the marvels of creation.[28] This is the strategy followed by al-Amiri (d. 992), who states:

Astronomy, as everyone knows, is a noble science. It examines the form of the upper world according to quantity and quality as well as the movement of every heavenly body. It seeks to discover the causes of eclipses and studies various phenomena, such as retrograde and rectilinear motions, movement and rest as found among "the receding, the running" (Qur'an 81:15–16) stars [planets] as well as the visibility and invisibility, the rising and the setting of the fixed stars. An intelligent man whose knowledge extends to heavenly phenomena, undoubtedly possesses a considerable share of bliss. Hence God has rebuked all who refrain from occupying themselves with this noble science and said (Qur'an 30:8 / 7, cited not quite literally): "Did they not think about

the creation of the heaven and the earth? God created these only for truth."
On the other hand He has praised those blessed with an interest in noble astronomy and said (Qur'an 3:191 / 188): "Those who mention God when stand-
ing, sitting and on their sides and reflect on the creation of the heavens and
the earth, etc."[29]

Islamic thinkers could also combine those two approaches to form a
third argument: Studying nature is obligatory because such knowledge
leads to knowledge of God. This argument is developed forcefully in the
Decisive Discourse (*Fasl al-maqāl*) of Averroes (d. 1198), who begins with an
ad hoc definition of philosophy that sounds much like the definition of
i'tibār that we have already seen: "We say . . . the activity of 'philosophy'
is nothing more than study of existing beings and reflection on them as
indications of the Artisan, i.e., inasmuch as they are products of art (for
beings only indicate the Artisan through our knowledge of the art in them,
and the more perfect this knowledge is, the more perfect the knowledge of
the Artisan becomes)."[30]

The Jewish thinkers who followed Averroes picked up similar definitions. Falaquera, for example, states: "It is known that philosophy is the
study of created beings and the investigation of them insofar as they point
to the Creator. . . . Therefore, the more perfect the knowledge of their
creation, the more perfect will be the knowledge of the Creator."[31]

Maimonides' strategy is even more powerful, given that he implies that
knowledge of nature is not only one way among others to know God, but
indeed the only way that can lead us toward any knowledge of the attributes of God. He writes:

> There is, moreover, no way to apprehend Him except it be through the things
> He has made; for they are indicative of His existence and of what ought to
> be believed about Him, I mean to say, of what should be affirmed and denied
> with regard to Him. It is therefore indispensable to consider all beings as they
> really are so that we may obtain for all the kinds of beings true and certain
> premises that would be useful to us in our researches pertaining to the divine
> sciences. . . . As for the matters pertaining to the astronomy of the spheres
> and to natural science, I do not consider that you should have any difficulty in
> grasping that those are matters necessary for the apprehension of the relation
> of the world to God's governance as this relation is in truth and not accord-
> ing to imaginings. There are also many speculative subjects that, although no
> premises can be obtained from them for the use of this science, nevertheless
> train the mind and procure it the habitus of drawing inferences and knowl-
> edge of the truth in matters pertaining to its essence. They also put an end to

the confusion in most of the minds of those engaged in speculation, a confusion mistaking things that are accidental for those that are essential; hereby an end is also put to the perversion of opinions arising out of this confusion. All this is achieved in addition to the representation of these subjects as they really are, even if they in no way belong to the divine science. These subjects are also not devoid of utility in other points, namely, with respect to matters that lead up to that science.[32]

Physics compensates for the impossibility of an affirmative theology. Or, to put it the other way around, negative theology opens the way to physics. I might perhaps go so far as to say that physics is the sole affirmative theology that we can have.

The Direct Interest of Physics

However, this model of argumentation does not respond to the question of whether physics is only indirectly interesting. We are given no direct legitimation of the study of nature. Such study is interesting, not in itself, but because it sets us on the way to what is intrinsically interesting, which is God. One might call this an *instrumental* model: the study of nature is a means in view of an end. The real goal is to know God, the Creator, through his creation. To a certain extent, extremes meet here: the least and the most noble ways to legitimate the search for physical knowledge have in common that both subordinate the study of nature to something other than itself, in the first instance, practical advantage; in the second, knowledge of a higher object.

But can we find arguments in which the study of nature is shown to be directly interesting? I have located three examples of this sort of argument. The first coincides with Simplicius's third argument that physics has moral pertinence. To my knowledge, however, the two others are new.

The Timaeus *and Its Posterity: The Virtues of Nature*

The first of these originates in the *Timaeus*. In this dialogue, Plato does not explicitly exclude the notion that we are capable of using reasoning to rise from the visible universe to the creator of the universe. More simply, he remains silent regarding that possibility. He even stresses, in a passage that is often quoted, how difficult it is to know "the Maker and the Father of the universe," and, if we did know him, how difficult it would be to reveal that knowledge to all humanity.[33] Nonetheless, the study of nature is useful for another reason. It is the principal reason or, more exactly, the most fertile reason, since it dominated the history of thought for centuries to come. Toward the end of the first part of the *Timaeus*, Plato sings the praises of the eyes and the sense of sight in these terms: "God devised and bestowed upon us vision to the end that we might behold the revolutions of Reason in the Heaven and use them for the revolvings of the reasoning that is within us, these being akin to those, the perturbable to the imperturbable; and that, through learning and sharing in calculations which are correct by their nature, by imitation of the absolutely unvarying revolutions of the God we might stabilize the variable revolutions within ourselves."[34]

In a word: we should imitate nature; more precisely, what is the most highly worthy of our imitation, which is the majestic order of the army of the skies, so as to put order into our lives. The heavenly bodies are like our elder brothers. Their matter is purer than the matter of which we have been made. Moreover, they were made by the divine Demiurge in person, whereas our bodies were fashioned by second-rank divinities, his under-lings. It is not surprising, then, if the heavenly bodies move with perfect order and obey laws that admit no exception. Our soul, the circular struc-ture of which is analogous to that of the Soul of the World, must strive to move with like order. Our perfection should reflect that of the world.

Throughout the Middle Ages, this idea had an immensely positive re-ception in all three cultural worlds.[35] By imitating the order and beauty of nature, we ennoble our souls and become more worthy of our own humanity. Physics is a mediation for anthropology. This implies that the moral virtues, by which man becomes what he must be, are present in the physical universe. Justice is not the province of man; it is present in the inner structure of objective reality. Bernard of Chartres (d. 1126), for example, says that the subject of Plato's *Timaeus* is none other than natu-ral justice (*naturalis justitia*): "Because Plato wanted to treat [the topic of] natural justice thoroughly, he began with the birth of the sensible world, in its creation, in the just ordering of its parts, in the distinction between celestial and non-celestial things he taught the power of the natural jus-tice of which the Creator showed proof toward the created, out of pure love, in attributing to each being without exception what appertains to it naturally (*tribuendo cuique quod suum erat*)."[36] Averroes makes an analogous declaration in the preface to his commentary on the *Physics*. Sages study physics "because they know that the nature of justice resides in the essence of things (*naturam justitiae existentem in substantia rerum; teva' ha-yōsher han-nimtsa be-'etsem ha-nimtsa'oth*), which is why they desire to imitate nature and acquire that form."[37]

As a result, physics is quite immediately interesting for us. In investigating physics, we become conscious of who we are; we even become what we really are. I have been unable to find a better expression of the literal manner in which thinkers of the ancient and medieval world were *interested* by physics than a text of Seneca's in which he praises knowledge of celestial phenomena: ["When the mind contacts those regions it is nurtured, grows, and returns to its origin just as though freed from its chains. As proof of its divinity it has this: divine things cause it pleasure, and it dwells among them not as being alien things but things of its own nature *(nec ut alienis sed ut suis interest)*. . . . It knows that these things pertain to itself *(scit illa ad se pertinere)*."[38]

This first response is impressive, but it has at least one drawback: it does not succeed in legitimating the study of nature except in a general way. In fact, being persuaded that the universe is well ordered ought to suffice to incite us to conduct ourselves in an orderly fashion too. But informing ourselves thoroughly about the details of that order is superfluous and cannot fail to make us appear pusillanimous. Moreover, the argument pertains only for celestial things; it is less convincing regarding the study of the inferior realities that surround us. Why should we study worms and insects? And is man himself all that worthy of our interest?[39]

Thomas Aquinas: Safeguarding Human Dignity

My second example is from the works of Thomas Aquinas. He devotes two chapters of his *Summa contra Gentiles* to the question of the pertinence of the study of nature for theology. He does so at the beginning of the Second Book, written between 1261 and 1264, which discusses the created world. Article 2 shows, positively, *"quod consideratio creaturarum utilis est ad fidei instructionem"* (that the consideration of creatures is useful for building up our faith). Article 3 shows, negatively, *"quod cognoscere naturam creaturarum valet ad destruendum errores qui sunt circa Deum"* (that the knowledge of the nature of creatures avails for refuting errors against God). Most of Thomas's arguments are traditional and strongly resemble those that we have found in Simplicius or elsewhere. In spite of all, however, his final argument, given in the last chapter, is perhaps original: "Man, who is led by faith to God as his last end, through ignoring the nature of things, and consequently the order of his place in the universe, thinks himself to be beneath certain creatures above whom he is placed: as evidenced in those who subject man's will to the stars, and against these it is said (Jerem. 10:2): *Be not afraid of the signs of heaven, which the heathens fear*; also to those who deem the angels to be the creatures of souls, and human souls to be mortal; and in those who hold any like opinions derogatory to the dignity of man."[40]

The same complex of ideas appears in another work, a commentary on the Credo compiled on the basis of vernacular sermons preached during Lent 1273, one year before Thomas Aquinas died.[41] In this sermon, Thomas offers a commentary on the first article of faith, the existence of one God, creator of heaven and earth. Once we believe that all that exists in the universe is the work of God, we are cured of three errors: Manichaeism, the doctrine of an eternal universe (in this context, Thomas cites the parable narrated by Maimonides of a child who cannot accept the idea that he had ever been in his mother's womb),[42] and the doctrine according to which God created the world out of preexistent matter. Moreover, faith in creation confers five rewards on us: recognizing the majesty of God; experiencing gratitude to God; supporting evil with patience, in an awareness that created beings cannot be harmful in themselves; using created beings correctly (that is, to the praise of God and for our own use); and knowing our dignity as human beings. Man alone has been created in the image of God, which is to say, free and immortal. Awareness of our own dignity encourages us to conduct ourselves in conformity with our vocation.

Thomas ends his chapter by denouncing the error of those who think that opinions about the creatures have nothing to do (*nihil interesse*) with the verity of faith. Those people, he adds, are mentioned (*narrare*) by no less a personage than St. Augustine. Although Thomas Aquinas is not much given to irony, I cannot help thinking that this passage is ironic, given that Augustine was precisely the sort of man who thought that only God and the soul, and nothing else, are worthy of interest, as shown in the famous opening passages of the *Soliloquies*.[43]

The overall context here is the traditional refutation of astrology, a topic to which medieval thinkers ceaselessly return. But it is interesting that Thomas, among the many passages in the Bible against the cult of idols, should have chosen a passage that emphasizes the phenomenon of fear, in which the prophet Jeremiah tells us not to fear the celestial signs: *me otōt ha-shamayim al-tehattū*. Thomas's intention is not that far from that of Epicurus, who sought to calm human anguish, one of the most dangerous types of which is anguish before celestial phenomena. Thomas attempts to produce something like a Christian version of "absence of trouble" (*ataraxia*). The theologian and the philosopher treat the same malady, but not in the same manner.

Thomas works to defend human dignity, an idea that is hardly Epicurean. He does not do so with the aid of anthropology, but, rather, indirectly, through physics. The task of physics is not imitation in the Platonic or Stoic sense, and even less is it the modern Cartesian project of domination. Conducting oneself with dignity and controlling nature are not the same thing. Nor is there any question here of Epicurean distance: physics only plays its helpful role if it gives us the truth. Not just the truth regarding the object of physics but also, in a reflexive manner, about the investigating subject.

The argument has some advantages. It explains why we would never be content with general knowledge (Plato) or with just any explanation (Epicurus), but feel impelled to seek precise and exhaustive knowledge. Moreover, although Thomas Aquinas concentrates explicitly on such superior realities as celestial phenomena or angels, his argument could easily be adapted to the study of terrestrial nature. The study of nature, instead of showing that we are not puppets in the hands of astral conjunctions, now had the task of showing, for example, that we are nobler than the upper primates. On the other hand, the principal drawback of this argument is that it fails to justify the study of everything in nature that does not lead—directly or indirectly—to anthropology, as, for example, chemistry or mineralogy.

Gersonides: Forming the Subject of Beatitude

My third and last example comes from the French Jewish philosopher Gersonides (d. 1344). That he comes third fits with the chronological order of the thinkers I am discussing, but also with the internal development of ideas. No thinker, ancient or medieval (to my knowledge, at least), considered the study of nature as important as he does. Gersonides, in fact, went so far as to found his entire doctrine of the ultimate purpose of man on an epistemological base, a doctrine that was to lead to a stunning refutation on the part of his successor, Hasdai Crescas.[44] Gersonides carefully excludes the possibility that the intellect can have anything to do with the pursuit of practical interests. He defends its purely theoretical nature, arguing against a passage of Averroes, which he probably misinterprets.[45] Speculation, he writes, is the deepest aspiration of humanity: "Nature has endowed us, the human species, with the desire for theoretical knowledge rather than for the attainment of practical skills."[46] As a result, the intellect is in a certain sense disinterested, at least as long as we differentiate between the interesting and the gratifying.

From another viewpoint, however, knowledge serves our highest interest. What is at stake in it is our ultimate beatitude. Indeed, our perfection is knowledge: "Human happiness is achieved when a man knows reality as much as he can, and it becomes more noble when he knows the more superior things than when he knows only the things of inferior rank and value."[47]

At the least, if happiness is not found in the possession of knowledge, it can be found in the very process of the search for knowledge.[48] This is an idea that admittedly has a modern ring to it. It recalls Pascal's bon mot that we prefer the hunt to the capture and Lessing's famous parable: If God gave him a choice between the truth and the search for truth, he would choose the second.[49]

Knowledge reaches its highest point in knowledge of God: "Happiness for man consists in grasping and knowing God in the measure of the possible. We attain this goal by the observation of things, their order and their submission to the laws, and of the way in which divine Wisdom puts them in order."[50] This argument is already familiar to us. There is an added element, however: for Gersonides, who follows Themistius on this point, that order is closely associated with God and, up to a point, is even identical with God.[51]

The knowledge of physical reality leads not only to the highest *object* of knowledge, which is God; it also constitutes the *subject* of knowledge. In fact, the very quality of eternal beatitude for any one person depends on the quantity of knowledge he has acquired. In more technical language, it depends on the quantity of intelligibles that a person has been able to transfer from power to act and has stored up in the acquired intellect. It also depends on the quality of those intelligibles: the more the object of our knowledge is sublime, the greater the beatitude that we achieve. Gersonides observes that it is impossible for us to actualize all the intelligibles, down to the very last, which is why union with the Agent Intellect is impossible.[52] Our range is narrower, for example concerning the heavenly bodies.[53] In spite of all, we must attempt to acquire the greatest possible number of intelligibles.[54] The only reason for wanting to prolong life is that we augment our chance of multiplying the intelligibles accumulated in us. I could summarize Gersonides' doctrine of beatitude by quoting a phrase of Rainer Maria Rilke, quite obviously written in a different context: "We are the bees of the invisible. We madly gather the honey of the visible so as to accumulate it in the great golden hive of the Invisible."[55] Gersonides' beatitude resembles that of the collector complacently surveying his purchases. There is more, however: the synthesis of the intelligibles that we achieve is none other than our very personality.[56] That synthesis does not coincide with the totality of what the Agent Intellect knows. With death, our acquired intellect is not absorbed into a unique and same universal intellect in such a way that our personality evaporates.

We *are* our knowledge; we are the particular style that we have given to a system of intelligibles; we are the particular point of view on the basis of which we consider the intelligible structure of the world. As long as we live this present life, as long as we are *in via*, we are not yet truly ourselves. We are still in the process of working in a construction site where what we are building is ourselves; we tend toward the definitive plenitude of our own being as persons until the moment when death will put the final touch to our portrait. Thus it is in the most literal way that we become ourselves through our knowledge of nature. It is said that we "do physics," but on a deeper level, it is physics that makes us.

This last argument perfectly satisfies what we were waiting for: it explains why physics is interesting in the fullest sense of the word. It explains why our knowledge of nature must be as precise and exhaustive as possible.

Conclusion

In guise of conclusion, I would like to leave my reader with a question and a paradox. The question is addressed to modern physics: Did it invalidate all the arguments that the preceding ages mobilized in its favor when it rejected what they were founded on in the ancient and medieval vision of the world? If this were the case, we would be faced with a paradox: The study of nature is more and more *fascinating* as it opens up broader and broader fields; it is more and more *gratifying*—or at least one can hope so—as its technological applications increase and diversify. But if we want to take words seriously, the study of nature is, strictly speaking, no longer *interesting*.

5

The Flesh

A Medieval Model of Subjectivity

One might argue in favor of medieval studies on the basis of what is called the "postmodern" movement. If we admit, as a hypothesis, that we are living after the modern age, we acquire new liberty in our practice of the history of philosophy. We disengage ourselves from the very idea of a teleology and from a necessary orientation to progressively more "modern" ideas. This means that premodern ideas, and medieval ideas in particular, would no longer be any more superannuated or old-fashioned than other forms of thought. Moreover, we would not have to plead—as some medievalists used to do—for a return to the Middle Ages. And for the excellent reason that the very idea of a return, of a *zurück zu*, itself supposes that there is a teleology in history. One can of course brush the warp of history across its threads, to borrow an image from Walter Benjamin.[1] But that would suppose that history has a thread. As it happens, that is the very presupposition that postmodern thought challenges.

As far as my problem is concerned, if that hypothesis were proven true, certain elements of premodern thought could become pertinent once more. And not only ancient thought, but medieval thought as well. The modern project might be said to center on the idea of subjectivity. Might a premodern period in the history of philosophy, and in particular the period that modernity attempted to empty of its content—the Middle Ages—have something to say to us on the topic? Can we discern in the attitude of the medieval mind elements that we can use for a postmodern synthesis? In particular, could those elements help us to elaborate a more adequate model of subjectivity? Quite understandably, a battery of questions of this sort remains more a program for investigation than a pretext for ready-made answers.

A Program of Investigation: Heidegger, Subjectivity, and Modernity

Let me begin by clarifying the concept of subjectivity and how it connects to the nature of modernity. There is nothing exceptional, or even anything novel, about positing a link between modernity and subjectivity. Hegel makes just such a connection. He does so with certain nuances, however, as he states that subjectivity was already present in Judaism and in the Roman world, with the rise of Christianity, although it became aware of itself as liberty only in the modern age.

A group of texts by Martin Heidegger contains the strongest brief for a quasi-identification between modernity and the domination of subjectivity, along with the most thorough analysis of the phenomenon. All of these texts date from the mid-1930s, when Heidegger, slowly recuperating from his intoxication with Nazism and working on his *Contributions to Philosophy*, sketched out a preliminary analysis of the modern world in two courses, one on "The Question of the Thing" (winter semester, 1935–36) and the other on "European Nihilism: On Nietzsche" (second trimester, 1940, later published in volume 2 of his *Nietzsche*), and in the essay "The Time of the World Image" (June 1938).

In these texts, Heidegger questions the common interpretation that presupposes man to be a subject—Husserl's famous "[we] men as subjects."[2] The question to ask is: How did it happen that man has become a subject? Or, put the other way around, how did it happen that the place of the subject, which is decisive from a very early date (more precisely, since Aristotle's concept of *hypokeimenon*) came to be occupied by man? More generally, how did it happen that the role of subjecticity (*die Subiectität*) came to be played by subjectivity (*die Subjektivität*)?[3] Heidegger's answer recalls Kant's formulas on the I, which must be able to accompany all representations: man is a subject because he must necessarily belong to any representation at the same time as the object that is the content of that representation.[4] Or, to put it differently, because he is the first object of certitude: "The I that represents is much more essentially and more necessarily co-represented in any 'I represent'—that is, as the one toward which, in return toward which, and before which all that is re-presented (*das Vor-gestellte*) is presented (*hingestellt*)."[5] Or, to put the matter in still another way, the subject itself is above all an object, the object of certitude (not the object of the "I"). The I must assure itself of its own being before it can become the "subject." The subject is the I, but only once it has been determined by certitude. The subject reigns, but it does so only to the extent that it is itself determined by certitude. If I may be permitted a play on words, the subject-king is itself subject to and subjected to certitude.

In the longer essay "The Time of the World Image," we find a declaration of capital importance: Man becomes subject to the very extent that the world becomes an image. This furnishes us with an important indication: What already is, or is not yet, a subject has something to do with the world. The world, for its part, can already be an image or else not yet be one. There has to be something like a pre-subjective modality of the I. And this mode of being that is proper to the I before it becomes a subject corresponds to a mode of being of the world when it is not yet an image. We can thus ask: What was the world when man was not yet a subject? And, symmetrically, what was man when the world was not yet an image?

The way in which Heidegger accounts for modern subjectivity is, from the point of view of the history of ideas, far from being exhaustive. It has been remarked, for example, that Heidegger pays little attention to the "I" of English empiricism or to that of Kant.[6] He devotes a lengthy and painstaking analysis to the Greek *ego*, of which he sees a typical example in the Sophist Protagoras. What is more, long segments of the *Introduction to Metaphysics* can be read as the study of the Greek *ego* that Heidegger promises elsewhere.[7] In contrast, Heidegger says little about the way in which the *ego* was experienced between the ancient Greeks and the Cartesian revolution. Nor does he explain how the world was experienced. Medieval thought does little more than furnish him with a background before which modern thought becomes visible, without receiving a definite content, and even without needing one. Thus Heidegger often alludes to the Christian certitude of salvation, but only as a distant precursor of the modern certitude of subjectivity.[8] Accentuating the certitude of salvation is less medieval than Protestant, what is more, thus already premodern. However that may be, despite his past as a medievalist, the Heidegger of the 1930s (as distinct from the 1920s) does not treat the Christian experience of the I as such, and even less the medieval version of that experience.

The Flesh as an Anthropological Criterion: Man and Angel

This means that my task might be to describe the medieval experience of the I and of the world. It goes without saying that the domain that opens before our eyes is limitless. To avoid losing my way, I shall follow the thread of a specific theme. I could have chosen others, and perhaps more pertinent ones, but the one I have chosen is not arbitrary. My Ariadne's thread through the medieval labyrinth will be the flesh, carnality, and the carnal nature of man.

I shall begin by studying three aspects of the medieval experience of the flesh: its pertinence for a definition of man, its connection with the medieval theory of knowledge and self-knowledge, and its reflection in the domain of ethics through the virtue of humility. After that, I shall sketch several possible points of contact between this experience and certain contemporary currents of thought.

First, a historical remark: the carnal dimension of man has acquired an anthropological pertinence thanks to authors of the age of primitive Christianity and the patristic age, who argued forcefully against Platonic dualism.[9] However, since I limit myself (if that is the proper term) to the medieval period, and in order to avoid enlarging it unduly, I will not treat the historical aspect of the problem, supposing it to be known.

In medieval thought, man is defined in various ways. According to the classic and most influential definition, the one passed on by Greek thought, man is a "rational mortal animal." The formula belongs to the treasury of ready-made definitions common to all medieval thinkers, whatever their other orientations. Its ultimate source is Aristotle's *Politics*.[10] It can be encountered, well before the Aristotelian renaissance of the thirteenth century, among a wide variety of authors.[11] To be sure, we also find another, more Neoplatonic, formula in Augustine and in the tradition that follows from him: man is a rational soul making use of a body that is mortal and made of clay.[12] Unlike the Neoplatonists, however, Augustine insists on the fact that the connection between the soul and the body is not counter to nature.[13]

Medieval thought envisioned the existence of other living and intelligent beings, hence other rational animals, the angels. The existence of angels was based on two sources, from which currents emerged and mixed in a number of ways. For one thing, the revealed religions were unanimous in granting the existence of intermediate beings between man and God, an idea that they may have borrowed from the religion of ancient Iran. For another, the same idea is among the theses of Neoplatonic philosophy, which uses it to give a philosophical respectability to the Olympic gods of mythology, but also to remain faithful to the rule formulated by Plato himself according to which the divine and the human do not mix.[14]

The existence of angels means that man is situated at the frontier between two worlds, that of the angels and that of the animals. The idea of man as a *methorion*, a boundary, or as an amphibious being, is older than the Middle Ages. We find it in a number of texts of late antiquity.[15] What is new is that the beings that are placed above man are henceforth angels and not, for example, celestial bodies.

As for the angels, their existence is required by a logical need underlying the definition of man. We can see this, for example, in a passage of Augustine: "Man is a kind of mean (*medium*) between beasts and angels. The beast is an irrational and mortal animal, the angel is a rational and immortal one, and man is between them (*medius*), lower than the angels but higher than the beasts, a rational and mortal animal."[16] Half a millennium after Augustine, and far from him, a Muslim, Farabi, deduced a more complete structure covering all the created living beings by adding jinni to the Augustinian scheme. In doing so, he exhausted the possibilities of the double-entry tabulation of combinations of the two basic properties of rationality and mortality: the angels are rational and not mortal; men are rational and mortal; the beasts are not rational and mortal, and the jinni are not rational and not mortal.[17]

The ontological status of the angels remained a disputed point throughout the Middle Ages. Thinkers agreed to call them immortal, but they disagreed when it came to knowing if they were corporeal in nature or purely spiritual. The latter was the dominant opinion among authors influenced by philosophy and, in particular, those influenced by Neoplatonic speculations on pure intelligences as forms without matter. This is the case of Dionysius the Areopagite (or Pseudo-Areopagite), who, as is known, borrowed much from Proclus.[18] On this point the Muslim authors also followed the wake of Neoplatonism,[19] as did Jewish authors.[20] It is hardly surprising that many Christian authors should have followed their example.[21]

For medieval man, the angels are not necessarily creatures whom one encounters easily. On this point we today are in the same boat or, at any rate, no better off. According to Augustine, the difficulty of contact with the world of the angels and the loss of familiarity with that world is even one of the heavy burdens (*aerumnae*) of this life.[22] Kant's ironic remark about the good angels who prompt little talk about them is thus less typically modern than one might think, as is de Tocqueville's odd and probably ironic "we miss the angels."[23] The fact remains that in the medieval vision of the world, the angels have a clearly determined place in the intellectual schema of being. Hence we have to take their existence into account. Man is situated between the animals, who have a body, and the angels, who are either totally incorporeal or are endowed with a body inaccessible to corruption. If the superior beings are incorporeal, what distinguishes them from men lies in whether they have a body or not. If they have a body that is purer than our own, the difference resides in the fact that our body is of flesh and the angelic body is not.

If this is true, the carnal nature of man acquires a great importance. One cannot define man or situate him on the scale of beings without taking into account the fact that he is flesh. Among the creatures, man must thus distinguish himself from what is not him on two fronts. It is not enough to stress his difference from the brute beasts because he participates in rational discourse; he also has to be distinguished from the angelic creatures who share his use of reason. And the only criterion for that distinction is man's carnal dimension, a characteristic that he alone possesses among the rational creatures. Thus it is by his flesh that man is unique.

Flesh and Body

"Flesh" does not signify "body" even if the human body is carnal. The word *caro* underlines the weakness and the fragility of the human body as it pursues its terrestrial pilgrimage, thus remaining "on its way" (*in via*). Augustine express this clearly: "The body, you see, that is not subject to decay is not properly called flesh and blood, but simply body. If it's flesh, I mean, it's subject to decay and mortal; but if it now dies no more, it is now no more subject to decay; and therefore, while retaining its own specific nature (*species*) without being subject to decay, it is not now called flesh, but body; and if it does happen to be called flesh, it is not now properly so called, but on account of a certain specific similarity."[24] The flesh is the body inasmuch as it is sensitive and mortal.

On the other hand, whereas our body makes each of us a singular individual, our flesh is a principle of continuity that is situated beyond individuation. It links us to what we are not but becomes what we are, or it helps us to become what we are. Flesh is made from the nourishment that we borrow from the nature that surrounds us. It is transmitted to us by other members of our same species, and we transmit it to still other members of our species: the flesh is what links us to our parents, to our brothers and sisters, to our children. Even after our resurrection, it connects us to the body that we formerly possessed, to the point that it is the inheritance of the entire fabric of humanity. This is, in any event, what underlies the doctrine of the "radical flesh" (*caro radicalis*) that we keep as resuscitated bodies.[25]

This idea of a frailty of the flesh does not mean that the flesh must be considered bad. Quite to the contrary, the Fathers of the Church insisted on the intrinsic goodness of the body, against Neoplatonic scorn and gnostic hatred of the body. St. Augustine recalls this notion forcefully: It is not the flesh that causes sin, even what is deemed a "sin of the flesh." It is always the soul that drags the body into sin. And Satan, the evil spirit par excellence, is not carnal, but is, to the contrary, pure spirit.[26] Not only do medieval thinkers state that the flesh is not evil, but medieval thought includes a completely positive vision of it that emphatically declares it to be good. I shall leave aside the precursors of this idea in primitive Christianity to concentrate on the way in which the positive vision of the flesh was brought to center stage during the early Middle Ages—that is, in the twelfth century.

We can see this in St. Bernard of Clairvaux. The context of the passage that I will summarize is important: Bernard is giving a line-by-line commentary of the *Song of Songs* in a series of sermons to the monks whom he serves as abbot. He interrupts the sermon series because of the death of his brother Gérard, who was also a monk. The funeral oration that he gives on that occasion forms the twenty-sixth of the sermons on the *Song of Songs*. It is also interesting to note that Bernard's homily, although preached for a particular occasion, was retained as an integral part of what Bernard had to say about the *Song* and about the love that is its principal subject. What is more, Bernard had to interrupt his sermon a second time to give free course to his sorrow with a flood of tears. Returning to his homily, he says that he was attached to his brother, not only by a kinship of the body (*carnis necessitudo*), but by a deeper unity, so that his brother's death undid the ties between two parts of one body. Before such a sorrow, Bernard's own flesh is not of steel (*nec caro mea aenea est*). If his affection (*affectus*) should be called carnal, he would not complain and would admit that he is human. He even goes a step further: "I have made public the depth of my affliction, I make no attempt to deny it. Will you say then that this is carnal? That it is human, yes, since I am a man. If this does not satisfy you then I am carnal. Yes, I am carnal, sold under sin, destined (*addictus*) to die, subject to penalties and sufferings. I am certainly not insensible to pain; to think that I shall die, that those who are mine will die, fills me with dread."[27]

Continuing my reflection on this text, I would like to draw attention to the subtle way in which it intertwines several dimensions of carnal existence. First, Bernard senses a break in the tissue of carnal kinship between men. A brother is closer to me than anyone else because he is born of the same flesh. Second, Bernard expresses an awareness of his own finitude and of his mortality. The flesh is there to be torn asunder. Third, the disruption reveals that this sort of affection—of oneself for oneself—is essential to man. The angels cannot suffer in this manner, not only because they soar in a sphere that transcends our mortality, but also because, since each of them constitutes a genre apart, they do not communicate with one another in membership in a same species. They cannot experience, as we do, the tearing of the tissue that binds us to those close to us.

This conception of the flesh explains one of St. Bernard's principal theses in his theory of love, which is the familiar idea that all love necessarily begins by being carnal. Carnal love is a first and completely positive step on the road that leads love to its ultimate flowering, which is charity toward oneself for the love of God.[28] Thus it is remarkable to see the carnal nature of man appearing, in a great many passages, as something positive in itself, and not only to the extent that it is counterbalanced by a human dignity founded on the spiritual. The flesh is present in heaven: even in Paradise, we were originally made of earthly clay. But it is "the clay of paradise (*limus paradisi*)."[29]

Which creature was better, the angel or man, remained an open question throughout the Middle Ages. Moreover, the most commonly admitted response to it varied both according to religious tradition and within each tradition. Among Jewish thinkers, a majority pronounced in favor of the angels.[30] In Islam, the Qur'an opted quite decidedly in favor of man.[31] In the Christian world, one hears a discreet but novel tone, with a decided accent on the historicity of man. The latter is a consequence of man's carnal nature. Human love needs to mature into charity, which implies the passage of time. The angel decides outside of time what he will be, a good angel or a demon, and once he has chosen, he will remain so for eternity. Man can of course fall, but he can also be redeemed. From this point of view, man is worth more than an angel. This is why angels have something to learn from men, because what happens within human history is not accessible to the angelic mind (Ephesians 3:10). This is one of the reasons that led medieval authors to recognize that man has certain advantages over the angel.[32]

Flesh and Conscience: The Sense of Touch

The carnal nature of man is implied by the theory of knowledge commonly accepted in the Middle Ages. According to it, all knowledge is necessarily based in sense knowledge. This is even true when knowledge is thought to grasp the immaterial.[33] This theory is of course Aristotle's, and it is not surprising to encounter it in the great Scholastics who were influenced by him. But a similar theory is attested even before Hellenic knowledge entered Western thought (via the Arabic route) in the twelfth and thirteenth centuries. It is thus that we find it in St. Bernard of Clairvaux

(d. 1153), in a passage taken, once again, from his commentary on the *Song of Songs*, more exactly, in the fifth sermon, probably delivered in 1135. The context is a comparison between four sorts of spirits: God, the angels, men, and the animals. The doctrine probably came from Dionysius the Areopagite, although we cannot determine its precise intermediaries. Man is corporeal. He needs a body in order to grasp the material world. But he also must pass through the body to attain the superior, spiritual realities (*ad spiritualia et intelligibilia proficiendo pertingere*). Man is a spirit wrapped in flesh and an inhabitant of the earth (*involutus carne ac terrae incola spiritus*). He thus needs to begin with the consideration of sensible things (*ex consideratione sensibilium proficiens*) in order to accede—slowly and by stages (*gradatim quodammodo paulatimque*) to where the angels arrive effortlessly.[34]

Can we be more precise regarding sense perception? Often cultural worlds are characterized by the central role that a certain sense organ is supposed to play in them. For example, the Greeks are supposed to have been eye people.[35] The ancient Hebrews, on the other hand, are supposed to have been ear people. I have little fondness for this sort of generalization, but they can have a certain heuristic value. Thus if forced to find the sense that could help us to characterize the medieval world, it seems to me that the sense of touch would be a good choice.

Touch is in fact the sense that we cannot help but possess: to lose it would be to lose life.[36] We will never cease to have it, even in our glorious body, when we are resurrected.[37] Knowledge is fundamentally sense perception, and sense perception is fundamentally touch.[38]

One could even go further and say that knowledge is conceived on the model of tactile knowledge. For Aristotle, knowledge is the encounter of a knower (subject) and a known (object). The two attain their perfection, and even become what they are, through that encounter. Knowledge is the common act of the knower and the known. By that same token, the knower knows himself in the very act of knowing something other than himself and through that other object. This occurs because the knower as such is produced only by none other than the act of knowing. Hence, in any attempt to know the knowing subject, the act of knowing furnishes the object.

As it happens, this structure is also found in the case of tactile perception. In touch, we perceive the resistant object that we touch, and at the same time we perceive what makes us sensitive to touch—that is, our flesh, compressed by the encounter with the object that resists it.[39] We do not see our eye when it sees; we do not hear our eardrums when they hear; we do not smell our nostrils when they smell. In contrast, we touch our flesh at the very moment that we touch an object. We perceive, not only the fact that we perceive, but also and simultaneously what makes that perception possible. Touch is thus something like a "transcendent perception": perception contributes to it something about the condition of possibility of perception. In touch, the I knows itself. But the I does not grasp itself in the same manner as does the modern subject—or at least not if we follow Heidegger's analysis. The subject does not make sure of itself before knowing things.

The situation is totally different for the medieval subject, for whom self-knowledge is marginal in relation to his sensorial perception or his intellectual grasp of other things.[40] If knowledge and self-knowledge are founded on the sense of touch, we cannot grasp ourselves without our body. In my opinion, what is at stake here is not so much an implicit thesis regarding the "mind-body problem" as a phenomenological given regarding our experience of the body. That experience can also find expression in the ancient and medieval idea that our body is made of earth or clay. That image contains more than a declaration about the chemical composition of the organism, a declaration that, what is more, has been contradicted by modern biology and had already been voided by the demise of the doctrine of the four elements. That idea bears on the relation that we have with our body. The earth is what we are obliged to presuppose, what we cannot create, the ground on which we build, the base on which we walk. It is analogous to the absolute immobility of the Prime Mover.[41] In like fashion, we awaken to conscious life and we discover ourselves already inhabiting a body that we have not created. According to a famous text of Husserl's in which he relativizes Copernican astronomy, our relation to the earth is analogous to our relation with our own bodies.[42]

This can be confirmed *a contrario*. Modernity began, or at least first found expression, with the Cartesian *ego*. But even in the Middle Ages, one can find an interesting term of comparison and perhaps a prefiguration of it—as I have already remarked—in an argument of Avicenna's traditionally known as the "flying man." It has drawn the attention of a number of philosophers and historians of thought, some of whom even see in it the indirect source of Descartes' *cogito*.[43] I shall examine only one aspect of the question here, basing my remarks on the earliest formulation of it in Avicenna's *Book of Health* (*Kitāb al-Shifā'*):

One has to imagine one of us as if he had been created all at once and created perfect. Except that his sight is veiled, and he cannot perceive exterior things. He has been created floating in the air or in the void, so that the

existence of the air does not affect him in any way that he can feel. There is
a separation among his members, so that they are neither attached to nor in
contact with one another. One asks then if he would assert his own existence.
Now, there is no doubt that he would assert his own existence, without going
so far as to assert that the existence of any extremity of his members or any
internal part of his viscera, heart, brain, or anything external. Still he would
assert his own essence without asserting any length, width, or depth.[44]

This experiment in thought is not totally honest. In reality, no one can
know what he would feel in a situation of the sort. But even leaving aside
that objection, the text helps us to better understand what is at stake concerning the sense of touch. Indeed, what Avicenna's example excludes with
such great care is above all the possibility of tactile perception. It supposes
that self-awareness remains when physical continuity with oneself is removed. The modern (or at least premodern) tone of this text derives from
the exclusion of the body operated upon. The body is excluded, not because of its material nature, but because it symbolizes what consciousness
must receive from the outside and cannot construct out of itself.

Humility as Awareness of Carnality

The virtue that enables us to become conscious of our carnal condition
and draw the consequences of it is humility.[45] By what right can we connect humility with carnality? In the Latin-speaking world—the world of
Western European clerics—the word humilitas was felt as deriving from
humus, or earth. Humilis is etymologized as humo clinis, or "leaning towards the earth."[46] In like fashion, the word for "man"—homo—is felt (and
today's philologists agree) as deriving from humus.[47] The same etymological play on words can be found in other languages, Hebrew for one: adam
is connected to adamah, or earth. The connection between humility and
earth even occurs where the language does not permit close verbal connections, for example, in the Persian poet Sa'dī.[48]

The earth—as we call our planet (remembering that it was not a planet
in the Middle Ages)—is not only the dwelling place of man. It is also, as
an element, the stuff of which our bodies are made. Bernard of Clairvaux
writes: "There is another earth that is closer to you," and that earth is caro,
the flesh.[49] Elsewhere Bernard states, "By this earth I mean our body."[50]
A contemporary of Bernard's speaks of "the flesh, which is like the earth
in man."[51] This connection between the flesh and humility can be demon-

strated in greater detail on three levels, which, to simplify matters, I shall call anthropology, theory of knowledge, and ethics.

From the viewpoint of anthropology, humility signifies our becoming aware that we are not angels, but terrestrial beings made of flesh and blood. We are above all earth-dwellers, inhabitants of the lowest point in the entire universe, the receptacle of all sorts of influences coming from above in a sort of cosmic draining process.[52] Furthermore, our body is made of earth, a rough and impure material that clashes with the vivacity of thought.[53] Our carnal nature is expressed in living terms by the ceaselessly recurrent image of "earthen vessels" (ostrakinon skeuos) originated by St. Paul and repeated in a large number of texts.[54] For example, people say that virgins transport a treasure beyond price in an earthen vessel, knowing that it is extremely difficult to live the life of an angel among men, to live on earth in the same way as celestial beings, or to live a life of chastity in the flesh.[55]

Humility is less an affect than a sort of knowledge.[56] It is above all self-knowledge. That is even what defines it: "Humility is that thorough self-examination which makes a man contemptible in his own sight (humilitas est virtus, qua homo verissima sui cognitione sibi ipse vilescit)."[57]

The structure of the knowledge that is implicit in knowledge of the self, as set into operation by humility, is the same as what we have seen in the case of the sense of touch. For the theory of knowledge, the primacy of touch signifies that we know ourselves because we know other things. We would not become conscious of ourselves if we were not ourselves affected, touched by other things. In similar fashion, humility is mediated self-knowledge, a knowledge of oneself that recognizes that the I does not receive its "I-ness" from itself. This sort of knowledge is thematized and is called "consideration." In consideration, the subject assures its own continuity and purifies itself so as to know itself better. But, unlike the modern subject as Heidegger describes it, this does not imply any effort to take control of oneself.[58]

Two Contemporary Problematics and the Medieval Model of Subjectivity

Up to this point, I have attempted to describe certain dimensions of medieval subjectivity through the concept of flesh and others that it seems to me are tied to that concept. Now I would like to present a brief reflection on the possible pertinence of these ideas for our own philosophical scene. I shall limit myself to two examples.

Anthropology

One might perhaps characterize modernity—not without a touch of pedagogical exaggeration—as the age without angels. It would be an intriguing task to narrate in some detail how the angels disappeared beyond the
horizon of human consciousness and to write the history of that disappearance. As we have seen, St. Augustine had already remarked that experience with angels is not comfortable.[59] But the modern age goes one step
further: angels are not only difficult to contact; they simply do not exist;
they have no place in our vision of the world. Schopenhauer laughs at
Kant, who, according to him, would have enlarged moral law to all rational beings whatsoever, just to include the angels.[60] His sarcasm might well
represent the final page of the history of angels among the philosophers.

Whether or not we return to the traditional definitions of living and
rational beings in relation to other beings, the consequence of the disappearance of the angels is that we are placed before an alternative: either
man is alone, or man and God stand face-to-face in an exclusive possession
of rationality. Modernity can be defined as the period in which we humans
are—or, supposing that we are no longer modern but postmodern, were—
the only creatures supposed to have a share in rationality. As it happens, it
is not a matter of indifference to know whether the only specific trait (or
at least the most heavily accentuated difference) defining man is rationality, or whether rationality is also a certain style of affectivity. Accentuating
the first can lead to excluding irrational humans from humanity, strictly
speaking. One can find traces of an attitude of this sort even in ancient and
medieval thought.[61] But modern thought gives it abundant justification.

The rediscovery of the flesh is perhaps a philosophical task decisive for
our own age. In his later works, Maurice Merleau-Ponty took several steps
toward a phenomenology of carnality. For him, the French word *chair*
is, first and foremost, a translation of the German *Leib*, the most current
French equivalent of which is *corps propre*. But since French and English
(unlike German, Italian, or Spanish) distinguish between living flesh and
meat—flesh that we eat—Merleau-Ponty's reflections on *la chair* take on
an original cast, often leading him to formulas strangely reminiscent of
Aristotle's *De anima*.[62] One might pursue this reflection, and in fact that
has been done.[63] The theme of the flesh has even become somewhat fashionable.

It is interesting to note that this enterprise of thinking about the flesh,
both in its realizations and in the tasks that still remain for it to do, is a
medieval enterprise. For the thinkers of the Middle Ages, the importance
of carnality was a consequence of the existence of a non-carnal rationality

in angelic nature. Man could not receive a complete definition unless one considered in him not only his rationality, but also, and just as decidedly, his carnal nature. Can we recapture a sense of that importance? Certainly, angels no longer figure in our vision of the world. But we have computers. And we have philosophers who wonder about what exact status to assign to what is called "artificial intelligence." The computer can offer us an opportunity to recover something of the significance of the fact that rationality is not man's only specific difference. Computers possess—or do not possess, according to how we look at it—something like "reason." But if we go back to the etymology of the word "reason," which is the ability to count (*reor*), those machines undoubtedly possess enough *ratio* to be able to count. They are material, but even the "soft" ware in them is not a flesh.

Amusingly enough, the status of the thinking machine was evoked in the Middle Ages by the Franciscan Pierre de Jean Olivi (Olieu) in the latter half of the thirteenth century. Olivi writes that to deny free will would be to take away from us what is most essential in us, which is personality or personhood, and grant us little more than being a sort of intellectual beast—that is, beasts endowed with an intellect (*quaedam bestiae intellectuales seu intellectum habentes*).[64] If he had lived in our own times, Olivi would certainly have had much to say on questions relating to computers and "artificial intelligence."

Hermeneutics

Often historians of hermeneutics seeks precursors of this highly contemporary branch of philosophy, which really exists as an independent discipline only since Schleiermacher. Most of the time they neglect the Middle Ages, on occasion not without a certain scorn, and jump directly from St. Augustine's *De doctrina christiana* to Luther.[65] It would be worthwhile to show that the hermeneutic problem already existed in the medieval period. From antiquity, the possibility of communicating was not naively taken for granted. Thus Gorgias was already wondering—supposing that there was something, and supposing that such a "something" could be known—whether one could communicate it to others, a question to which he responded negatively: it would be "incommunicable to the neighbor (*anermeneuton tō pelas*)."[66] Far from displaying any naïveté, the ancient and medieval thinkers were attempting to guarantee the possibility of communication because they felt that it needed to be established. This was the case in antiquity with Plato and Aristotle, the two founders of the classical tradition of philosophy, and later among Aristotle's commentators.[67]

Nor was the problem forgotten during the Middle Ages. Thomas Aquinas treats it explicitly in his treatise *On the Unity of the Intellect*. The fundamental phenomenon that he feels must be taken into consideration is that "this man understands (*hic homo singularis intelligit*)."[68] His audacious response is that, just like the other functions of the soul, the intellect is the form of the body, and of a physical, individual body.[69] Understanding pertains to the individual. This makes Thomas a distant precursor of the Romantic idea of hermeneutics, which takes as its point of departure a formula that sounds like Scholastic Latin but was probably coined by Goethe in a letter to Lavater: "the individual is undescribable (*individuum est ineffabile*)."[70] If the act by which I understand is not the same as the one by which my neighbor understands, and even less the act of some impersonal principle common to humanity as a whole, if we want to understand, to seize what we want to know and assimilate it, we need to make a special effort, one that each one of us must take on personally and accomplish in an absolutely individual manner.

Moreover, the hermeneutic problem, as the medieval thinkers viewed it, was linked to the problem of the carnal status of man. Man speaks because he is carnal. The angels do not speak because they have no need to do so.[71] Our understanding can only be purely negative: the coarseness of our flesh prevents us from having direct access to the thoughts of others. But at the same time, there is something positive about it: we express ourselves through what we say to our neighbor. Knowledge is mediated through a social flesh. Self-knowledge is possible only through the mediation of a friend.[72] Thus there is some sort of analogy between the individual and society. The city plays the same role as the flesh. Social realities are carnal in nature.

Thomas Aquinas echoes Aristotle when he reflects on what his adversaries threaten, given that, as he understands them, the act of "intelligating" is collective. That idea threatens what he calls *conversatio civilis*, which we would probably translate as "social life."[73] The expression is interesting, and even more so from the viewpoint of modern hermeneutics, beginning with Schleiermacher's *Dialektik*, which states that conversation is the model for linguistic communication. Conversation has to continue, and that conversation is *civilis*, of a political nature: it even constitutes the city as such.

Thus we can note that medieval hermeneutics has a political dimension. It is situated beyond explicit political theories, as they are expressed in the various commentaries on Aristotle's *Politics*, then recently rediscovered. Ultimately, the city is possible and necessary because we cannot communicate in any other manner than by language, to the extent that we are individuals incapable of communication with an intuitive grasp of a sole and unique truth, but feel a need to share it by exchanging our thoughts.

Conclusion

I have sketched out a possible approach to subjectivity in medieval thought by making use of the concept of flesh. I have stressed a few points of contact with certain contemporary problems that might render that concept pertinent for our concerns today. In doing so, I make no claim to enroll the history of philosophy in the service of one or another of our intellectual fashions. I do think, however, that contemporary thought should not be limited to a dialogue with ancient and modern thinkers, and that medieval authors ought to be considered as partners who are quite deserving of being heard.

6

The Denial of Humanity

On the Judgment "Those People Are Not Men" in Some Ancient and Medieval Texts

Few phenomena are harder to bear than racism. Unless it is, perhaps, the clear conscience of those who believe themselves not prone to that error. Philosophers are prominent among representatives of that self-satisfaction. My aim here is to invite them—that is, my colleagues and myself—to a historical and corporative examination of conscience.

Some Precautions

I have no intention of drawing up a catalog of the declarations of philosophers we might call "racist." Even the greatest of them made statements that are explicitly and tranquilly racist. There are, for example, well-known passages in Aristotle about the superiority of the Greeks over the Barbarians.[1] Nietzsche, at the other end of the history of philosophy, is clearly rabidly anti-Semitic—or perhaps one should say he displays a slightly bothersome philo-Semitism prefiguring the *Protocols of the Wise Men of Zion* (a work written only in the beginning of the twentieth century, a few years after Nietzsche's death). He did not escape sharing the prejudices of his age toward the black race, however.[2]

Nor need we speak of the great philosophers' imitators, who can cast retrospective suspicion on the master they claim to follow. It is just as irresponsible to blame the masters for the erroneous ideas of the disciples as to credit them with their followers' virtues. I shall take care, for example, not to present the anti-fascism of an early translator as a benefit of Spinoza's ideas. The Count of Boulainvilliers, the first (but clandestine) French translator of the *Ethics*, could be seen as a typical disciple of Spinoza, but he was a leading exponent of the idea of the supremacy of the nobility over the Third Estate, a supremacy founded on a right of conquest.[3]

As for the masters themselves, it will always be easy (too easy perhaps) to attribute their failings to the man rather than the thinker, in the interest of defending the purity of the discipline that the thinker represents. To take Heidegger as an example—which I obviously cannot claim will give him his just deserts—we can draw a distinction between the one text in which he speaks of "the Jew Fränkel," on the one hand, and his thoughts about the essence of man as *Dasein*, sketched out in his *Sein und Zeit* (*Being and Time*), which makes any biological determination of the humanity of man impossible, on the other hand. It remains to be seen to what extent the other evidence of anti-Semitism in Heidegger is worthy of credence and whether racism can be reduced to a biologism.[4]

What I shall present here is a series of texts in which the author states that certain beings, although they have a human figure, "are not men." I have found a certain number of these, but my list is far from exhaustive.[5] They will be offered here as I have chanced upon them in reading that I have pursued for other reasons, and will be arranged in chronological order, the most neutral. Finally, I will limit myself to passages taken from ancient and medieval authors writing in a span of time from the third century BCE to the end of the Middle Ages in the fourteenth century.

That time period has the interest of preceding the Iberian emphasis on "purity of blood" (*limpieza de sangre*); it also precedes the discovery of the New World and its indigenous peoples and the theoretical and practical problems that arose with them. For even greater reason, it precedes the emergence of evolutionary biology and the form of racism that claims to be founded on it. Hence the idea of the non-humanity of certain men is presented by these authors in what might be called a state of chemical purity.

Some "Pagan" Texts

(1) The first philosopher cited here will be Aristotle, the Philosopher par excellence. A well-known passage of the *Politics* states: "A man who is incapable of entering into partnership, or who is so self-sufficing that he has no need to do so, is no part of a state, so that he must be either a lower animal (*therion*) or a god."[6]

We have no Greek commentary on this passage, nor any Arabic commentary, given that this work does not seem to have ever been translated into Arabic.[7] We do have a commentary in Latin by Thomas Aquinas, however, who takes the edge off Aristotle's assimilation of man to a lower animal: "If it should happen that someone is unable to participate in the society of a political community (*communicare societate civitatis*) because of the individual's depravity (*pravitas*), such a one is worse than a human being and a beast, as it were (*quasi*)."[8]

Later in the *Politics*, Aristotle declares: "It is not indeed clear whether this collective superiority of the many compared with the few good men can possibly exist in regard to every democracy and every multitude, and perhaps it may be urged that it is manifestly impossible in the case of some— for the same argument would also apply to animals (*theria*), yet what a difference is there, practically, between some multitudes and animals?"[9] As is known, the commentary on this passage that is printed in the works of St. Thomas Aquinas is no longer by him after book III, chapter 7, but by Pierre d'Auvergne. The passage speaks of a bestial troupe whose members have a propensity to commit beastly actions, but it does not cast their humanity in doubt.[10]

Next I would like to cite several texts that can be taken as representative of a certain moral vulgate, Stoic for the most part, of the Hellenistic and Roman periods.

(2) Cicero:

It is essential to every inquiry about duty that we keep before our eyes how far superior man is by nature to cattle and other beasts: they have no thought except for sensual pleasure and this they are impelled by every instinct to seek; but man's mind is nurtured by study and meditation; he is always either investigating or doing, and he is captivated by the pleasure of seeing and hearing. Nay, even if a man is more than ordinarily inclined to sensual pleasures, provided, of course, that he be not quite on a level with the beasts of the field (for some people are men only in name, not in fact) (*sunt enim quidam homines non re sed nomine*)—if, I say, he is a little too susceptible to the attractions of pleasure, he hides the fact, however much he may be caught in its toils, and for very shame conceals his appetite.[11]

(3) Seneca: "Put in the same class [as beasts of the field] those people whose dullness of nature and ignorance of themselves have reduced them to the level of beasts of the field and of inanimate things. There is no difference between the one and the other, since in one case they are things without reason, and in the other their reason is warped, and works their own hurt, being active in the wrong direction."[12]

(4) Epictetus: "Where do they put their interest—outside themselves,

or in their moral purpose? If outside, call them not friends, any more than you would call them faithful, steadfast, courageous, or free: nay, call them not even human beings, if you are wise. For it is no judgement of human sort which makes them bite (that is, revile) one another, and take to the desert (that is, to the market-place) as wild beasts take to the mountains, etc."[13]

Elsewhere Epictetus writes: "Why, then, did you call him a human being? For surely everything is not judged by its outward appearance only, is it? . . . Therefore, neither are the nose and the eyes sufficient to prove that one is a human being, but you must see whether one has the judgements (*dogmata*) that belong to a human being. Here is a man who does not listen to reason (*ouk akouei logou*), he does not understand when he is confuted; he is an ass. Here is one whose sense of self-respect (*to aidemon*) has grown numb; he is useless (*akhrestos*), a sheep, anything but a human being."[14]

These passages are followed by others that express the idea that the humanity of man resides above all in his religiousness, a theme that was to be highly popular in the Middle Ages.[15]

(5) In the *Corpus Hermeticum* attributed to Hermes Trismegistus, we read: "The intellect cannot support a torpid soul, but it abandons such a soul attached to the body and stifled by it here below. Such a soul . . . does not possess intellect: thus one should not even call such a being 'man.' For man is a divine living being, who must be compared, not to the rest of the terrestrial living beings, but to those on high, in the heavens, who are called gods."[16]

The Beginnings of Monotheism

(6) The Babylonian Talmud interprets Ezekiel 34:31 as meaning: "And you, my flock, the flock of my pastures, are men." Rabbi Simeon bar Yohai says to the Israelites, "You are classified as man, and gentiles are not classified as man."[17] Since the author of that assertion is Simeon bar Yohai, it is hardly surprising that the statement is repeated in the *Zohar*, supposed to be his work.[18]

The English translation of the second passage explains it in a note in a manner that seems satisfactory: "Only an Israelite, about whom one can say, given than he is a worshiper of the true God, that he, like Adam, was created in the image of God. Idolaters, who have disfigured the divine image, lose all claim to be called so."[19] Taking a different approach, Moritz Lazarus explains that: (a) "'not called men' is a favorite phrase to denote that the life of such a one is unworthy a human being," and, (b) in "all European languages," it signifies "inhuman" in the sense of "cruel or vengeful."[20] The argument, which recalls that of "the cauldron," can be explained by the author's protests against the polemics of the age, which rested on an old tradition of anti-Jewish interpretation of these passages.[21] The most sober response to this sort of attack seems to me to be the chronological approach offered here.

(7) Boethius: "Whatever falls from goodness, ceases to be; wherefore evil men cease to be what they were—but that they were men till now their still surviving form of the human body shows—and therefore by turning to wickedness they have by that same act lost their human nature. . . . So it follows that you cannot adjudge him a man whom you see transformed by vices. . . . So he who having left goodness (*probitas*) aside has ceased to be a man, since he cannot pass over into the divine state, turns into a beast (*bellua*)." Boethius then lists eight animals that vicious men resemble: the greedy man is a wolf, the slanderer a dog, the wily man a fox, and so on.[22]

Boethius seems to have taken inspiration here from the idea mentioned (and criticized) in a treatise attributed to Aristotle that claims that physical resemblances in the faces of certain men shared by animals reveal the presence of traits that those animals represent.[23] He may also have been thinking of the Platonic myths of reincarnation. There is an important difference, however: Plato takes the viewpoint of a temporality previous to all possible experience, so that what has the figure of a man must necessarily be a man, and what looks like an animal must be an animal, even if its soul had been human in an earlier existence. Boethius supposes in man a degeneration situated within empirical life.

(8) The Qur'an: "O you who believe! Obey Allah and His Messenger, and do not turn away from him when you hear (him speak). Nor be like those who say, 'We hear,' but do not listen. For the worst of beasts in the sight of Allah are the deaf and the dumb—those who do not understand."[24] The word translated here as "beasts" (*dābba*) signifies crawling creatures and is usually applied to animals. Other translations read: "Unbelievers are the worst of animals." This is the basis for the notion that can occasionally be found in Islam that unbelievers are to be classed with the animals, below common humanity.[25]

The Apogee of Medieval Aristotelianism

(9) In Muslim Spain, the philosopher Ibn Bājja (Avempace) had this to say: "And for that reason also, the one whose animal soul dominates the rational soul to the point that it lets itself always get carried away by its pas-

sions, contrary to what his reason dictates to him, is indeed a man, but the worst of the beasts is better than he. And it is even just to say that he is a beast, although he is endowed with the human reason with which he produced that act. Indeed, in this case, his reason is an evil that is added to his own vice."[26]

(10) Ibn Bājja's somewhat younger contemporary Jehuda Halevi places at the head of the list of persons interrogated by the king of the Khazars in connection with the latter's search for the true religion a philosopher whose doctrine is that of the Arab Aristotelians, especially Ibn Bājja (in book I) and Avicenna (in book V). This fictive philosopher explains that men can realize the potential of their nature to differing degrees. At the bottom is "the negro (*habashī*; Ethiopian) who is able (*yuhayya'u*) to receive nothing more than the human shape and speech in its least developed form."[27] The opposite extreme is represented by the philosopher himself (probably speaking for the Philosopher, Aristotle, who represented the unsurpassable summit of the human mind for several of his medieval disciples).[28] Jehuda Halevi's disciple and spokesman nonetheless recognizes that the black man has the form (*surah*) of humanity. However, if that word can designate external appearance, the philosophers also used it to designate what gives a being that of which it is the form (*forma dat esse rei*), or what gives substance. In that case a black man is indeed a man, and not in appearance only. Which is an invitation to think about the fact that he also possesses speech (*nutq*), articulated language, and reason.[29]

The idea is far from being exceptional in the cultural context of the age, and we can find analogous texts among the Muslim medieval writers. Thus Ibn Khaldūn writes tranquilly: "The Negro nations (*Sūdān*) are, as a rule, submissive to slavery because [Negroes] have little [that is essentially] human and have attributes that are quite similar to those of dumb animals."[30] The classic commentators on the *Kuzari* do not seem to have been particularly shocked by this passage, nor did they attenuate it. Thus the Italian erudite Judah ben Joseph Moscato (1530–1590), in his *Qol Jehudah*, limits his remarks to referring to a passage in Maimonides' *Guide for the Perplexed* (quoted below). A later commentator, during the Enlightenment, had a good deal more to say.[31] In his *Otsar Nehmad*, Israel ben Moses Halevi (Zamosc) (ca. 1700–1772) writes:

HE WHO IS INCAPABLE OF . . . MORE: because of the great heat, their temperament (*mezeg*) does not arrive at a perfect equilibrium, but according to the opinion of our Law, the majority of them are of the posterity (*zera'*) of Ham (Genesis 10:6), and human perfection is only given to the posterity of Shem, whereas the posterity of Ham is imperfect (*haser*) from the fact that they are cursed [by Noah: see Gen. 9:25]. OF RECEIVING HUMAN FORM: for, in fact, "Man . . . resembles the beasts that perish" (Psalm 49:21); they have no figure (*to'ar*) of a man; they go naked outdoors. When he says HUMAN FORM, he means the shape that man possesses in the whole of his members; it is uniquely in that respect that they resemble man. Or else he means that he [the black man] is not capable of receiving the form of man—that is to say, the soul—unless at the extreme of imperfection, for they have no religion (*dath*), intellectual or traditional. [There follows a reference to the same passage in the *Guide for the Perplexed*.] AND THE DISCOURSE AT THE EXTREME OF IMPERFECTION: by the articulation of the vowels and the proper pronunciation of the words.[32]

It is worth noting, however, that the words given above in capitals are not directly stated by Jehuda Halevi, but placed in the mouth of his philosopher. The two protagonists of the dialogue, who are closer to the author's own thought, do not seem to hold similar doctrines. This is implied, in any event, in a reply of the king of the Khazars (if I understand it correctly), who states that he bases his judgment on the philosophers, and not on an authority that he, quite rightly, finds it difficult to define, designated as *'āmma dahmā*. Hartwig Hirschfeld renders this as "a negro people"; Ibn Tibbon as "a nation left to its own devices that agrees on no opinion (*mufqereth*, or, literally, *res nullius*)." Charles Touati translates it as *"une populace abêtie"* (a sluggish or bedazed populace).[33] It seems to me simpler to understand the expression without any reference to race or religion, following its stated meaning: the vulgar masses, as opposed to the philosophers, who constitute the elite of humanity and are in agreement with one another.

(11) Maimonides writes in the introduction to his first work, the *Commentary on the Mishnah*: "A man, before he activates his dormant understanding and knowledge, is no more than a beast. He is indistinguishable from the other species of living beings except for his powers of logical reasoning (*nutq*), i.e., in that he forms thoughts in his mind, the most profound of thoughts being the picturing in his mind the One-ness of The-Holy-One-Blessed-be-He and all G-d-related ideas which accompany this concept."[34]

In the body of the same work, Maimonides comments on a case of the goring by a steer in which the *Mishnah*, all other things being equal, gives the Israelite an advantage over the pagan. This elicits a malaise that Maimonides seeks to smooth over:

If a trial is engaged between an Israelite and a pagan, let the manner of the sentence between them be as I shall explain: If there is for us an advantage in their laws, we judge them according to their laws and we tell them: "Such are your laws." But if it is better for us that we judge according to our laws, we judge them according to our laws and we tell them: "Such are our laws." Let that thing not seem difficult in your eyes, and do not be astonished by it, just as you are not astonished by the slaughter of animals, even if they have done no evil. Indeed, someone in whom human dispositions have not been led to their perfection is not truly a man, and he has no other aim than the [true] man. To speak on this question requires a special book.[35]

Maimonides' philosophic masterpiece—the *Guide for the Perplexed*—ends with a famous parable on the different classes or levels of men, whose greater or lesser knowledge of God in his reality is compared to the proximity or distance of the inhabitants of a city from the king in the throne room of his palace:

Those who are outside the city are all human individuals who have no doctrinal belief, neither one based on speculation nor one that accepts the authority of tradition: such individuals as the furthermost Turks found in the remote North, the Negroes (*sūdān*) found in the remote South, and those who resemble them from among them that are with us in these climes. The status of those is like that of irrational animals. To my mind they do not have the rank of men, but have among the beings a rank lower than the rank of man but higher than the rank of the apes. For they have the external shape and lineaments of a man and a faculty of discernment that is superior to that of the apes.[36]

It is noteworthy that the polar opposition between the Turk who lives at the extreme north and the black man who lives at the extreme south, both of whom were considered "naturally slaves," is utterly banal at the time and in the cultural world of the southern Mediterranean.[37]

The attitude of Maimonides' classic medieval commentators—Ephodi, Shem Tov, Bunan Crescas, Falaquera, Joseph Ibn Caspi, and Moses of Narbonne (Abravanel did not write a commentary on the third part)—is also noteworthy. They express their opinions on the controversial point contained in the parable, which is the superiority of the philosopher over the Talmudist that Maimonides seems to recognize. But they have not a word to say about the phrases that I have picked out, which seem to present no problems for them.

(12) Meister Eckhart: "[The inner man] guards [the five senses] against animal diversions—such as people choose when they live like animals

without intelligence. Such people are more properly called animals than persons (*und solhe liute heizent eigentlicher vihe dan liute*)."[38]

A Few Reflections

These texts, let me repeat, by no means constitute an exhaustive enumeration. They come from a variety of sources: from polytheists ("pagans") and monotheists, and, among the latter, from Jews, Christians, and Muslims. The attitude that I have noted does not imply a specific "world vision." It is not found only among philosophers, as certain texts come from the literary genre of religious law (the Talmud) or revelation with a Gnostic cast (Pseudo-Hermes). But philosophers give it expression—both those who came before the great monotheistic religions and those contemporary to them. Thus it cannot be confused with the "intolerance" that often passes for the sorry privilege of those religions.

The attitude that I have focused on does not coincide with racism, but can include discrimination between peoples, as with the texts of Jehuda Halevi and Maimonides. Rather, it makes up something like the genre of which racism is the species, unless it operates as a condition of possibility for racism. If we limit ourselves to what is explicit in the passages quoted, we can remark that although they do on occasion name particular peoples (blacks or Turks), they do not linger over so-called racial characteristics as such. Black people, for example, are not typed by their physical characteristics. Such characteristics serve for recognizing such peoples, but no theory about their cause or the peoples' claimed inferiority is attached to them.

There is a paradox here: although the philosophers deny humanity to certain beings, they nonetheless are forced to consider them as human, or else refusal would be superfluous and would have to give way to simple recognition of a fact. When non-humanity is manifest, it is not necessary to express it. "Considering like" in this fashion is the affirmation of an appearance and of what is only an appearance: the human figure is not the face of man.

Thus, despite the thematic genealogy that connects them, these texts should not be placed in the same series as other texts (like certain Platonic myths) that suppose that animals have been derived from the fall of a spirit or the degeneration of a primitive man. Plato makes it clear, in fact, that in order to become a man, one must have seen the supra-celestial truth, in which case it is precisely vision that conditions the possession of the human form (*skhema*).[39]

What stands opposed to "man" can be either his opposite (non-man) or something contrary to him, which can be given as the monkey, for example, or the whole bestiary mobilized by Boethius. There is no need for any reference to the modern theory of evolution: the much older idea of a gradation of living creatures suffices.

Within the works of these philosophers, such texts are not the product of a slippage due to the intrusion of biographical elements that can be charged to the man rather than the thinker—supposing that to be a legitimate distinction, of course. They can be deduced from the very act by which the philosopher defines himself as such—that is, as a man of reason, hence the man most worthy of his own humanity. For the philosopher, placing reason on the throne of the universe automatically exalts him above the world of living creatures.[40] And in fact it is indeed the philosopher, in the polarization of humanity he proposes, who occupies the summit of a pyramid, the base of which (or perhaps the basement) is represented by those whose humanity he values least, as is clearly seen in the passage from Jehuda Halevi.

These texts are in fact the direct consequence of the classic definition of man by the closest genre (animal) and a differentiation of species (reasonable). If the specific difference is absent, we return to the close genre alone: a non-reasonable animal is not a man, or is one only by abuse of language.

More generally, and even more disquieting, one might wonder just what purpose a definition of man might serve.

The specific difference—that is, the concept of "reason" that is operative in these texts—is two-pronged, including both theoretical reason and practical, or moral, reason. One ceases to be a man either because one is incapable of grasping the intelligibles, or because one behaves in a bestial fashion. The texts hesitate between the two determinations of reason. Maimonides pronounces clearly for theoretic reason as a grasp of the intelligibles. The others are less clear. In like fashion, the texts hesitate between two styles: that of a moral exhortation that is not without a certain nobility ("Be worthy of your humanity"),[41] and that of a cold descriptive classification of intellectual levels.

The "religious" determinations themselves oscillate between those two conceptions of the *logos* that makes man: certain texts say that those who are strangers to religion drop out of humanity. The question arises of whether religiosity is conceived, roughly speaking, as the presence of a moral sense or as the presence of intellectual illumination. In other words, if we are dealing with an ethical or philosophical religion.

Such texts show the limits of a type of anti-racist argument that is in other respects totally well-intentioned and that states that "the soul has no color," an argument that reappears in various forms in current debate today ("To be French is a state of mind, not a skin color"). The negation of the pertinence of bodily determinations to the profit of the mind, which is invisible, hence colorless, ought to make racism impossible. As it happens, we see that the privilege unilaterally accorded to the mind can also end up with a refusal of the humanity of the "other" man. It is possible, on the other hand, that the body, in that which makes it human and cannot be reduced to the intellectual, can take the role of an ultimate guarantee before attitudes such as those displayed in the examples I have taken from the philosophers.

PART III

Comparisons

7

Three Muslim Views of
the Christian City

It has become a commonplace to contrast Islam and Christianity by remarking that the first makes no distinction between the spiritual and the temporal. That observation is most often made by Christians, who draw satisfaction from it. Which is enough to render it suspect. I shall thus take care not to claim to know if it is true or not. It would be interesting to ask whether that difference between the two religions has been perceived in Islamic lands. What I would like to do here, without any claim to being exhaustive, it to place three items in the dossier. I have found them as I pursued readings that led me, above all, to the philosophers. I am aware that they are not representative, and that they are even frankly atypical. Philosophers are known for giving in all too often to a malady that finds delight within the sphere of common representations and is called genius.

Biruni: A Faith without a Law

The first text is from the early eleventh century, probably close to the year 1000. It is by Biruni (973–1050), a universal genius, astronomer, geographer, and the author of a book about India that is exceptional from many points of view. Here, however, I am interested in another of his works on the various ways to calculate dates. This utterly factual inquiry permits Biruni, whose subject obliges him to speak of various religious holidays celebrated in the different communities, to make a number of digressions that, from reading with our criteria of today, reveal much about the history of religions.

Thus Biruni includes a chapter on the Melchites, Christians who accepted the dogma defined at the Council of Chalcedon (451), and on their use of the Syriac calendar. On the third day of the first month of Kānūn, this group remembers a personage called Father Johannes, who gathered together the directives of their Christian faith (*mu'allif rusūm al-nasrāniyya*). Biruni notes that the title of "Father" is the highest form of address, because it implies that the people's roots (*usūl*) are tied to veneration of him. He adds: "Their laws (*rusūm*; *mashrū*) [of their religion (*dīn*)] are derived and developed (*istakhraja*) by their most venerated men from the canonical sayings (*qawānin*) of Messiah and the apostles (*salīhūn*)."[1]

Biruni speaks of Christianity elsewhere as well. He compares its ideal to the Indian ideal and alludes to the words of Christ in terms that recall the Gospel of St. Matthew: giving your shirt as well as your coat, turning the other cheek, praying for your enemies (Matthew 5:39–40, 44). He remarks that such precepts are good for philosophers, but not for flesh-and-blood men. What is needed for the latter is constraints: "the whip and the sword." He ends with the sarcastic note that since Constantine gained power, those constraints have been busy indeed.[2]

The classic response of Christian authors to sublime but troubling words such as these is that precepts like those cited by Biruni are applicable only where the attitude asked for does not lead to scandal.[3] This is particularly true when that attitude does not endanger the good order of the city. If such precepts were supposed to serve as laws for a political society, they would be flagrantly inadequate. It is thus interesting that Biruni does not apply this distinction, but instead spontaneously interprets the Gospel counsel in a political sense.

In the brief passage quoted above, Biruni draws attention to the origin of the rules that govern the Christian community. These are not revealed and imposed by God in such a way as to form a *sharia*. They are simply deduced from words that might have been said by Christ, who, for Islam, was a prophet, but also from the words of the apostles, whom no one has ever taken for prophets.

Averroes: Laws Founded on the Interest of the Moment

The second text dates from the second half of the twelfth century. It is by Averroes (1126–1198). On reading Aristotle's *Rhetoric*, he encounters the chapter in which the Philosopher explains that the orator must know what public spirit reigns in the cities.[4] That spirit depends on the regime, and one would not address a democratic assembly in the same way as a senate whose membership was limited to an aristocracy. Aristotle thus offers a rapid outline of the various political regimes. The passage may not plumb the deepest philosophic depths, but since Aristotle's *Politics* was not translated into Arabic,[5] it is the only summary of the politics of his principal teacher that Averroes had available to him. In his commentary on it, Averroes remarks: "It may be that the laws (*sunan*) instituted (*mawdūʿa*) in these cities is determined (*mahdūda*), invariable, one for all times, as is the case with our Islamic law (*sunna*). And it may be that those cities do not have determined laws, but that one relies on the subject of those [laws] to those who hold the power (*amr*) in those [cities] according to what is the most useful (*anfaʿ*) at each moment, as is the case today for many Byzantine (Rūm) laws."[6]

The term "Byzantine" with which this passage ends raises some problems. Precisely what does it refer to? "Romans" usually signifies those whom we would call Byzantines. Averroes mentions Rūm elsewhere, when he explains that the scholars of the land of Rūm became Christians when the religion of Jesus was brought to them, just as the scholars of Alexandria became Muslims when Islam reached them.[7] In contrast, Arabs usually use the term "Franks" (*Ifranj*) to refer to the Christians of Latin Europe. And in fact Averroes, writing about Pythagoras, notes that he lived in Italy, which is now called the land of the Franks (*Ifranj*).[8] One might thus ask how Averroes had knowledge of the Byzantine regime of his age. I wonder whether Averroes was not inspired by Farabi, whom he quotes on the preceding page.[9] For the latter, the Byzantine world was closer to hand. He may even have had direct experience of it through living in Greece, if we can believe one of his biographers.[10]

Whatever the facts, it is important to stress that the idea of a regime that is based on nothing other than the utility of the moment is projected on to Byzantium, which Islam saw as an "other," if not as its principal enemy. The sketch that Averroes gives of it is brevity itself (one line!), but it emphasizes a basic trait, which is an exclusive interest in the utility of the moment. For us, there is something obvious about this. What we see here is something like an elementary liberalism, prior to the nature of the regime. Let me try to formulate the notion: The city does not have for its purpose any other thing than the good of its citizens, but such as the citizens determine it to be. In the medieval worlds of Muslims and Jews alike, such ideas were rare indeed.[11] In Averroes, a simple mention of them seems equivalent to an implied criticism.

Ibn Khaldūn: Laws without *Sharia*

The third text, which I will treat at somewhat greater length, goes back to the second half of the fourteenth century. It is by Ibn Khaldūn (1332–1406) and figures in his master work, the *Muqaddima*.[12] Although Ibn Khaldūn does not seem to have been aware of Biruni's work, he knew Averroes, and he even quotes a phrase from the *Commentary on the Rhetoric*, another passage from which is quoted above.[13]

Ibn Khaldūn devotes a chapter of this work to the titles of "pope" and "patriarch" within Christianity and "Kohen" in Judaism. He speaks of the pope elsewhere, for example, when he mentions Rome as the seat of the papacy.[14] He states:

> After the removal of its prophet [*nabī*], a religious group [*milla*] must have someone to take care of it [*qāʾim bihā*]. (Such a person) must cause the people to act according to the religious laws. In a way, he stands to them in the place (*khalīfa*, caliph) of their prophet, in as much as (he urges) the obligations [*taklīf*] which (the prophet) had imposed upon them. Furthermore, in accordance with the afore-mentioned need for political leadership in social organization [*ijtimāʿ*], the human species must have a person [*shakhs*] who will cause them to act in accordance with what is good for them [*siyāsa*] and who will prevent them by force [*bi ʾl-qahr*] from doing things harmful to them. Such a person is the one who is called ruler.
>
> In the Muslim community [*milla*], the holy war is a religious duty [*mashrūʿ*], because of the universalism of the (Muslim) mission [*li-ʿumūm al-daʿwa*] and (the obligation to) convert everybody to Islam either by persuasion or by force [*tawʿ an wa karhan*]. Therefore, caliphate [*khilāfa*] and royal authority [*mulk*] are united in (Islam), so that the person in charge can devote the available strength to both of them at the same time.
>
> The other religious groups did not have a universal mission, and the holy war was not a religious duty to them, save only for purposes of defense. It has thus come about that the person in charge of religious affairs [*al-qāʾim bi-ʾamri d-dīn*] in (other religious groups) is not concerned with power politics at all. (Among them,) royal authority comes to those who have it, by accident [*bi ʾl-ʿarad*] and in some way that has nothing to do with religion [*li-amr ghayr dīnī*]. It comes to them as the necessary result of group feeling [*ʿasabiyya*], which by its very nature seeks to obtain royal authority, as we have mentioned before, and not because they are under obligation to gain power over other nations [*mukallifūn biʾl-taghallub ʿalā ʾl-umam*], as is the case with Islam. They are merely required to establish their religion [*dīn*] among their own (people) [*fī khāssatihim*].[15]

Ibn Khaldūn begins by making two general remarks that are based on doctrines that he has expressed elsewhere. A religious community needs to have someone who takes charge of it. He compares this with the need that all human communities have for governance, a fact that he has already established. Ibn Khaldūn does not explain the relationship between these two needs: is one a special case of the other?

A third part of the work treats non-Muslim communities. Here Ibn Khaldūn presents a historic summary of the way in which the relationship between power and religion was worked out in Judaism, then in Christianity, to the examination of which he devotes twice as much space.[16] The historical exactitude of Ibn Khaldūn's description matters little here. One might suggest changes in it or compare it to what he says about the same topics on other occasions. For example, in speaking of Judaism and the Jews, he gives an explanation of their sojourn in the desert that recalls a passage of Maimonides in a very interesting manner.[17] He seeks the reasons for their inability to form a kingdom.[18] Finally, he wonders about the reasons for the character traditionally attributed to them.[19]

One might also compare what Ibn Khaldūn says with what we know of the historical reality of the civilizations that he studies. For example, can one ignore—as he does—the difference between the Latin opposition of the pope and the emperor and the "symphony" of the two powers of the Basileus and the Patriarch in Byzantium? For Ibn Khaldūn, in any event (as is true, what is more, of the common opinion of Muslims of his time), that separation of powers existed and—this is the important point—it was a bad thing. A purely secular politics can only be deficient.[20]

However one might judge the Jewish and Christian "city," the fact is that in both versions, political power and religious authority were separate entities. They remained subject to the necessity to seek power for reasons of solidarity, as Ibn Khaldūn states that he has explained elsewhere, which is indeed the case.[21]

A second part of this discussion explains the situation in Islam. Here the two needs are satisfied by a sole authority. This is a particularity of Islam, something that Ibn Khaldūn recognizes on another occasion.[22] But why should what is unified in Islam be separated in Judaism and Christianity? That is the enigma that Ibn Khaldūn attempts to resolve. His response is contained in one long phrase, or, rather, a long subject followed by a one-word predicate. That interminable subject, as it seems to me to require retranslation, is militancy in view of the generality of the appeal and in order to bring the totality of the people, willy-nilly, to the religious duty of Islam.

Militancy (*"Jihād"*)

We need to examine this notion more closely. "Militancy" here expresses the well-known concept of *jihād*, a subject on which we now have available a voluminous and excellent monograph by Alfred Morabia.[23] Finding an equivalent for "militancy" has given me some trouble. To translate the term as "holy war," as is often done, ignores its etymology, which implies the idea of effort. On the other hand, that translation restricts the meaning of what is a global effort on the part of the entire community. This is the sense on which Muslims of goodwill insist today when their intent is apologetic, as, for example, in the famous *Manual* of Maulana Muhammad Ali (1875–1951).[24] We are all aware of the often-repeated hadith on greater and lesser *jihād* attributed to the Prophet. "Militancy" thus seems to me to have a dual advantage: it expresses the two aspects of the term, but it also echoes its "military" aspect.

Whether we find it astonishing or scandalous or not, Ibn Khaldūn, for his part, is in no way ashamed of the military dimension of *jihād*, and in fact stresses it. For him, *jihād* designates a quite concrete war, which he enters into his classification of types of wars.[25] One might ask whether that war was for him a principle or a present reality. He goes as far as to assert that militancy is henceforth empty of meaning (*butlān*).[26] But elsewhere we read a highly interesting passage on the way in which the sovereigns of the Maghreb employed mercenaries come from Europe ("Franks") to deal with Arabs or Berbers, but avoided hiring them for a *jihād* out of fear that they might take sides with their coreligionists.[27]

At the level of principles, in any event, Ibn Khaldūn conceives of a war that aims at dominating the adherents of other religions, "willingly or unwillingly." The expression, which became a commonplace, comes from the Qur'an, which does indeed say "willingly or unwillingly," but in another context, to speak of the way in which nature is subject to God.[28] Ibn Khaldūn calmly summarizes the situation of Christians and Jews: "It is (for them to choose between) conversion to Islam, payment of the poll tax, or death."[29]

Ibn Khaldūn states that the idea of holy war exists only in Islam. What about the other religions? He is in fact thinking only of Christianity, given that Judaism of the time had no military strength. In Christianity and Judaism, militancy is purely defensive. One might quarrel with that statement, even though it is true that cases of forced conversions obtained by arms are rare in Christian areas, Charlemagne's forced baptism of the Saxons being a nearly unique exception. In any event, it is remarkable that Ibn Khaldūn does not mention the Crusades in this context, since he knew about them and twice speaks of them elsewhere.[30] Where Byzantium is concerned, in any event, Ibn Khaldūn was quite right. For that profoundly peaceful empire, the idea of holy war was unthinkable, even horrifying to contemplate when waged by other Christians.[31]

Ibn Khaldūn connects the refusal to distinguish between what we call temporal and spiritual powers to what he terms, here and elsewhere, "the generality of the call (ʿumūm al-daʿwa)."[32] Here as elsewhere, to translate is to interpret. The generality of that call is not universal, addressed to all men. For although Judaism does not claim that it would be a good thing if all men were Jews, Islam is not the only universalist religion. That is also true of Buddhism, about which Ibn Khaldūn ought to have had at least as much knowledge as the average Muslim, and which he may have included among the idolatrous religions that, according to him and contrary to an opinion common at the time, prevail among the majority of humanity.[33] But universality is above all an aspect of Christianity, which is expressly targeted here, and which is even missionary.

Should Ibn Khaldūn's admittedly difficult expression be translated as "all-inclusive in its appeal," as the author of an anthology of the *Muqaddima* has done?[34] If we do, it makes sense that Ibn Khaldūn should seek to regulate all aspects of life, whereas Judaism and Christianity are closed in within the realm of spiritual affairs. One might think so on reading the passage on the private character of religious duty—all the more so since the expression he uses is part of the classic opposition between what is general, even common, and what is particular, made for the "happy few" (ʿamma / khāssa).[35]

The two explanations should probably be connected: what makes Islam singular is not its claim to universality, but rather its means for attaining universality, which include war. It is the necessity of war that requires a political dimension in the direction of the community. Politics is founded on war, not on the maintenance of peace. But where does the obligation of war come from? As for what we can know of its history, I might recall that historians still debate the exact motive for the Muslim conquest of the first century of the Hegira.[36]

The Nature of the Revealed Contents

For Ibn Khaldūn, the reason for war lies in the one word that serves as a predicate that follows the long phrase that I have just examined: war is itself the object of a religious commandment. Ibn Khaldūn says this on two occasions: it is *mashrūʿ*, "imposed by the *sharia*." Muslims are *mutakallafūn*, "charged (by this commandment)." The law derives from the *sharia*, which is to say that it is drawn from a divine word. This is what makes Islam unique, and what joins Ibn Khaldūn to Biruni in the text we have already examined.

What is the nature of that law? To my knowledge, Ibn Khaldūn does not speak elsewhere about the nature of Jewish law. But he does make a very interesting remark about Christian law, as seen in the four Gospels: "These four recensions of the Gospel differ from each other. Not all of it is pure revelation [wahī], but (the Gospels) have an admixture [masūba] of the words of Jesus and of the Apostles. Most of (their contents) consists of sermons [mawāʿiz] and stories [qisas]. There are very few laws [ahkām] in them."[37]

Ibn Khaldūn—and the same could be said of Islam in general—sees the writings of the "peoples of the book" on the model of the Qurʾan, and he judges them by the Qurʾan's standards. For Islam, revelation must be divine dictation passively captured, without distortion, by the prophetic receptor. This is why, when the message is transmitted definitively, its receiver must be virgin of all previous knowledge. Thus Islam tends to interpret a somewhat unclear adjective designating Muhammad—ummī—as meaning "illiterate" or "unlettered" so that "the 'inlibration,' the revelation of the Divine Word in the Book, can happen without his own intellectual activity, as an act of pure grace," just as Mary must be virginal "so that she can immaculately bear the Divine Word to its incarnation."[38] For both Judaism and Christianity, in contrast, the revealed text is an inspired word, passed through the prism of a human liberty, which stamps it with its particular style, its particular bits of knowledge, and so on.

It is that conception of revelation that explains Ibn Khaldūn's formula, which anyone marked by Christian culture finds so striking and so strange: the Gospel narratives are "mixed" (the Arabic term often denotes "made impure, adulterated, dirtied") with the sayings of Jesus. A law must contain rules. Thus Ibn Khaldūn supposes, for example, that the translation of earlier holy books had the aim of extracting "rules" (ahkām) from them.[39] From that point of view, the Gospels are in fact very disappointing. This is a fairly old reproach, and it was aimed at some Christian authors, for example, the authors of certain codes of Nestorian law.[40]

But everything happens just as if Ibn Khaldūn, naively but very cleverly, had put his finger on the absolutely central characteristics of Christian revelation.[41] And this is true even though he saw those characteristics purely negatively. He mentions two traits:

First, the Gospels contain "sermons" and "exhortations." In stating this, Ibn Khaldūn grasps the particular style of what is called Christian "morality," a style that might be called paraenetic. The point is not to furnish new laws to regulate conduct, but rather to encourage obedience to rules already known, rules dictated by the conscience and that can, in principle, be followed perfectly. The object that these exhortations seek is not submission, but turning hearts around, freeing a captive liberty.

Second, the Gospels contain "stories." These are not the parables, which are rendered by another word in Arabic, but relations in general. The word that Ibn Khaldūn uses is the same one used, for example, by Avicenna to speak of his own philosophical tales or, earlier, the one chosen by the translators of Aristotle's *Poetics* to render *mythos*, in the sense of the plot or "intrigue" of a tragedy.[42] The content of Christian writings is narrative, not prescriptive: they relate a "story," not a "message." A message would prescribe what man must do for God; a story relates what God has done for man. In his people and, according to Christians, in Jesus Christ. This is why the first of what are known as the "Ten Commandments" (Exodus 20:2; Deuteronomy 5:6) recalls what God has done for his people: he liberated them from slavery in Egypt.

In this manner, Ibn Khaldūn grasped, perhaps without being aware of it, the way in which, on the one hand, the nature of revelation and, on the other, the conception of the link between the political and the religious form one unified system.

8

The *Jihād* of the Philosophers

In Lieu of an Introduction

The theme of *jihād* has become fashionable. The word evokes somber associations. By putting it into the title of a book, the publishers hope for a smash success. Phenomena such as this belong in the domain of psychopathology. As a consequence, I do not intend to say a word on the subject. To the contrary, I am going to limit myself to the reality that can be documented historically. I shall not penetrate very deeply into the unfolding reality of the history of Islam, but only treat its reflection in the works of the Islamic philosophers.

As it happens, the philosophers are not the only ones who have taken on *jihād* as an object of reflection. An adequate treatment of the theme would lead to a comparison between the philosophers and the other currents of thought in Islam, a topic that must remain in suspense here. I can spare myself the task all the more easily because we now possess an authoritative synthesis of the multiple questions tied to *jihād* by the late Alfred Morabia.[1] But his book, which covers a vast terrain, concentrates on Islamic law and neglects the philosophers. This is not the result of chance, given that philosophers never occupied more than a marginal place in the overall framework of Islamic civilization.

The theme of the philosophers' relationship to *jihād* has already been discussed, in particular by Joel Kraemer, an American scholar who has taught for a number of years in Israel.[2] I owe to Kraemer's excellent article many texts and ideas. Still, it seems to me legitimate to return to the theme again. In spite of the title of Kraemer's article "The Jihād of the Falāsifa," *jihād* is not its focus: he shows—to my mind convincingly—that the philosophers, rather than following the path laid out by Islamic theology, went their own ways. Kraemer touches on the example of war in passing and treats only Farabi systematically. All of this justifies a new approach to the topic.

An Antimony: Clemency or Toughness in the Philosophers?

The Clemency of the Ideal-Type of the Philosopher?

As a point of departure, I have chosen an antimony. In the eleventh century, the poet and Jewish apologist Jehuda Halevi stages a discussion between the king of the Kazars and representatives of various schools of thought in which adepts of the three monotheistic religions and a philosopher take turns speaking. Halevi places in the mouth of this purely ideal-typical character a summary of the *falsafa* of his time, which does not totally coincide with what we call "philosophy." What we understand by "philosophy" is above all a program, an effort to reach the truth that is made possible only by free investigation. *Falsafa*, on the other hand, designates a system of available truths. These are found, for the most part, in the works of Aristotle and his commentators and those who continued his train of thought within Greek culture—men like Alexander of Aphrodisias or Themistius—or within the Arab world—Farabi, Avicenna, or Ibn Bājja, Halevi's contemporary and compatriot.

In the course of his discussion with the "philosopher," the king mentions the fact that the two major religions—Christianity and Islam—fight one another. The philosopher then remarks, "The philosophers' creed knows no manslaughter, as they only cultivate the intellect (*yaʾummūna 'l'aqla*)."[3] The question immediately arises of the source of the particular doctrine that Halevi puts into the mouth of his imaginary philosopher.

The Toughness of the Real Philosophers

But that is only the first point. The second is that the real philosophers were not exactly tender to those who thought differently from themselves. One example of this is a passage in which Averroes refutes Ghazali, saying that only the heretics (*zanādiqa*) in Islam deny the miracles of Abraham. The wise men among the philosophers do not permit themselves to dispute the principles of the religious laws (*sharāʾiʿ*). Anyone who does so deserves harsh punishment. Averroes gives a reason for this: One has no right to contest the principles of the sciences, but must accept them—a very Aristotelian viewpoint. Even less, Averroes continues, should one contest those of the practical sciences of religious legislation (*sināʿa ʿamaliyya shar ʿiyya*). Conformity to the virtues prescribed by the Law is necessary, not for the existence of man as such, but to the extent that man is wise. Because of that, all men are held to accept the principles of the Law and submit to them, and also to esteem the legislator. To protest or revolt against the dispositions of the Law is to demolish the existence of man. As a consequence, heretics must be killed.[4]

Averroes approves, without reservation, of the slaughter of dissidents. A few centuries ago, Averroes was considered a caricature of the unbeliever by the author of the *Book of the Three Imposters*, a person of sinister reputation who was probably more imaginary than real. Today Averroes is praised as the precursor of the only virtue that is left to us in our "enlightened" age, which is "tolerance." Both of these evaluations are false. Dominique Urvoy expresses the paradox with admirable precision. In his biography of Averroes, Urvoy writes that Ibn Rushd would have condemned—and would have had to condemn, what is more—his quasi-homonymous Salman Rushdie.[5] But the real question is to know whether he would have been acting as a judge or as a philosopher. As a judge aware of his duty, he must apply the law, come what may. But Averroes wrote his statement about the killing of heretics in a work in which juridical questions play absolutely no part, but is instead wholly philosophical in nature.

The question that arises here is the one that Karl Popper posed some years ago regarding Plato and Hegel: Why is there an ambiguous relationship between philosophy—or at least certain philosophies—and tyranny? Why have some major philosophers been hostile to an "open society"?[6]

I shall leave this question in the background here and simply interrogate three philosophers concerning their relationship with war. The three philosophers who demand to have their say here are Farabi, Avicenna, and Averroes. As well as their profession of belief in Islam and in Aristotelian philosophy, they have at least one thing in common. For all three, *jihād* is not only an intellectual construction but an everyday reality. For Farabi and Averroes, war was directed at Christians. Farabi lived in the ninth century in Iraq and later in Syria. In those lands the enemy was the Byzantine Empire. The highest-ranking military chief in the region of the front, Sayf ad-Dawlah, was also Farabi's protector. Averroes lived in Spain—that is, at the farthest western part of the Islamic Empire, at the end of the twelfth century. Islamic Spain, known as al-Andalus, was under pressure from the Christian kingdoms of the north, which were nibbling into Islamic territory. It was only fourteen years after the death of Averroes in the year 1212 that the decisive battle of Las Navas de Tolosa was fought. The Christian victory was a watershed moment. Avicenna, who was older, lived at a time—the early eleventh century—and in a region—Persia—in which a *jihād* against the "pagans" had become a reality. Mahmūd of Ghazna had attacked the Indian Punjab in the name of Sunnite Islam, annexing it in 1020. So much for the general framework: let us turn to the three witnesses and interrogate them in chronological order.

Farabi

The Ideal Statesman as a Warrior

Farabi mentions military affairs in a number of contexts.[7] He does so especially (and this is hardly surprising) in his politico-philosophical works, where he attempts to describe a perfect state. The capacity to fight depends on the same qualities necessary for leading that state; it does not matter whether those qualities are found in one person or are dispersed among many, as in the case of a council whose members include a minister of defense. Farabi describes the courageous combatant.[8] It may be that, for lack of time, the "first chief" has not been able to complete his legislation. Farabi gives only one example of such a situation, which is war.[9] The conduct of war thus seems to be an obstacle, but at the same time war is also a necessary activity of the head of state. Two texts call for more detailed discussion.

The Just War

In a collection of aphorisms that he states he extracted from the works of ancient writers, Farabi draws up a list of justifications for a war.[10] He offers seven of these:

(1) The first is defense against an enemy that attacks the state from the outside. Thus far, we would have no objection.

(2) Immediately after, however, comes something a bit more dubious: One has a right to conduct a war in order to acquire something that the state deserves to have but that is in the possession of others. In clear terms, this implies a war of appropriation and pillage.

(3) The third case is war to force people to accept what is better and more salutary for them, if they do not recognize it spontaneously and if they refuse to accept the leadership of someone who knows what is good for them and procures it for them. This corresponds roughly to the French concept of a *mission civilisatrice*. Farabi insists on the point, explicitly stating that the aim is the good of the conquered, not the conqueror.

(4) The fourth case is combat against people for whom it is better to serve, but who refuse the yoke of slavery.

The remaining cases are combinations of the first four.

(5) The fifth case is combat against a group that refuses to give restitution of something that the citizens of the state have a right to receive. It differs from the second justification for war only by the element of justice.

(6) In the sixth case, war serves to punish evildoers so that they cannot repeat their wrong deeds, but also to intimidate others who might have thought of attacking the state. This justification combines the four first cases.

(7) The seventh case is the extermination and total elimination of people whose continued existence might harm the state. Since this turns the virtuous state toward the good, it is connected with the first category.

In his *Virtuous City*, Farabi rejects the viewpoint that the highest goal of the state lies in the conquest and exploitation of other states, however.[11] The source of this passage—if indeed there is one—is difficult to find. One might think, for example, of the critique of the military ideal of Sparta in the early pages of Plato's *Laws*, a work of which Farabi wrote a summary.[12] It is hardly surprising that he is so resolute in his rejection of the practical consequences of such a cruel attitude. A war that serves no purpose other than a desire for power or the ambition of a tyrannical sovereign is not permitted.

War as Pedagogy

The longest passage on war in Farabi is in a work titled *The Attainment of Happiness*. The practical virtues that lead to happiness are acquired by exercise, by repeated virtuous acts. This occurs in two ways. The first is persuasion: among other means, discourse can be used to excite the passions, thus producing voluntary (*taw'an*) submission. The second means is constraint (*ikrāh*).[13] Constraint is appropriate for all those who cannot be incited to admit the just (*sawāb*), either spontaneously or by instruction. The same holds true for anyone who refuses to communicate his knowledge in the speculative sciences.[14]

Two groups of people are needed to accomplish this goal: one uses competent specialists to instruct willing students; the second aims at the instruction of those who are educated only unwillingly. These operate just like the father of a family or a schoolmaster. The king is the educator of the people. Thanks to education, the military arts (*mihna harbiyya*) reach a high point.[15] They serve to conquer the nations and the states that refuse to submit, thus permitting the attainment of happiness, which is the final goal for which man is born.[16]

The ideal leaders of the state should have available both of these means so as to educate their fellow citizens by both persuasion and constraint. In cases in which these means prove impracticable, a system must be created by means of which every group of citizens is instructed by a corresponding group of functionaries.[17] It is impossible not to be struck by the resemblance between Farabi's outline and our experience of the totalitarian state, in which every citizen spies on his fellow citizens and inculcates the official ideology.

Farabi uses the word "compulsion" to speak of this constraint, echoing a passage in the Qur'an much cited in our own day, which states, "Let there be no compulsion in religion."[18] As the Qur'an text indicates, it is not a question of *forbidding* the use of force, but only of *ascertaining* that it is not efficacious. According to Farabi, in any event, that compulsion is manifested by war. In the ideal state, there must also be warriors, exactly as in Plato's ideal city. But there is an essential difference between Plato's Callipolis and the perfect state according to Farabi: Platonic warriors make up a caste of governors who act only to defend the state against possible external aggression. According to Farabi, pedagogy is directed outward as much as it is inward. This does not produce a true war of religions, however. What must also be attained by constraint is not men's submission (in Arabic, *islām*), but the transmission of knowledge.

Avicenna

"A Good Badly Acquired Never Profits Anyone"

In his monumental "encyclopedia of philosophical sciences," *The Book of Health* (in Arabic, *Kitāb al-Shifā'*), Avicenna devotes a few pages to political theory. He does so within the framework of his metaphysics, toward the end of which he includes a passage on war.[19] The leader of the ideal society turns against enemies and those who revolt against the *sunna*. The *sunna*, to which the leader feels himself obliged, demands combat against its enemies, and even their annihilation (*ifnā'*); but that can only occur after those enemies had been called to the truth. Then their fortunes and their women (literally: their women's vulvas) are declared free booty. As a reason for this, Avicenna states that those goods are not managed as the perfect state determines they should be; consequently, they do not turn their possessors toward the good, and they even conduct them to ruin and to evil. "A good badly acquired never profits anyone" means that someone who does not belong to the perfect state (*madīna fādila*) is not the legitimate possessor of his own goods.[20] This legitimates pillage expeditions.

Men need servants. Possible servants must be constrained to serve the members of the just state (*madīna ʿādila*). The rule also applies to men who may not be capable of acquiring the virtues. As an example Avicenna mentions the Turks who once lived in the far north as nomads, black people, and, more generally, those who live in climates unpropitious to those virtues. Only balanced climates produce peoples whose temperament is noble and whose souls are healthy.[21] This permits him to found slavery on reason.

A Claim to the Absolute

In a long paragraph, Avicenna discusses more complex situations. If another state has customs (*sunna*) that are praiseworthy, the head of the perfect state has no right to attack that other state immediately. He has that right only if it can be announced at that moment that only revealed law (*sunna nāzila*) applies. But if the peoples for whom that law is prescribed persist in their error (that is, if they reject it), it must be imposed on them by force. The total application of the law can, consequently, presuppose the occupation of the entire world.[22] Why should this be so?

Let us imagine that the citizens of a state who lead an irreproachable life (*ahlu madīnatin hasanati ʾs-sīra*) recognize the new law as good and praiseworthy, and that they even agree that accepting that law will help corrupt states to improve. Let us also admit that they declare that they are not obliged to apply that law, claiming that the author of that law was wrong to consider it universally valid. This case would present a danger for the law: Avicenna says "a weakness" (*wahn*), a defect. Those who oppose the law and who live within the state in question might argue that others had already refused to submit to it.

This explains why the law has a tendency to expand, which one might argue can be satisfied only by conquest of the entire earth. The question is not to know whether the other state is well governed. Avicenna supposes that its inhabitants live morally, in an irreproachable manner. The simple fact that there are people who believe in something else or, to put it better, people who belong to other states, is intolerable.

In spite of everything, the combat against that other state must not be conducted in the same way as a combat against those who reside in absolute error. Combat is pedagogical in nature; it represents a punishment (*ʿaddaba*). The other state also has the right to choose to pay tribute as compensation for its stubbornness. For it is established that it must be counted among the naysayers: how could it be otherwise, given that it refuses, after all, to obey the direction (*sharia*) given by God?[23]

Ambiguity

It is fairly difficult to avoid the impression that Avicenna is describing what is in fact the Islamic practice of holy war. Is he simply deducing that practice from higher principles, in which case philosophy would serve merely to give the real Islam a varnish of philosophical respectability? The same question arises from a reading of his entire chapter on politics. On occasion one has the impression that Avicenna is limiting himself to describing, in deliberately ambiguous terms, the Islam that really exists, avoiding technical vocabulary or using periphrases. The dispositions of the law are all present, as, for example, the wearing of the veil for women. On the other hand, there are also passages in which Avicenna presupposes dispositions that have little to do with Islam and quite probably have more to do with the Platonic state, as when he divides the state, from the start, into three classes: administrators, artisans, and guardians.[24] Avicenna's entire enterprise is ambiguous: for example, his description of the perfect man could be interpreted as a portrait of the Prophet, but also as a self-portrait. This is at least what his immediate disciple, Bahmanyār, understood.[25]

Is this passage a sophisticated description of *jihād*, with a long discussion of the particular case of the members of the community of the book (*ahl al-kitāb*)? Whatever the case may be, the elements of Avicenna's presentation correspond to theories that can also be read in the works of Islamic theorists of *jihād*. To offer only one example: the theorist Ibn Taymiyya (who attacks Avicenna mercilessly, making the two strange bedfellows) expresses the idea that the goods of other communities represent what is basically an illegitimate possession.[26]

Averroes

Averroes writes explicitly, as a jurist, about holy war in his manual of jurisprudence.[27] His understanding of holy war as a very concrete affair is that of the Islam of his age and, what is more, that of Islam as a whole in all ages. The only exception is a very few Sufis, the same circles that invented and circulated the altogether too famous hadith about great and small *jihād*s, about which I might recall that it figures in *not one* of the six canonical collections of the declarations of the Prophet.[28] In this chapter of Averroes' juridical manual, in any event, he speaks—as any treatise about things military (*fiqh*) would have to do—about what should be the fate of captives, how booty should be shared out, and so forth.

Averroes approves of holy war as a Muslim conscious of his duty and as a respected head of a community. His biographer Al-Ansārī al-Marrākushī, relying on the testimony of an immediate disciple, Abū l-Qāsim b. at-Taylisān (1179–1244), relates that Averroes, in a sermon preached at the Great Mosque of Cordova, called for a holy war against the Christian kingdoms of the north.[29] There is nothing surprising or shocking here: it was wartime. Does anyone judge Henri Bergson for his anti-German statements in 1917, when he sought to persuade the United States to come into World War I on the side of the Allies?[30] Or his German colleagues of that same period for the brochures they wrote in support of their country's war effort?

Jihād *and Equity*

Averroes also writes of holy war as a philosopher. He devotes a short section to it in his commentary on book V of Aristotle's *Nicomachean Ethics*,[31] a digression in Averroes' chapter X (14) on equity (*epieikeia*). According to Aristotle, equity is an improvement of the law. The law should be ameliorated when it is shown to be too general, but such an amelioration must occur when the question arises of precisely what the legislator wanted to get at, hence what he would have said in one concrete instance or another. Everything is not regulated by a law for a simple reason: in certain cases, it is impossible to promulgate a law, and because of that, specific decisions must be made.[32] Averroes holds to that rule. The laws on the *jihād*, he states, are a striking example of this principle. The law contains the general commandment to exterminate one's adversaries totally (*mī shehōleq 'imman; qui diversi sunt ab eis*). There are, however, times when peace is preferable to war. The great mass of Muslims believe that this principle is obligatory in a general manner, even when the extermination of one's adversaries is impossible. This leads to great harm, because it misunderstands the legislator's intention.

At the same time, Averroes casts absolutely no doubt on the definitive character of the principle. Only its application must cede to another principle, which is the long-term good of the Islamic community. Should the latter be endangered because of the strict application of the law, that application must be suspended or limited. The ultimate goal is the good of Islam; in itself a war of annihilation is a perfectly legitimate means for achieving that goal.

War in general comes into question above all in Averroes' paraphrase of Plato's *Republic*.[33] His principal intention is always to understand Plato and to adapt Plato to his own ends. There are two passages on this topic that should be examined in more detail.

War as a Path toward God

A long passage in Averroes' commentary on the *Republic* discusses the virtue of courage.[34] Averroes remains close to the doctrine of Farabi that we
have already examined. Just like his predecessor, Averroes distinguishes
two methods of instruction, the second of which is constraint. War is a
species of that genus. In this context, he writes, "Yet for other nations
which are not good and whose [system of government] is not human[e],
there is no other way of teaching except by this method, namely coercing
them through war to be bound to virtue."[35]

Thus we read in this work, not without some astonishment, that war is a
road toward God. The expression requires commentary. First, it recalls the
language of the Qur'an, which mentions a "way of Allah," an expression
that can even be interpreted in a military sense: the adepts of Muhammad
fight, put their lives and their goods in jeopardy, and are even killed "on
the way of Allah" (*fī sabīli 'Llah*).[36] The expression can also simply mean
"according to the way of God."

But that way leads also to man. Averroes speaks of "laws which follow
the human laws." By "human laws" he might reasonably mean those that
are in conformity with human nature, to the extent that such nature is
known to philosophy. In this context, "human" signifies "good," not in the
current sense of the "humane" treatment of animals, for example, but in the
sense of "in conformity with man's essence." Hence the human becomes
the measure of the laws.[37] Islamic Law, which is held to be divine, is to be
considered human because it follows the demands of philosophy. The law
that demands war is human in that it helps to bring about what is essentially
human in man. As in Farabi, the ultimate end is wisdom, not Islam.[38]

Religion Adds to the Stakes in War

A second passage in Averroes' work on Plato's *Republic* merits consideration. Plato declares that the wars among Greeks are, strictly speaking,
civil wars. As a consequence, he proposes certain rules for the conduct of
war: setting the enemy's houses on fire should not be permitted, nor cut-
ting down their fruit trees, and so on. Averroes compares such wars to dis-
cord within the family.[39] He mentions Plato's rules, but he stresses the fact
that Plato disagrees here with many legislators. Concerning the content of
the laws, we can surmise that he was thinking of a familiar episode in the
life of the Prophet. Muhammad did in fact order that the palm trees of his
Jewish enemies, the Banū Nadīr, be uprooted, an act that Averroes mentions elsewhere.[40] Previously, that act had been held to be a serious crime.[41]

But, according to Islam, the acts and deeds of the Prophet are the model for what is permitted or forbidden. On the significance of this difference between the Greek philosopher and the prophet of the Arabs, Averroes says practically nothing. A response can be found between the lines, however, since he remarks that enemies, according to Plato, should be held to be people who are in error, not to be unbelievers. On this occasion he uses the words *tōeh* and *kōfer*. In Arabic these terms were probably *dāllun* and *kāfir*, technical terms of Islamic law. Therefore what is suggested here is that adding a religious dimension to quarrels poisons them—an idea that had its echoes among philosophers or the philosophically inclined.[42]

Conclusion

I shall conclude by summarizing my thoughts and advancing a thesis or two.

(1) The doctrine of the *falāsifa* corresponds roughly to that of their Greek sources. This is true for the measured versions of that doctrine, but also for the cases that we find the most scandalous. Aristotle had already distinguished three cases in which it is just to wage a war: to conserve one's own liberty; to acquire a command (*hegemonia*) that contributes to the needs of those who are commanded; to dominate (*despozein*) peoples who deserve to be enslaved (*axios douleuein*).[43] These three cases correspond to the first, third, and fourth on Farabi's list. Aristotle applies this distinction in book VII of the *Politics*, a work that, according to all known evidence, was never translated into Arabic.[44] But it is not to be excluded that fragments of it or notions from it reached the Islamic world. Be that as it may, I should note that the two last cases seem to me highly disputable. Whether we like it or not, neither the Greek philosophers nor the Arabic philosophers were pacifists.

(2) In Islam as a historical reality, and even in contemporary Islam, the philosophers found themselves confronted with the fact of wars of conquest with a religious dimension. Similarly, they found themselves confronted with a doctrine that was already in the course of development and that was intended to limit that warfare by providing norms for it but at the same time justify it. On many points they supported that theory.

(3) Still, one must agree with Kraemer: the philosophers developed no theory of Islamic war as such. Among them the word *jihād*, when it occurred, signified "war" in general. Most of the time, they avoid the technical term in favor of a neutral word *harb*, which speaks of all sorts of war.[45] This notion is all the more persuasive because, according to the classic doctrine, after the arrival of the Prophet, no "profane" war could take place.[46]

Avicenna flirts a bit with the technical terms of theology. He does so, what is more, throughout his oeuvre. Averroes notoriously reproached him for betraying a purely philosophical interest in order to put himself in the service of the theologians of the Kalām.[47]

(4) The philosophers chose a particular tactic in their treatment of the strict sense of *jihād*. It might be best described by means of a comparison with other solutions, such as that of the Sufis. Islamic mysticism transposes combat into the *combattimento spirituale* of one who prays, against himself, against his inclinations. That led to false statements, for example, the much-cited supposed declaration of the Prophet regarding lesser and greater *jihād*, a pious invention, as we have seen, not to be found in any of the six classic collections.[48]

The philosophers change the end, but the means remained resolutely military. In general, they express no remorse about widespread bloodletting. Farabi has nothing to say against the murder of "bestial" men.[49] Avicenna suggests that the skeptic should be tortured until he admits that the difference between the true and the non-true is indeed pertinent.[50] Averroes advocates the elimination of the mentally handicapped. He refers, without comment, to Plato's proposition that the ideal state should be founded by chasing out adults.[51] These medieval thinkers are neither more cruel nor more kind than their ancient masters, or than a good many of their colleagues among thinkers of the modern age. On the subject of eggs needing to be broken in order to make an omelet or innocent little flowers that are crushed as the cart of universal history passes over them, the modern philosopher, too, sheds scarcely a tear.

In his approval of war, the *falsafa* is even more radical than ordinary, non-philosophical, Islamic practice. The goal of the latter is conquest and the control of the state, not control of minds. The point is to gain and hold power. According to ordinary Islamic doctrine, the long-term conversion of conquered peoples is highly desirable, but it is not the prime goal. In practice, in any event, conversion takes place at a second stage. The principal goal is peace (*salām*)—that is, Islamic domination over a "pacified" (*dār as-salām*) domain. The philosophers developed a doctrine according to which holy war can lead to philosophy, by which means they wanted to conquer souls as well.

Thus we can return to the antinomy with which we began. The philosopher invented by Jehuda Halevi forbids only the murder of Christians or Muslims as Christians and Muslims—that is, religious war—and not the murder of people in general.[52] The philosopher rejects *holy* war, not war in general. Or, to put it more precisely: for him, it is not religion, but only philosophy, that can sanctify war.

PART IV

Filiations

Inclusion and Digestion

Two Models of Cultural Appropriation
In Response to a Question of Hans-Georg Gadamer
(Tübingen, September 3, 1996)

Literary hermeneutics—hermeneutics in the strict sense, to which I shall limit my remarks here—supposes (at the least) the existence of a text that is to be understood. More exactly, because a text is not something that simply "is there," it supposes the existence of its material support. Interpretation of the text can take place only if access to it is arranged. As it happens, this presence of the text can by no means be taken for granted. It is not just any appropriation that conserves the text that it absorbs. It is not just any civilization that encourages a style of appropriation that permits the transmission of the object of that appropriation to future generations so that they can newly appropriate it themselves.

Two Styles of Appropriation

Within the genus "appropriation," we can distinguish two manners of appropriating. I propose to call them "inclusion" and "digestion."[1]

As a child I was fascinated by the baubles found in souvenir stores at the beach or in the mountains in which an edelweiss, a gentian, or a small sea horse was immobilized in a globe of transparent plastic. In this domain as in others, art imitates nature. We know, in fact, about the pieces of amber frequently found on the shores of the North Sea in which flies, spiders, and even tiny snails are trapped, prisoners of the resin on which they had ventured thousands of years ago and which closed over them before hardening. Aristotle was familiar with that diaphanous quality, although he preferred less resistant mediums such as air or water.[2] Its fascination lies in the paradox of a transparent solidity. Usually what is transparent offers no resistance, and when it does, it is fragile, like the glass of a container or a windowpane. In that case its interest lies in the contrast between the two extremes of manifestation and the risk of seeing the object disappear. That object is boldly exposed only to throw the possibility of its loss more strongly into relief.[3] In the case of inclusion, on the other hand, what permits vision can also be solidly grasped, hard as a precious stone.

It is hardly astonishing that this sort of phenomenon has attracted the attention of writers, who have given it a strong symbolic charge. Thus Günter Grass sees in inclusion the symbol, among other things, of the way in which the "I" is enclosed within itself: "She gave me a piece of amber, that's all. With an insect enclosure. I'm the enclosure. In case of doubt, I, late-enamored and kept in reserve. Beside me: I. Outside me: I. Foisted on me like a hoax, the obedient but grumbling I. Always escaping, fleeing the times, devious."[4]

Artificial inclusions are produced by pouring transparent plastic around the object, and I shall use the term "inclusion" for the activity that produces those objects.

In either case, natural or artificially made, the transparent mass has a double effect. On the one hand, it protects the object: the surrounding mass safeguards it from all direct grasp. Moreover, it eliminates the action of the air, contact with which would inevitably lead to the decomposition of the object's organic matter. This is why the insects enclosed in amber have managed to last for thousands of years. In the case of an artificial inclusion, the enclosed object is maintained in one particular position chosen because it facilitates observation. Thus, if the object is a beetle, the wing sheaths and wings may be deployed; if a flower, the petals can be perfectly open. This produces a paradoxical relationship between the interior and the exterior, the inherent and the foreign. What becomes interior does not lose its alterity for all that. It is even precisely by its internalization that the object is conserved in its alterity.

Thus I shall take the word "inclusion" in a technical sense, to indicate an appropriation in which what is appropriated is maintained in its alterity and surrounded by the process of appropriation itself, a process whose very presence reinforces the alterity of what has been appropriated.

In contrast, I shall call "digestion" the process of appropriation in which the object is so profoundly internalized that it loses its independence. In this case, the appropriation does away with all difference between the subject that does the appropriating and the object appropriated: at base, a wolf consists of sheep it has digested and that have become wolf. Unlike inclusion, which is a highly artificial procedure, digestion is a natural process; it is even among the most elementary mechanisms of life.

Two Metaphors for Cultural Appropriation

Digestion has long been used as a metaphor for cultural appropriation. Using the image of taking food to stand for learning is attested early in history, in ancient Egypt as in the Bible.[5] The invitation to assimilate what is read so intimately that it becomes the very substance of the reader is a common notion. It can be found, for example, in Montaigne: "Now we must not attach learning to the mind, we must incorporate it; we must not sprinkle, but dye."[6]

Nietzsche placed the organic metaphor into the framework of a systematic theory of culture, using it, in particular, in his reflections on historical knowledge and on the "plastic power" that such knowledge required.[7] Later on, he assigned the idea of "incorporation" a central place in his doctrine of the eternal return of the identical as a justification of the past.[8] At the same time, he developed a theory of culture in which the mind is compared, quite deliberately, to a stomach.[9] If we look at it more closely, the image is in itself surprising: what we expect from a good memory is not that it attacks its contents and even dissolves them, which is what a healthy stomach does. And yet, the image, too, is an old one, given that it can be found early as Augustine.[10] Similar remarks have also been applied to the theory of literature. Thus Paul Valéry remarked, "Someone who has poorly digested the substance of others is a plagiarist: he renders up recognizable pieces of them. Originality: an affair of the stomach."[11]

On the other hand, the idea of inclusion—as far as I know—is almost never used as a category in the theory of culture. I have found only one exception to this rule: the medievalist Kurt Flasch uses the closely related idea of "insertion" (*Einsetzung*) to designate a cultural phenomenon. He uses the term first in the context of an analysis of an art object, the Cross of Lothair in the treasury of the cathedral of Aix-la-Chappelle. The arms and the staff of the cross are set with precious stones, but at the center, surprisingly enough, there is not an effigy of the Man of Sorrows, but an ancient cameo bearing the profile of a Roman emperor. According to Flasch, this example, and with it the whole of the cathedral, which is a "citation" of the Church of San Vitale in Ravenna, permits us to understand the cultural project of the Carolingians: "'Insertion'—there is the key to Carolingian civilization. . . . 'Insertion' was not only a conservation; it does more than conserve a few fragments of ancient art objects by inserting them into cult objects. It replaced the past in the present. . . . Even when the ancient fragment was inserted without changing it, its effective function was changed. It became a part of a new historical world: insertion."[12]

Here I would like to broaden Kurt Flasch's intuition. In doing so, I shall nonetheless accentuate it in an essentially different way. The thesis that I shall attempt to defend here is this: The way in which the sources of European culture are present within that culture is inclusion. The legacy of the ancient world, and with it our biblical heritage, are inserted as is— that is, as they are and remain "other"—within the diaphanous milieu of European culture.

Different Ways of Commenting

I support my thesis with the concrete example of written works. When the object to be received is a text, each of the two methods of appropriation that I have outlined above finds its equivalent in a literary genre. The first is the *commentary*. In it the classical text is reproduced in its literal entirety, broken down into units of meaning called "lemmas," after which each lemma is studied and explicated. The second method is to rewrite the text so that it comes to be integrated into a new work, thus losing its independence. This is the method of *paraphrase*.

I am distinguishing only two methods here. I do not consider the procedure of adding a series of notes to the text to be a third method that should be placed on the same plane as the two others, but rather as a species of the genus "commentary." Indeed, the only difference consists in the fact that adding notes does not explain the entire text to be commented, but only certain passages, considered to merit special treatment because of their obscurity or their intrinsic interest. In theory, the original text remains, whereas it disappears in the case of paraphrase.

For us, paraphrase is no longer a current practice. We even find it hard to imagine that one could write about a text otherwise than in the style that has become obvious to us—that of the commentary. This means that it is worth taking the trouble to remind ourselves of the historical importance of the paraphrase. It is a style we can encounter in various cultural domains and in a variety of forms.

Paraphrase can vary too, however. In certain cases one can almost recover every phrase of the original text in the paraphrase, to the point of being able to reconstitute the original. I am thinking, for example, of the Hebrew paraphrase to Maimonides' *Guide for the Perplexed* written in the fourteenth century by Shem Tov ben Yacob, one of the classic commentaries often printed at the foot of the page in editions to the *Guide* in the Hebrew translation by Ibn Tibbon.[13] One might also mention the Greek paraphrase by the Byzantine author Georgios Pachymeres (d. 1310) of the works of Dionysius the Areopagite.[14] In the latter, the paraphrase consists basically in a series of minuscule inclusions floating throughout in the commentary.

In other cases, on the other hand, few if any words are simply repeated: the text is completely rewritten, the demonstration proceeds more systematically, the exposition is clearer, and examples that are out-of-date or have become hard to comprehend are replaced by others that are more current and easier to grasp. This is where paraphrase appears in its purest form. A technical term in Arabic with the literal sense of "liberation" (*tahrīr*) refers to this method.[15] There are a number of examples of this in monumental "edited versions" of classic works, such as, for example, Ptolemy's *Almagest*, rewritten by Nasīr ad-Dīn Tūsī (d. 1274), among others.

In certain cases, opinions are attributed to the author whose work is commented on that he never held, but that correspond to the current state of knowledge. Thus Averroes claims to find mention of nerves in Aristotle, whereas their role in perception was not discovered until Galen, half a millennium after Aristotle.[16]

What I am getting at ought to be apparent by now: Commentary is a model of inclusion; paraphrase represents a digestion.

Aristotle as an Example

Let us examine for a moment an even more particular example, that of the various ways in which the works of "the Philosopher," Aristotle, were commented on, and try to draw up a typology of those methods according to place and time period. What we find, roughly speaking, is that the "pagan" commentators of antiquity practiced both commentary and paraphrase. At the end of the third century of our era, Alexander of Aphrodisias composed commentaries. In the fourth century, Themistius seems to have written only paraphrases.[17] The great commentators of Neoplatonic inspiration of the early sixth century—Simplicius, for instance—preferred the commentary style. The Syriacs wrote summaries, but they also dictated commentaries to the works they used in their teaching.[18]

Early in the Arabic reception of ancient texts, the situation remained unchanged: Farabi (d. 950) wrote both commentaries, such as the one on *De interpretatione*, and shorter texts reiterating the contents of certain treatises of the *Organon*, at times using the same title as the original. Thus we have an *Isagoge* by him, a treatise on the *Categories*, and a *Book of Apodictic Demonstration* (*burhān*), corresponding to the *Second Analytics*, that became the traditional title in Arabic, and more.[19]

The works of Avicenna (d. 1037) represent a watershed moment. He systematically used the method of paraphrase. In his monumental encyclopedia of the philosophical sciences, *The Book of Health* (*Kitāb al-Shifā'*), he rewrote the entire edifice of Aristotelian knowledge, thus breaking with the tradition of commentaries on Aristotle. The only commentaries of his that we have are notes to book lambda of the *Metaphysics*, to the *De anima*, and to the so-called "Theology of Aristotle," all texts that Avicenna does not seem to have dreamed of publishing himself.[20] His intention in writing his encyclopedia was instead to take over the whole of Aristotelian knowledge and express it in a new way. I should have no need to repeat the obvious—that Avicenna added to an authentically Aristotelian base a good number of elements from elsewhere. This is especially true of the Neoplatonic pseudepigraphy that, at the time, accompanied the *corpus aristotelicum* like a shadow.[21] Moreover, it is quite clear that Avicenna's synthesis is the work of an uncontested philosophical genius, which gives it a profound originality. But what seems to me important is that Avicenna's method of rewriting carries the style of the paraphrase to its perfection and constitutes an extremely pertinent example of the Islamic habit of appropriating a cultural good and incorporating it, a notion to which I shall return.

Avicenna's enterprise was strikingly successful. With him, the very term "philosophy" received a new reference. Before Avicenna, a *faylasūf* was a disciple of Aristotle; after him, a *faylasūf* was a disciple . . . of Avicenna himself. Aristotelianism became Avicennism.[22] Avicenna himself achieved the status of a classic author whose works require commentary. Before him, the philosophers wrote commentaries on the works of Aristotle; after him, exegesis focused on his own works. I am thinking, for example, of the notes on the *Book of Directives and Remarks* (*Kitāb al-Isarāt wa l-tanbihāt*) of Fakhr ud-Dīn al-Rāzī (d. 1209), of Nasīr ad-Dīn, and many others.[23]

With Avicenna, the receiver has so profoundly absorbed what he assimilates that he has quite simply taken its place. The consequence was that the original source, the *corpus aristotelicum*, became inaccessible. This made any new direct reception impossible. Avicenna put a final period on the hermeneutic practice that had been dominant until his time. After him, the Islamic East shows hardly any trace of a direct relationship with the letter of Aristotle's works. The one exception proves the rule: the one commentary that we do have does not concern an authentic work of the

Philosopher, but the pseudepigraphic work mentioned above, the notes of Qadi Saʿid Qummi (d. 1691) on the "Theology of Aristotle."[24]

In the eleventh century and at the other end of the Islamic world, Averroes (d. 1198) took on the task of interpreting the whole of Aristotle's oeuvre in a new fashion. His aim was to return to authentic Aristotelianism by cleansing it of the sedimentations due, in particular, to Avicenna. To a certain extent, Averroes went back to the method of Farabi, but he applied that method systematically. His commentaries are in the two literary genres: paraphrase (that is, digestion) when he summarizes in abridgments (*jawāmiʿ*) and the "middle" commentaries; inclusion in his "Great Commentaries" (*tafsīr*).

In the Latin Christian world, the process of the appropriation of Aristotle, which had come to a halt with the death of Boethius (524), started up again in the twelfth century. Albertus Magnus (d. 1280) applied Avicenna's method. His vastly long works at times repeat Aristotle's titles, and in his *Metaphysics* he follows the outline of Aristotle's work of the same title. He gives a consistent paraphrase of the Aristotelian text, not without permitting himself long digressions. His immediate disciple Thomas Aquinas (d. 1274), on the other hand, totally renounces paraphrase, writing only great commentaries, all of which reflect the method of Averroes. However, surprisingly and unhappily for us, "at no point" does he say "anything about the intention that he was pursuing in his commentaries of Aristotle,"[25] and he says even less about his method.

The great exegetes who came after Thomas Aquinas also preferred commentary as a style. The Jesuit Pedro Fonseca chose a complex form for his commentary on the *Metaphysics*: after the text and his translation come notes, objections and responses to those objections, and finally dissertations (*quaestiones*) on certain salient points.[26] Sylvester Maurus, also a Jesuit, may have titled his commentary on Aristotle's works "Paraphrase," but it was in fact an exhaustive exposé of the contents following the translated text. It is interesting to note that this work was republished only a little more than a century ago.[27]

The decisive step was not taken, though, until the rise of philology, which delivered a death blow to the paraphrase as a style. The entire enterprise of philology could be described as an explication of the entire written heritage of the ancient writers in the style of the commentary. It does this, as is known, by elaborating on the classical texts and, later, any text, using tools that had been forged for the analysis of sacred texts. Not all sorts of sacred texts make philological treatment necessary (or even possible), however. In order for something like a philology to arise, the sacred text that it deals with must present quite specific characteristics.

The Christian and Islamic Contexts

In each particular instance, we can discern something like an affective affinity between the style of appropriation chosen and the corresponding
religious background. There is, to begin with, a group of facts that we can
note flatly. Avicenna develops his new style of reading Aristotle in opposition to the style that was practiced in his day, as represented by the Aristotelians of Baghdad, who were Nestorian Christian Arabs.[28]

Avicenna also stands apart from his distant successor Averroes, who returned to the great commentaries of Farabi. Averroes, despite his Muslim
origin and an attachment to Islam that no one today doubts, has remained
almost unknown in the Islamic East. In contrast, he was read and commented on with passion by the Jews and Christians of Europe. The reception of his thought did not take place in the Muslim world, but almost exclusively among Jews and Christians. There is a striking example of this in
the fact that we have one manuscript in Arabic of his great commentary on
the *Metaphysics*, whereas we have fifteen or so of the Hebrew translation,
and the Latin translation exists in many manuscripts and printed books,
including incunables.

An extremely interesting reversal of the usual relationship between Jewish and Christian philosophers can be observed concerning Averroes' exegetical works. In the twelfth century, as is known, a population upheaval
took place that had far-reaching consequences for the intellectual centers of
the Jewish world. The Almohad rulers of Spain gave Jewish communities
that had lived up to that time under Islamic domination the choice between
conversion to Islam or exile. It was in such circumstances, for example, that
the family of Maimonides was obliged to leave Cordova, finally settling in
Egypt. Many Jewish families chose to emigrate to the north, however, settling in Christian lands in Catalonia or in Provence. This means that Jewish
thinkers gradually entered into the zone of influence of Christian thinkers.

This geographic shift was followed by an evolution in style of appropriation. At first, the Jews neglected the great commentaries and used abridgments, which replaced the original text for them. Thus, every time that a
Jewish thinker such as Gersonides cites Aristotle as an authority, or even refers to one of the latter's works, he is in fact using the summary of that work
by Averroes. The Christian appropriation of Aristotle occurred in a symmetrically opposed manner: from the start, Christians used the great commentaries, and abridgments were hardly ever used until the Renaissance.

It was only in the wake of Christian Scholasticism that Jews became
interested in the great commentaries of Averroes and, by that token, in the
original text of Aristotle's writings.[29] With the Jews' shift from the Islamic

domain of cultural influence to the Christian domain of influence, the Islamic model of appropriation switched to the Christian model—that is, digestion gave way to inclusion.

Islam as a Culture of Digestion

The example of the reception of Aristotle in the Middle Ages can help us to define the style of Islamic reception. One can in fact identify the same traits regarding the overall process of appropriation of the legacy of the ancient world. In that way—that is, indirectly—we can better perceive the extent to which the sort of appropriation that operated in the European domain was produced in what was basically quite a strange manner.

Friedrich Schlegel once attempted to define the Islamic style of appropriation. He writes: "The Arabs are of an extremely polemical nature; they are the annihilators among the nations. Their mania (*Liebhaberei*) for effacing the originals or for throwing them away once the translation is finished characterizes the spirit of their philosophy. This is why they were perhaps infinitely cultivated but, despite all their culture, more purely barbarian than the Europeans of the Middle Ages. Barbarian is, in fact, what is at the same time the adversary of both classicism and progress."[30] The overall judgment of Arab culture that Schlegel formulates here need not be of interest to us. Even if we take seriously his distinction between the "cultivated" and the "barbarian," his judgment remains extremely unjust. What would be more interesting would be to establish from what source Schlegel, who had no particular competence in this domain, drew such an opinion, which is something that I have been unable to establish.

Concerning the facts, however, Schlegel is right up to a point. The Arabs did not conserve the manuscripts from which they made their translations. On the other hand, one can hardly speak of a positive decision in favor of their destruction. The fact of the matter is less spectacular: after a translation was made, the manuscripts were neglected because they had become useless.

In the fifteenth century, a Muslim, the great Tunisian historian Ibn Khaldūn, makes a similar remark regarding the disappearance of the originals of Arabic translations. In the famous first volume of his historical work, he writes, in this context, several phrases to which I will add literal translations:

> [The Muslims] desired to learn the sciences of the [foreign] nations. They
> made them their own through translations. They pressed them into the

mold of their own views. They took them over into their own language from the non-Arab languages [literally: they peeled off (*jarrada*) those foreign languages] and surpassed the achievements of [the non-Arabs] in them. The manuscripts in the non-Arabic language were forgotten, abandoned, and scattered [lit. "a forgotten object, a deserted ruin, and a scattered particle of dust." Cf. Qur'an 25:23]. All the sciences came to exist in Arabic. The systematic works on them were written in [Arabic] writing. Thus students of the sciences needed a knowledge of the meaning of [Arabic] words and [Arabic] writing. They could dispense with all other languages, because they had been wiped out and there was no longer any interest in them.[31]

What Ibn Khaldūn is saying here in images and in a tone totally different from Schlegel's nonetheless amounts to the same thing. Every image is telling: the manuscripts remained like the vestiges left in a camp after the departure of those who had used it, a theme that is part of the required figures of Arab poetry. Manuscripts continued to be vestiges because they were no longer useful. Their contents had been poured into a new vessel, a new mold, which implies the loss of their original form. But what is most revealing is the metaphor of peeling, which Franz Rosenthal renders less satisfactorily with the image of "the mold of their own language." Language is the skin or peel that is removed and thrown away after we consume what was edible or drinkable in the fruit.

A similar remark could be made and we could trace the same procedure in other domains of Islamic knowledge. In the law, for example, Roman law was absorbed, with the variants that the Arabs had found in place in the lands that they conquered. But the jurists credited Islam with what they appropriated in this manner: the hadiths place in the mouth of the Prophet the juridical practice in vigor at the time.[32] By this means practice was clothed in a new authority that gave it religious legitimacy. Moreover, this process tore such usages from their roots, for example, in the metaphysics and the cosmology of law sketched by the Stoics, to be attached on to a historical origin. The Islamic method of appropriation can be deployed only at the price of a denial of origin: Islamic culture claims to be an absolute beginning, and it crushes any awareness of owing something to an earlier situation, which it characterizes as the age of ignorance (*jāhiliyya*).[33]

I might remark that this attitude regarding what had been handed down is not a chance occurrence. Its roots plunge deep into the very essence of Islam, the religion that has marked Arab culture. We can find it, in fact, at the heart of the Islamic message: the books that bear witness to earlier revelations were, according to that message, falsified by the communities that had been charged with keeping them, the Jews and the Christians, but their authentic content was conserved in the Qur'an. In that way, earlier writings lose their interest, and the disappearance of their authentic contents loses its gravity. The Holy Book of Islam replaces the books that preceded it. Moreover, it does so to the extent that it incorporates those other books. The Qur'an is thus like a paraphrase of the Old Testament and the New Testament.

One might even go so far as to speak of a *paratext*: in the Qur'an, the biblical narratives are presupposed. The narratives about the great figures of the Old Alliance are almost incomprehensible with no knowledge of the Bible, and especially of the Jewish Midrash. But, according to Islamic dogmatics, there can be no literary influence. The Prophet must have received everything directly from Allah.

Europe as a Culture of Inclusion

I have shown elsewhere how Europe launched itself on another and diametrically opposed route.[34] I might add to the examples studied there that of the law, just mentioned in relation to Islam. European law emerged from a systematization of a juridical corpus that came from an earlier civilization, from Roman law rediscovered in the wake of the papal revolution of the late eleventh century.[35]

We can see a comparable attitude regarding the Other in the Bible, the most exemplary text in European religion. For Christians, the Bible is made up of two parts, a fact that for a long time Christians have not considered strange. And yet! It is unheard of in the history of religions that the holy book of a religion contain, at its side, that of an earlier religion. Moreover, the second book, the New Testament, constitutes something like a commentary on the first. More exactly, and using the technical term of Jewish exegesis, the New Testament is like a *pesher* of the Old, which is to say an interpretation that applies the text to the present situation and interprets it in function of a key event, here the Passion and the Resurrection of Jesus.

We could apply this concept to many phenomena in European culture. We might even describe that culture globally as a *pesher* of the cultures that preceded it. It constantly tries to show that Greek thought and the Old Testament throw light on current situations, a process that in turn opens up new possibilities for interpretation. From time to time, this tendency is manifested with a special, if not a spectacular, clarity, as for example in periods of religious renewal and political upheaval. Examples include the

English Puritans' obsession with the Old Testament, or the way Napoleon's empire imitated everything Roman. Even without those crises, however, the entire uninterrupted chain of renaissances that determined European cultural history bears witness to a relationship of this sort.

European civilization, according to my thesis, is based on the model of inclusion. But if that is the case, how can that attitude, which is at base conservative, be compatible with the clearly observable dynamic of European history? Has not that history been marked by a structural instability that tirelessly urges it to conquest, to technical innovation, and to political and social revolutions?

The same paradox exists in the domain of written culture, as does its solution. At first sight, literary exegesis gives the impression of being opposed to progress. But in reality it has produced the exactly opposite effect, perhaps against the wishes of its promoters. To measure the traditional in relation to what is new supposes that the doctrine transmitted has been crystallized into a stable form. Only when this has occurred can that doctrine become the object of a critical regard and, by the same token, can it be surpassed.[36] Progress and conservation run parallel to one another and even reinforce one another. To the contrary, an assimilation by intussusception (that is, by digestion) does not show the line of demarcation between the old and the new, thus making it more difficult to stand at a distance from oneself.

Cultural life in Andalusia in the twelfth century offers an example of this. Thinkers like Ibn Bājja (d. ca. 1138) or Averroes intended to impose an authentic Aristotelianism there, cleansed of the dross deposited on it by Avicenna. In astronomy that led al-Bitrūjī (Alpetragius) to an attempt to correct Ptolemy's system, a move that consisted essentially in hypotheses aiming at "saving the phenomena" by constructing a mathematical model capable of accounting for appearances, but that did not claim to represent reality. Al-Bitrūjī set himself the task of making this theory compatible with Aristotelian physics—that is, with what was considered at the time to be an adequate description of the real world.[37] It was only after the failure of the Andalusian reform of astronomy that scholars felt they were at an impasse, an admission that, in the long term, led to a new astronomy.

The Literature on the Stomach

This leads me to the problem of human consciousness. What is a culture (like European culture) that embraces elements from other cultures, but that does not consume them, and even takes all possible precautions to

prevent those elements from dissolving and merging with itself? Our mu-
seum technology has invented a convenient way to multiply such inclusions: in even the most modest collection, each display window transforms
the objects exposed in it into inclusions. But what is a culture that gives
itself the goal of conserving, right in the midst of its own present, bubbles
from or reserves out of the past? Here we are obliged to take Nietzsche's
objections seriously. It may very well be that historical science (*Historie*) is
harmful for Life.[38] And just as harmful for life with a lowercase "l," for life
in the literal and most elementary sense, as prolonged by the biological
process of nutrition. The most adequate model of a healthy life, even on
the cultural level, may well be not inclusion, but—precisely—digestion.
Living tradition is a digestion of the past to the profit of the future. Does
this mean that European culture is intrinsically sick?

The attempt simply to eliminate tradition can (and even must) put life
in danger, to the extent that it destroys the works that bear witness to it
and express it. Michel Henry has given a fascinating example of this. In his
highly impressive book *La Barbarie*, he speaks of the supposed "restoration" of the Byzantine mosaics of the Greek monastery of Daphne.[39] Restorers made quite clumsy attempts to remove the tesserae that had been
placed in the mosaic over the course of centuries to replace damaged parts.
The hope was to return the work to its primitive state, but the result was
that the mosaics were so disfigured that they became illegible and the
spectator receives none of their former impact. Henry brilliantly analyzes
this failure as symptomatic of a loss of meaning connected with historical
awareness, a question he pursues more deeply than I can here.

Be that as it may, there is another route to follow, as can be demonstrated
by another example of the restoration of a work of figurative art. When
a fresco has been damaged by humidity in its supporting walls, restorers
use the technique of *tratteggio*.[40] The colored portions that fell off from the
damp plaster are replaced with colors that complete the painted forms and
permit the eye to grasp their contours, but those colors are applied only in
very fine hash marks. When the work is viewed from afar, as is the usual
case with a spectator looking at a ceiling situated several meters above
the head, this gives the impression that the paintings remain intact. The
image becomes readable; the mythological scene is identifiable, without
spoiling the naive pleasure of enjoying a work of art. But a connoisseur
who examines the details, for example, to evaluate the artist's technique,
analyze the chemical composition of the pigments used, et cetera, has no
difficulty distinguishing the original portions of the work from the ones
that have been restored.

Tratteggio provides an image for the way that the entire activity of historical investigation can be understood. The historian attempts to give back life to the past, but he does so only in vitro. He makes the past newly present, but he does not introduce it into the present. He must give the reader the impression that his narrative speaks of contemporary events, and the more talented he is the better he attains that goal. But the illusion is compensated by a feeling of distance. It is only when we read superficially that we can imagine we are living a bygone past. The connoisseur, on the other hand, can measure the abyss that separates us from that past.

According to Nietzsche, European culture suffers from dyspepsia.[41] In other words, for the West, the sources of its culture remain undigested—in French, they remain *sur l'estomac*. One might respond, if I may be permitted to take Nietzsche's image, which is already a bit much, and push it even further: for a long time now, that stomach—precisely because of all the undissolved inclusions within it—has become more like a gizzard. In other words, thanks to the model of appropriation that Europe developed with its sources, it can appropriate other cultures without feeling obliged to digest them.

10]⌐··

The Interpreter

Reflections on Arabic Translations

The history of medieval philosophy—and even modern philosophy—would not have been what it was without a vast movement to transfer knowledge from one language and one culture to another. This occurred in successive waves of translation that began well before what we call the Middle Ages.

A Thousand Years of Transfer

The first episode lies in the extremely long-term passage from Greek to Latin. It began when the Roman elite began to learn Greek after the armies of Rome conquered southern Italy, then continental Greece, in the second century BCE. That acculturation was, moreover, simply the linguistic aspect of a broader movement that led Rome to rethink itself in all of its dimensions.[1]

That episode lasted a good six centuries, from Cicero (d. 43 BCE) to Boethius (d. 524), and it included Latin-speaking Christians of the fourth century. The latter translated Christian authors: one such was Rufinus, thanks to whom we possess more than just scraps of Origen. But they also translated the pagan authors: Marius Victorinus, for example, may have translated some of Plotinus's works. We might even say that this all-over movement lasted almost a thousand years, if we include the translations of Nemesius of Emesa (whom people took for Gregory of Nyssa), of Pseudo-Dionysius the Areopagite, and of Maximus the Confessor, whose works were translated into Latin from Greek by John Scotus Erigena (d. 877), who integrated them into his *De divisione naturae*. As his double surname indicates, John came from Ireland—the far ends of the world, therefore which had not been troubled by migrations (the so-called "barbarian invasions") and where smatterings of Greek culture had survived in the monasteries.

Translations were not made uniquely into Latin: in parallel fashion, there were translations from the Greek into the languages of the Christians of the East. This was the case above all for Syriac, the Aramaic spoken by Christians of the Middle East from the sixth to the eighth centuries. There were also translations into the national languages of other Christian peoples, such as Armenian and Georgian. Thus there exists a text of a Greek writer, St. Irenaeus, bishop of Lyon, the *Demonstration of the Apostolic Preaching*, which we possess only in Armenian and in translations from Armenian.

The second episode in our history, and the first situated incontestably in the Middle Ages, is the movement of translations into Arabic in the ninth and tenth centuries. I shall speak here only of translations from the Greek, because they are the ones that concern works of philosophy. The very first translations, however, were made from Pahlavi, beginning with the masterwork of Arabic prose, the *Kalila wa-Dimna* of Ibn al-Muqaffaʿ (who was executed in 756).

Vast numbers of works were translated from the Greek. We possess many monographs and a number of good syntheses.[2] These translations stretch over a period of from one to two centuries, roughly from 800 to 950. The first is thought to be Aristotle's *Topics*, in 782. The movement stopped when the Arabs decided that they had assimilated all of Greek knowledge, even that they had prolonged and surpassed it.[3]

In the next chapter, I shall treat the third episode, in which Europe appropriated—or reappropriated—the Greek heritage, but also the Islamic heritage, by means of translations.

The Background

If we try to reconstitute the overall context of the movement to translate works into Arabic, we can place ourselves on at least three scales. Let us begin with the broadest one.

The general, long-term framework is the Arab conquest. It stands as an exceptional historical phenomenon. Not infrequently, the peoples of a less advanced civilization conquer more advanced civilizations. The Romans had conquered Greece, the Franks, Gaul, and so on. But the conquerors usually become assimilated into the conquered: the Franks neglected their original language and religion, learned the vernacular Latin spoken by the Gauls, and adopted the Christianity that they practiced. But although the Arab conquerors borrowed the culture of the peoples they defeated, they imposed their own language and their religion on them.

It should be noted that the Arab conquest was aided by an economic rise in the conquered territories that lasted for several centuries.[4] The Arabs had taken over regions of a high, long-established culture: from classical antiquity, the Middle East was an economic and cultural center of gravity; in the Roman Empire, the eastern half was already the more prosperous. Conquest put an end to the rivalry between the Byzantine Empire and Persia to the advantage of a "third thief," who gobbled up the second and the richest part of the first. Commercial routes were redefined to suit the new empire. Pillage put back into circulation the gold that had slumbered in Egyptian tombs and on icons, giving a new breath to economic affairs. A class of merchants and functionaries developed who had leisure, an indispensable condition for high culture. These men learned Arabic, the language in which they did business and carried on administration, thus enabling them to prolong the cultural tradition of the region, already centuries old.

The narrowest scale is the Abbasid dynasty, in power since the revolution of 750. It reflected Persian more than Arab influence. According to a fascinating hypothesis of Dimitri Gutas, their policies favoring translation may have been prompted by a desire to further the Zoroastrian heritage of ancient Persia. Zoroastrianism had been the national religion of Iran before the Arab conquest. It supposed that religious truth was scattered in a number of books and should be gathered into one whole. Gutas suggests that this is what the Abbasid caliphs, the heirs of the Persian sovereigns, attempted to do, extending the project to Greek philosophical knowledge.[5]

Another element, also linked to the character of the new dynasty, deserves mention. Umayyad Islam had remained the exclusive religion of the governing class that had emerged from the conquest. In contrast, Abbasid Islam was proselytizing. It thus sought to respond to the objections of the Zoroastrians (in particular of those among them who had only superficially adopted Islam) and of Christian theologians trained in Aristotelian logic. As a consequence, the people of the Kalām needed manuals on how to pursue controversy, and Aristotle on logic fulfilled that function. A motivation of the sort might explain why the first text of the Philosopher to be translated was one whose translation we would never dream might be urgent, but that could in fact do what was expected of it—the *Refutations of the Sophists* (*Sophistici Elenchi*).[6]

What Was Translated?

We possess a literary translation, the *Kalila wa-Dimna*, but, as we have already seen, it was translated, not from the Greek but from Pahlavi, thus it falls outside the limits of our survey.

One important fact is negative in nature: no earlier sacred text was translated. Muslim dogmatics in fact resolved the problem of the incompatibility of the Qur'an and the Bible by declaring that both the Old and New Testaments had been falsified by their possessors: Jews for the Torah, Christians for the Gospel. This dogma is known by the technical term *tahrīf*.[7] As a consequence, biblical texts are hardly ever studied by Muslims; even reading them is forbidden, on the basis of certain hadiths, and in any event there is no translation made for Muslim use. There is no Muslim equivalent of the Septuagint or the Vulgate. The Bible was translated into Arabic by and for Jews (by Saadia Gaon, for example), or by and for Christians. Moreover, it is not to be completely excluded that a translation may have existed before Muhammad, for the use of the Christian tribes of Arabia.[8] But we do not possess any fragment of it.

What was translated from Greek into Arabic was, generally speaking, useful knowledge. We find no aesthetic concerns in such works. No literature was translated and no history. The name of Homer was known, but his works were stripped down to a few moral maxims. The tragic poets, lyric poets, and historians were ignored. What was translated, and in abundance, were works of science and philosophy (to the extent that any clear distinction was made between the two at the time).

As for what we call "the sciences," translations into Arabic permitted the appropriation of Greek knowledge by the Middle East and Islamic Andalusia. That knowledge was enriched by the personal contribution of Arab scholars, a contribution that permitted notable progress in mathematics, optics, astronomy, and more. Since I am hardly competent in those domains, I shall not speak of them, contenting myself with mentioning that several good and recent summaries are available.[9]

The Role of Translation in Building a Culture

In Islam, there is no line of demarcation between knowledge and another domain (faith, religion), but rather between two types of knowledge: Islamic sciences and outside sciences.

The Arabic word for "knowledge" (*'ilm*) has a religious connotation from the start. Reciprocally, religion represents a "knowledge." The period that preceded Islam is classically designated as "the ignorance" (*jāhiliyya*). There is a much-repeated hadith praising "knowledge": "Seek knowledge, even in China."[10] Nothing could better propagate the image of an Islam friend of the sciences, compatible with modernity, even a factor of progress. In fact, however, when the hadith was put into circulation, its intention was by no means to legitimate physics or geography. The word *ʿilm* signified science only when used with an annexed term, such as "the science *of* nature" or "the science *of* language." Used absolutely, it designates religious knowledge, more precisely, the knowledge, revealed by God, of the duties of man. The hadith in question is part of a series of declarations put into the mouth of Muhammad and telling the merits of those who embark on long voyages to gather from the very mouth of the transmitters traditions regarding the Prophet.[11] It is thus a hadith that brings legitimacy to the hadith itself, not to knowledge in general. A description of the Far East for the use of traders remarks with surprise that the Chinese have no *ʿilm*. The French translator adds, quite rightly: "The Chinese have no science [of the Law]."[12]

Religious knowledge—like the *fiqh*, the hadith, and exegesis of the Qurʾan, along with the auxiliary disciplines of grammar, poetics, and so on—*must* be internal in origin. In reality, the law comes either from earlier Arab practices or from the conquered peoples, and it is fictively attributed to the Prophet. The task of inscribing the cultural heritage affected, primarily and paradoxically, the Arabic language itself, and did so in its supposedly normative document, the Qurʾan. It would only be a slight exaggeration to speak of an Arabization of Arabic itself. The language of the Qurʾan is the language that was spoken in the Arabic Peninsula in the seventh century: a mix of dialects, with a strong injection of words and turns of phrase borrowed from the language of high culture, Syro-Aramaic, or Syriac. It was the job of the commentators of the Qurʾan and the grammarians to explain every passage solely on the basis of the resources of an Arabic in great part postulated ad hoc.[13]

In contrast, profane knowledge *has the right* to be of foreign origin. It comes from Persia or from Greece. Persia itself often functioned to relay material from India. This is the case, for example, for the numerals that we still call "Arabic." This knowledge came by means of translations.

The Place of the Other in the Constitution of a Public Space

All societies are defined by a unique style of negotiating their relations with others. Medieval Islamic society emerged from the conquest by a warlike Arab minority of vast populations that already had other religions. It was thus an exception to the rule because in it the other was already present. But, if I may be permitted to put it this way, all others are not as other as other others. Within Islamic space, in principle, pagans had no place. In contrast, the Jew and the Christian did have a place, regulated by the rules of the *dhimma*, or "protection."

In like fashion, the translators who participated in the translation movement were never Muslims. For the most part, they were Christians of the three dominant denominations, with a few Sabians. The language of culture for these Christians was Syriac, and their liturgical language was Greek.

The translators already knew the languages they were to translate. We do, of course, have examples of translators who traveled to Greece to perfect their skills, but they were Christians for whom Greek was already at least a liturgical language.

This reflects a fundamental structure of Islamic civilization, here transposed to the level of culture. That civilization was particular in having foreigners within it. This corresponds to a current practice in the Muslim states: it is not the Muslims, but the "protected" peoples who are charged with non-political, non-military contacts with their equivalents on the outside. They were the ones who engaged in commerce and more. Thus there is evidence of entire Christian families who, from father to son, were interpreters (*drogman*) for the Sublime Port.

Neither were there any Muslims among the ninth-century translators. Almost all of them were Christians of various Eastern denominations: Jacobites, Melchites, and, above all, Nestorians (though I am not sure why the latter predominated). A few others were Sabians, a somewhat bizarre religious community with an intriguing history, whose elites were perhaps the last heirs of the pagan philosophers of the School of Athens.[14] No Muslim learned Greek or, even less, Syriac. Cultivated Christians were often bilingual, even trilingual: they used Arabic for daily life, Syriac for liturgy, and Greek for cultural purposes.

The translators that helped to pass along the Greek heritage to the Arabs were artisans who worked for private patrons, without institutional support.[15] One often hears tell of the "House of Wisdom" (*bayt al-hikmah*), a sort of research center subsidized by the caliphs that specialized in producing Arabic translations of Greek works. This is pure legend. The further back in time we go, the less the chroniclers connect the activity of translation with that "house."[16] As an institution it was above all a propaganda office working for the Muʿtazilite doctrine supported by the caliphs.

The Vocabulary of the Act of Translation:
Transporting, Imitating, Rivaling, Et Cetera

Does the way translations were spoken of and the words used to speak of them teach us something about the way they were experienced? The dictionary that is perhaps the best on this question, the German-Arabic dictionary of Götz Schregle, renders *übersetzen* as *tarjama* and *naqala*.[17] *Tarjama*, or "to interpret," is an old Aramaic, subsequently Hebrew, verb, undoubtedly formed on the Akkadian substantive for "interpreter." The related Arabic word, *turjuman*, is the origin of the French *truchement* (interpreter, go-between). But we also have *naqala*, "to transport," or do a translation. Among the translators of Aristotle, this was the root chosen to render the third of the three types of movement per se: movement according to place, or displacement (*phora*). One can also find *akhraja*, "to bring out," not always in the sense of "to publish."[18]

The connotations of these terms are significative: "to transport" implies the displacement of a contents that remains the same; "to bring out" implies that only the translation brings the text out of its hole to introduce it into a public space.

All of this is supposed to have happened as if knowledge were composed of movable objects that could be imported from one region to another just like goods in international trade. The transport of manuscripts is narrated as if it were a mission of exploration bringing back exotic curiosities. Some texts take up these representations and give them expression.

The idea of *translatio studiorum* from Alexandria to Baghdad can be read in Farabi, along with the affirmation of a perfect continuity of teaching from master to student. The philosopher is expected to present himself as the heir to a knowledge that he is supposed to have received, without loss, from its Greek origins. Relations of this transfer of knowledge lend credit to what is perhaps more legend than reality.[19] Translation is not mentioned as a significant intermediate stage.

Ibn Khaldūn implies that translation is a simple process of peeling the linguistic shell off a work, something that is supposed not to affect the contents. He explains why the manuscripts that were translated have not been conserved.[20] No feeling of loss in relation to the original appears in the translation. The adage *traduttore tradittore* was unheard-of. Quite to the contrary, a text of Biruni's explains that translation into Arabic ennobles the texts translated.[21]

The Relationship with the Greeks in Each Culture

Knowledge is Greek in origin. In a very concrete manner, it is supposed to have come from the land of the Greeks, which means the Byzantine Empire. But the Arab authors carefully distinguish between the Greeks they want to translate and actual Greeks. Actual Greeks were considered less worthy than the ancient Greeks. This attitude verifies a sort of historical law according to which conquerors eventually appropriate the past of the natives of the conquered lands, but scorn the present natives. The Romans translated the Greeks, but scorned the *graeculi*. Colonizers have a tendency to pin the colonized land down to its historical past. The colonial administrator and Orientalist Octave Houdas imposed teaching in classical literary Arabic in the Algerian madrassas, where the professors would have preferred dialect.[22]

There was thus a double movement to appreciate the Greeks of the past and devalue the present Greeks: those of the eastern Roman Empire, the Byzantines who were the real adversaries of the caliphs.

The ancient Greeks were judged by their highest representatives. When "Greeks" were spoken of, that generally meant "the philosophers," and even just "Aristotle." Thus the physician and freethinker Razi writes that the Greeks were a chaste people.[23] He had never heard of Aristophanes or the Greek love stories, and even less had he seen any obscene graffiti. Maimonides distinguishes between the "laws of the Greeks" and the "follies of the Sabians." Such imaginary Greeks were thought not to have believed in astrology.[24]

Contemporary Greeks—the Byzantines—on the other hand, were thought mere degenerates. The tone is moderate at first: in the ninth century, Jāhiz writes that the "Romans" of Byzantium are great scholars, which makes him wonder how they could believe in the Incarnation, which involves a thousand absurdities and inconveniences for God.[25] It is noteworthy that the inverse hypothesis—that Christian dogma, given that it had been accepted by very gifted people, might not be as absurd as it seemed—does not seem to have to entered the mind of this polemicist. The more time went on, the sharper the tone became. Thus at the end of the fifteenth century, Suyuti relates an anecdote according to which the works of the ancient philosophers were buried by the Byzantines, who were just delighted to get rid of them when the caliphs came to ask for them.[26]

The meaning of such calumnies is clear: contemporary Greeks are no longer deserving of their own ancestors. The only legitimate heirs of the ancient Greeks are not their blood descendants, but the Arabs.

The Place of Translation in the Culture Studied

The Islamic world showed almost no interest in the other as such. That attitude lasted until the Ottoman age. Those who were obliged to sojourn in Christian lands, as ambassadors of the Sublime Port, for example, or as fighting men taken prisoner before being exchanged, seldom tell of their experiences.[27]

Inversely, the populations of lands under Islam found it difficult to understand that travelers could come from far away uniquely in order to observe them. This is what the French traveler Jean Chardin remarks about the Persians when he visited their land in 1686:

> Where voyages are concerned, those undertaken for simple curiosity are even more inconceivable to the Persians than promenades. They have no experience of the intense pleasure that we feel in seeing different manners than our own and in hearing a language not usually heard. . . . But they paused, in particular, over the words "gentlemen curious to travel," which could not be translated into their language without bearing the air of absurdity that all things not practiced or even unknown bear. They asked me if it were possible that there could be people among us who might want to take the trouble to travel two or three thousand leagues with so much risk and discomfort just to see how people are made and what they do in Persia, with no other purpose in mind.[28]

Thus we need to be aware of a fact that provides an invisible backdrop to the enterprise of translation. By this I mean the effort to translate *oneself* into another culture, to attempt to understand it and understand how it is made up. It seems that no one in the Islamic world—Muslim, Jew, or Christian—went beyond translation in the most concrete, most strictly linguistic sense of the term. No one sought to apply the translation to himself, so to speak, by transporting himself into another universe of thought.

This is why no one translated a vision of the world; at best it was transposed. That fact depends on the idea, more or less consciously held, that every culture can find in another culture term-for-term equivalents to its own. This is what permitted Herodotus, for example, to make a quite unceremonious connection between the names of the Egyptian gods and the gods of the Greek Olympus.[29] Thus when a Greek text that spoke of the gods was to be translated (for example, the Arabic texts of Plotinus), the gods become angels and demons become jinni.[30] Similarly, the translators of Aristotle's *Poetics*, who lived in a civilization without theater, rendered the word for "tragedy" as "laudative poetry" and the one for "comedy" as "satiric poetry." Averroes simply follows them, innovating in nothing, contrary to what Jorge Luis Borges relates when he makes the perplexity of the Commentator the subject of a famous novella.[31]

This means that we should not expect anything analogous to a modern historical sense from these translators.

Arabs and Latins

In this sense, the Islamic world represents a case symmetrical to that of the Latin world. The Romans adapted but translated little. On the other hand, they learned Greek.

The Islamic world translated a good deal, to the point that the Arabs can perhaps be called the inventors of translation. But the Muslims did not learn Greek. Those who knew Greek had been raised bilingual because they were sons of an Arab father and a Greek mother.[32] No Muslim seems to have ever learned a foreign language for theoretical reasons rather than, for example, commercial reasons.

The one exception is perhaps Farabi. One of his biographers relates that he is supposed to have spent seven years in "Greece" in order to study there. This information is all the more interesting because the word used is not "Rūm," which designated Constantinople, but rather "Yunan," which can mean only Greece. One might well wonder where, to what center of teaching, in Greece of the time might a student from the Muslim world have possibly gone. Farabi does not seem to have shown proof of a very profound knowledge of Greek. He does indeed cite a few words of that language. But the etymological explanations that he gives of the titles of some of Plato's dialogues are sheer fantasy.[33]

The only real exception is Biruni. But he is an exception that proves the rule: the language that he learned was not Greek, but Sanskrit. Biruni had learned that language to the point of being able to translate into it from Arabic. He made use of that ability to give the religion of the Hindus a presentation admirable for its impartiality.

The Entry of Aristotle in Europe

The Arab Intermediary

The texts that the Arabs had translated were in turn translated into Latin, either directly from the Greek or from translations that had been made by Arabs. Eventually certain philosophical texts that continued the Greek acquisitions but were written directly in Arabic were also translated into European languages.

A Spanish Itinerary

Let me begin by briefly recalling the facts. These are known, in their overall lines, thanks to solid studies, on which I have relied.[1]

Until the eleventh century, the Europe of Latin culture knew little about Aristotle: the first parts of the works on logic were known, the *Categories* and *De interpretatione*, in the translation by Boethius. The latter, one of the last Romans to be perfectly bilingual, set himself the project of translating all of Aristotle into Latin and commenting on it, but also all of Plato. His execution in 524 prevented him from progressing very far toward the realization of that immense project. For six centuries, that was all there was.

In the thirteenth century, Robert Grosseteste, the bishop of Lincoln, translated the *Nicomachean Ethics* (ca. 1246) and a portion of the *Treatise on the Heavens*. Then the Flemish Dominican William of Moerbeke set himself the task of a systematic translation or revision of all of Aristotle's works, which he accomplished between 1260 and 1280. These are the translations used by Scholasticism at its height. It is not true, as is often said, that Thomas Aquinas ordered translations from his fellow scholar: Thomas made use of works that William had already translated independently. These translations continued to be authoritative until the Italian humanists criticized their style, which they found lacking according to their criteria. They did their best to rival them in a more Ciceronian Latin. Thus Leonardo Bruni retranslated the *Nicomachean Ethics*.[2] After then, modern languages took over from Latin.

I would like to turn here to an epoch a good century earlier than William of Moerbeke. It was in fact in the twelfth century that attempts began to be made to fill the yawning gaps in what was available of Aristotle. For one thing, Boethius's translations of the *Prior Analytics*, the *Topics*, and the *Sophistical Refutations* were found around 1120—after six centuries! We do not know how, nor where, nor by whom. The rest of Aristotle's works were translated for the first time, either from the Greek, as was the case of James of Venice, who translated the *Metaphysics* and the *Posterior Analytics*,[3] or from the Arabic, in translations made in Spain, in Toledo, beginning around 1130, which were themselves based on translations from the Greek and/or from Syriac made in the ninth century in Baghdad.

We do not know exactly when the movement for translations from the Arabic began. At first it concerned texts that we would not classify as "philosophy," but rather as "science." The mission of Jean de Vandières (900–974, known in Lorraine as John of Gorze, where he served as the abbot of a monastery) is often mentioned. Emperor Otto III sent him to Cordova as an ambassador to caliph ʿAbd ar-Rahmān in 953. There he met scholars who knew Arabic, and he brought back books in that language, but the sources say no more about them. All we know is that mathematical and astronomical knowledge of Arab origin is attested in Lorraine of the time.[4]

Early traces of the influence of Arab astronomical knowledge can be found in Gerbert of Aurillac (b. ca. 940), who was pope from 999 to 1003 under the name of Sylvester II.[5] Here, too, legends snowball as writers for popular weeklies and tourist brochures borrow from one another. Gerbert spent three years in the monastery of Vich, in Christian Catalonia, where he learned mathematics and astronomy as they were cultivated on the other side of the religious frontier. But that is not enough: we are told that he studied in Muslim Spain. Next he is imagined to have been a student in a university of the Maghreb. But did Gerbert know Arabic? Could a Christian monk study in a Muslim establishment? Or in an institution of higher learning a century before the foundation of the madrassa by Nizam al-Mulk (d. 1092)? And can we speak of "universities" to designate those schools, where little else was taught but Muslim law?

To come back down to earth and to facts, the first translations were completely practical in their aim: what was put into Latin were manuals of medicine, arithmetic, or astronomy. In that manner, the medical school of Salerno, just south of Naples, made good use of translations by Constantine the African.

In Toledo, translation centered on philosophical texts. We know about the activities of certain translators: Gerard of Cremona (1114–1187) translated the *Posterior Analytics* (thus completing the corpus of Aristotle's writings on logic), the *Physics*, and *On Generation and Corruption*. Before 1220, Michael Scot translated works of biology, brought together under the title *De animalibus*. But the Arabic philosophers were also translated. Thus the archdeacon Gundissalinus (Domingo Gundisalvo) translated the works of Avicenna, with the help of Johannes Avendauth, who may have been Jewish.[6]

Some Reflections

The choice of the texts that were translated is significant. As we have seen, the wave of translations had begun with technical works, and things might well have stayed that way. This is what the example of Byzantium shows. There only treatises on medicine were translated from the Arabic, but nothing philosophical. This leads to an amusing paradox: the names of the Arab philosophers appear in Byzantine Greek only in the Greek translations of the works of Thomas Aquinas made in the fourteenth century. In contrast, in Latin Christianity, as was the case in Iraqi Islam of the ninth century, "practical" translations were accompanied by what might be called "theoretical" ones. The existence of the latter is not to be taken for granted and merits explanation.

The contents of such "theoretical" translations was not limited to the Aristotelian corpus. Far from it. Along with Aristotle, they included the works of commentators and of philosophers who followed in his wake. Aristotle's works were never separated from the "dressing" that helped readers to understand them, or from works in all branches of knowledge that showed similar intellectual preoccupations. At the limit, the whole of Greek knowledge entered into Europe, including authors who came after Aristotle.

The method of translation is interesting.[7] It is presented in the prologue to Avicenna's *De anima*. It supposes the collaboration of two people: a first translator reads the Arabic text and translates it orally into the vernacular. We do not know whether this was a dialect of Spanish or perhaps dialectal Arabic. Then a second person translates what he hears into Latin. The first translator is a Jew or a Mozarabic Christian; the second is a Christian cleric.

The translations produced in Toledo are useful as a first approach, but they are not yet fully satisfactory. In fact, translating a translation multiplies the risks of distortion. The drawbacks of these translations led to their being used only when nothing better was available, before there were direct translations or in places that the direct translations had not yet reached. The importance of the Arabo-Latin translations of Aristotle should thus not be exaggerated.[8]

There is one important consequence, however, that is not so much inherent in the movement to produce translations in Toledo as it is parallel to that movement. Indeed, aside from the translations addressed to Christian readers, another and equally vast movement occurred in Jewish circles. When the Jews were chased out of Muslim Andalusia by the Almohads in 1148, many Jewish families moved north and settled in Christian lands, Catalonia or Provence. One of these, the Ibn Tibbon family, produced three generations of translators, each one of whom—and the parallel is significant—corresponds to a stage in the appropriation of Arab knowledge on the part of the Jewish communities. Jehuda translated texts of spirituality or apologetics written in Arabic but by Jewish authors. His son Samuel's chief translation was the *Guide for the Perplexed* of Maimonides, a Jewish work, to be sure, but one that approves of the study of secular knowledge. Samuel also started translating the works of Aristotle, beginning (and we might find this surprising) with the *Meteorology*, a work that he needed in order to interpret the narration of creation in Genesis according to Maimonides' method. The third in the family was Moses, the son of Samuel (hence Jehuda's grandson), who translated massive amounts of scientific and / or philosophical works by pagan authors—Aristotle among them—and Muslim authors, above all, Averroes.[9]

Among the Jews of the northern Mediterranean, this movement to translate works into Hebrew began as and at least in part remained motivated by emulation: the point was to imitate the Latin translations made by Christians and even rival them.[10]

The Role of the Arab World

How should we evaluate the role of the Arabs in this transmission of knowledge? The first thing to agree on is the meaning of the word "Arab." A persistent misunderstanding has it simply meaning Muslims. But it can also refer to people who spoke Arabic and were of Arab culture, leaving aside their religious affiliation. In that case, we can include within our adjective Christians who lived under Muslim domination, such as the Mozarabs of Spain, the Jews who lived under the same conditions, and even a few "Sabians."

It might be amusing to apply the ancient and medieval theory of the four causes to this role.[11]

(1) The Arabs—and here I mean Arabic speakers—were the *material* cause of the translations, because the manuscripts that were translated were written down in their language. This concerns only a part, in fact a small part, of the works of Aristotle translated into Latin.

(2) Were the Arabs the *efficient* cause of the transmission of Greek culture to Europe? If we take "Arabs" to mean Muslims, their role was nil. They did not actively transmit anything, either by translating texts or by furnishing texts. In Iraq of the ninth to tenth centuries, translations were almost exclusively the work of Christians. If, on the other hand, we understand by "Arabs" people who spoke Arabic, they obviously made the Toledo translations possible, thanks to their knowledge of the language from which works were translated.

(3) Even more decisively, the Arabs were the *formal* cause of such translations. The works of Aristotle that were translated from the Arabic, even if they made up only a small part of the corpus, have a significance that transcends Aristotle himself. Beyond Aristotle the philosopher from Stagira and his works, there was in fact an "Aristotle effect" in which his name served as a banner for an entire and much broader tendency. Concerning the content of what entered into Europe, these works were primarily written by Arab philosophers who were in fact Aristotelians: a bit of al-Kindi and Farabi, a lot of Avicenna, and, later, nearly all of Averroes.

There is more, however: the central place accorded to Aristotle is also an Arab fact and, more precisely, an Andalusian fact. The Aristotelian renaissance began in the West, but not in a Christian land: it began in Andalusia under Islamic domination. Aristotelianism as faithfulness to Aristotle—to an Aristotle that was, or was supposed to be, "pure"—was the specialty of the region. The first philosopher about whom we know enough to consider him "Aristotelian" is Ibn Bājja (ca. 1085–ca. 1138).

Ibn Bājja wrote commentaries on the logical works of Farabi, but he was unaware of Avicenna, who was, in fact, closer to him in time. We do not know why. It is possible that he deliberately chose not to take him into account, to ignore him, so to speak. But it is also quite possible that the work of Avicenna had not yet reached Andalusia in the age in which Ibn Bājja lived. Thus the historian of sciences Sāʿid al-Andalusī (d. 1070) does not mention Avicenna even once in his *Generations of the Nations (Tabaqāt al-Umam*; 1068).[12] One might hazard a conjecture regarding the date of entry of Avicenna in Andalusia. On two occasions in his *Kuzari* (1140), the Jewish poet and apologist Jehuda Halevi (1075–1141) offers a summary of the fundamental theses of philosophy. In book 1, the model is Ibn Bājja, but in book 5 he refers to the system of Avicenna. It is thus possible that Halevi became aware of Avicenna while he was already engaged in writing his masterwork, which would indicate that Avicenna's works began to be diffused in Andalusia during the 1130s.[13]

Even after the reception of Avicenna's works in the Muslim West, we can sense the persistence of a sort of reserve toward them. To be sure, the first among the Jewish Aristotelians, Abraham Ibn Daoud, the author of *The Exalted Faith* (*Emunah ha-ramah*), was a follower of Avicenna. But Maimonides, in his letter to his translator Ibn Tibbon, places Avicenna second, behind Farabi.[14] As for Averroes, he attributes to the influence of Avicenna the corruption of Aristotelian philosophy, which he intends to restore to its purity.

(4) It seems to me that the Arabs fulfilled another role for which I have to replace the fourth of the Aristotelian causes, the final cause, by another drawn from Seneca: the *exemplary* cause. The transmission of knowledge is not accomplished in a purely hydraulic fashion: it requires a need, a demand. As it happens, that need was formulated even before anyone thought of satisfying it by borrowing from the Arab world. It is vast and embraces an entire way of life. Abelard, in his *Dialogue between a Philosopher, a Jew, and a Christian* (probably written between 1136 and 1140), presents a philosopher. This anonymous personage is given as a descendant of Ishmael and as circumcised.[15] Remarkably, he seeks a purely "lay" ethic and a purely "philosophical" happiness. It is not to be excluded that Abelard constructed this model on the basis of hearsay about Ibn Bājja that may have reached him when he was in Cluny, an abbey that had sustained contacts with Spain. That is—paradoxically—on the basis of a model that was already on the point of disappearing in the Muslim world that had given rise to it.

The fact remains that the portrait of the philosopher, as a human type, precedes its realizations by several dozen years. It matters little whether those realizations were actual people, hallucinatory (among certain radical Aristotelians of the Faculty of Arts of the Sorbonne in the thirteenth century), or nightmarish (among the ecclesiastical censors).[16] The model remained with Europe and continued to haunt it. When Europe appealed to Arabism, it already knew what it was seeking.

12

The Extra-European Sources of Philosophic Europe

European philosophy had external sources as well as sources from within its own continent.

Where Is Europe?

The answer to that question depends on where you set Europe's frontiers. The question is a current one for Europeans today. For a medievalist, the answer is easy enough if we listen to the interested parties themselves—that is, the people who told their neighbors "We are Europeans" and received the response "You are Europeans," and, at times, "You are dirty Europeans."

In the Middle Ages, Europe was the Latin West, the West that was Latin in language and culture. On occasion people in Constantinople called the inhabitants of the West "Europeans," but more often they called them "Franks" (*Ifranj*). The word "European" was not frequent at that time in Arabic. In no case did the people of either Constantinople or Baghdad think that they had anything in common with those rough and bloodthirsty people, whom some regarded as schismatics, if not heretics, and others thought quite simply miscreants.

Thus if we think of Europe in the same terms as people of the Middle Ages, Greece—both ancient Greece and the Roman Empire of the East (which we call "Byzantine")—was outside of its boundaries. We would have to count all of Greek philosophy as extra-European sources of our philosophy: the works of continental Geeks like Plato; Macedonians like Aristotle; Phoenicians like

Zeno, the founder of Stoicism; or Greeks of Egypt like Plotinus, to mention only some particularly important names.

That would leave only the Roman philosophers as internal sources of European philosophy. These would include, for example, two Italians, Lucretius and Cicero, and a Spaniard from Cordova, Seneca—that is, men who adapted and versified Epicurus, a Greek thinker, blithely sacked the Hellenistic thinkers or gave a somewhat declamatory version of Stoic ethics.

Does this mean that there is *no* European source of European philosophy? That is my opinion, but it will have to be the topic of another essay.

Translations from the Arabic

My present topic belongs instead within the context of reflections on the relationship between Europe and Islam. In the case that interests me here, Islam signifies the Arab world, which is only an approximation. Arab and Islam are two different things. In fact, since the seventh century—hence since its beginning—Islam included populations of other languages than Arabic: Persian, Turkish, Berber. In the Middle Ages, it had already penetrated into Africa and, after the campaigns of Mahmūd of Ghazna in the early eleventh century, it irrupted with violence in the Indian subcontinent. And yet. For one thing, Arabic is still the dominant language of Islamic culture; for another, it was in any event the Arab world that was in contact with Western Christianity in Spain and in Sicily. Toward the East, Byzantium—the Roman Empire of the East—still lay between Europe and the Turks.

Concrete philosophic contact with Arab sources was established by a movement to produce translations that traversed Christian and Jewish Europe.[1] It is that movement that I shall attempt to sketch here by responding to a series of questions.

When were translations made? Not for long, on the scale of the history of the world. In the twelfth and thirteenth centuries, after which the window closed. Only one meteorite slipped through: the philosophical novel *Hayy ibn Yaqzān*, of Ibn Tufayl (d. 1185), a work with an obviously symbolic title that could be translated as "Vital, the Son of Gregory" or "The Living, Son of the Awakened." This work was translated into Latin in 1671, then twice into English, once into German, once into Dutch, although never into French. It is not impossible that Daniel Defoe found inspiration in the work for his *Robinson Crusoe*, since it is the story of a man who grows up alone on an island and rediscovers, by the force of his mind alone, the entire philosophico-theological system of his age.

After this one exception, we need to wait for the "philological age" that began in the eighteenth century. Only then did people start to seek out manuscripts, print them, and translate them in a scientifically satisfactory manner. For example, Averroes' famous *Decisive Discourse* was printed and translated for the first time in Munich by one Marcus Joseph Müller in the mid-nineteenth century. Many printed versions of this text are pirated editions made in Arab lands at the time of the Arab renaissance of the late nineteenth century known as the *Nahdah*. There has been a steady stream of translations since then.

Where did translation take place? For medicine, at Salerno, south of Naples. For philosophy, in newly reconquered Toledo (after 1085), and in Sicily at the court of Emperor Frederick II. This was true only of the movement to translate Arabic works into Latin, however. That movement was in fact doubled by a vast move to translate works from Arabic into Hebrew that took place wherever Jews, and particularly Spanish Jews, took refuge from Almohad persecution after 1148. Some Jews moved north, but most remained on the shores of the Mediterranean, settling in Christian Catalonia or in Provence, for example, at Montpellier, Narbonne, and Lunel. And they brought with them, tucked under their arms, Arabic manuscripts that they intended to put into Hebrew.

Who translated? Who were these translators? Among the Christians, they came from everywhere, even from Scotland, which is hardly Mediterranean. Among the Jews, we have just seen an answer to the question. I might again signal the case of the three generations of translators in the famous Ibn Tibbon family. On occasion—for example, in Toledo—translation from Arabic into Latin was a shared task involving a Jew who translated from the Arabic to the local vernacular (Catalan, Provençal, et cetera) and a Christian cleric who translated from the vernacular into Latin.

Into what language were works translated? Given that the texts translated were scholarly, the target language was that of people of learning: Latin among Christians and Hebrew among Jews. Translation was not done into vernacular languages that had no relation to Latin or into languages, such as the Romance languages, that had already grown away from Latin.

Where did the translated texts come from? They were materially present in the territory of the target culture, as were Greek texts in the south of Italy and Arabic texts in Spain. Since the latter were obviously Arab in origin, they were perceived as being Islamic. But that Islamic origin was not a Muslim origin, in the sense that the religious affiliation of the authors who were translated mattered. I have recently realized, not without some surprise, that it is truly exceptional when a medieval philosopher explicitly mentions the fact that someone he cites or criticizes belongs to a particular religion.[2]

The knowledge that entered into Europe is thus a knowledge that is either religiously neutral or very little marked by religion: it was considered to be knowledge, period. Its entry set off an enthusiasm that turned to scorn the knowledge that the Latin world had possessed until then, which paled in comparison with the Greek and Arabized knowledge that the West rediscovered or discovered enriched. This is evidenced in the sharp remarks of Adelard of Bath or Plato of Tivoli.[3]

Content Transferred

What was translated? As I have just suggested, not the religious sources: the Qur'an was translated for the first time in Toledo, in the mid-twelfth century, under the encouragement of Peter the Venerable, the abbot of Cluny. But his translation had little circulation before the text was printed in the sixteenth century by the humanist Theodorus Bibliander.[4] The hadith about Muhammad's night flight was adapted, thanks to its marvelous aspect, as *Muhammad's Ladder*.[5] Very few literary texts were translated: at the most a few tales, thanks to the converted Jew Petrus Alphonsi (early twelfth century). The better part of the translations were scientific texts (medical texts such as the works of Razi) and philosophical texts, which is what interests us here.

Who was translated? Among the Greek philosophers, essentially Aristotle. To some extent, his commentators. Not Plato. The Middle Ages as a whole passed Plato by. In the thirteenth century, Henri Aristippe, who was active at the Sicilian court of Emperor Frederick II, did indeed translate the *Meno* and the *Phaedo*, but the manuscripts of these versions had little or no circulation. The Middle Ages possessed only the beginning of the *Timaeus* and portions of the *Parmenides*, thanks to the commentary of Proclus. Europe had to wait for the Florentines of the fifteenth century and their enthusiasm for the "Divine Plato" that inspired Marsilio Ficino to translate all of Plato's dialogues into Latin. I should also mention a few meteorites, such as the *Hypotyposes* of Sextus Empiricus: there is a Latin translation of the thirteenth century, but no one seems to have used it at the time.

I might also note a surprising phenomenon, dating from the fifteenth century, which is the Latin translation of the *Corpus Hermeticum*, writings attributed to the supposed "Hermes Trismegistus." These Greek treatises—some fifteen of them, of unequal length—seem to us a undigested jumble of popular Neoplatonism, mixed with mysticism and a few traces of Egyptian wisdom. Only one of these texts had been translated into Latin in antiquity, the *Asclepius*, cited by certain Latin Fathers of the Church such as Augustine.[6] Hermes' name remained known by certain Scholastics, such as Abelard, Albertus Magnus, and Bradwardine.[7] When a complete manuscript of the *Corpus* reached Florence, Marsilio Ficino, who was busily at work translating no lesser a personage than Plato, put aside that task and hastened to translate the Pseudo-Hermes into Latin. What seems monstrous to us can be explained by contemporary beliefs. It was in fact thought that the *Corpus Hermeticum* was the most ancient book in the world, pre-dating Plato and perhaps even Moses, who was considered to be the author of the Pentateuch. Proof that it was written later was only established in 1614 by Isaac Casaubon, and the idea was accepted only gradually.

Among the Arab philosophers, who was translated? I shall take them in the order that has become traditional in histories of philosophy, which begins with al-Kindi. Let me recall that later Arab philosophers, from Farabi to Averroes, totally ignore him and never cite him or even name him. As a result, al-Kindi was very seldom translated: two or three short treatises at best. Farabi was fairly unfortunate. He was perhaps the greatest Arab philosopher and the true founder of the discipline, but only two of his works were translated into Latin, and they are marginal in his production. He was somewhat more fortunate in Hebrew, with translations of several of his works on logic. Avicenna was translated a good century after his death in 1037. In particular, his *Metaphysics* was translated, well before Aristotle's work of the same name, as well as his *Psychology*.

The really fortunate Arab philosopher was Averroes. He had been almost forgotten in Arab lands, thus in the language that was his own, almost immediately after his death. He was seen as a shooting star, perhaps even a final bouquet. In contrast, only some twenty years after his death, translations into both Hebrew and Latin began to appear. That is about the same amount of time that it takes in our own days for a work to pass from Germany to France. Thanks to the predominance of Aristotle's works in the medieval intellectual world, it was above all Averroes' commentaries on Aristotle that were translated into both Hebrew and Latin. Later his response to Ghazali's criticisms of philosophy was translated as well. His

juridical treatises were not translated, however, and even less the famous
(perhaps too famous) *Decisive Discourse*. That work was translated into Hebrew and left some trace in Italian Jewish thinkers of the fifteenth century,
but no trace in Latin.

Why Translate?

Today that question seems to us a bit silly. For us, a text is translated because it is interesting, because it is fine. For the Middle Ages, things were
not so simple. How can we explain the need for translations? We have to
break with the naively hydraulic model of the superior that flows automatically toward the inferior. Even the word "influence," through its etymology, foments this sort of representation. It is highly superficial, however. In
reality, works were not translated because their authors were interesting or
because someone sensed their cultural superiority. Works were translated
because they were *needed*. But to cite a need is not to explain it.[8] Demand
precedes the presence of the product on the market, and it is that demand
that has to be explained.

This is what I think: The European intellectual renaissance preceded
the translations from the Arabic. The latter were not the cause, but the
effect of that renaissance. Like all historical events, it had economic aspects
(lands newly under cultivation, new agricultural techniques) and social
aspects (the rise of free cities).[9] On the level of intellectual life, it can be
understood as arising from a movement that began in the eleventh century,
probably launched by the Gregorian reform of the Church that certain historians with a good imagination call the "Papal Revolution." Gregory VII's
attempted reform brought on a conflict with the empire usually known as
the "Investiture Question." That conflict bears witness to a reorientation
of Christianity toward a transformation of the temporal world, up to that
point more or less left to its own devices, with the Church taking refuge in
an apocalyptical attitude that said since the world was about to end, there
was little need to transform it.

The Church's effort to become an autonomous entity by drawing up a
law that would be exclusive to it—Canon Law—prompted an intense need
for intellectual tools. More refined concepts were called for than those
available at the time. Hence the appeal to the logical works of Aristotle,
who was translated from Greek to Latin, either through Arabic or directly
from the Greek, and the Aristotelian heritage was recovered. This is shown
in a work by an American juridical scholar that I find highly informative,

Harold J. Berman's *Law and Revolution* (1983), recently translated into French.[10]

I should remark, to conclude, that these facts provide an excellent illustration of what, for me, constitutes a structural trait of European culture, and that I have called elsewhere "eccentric identity": it is *intrinsically* that Europe is based on what is external to it. The relationship with the exterior is internal to it.[11]

PART V

Pricked Balloons

13]&··

Some Mediterranean Myths

The title proposed for the day's discussion in the colloquy that gave rise to this piece was "The Reflux of Utopias of Coexistence." For my part, I see this as something positive and a reason, if not to hope, at least to act. A U-topia—a "nowhere," a "non-place"—is in fact an illusion, and the first condition for realizing one's dreams is to wake up.

The Mediterranean is the object of an entire series of legends. They are for the most part rose-colored. They go from the best to the worst, from Paul Valéry or Albert Camus to Gilbert Trigano, from the "Mediterranean spirit" to Club Med.[1] "Dialogue," *métissage*, "multiculturalism"—all the slogans in vogue with the beautiful people of the media—are anchored in the Mediterranean space.

A Conclusive Experiment

The examples of multicultural cities or regions have not had a very positive historical fate. If we consider the past as a series of experiments to show whether certain solutions to social problems were viable, the experiment is hardly conclusive. All regions that once were multicultural have a tendency to cease being so. And that movement is not a recent invention.

On the northern shores of the Mediterranean, Sicily was taken by the Normans at the end of the eleventh century, and Andalusia was reconquered by the Christian north at the end of the fifteenth century. The last Muslims in Spain (the Moriscos) were expelled a little more than a century later, in 1610. And do we really have to mention Bosnia?

On the southern shores of the Mediterranean, Alexandria, a city peopled from its foundation by a mix of peoples in which Greeks and Italians joined with Egyptians, has been almost exclusively Arabo-Muslim in recent decades. With Algerian independence, most of the Spanish, the Italians, the Maltese, and the French who had settled in Algeria as colonists—along with Jews who had been there forever and had, in the majority, accepted the French citizenship that the loi Crémieux of 1870 offered them,—all moved to *la Métropole*, continental France.

A Not So Rose-Colored Past

Should we regret that past? It should not be painted in rosy hues. Coexistence was never equality. It was not always mutual respect, nor even always reciprocal knowledge. The modern colonization of Algeria did not produce a society in which those values reigned exclusively. The reader can guess that I am fond of understatement.

Further back in the past, Alexandria was also the site of the invention of anti-Semitism, beginning with Flavius Josephus's response to a pamphlet of Apion's.[2] The city is even—if I may be permitted an anachronism—the birthplace of the pogrom, well before Christianity had acquired political influence. The first anti-Jewish riots in history date in fact from the year 38 CE.[3]

Cordova, another city whose praises have been abundantly sung, is nonetheless also the city from which its two greatest thinkers were exiled, the Jew Maimonides and the Muslim Averroes, the second for reasons that are unclear. He had perhaps simply fallen into disgrace.[4] When still a child, Maimonides had to flee before the Almohads, who in 1148 had given non-Muslims a choice of conversion, exile, or death—an exceptional move in Islam. Cordova is one of those cities that reclaim, after their death, citizens who were hardly happy there during their lifetimes, as Salzburg claims Mozart or Vienna, Freud and Wittgenstein.

Generally speaking, there were the dominators and the dominated in medieval Andalusia. Jews and Christians remained *ahl al-dhimma*, second-class subjects, and were therefore subjected by the Muslim *sharia* to all sorts of restrictions. These humiliating conditions were not always applied with equal rigor in all times or places, but control was exercised by the dominators with a perfectly clear conscience: the point was to make the dominated understand that it would be in their interest to join the true religion. Those who refused to do so lived under a fully developed system of psychological humiliation. Ibn Khaldūn offers a detailed description of this situation in the fifteenth century.[5]

There were of course exceptions, at times spectacular ones. One that is cited ceaselessly is that of Samuel Ibn Nagrila, called "al-Nagid" (d. 1056). A Jew who became vizier of the kingdom of Grenada, one of the smaller kingdoms (*taifas*) that emerged from the disintegration of the Umayyad caliphate, and who is known in particular through Ibn Hazm's attacks on him. In general, however, the situation of the tribute-paying populations was not essentially different from that of their like in the East: their work supported a governing class with enough leisure to pursue cultural development.

I should note a historical fact that is interesting because it is an exception to the rule: Christian communities disappeared from the Maghreb around the eleventh century, whereas in the East such communities still remain as minorities today. This is the case with the Copts in Egypt (which is a pleonasm, given that "Copt" simply means "Egyptian"). It is also the case of various Christian groups in Syria, Lebanon, Iraq, and Iran.

The Mediterranean as a Past Reality

We can console ourselves about this sobering image of the Mediterranean space with a paradox: Europeans are only slightly Mediterranean. Before we go on, we will need to reevaluate the importance of the Mediterranean in the dialogue between cultures that is supposed to be a Mediterranean theme.

The Mediterranean, as such, only played a central role when there was one culture all around its shores. That happened only with the Roman Empire, the beginning of which can be dated to a few dozen years before the Roman political system changed from the Republic to the Principate. The decisive date is perhaps 67 BCE, when Pompey subdued the last of the Illyrian pirates, after which Rome had undisputed control of Mediterranean commerce.

With the Arab conquest of the southern shores of the Mediterranean, that cultural unity ceased. According to a familiar thesis formulated by the Belgian historian Henri Pirenne in the 1920s, that conquest marked the true end of the ancient world.[6] According to him, the rupture of Mediterranean unity resulted in a dual recentering of the two remaining halves, somewhat in the same way that cell division produces nuclei by mitosis. The capital of the Arab Empire moved from Damascus to Baghdad;

the center of gravity in the Roman Empire of the West moved north to Aachen (Aix-la-Chapelle). To be sure, historical investigation did not stand still after Pirenne, and some historians have stressed that the recomposition of world space effected by the Arab conquest had beneficial results for Mediterranean commerce, which was given a second wind after the barbarian invasions.[7] We need think only of what happened in the ports of the northern Mediterranean, Venice in particular.

But if a renewal of the sort took place in the Mediterranean, its motor force—or, to change the metaphor, its epicenter—was not Mediterranean.

Three Ways Out of the Mediterranean

It might prove amusing to devise a purely amateur narration of the history of the medieval and modern world as three successive ways to break out of the Mediterranean basin. In geographical terms, these were ways to leave the Mediterranean behind. In historical terms, they are also three outgrowths of ancient culture.

Those three successive moves to prolong and extend the Mediterranean were launched from three regions: (1) Byzantium, which opened up the Mediterranean toward the Black Sea via the Bosporus, the site of Constantinople; (2) Islam, which opened it up in the direction of the Indian Ocean though the Strait of Hormuz (the key port here is Basra); (3) modern Europe, which opened it out in the direction of the Atlantic through the Strait of Gibraltar and the English Channel (through Seville, London, and Amsterdam). These civilizations expanded by taking advantage of commercial routes leading out of the Mediterranean basin.

A distinction can be made between strait-worlds and isthmus-worlds. Byzantium was a strait-world; medieval Europe and the Islamic Empire were isthmus-worlds. Europe is the entire group of isthmuses between the Mediterranean and the Atlantic. The Islamic Empire is the entire group of isthmuses between the Mediterranean, the Indian Ocean, and the great inland seas, the Black Sea and the Caspian Sea.

History has favored the isthmus-worlds. Byzantium, caught in a vise between two isthmus-worlds, was finally absorbed by the Islamic Empire. The two medieval worlds that won the struggle for life were both worlds whose center of gravity had moved far from the Mediterranean. The center of the Arab Empire was perhaps first Medina, later certainly Damascus, then Baghdad, and with the Abbasids (750) that empire became at least as much Persian as Arab. The center of the Roman Empire of the East was no longer Rome but Constantinople, which can be considered Mediterranean only by stretching the definition. The center of the Roman Empire of the West, first with Charlemagne and later, more firmly, with the Ottonians, was no longer Rome, but Aix-la-Chapelle, a city far from the Mediterranean.

The Mediterranean as a Retrospective Dream of Europe

From this point of view, not only is Europe, as such, not Mediterranean, but it is highly anti-Mediterranean. It is the site of the most decisive thrust outward from the Mediterranean space. It is in fact from Europe that the reorientation of world commerce emerged, first sailing directly toward Asia around the African continent, then in the Atlantic, and, finally, throughout the entire globe.

Connected with this is the presence of the Mediterranean in the European imaginary, first in the form of a nostalgia and eventually as a trauma. It is perhaps precisely because of its hallucinatory status that its affective value is so great. To borrow a phrase of Proust's that may even be too well known: The only true paradise is always the paradise we have lost.[8]

In the history of European sensibilities, these nostalgias occur successively as they fix on different lands from one age to another. They are perceived as conserving, as if embalmed, the worlds that civilization has left behind. Thus Italy was for the Middle Ages and the Renaissance the depository of the Roman heritage; for German classicism, Greece was the conservatory of paganism (Schiller, Hölderlin); later, for industrialized Europe, Spain was seen as conserving medieval customs (Mérimée, Bizet).

For today's Europeans, Morocco, Tunisia, and even Egypt are perceived as conserving a world that contained a number of things that had to be suppressed in the modern rationalization of conditions of life in those lands: a world of forgotten sensations and of bright colors, sounds, and odors; a world of human relations founded on homage, hospitality, and so on. Hence the Orientalist dreams of many writers and painters. I might cite in this connection, drawing from a range of disciplines, the names of Gustave Flaubert, Ignaz Goldziher,[9] Marshal Lyautey, T. E. Lawrence, and Paul Klee, among others. Without mentioning the promises of the travel agencies.

As for Venice, it is for all Europeans the marvelous memory of a city neglected by the first capitalist economy, a splendid and pearly shell abandoned by a mollusk that proved capable of adapting to all forms.

Was There Dialogue among Mediterranean Civilizations?

In a literature that has become almost a literary genre, some have stressed the cultural exchanges that took place in the Mediterranean during the Middle Ages. I have evoked them myself elsewhere.[10] I have been well repaid (and I am in fact paid) for knowing about them.

There is an incontestable reality here, but we need to understand what is involved. Cultural elements borrowed by one civilization from another are realities. Moreover, this has been the rule for a very long time, in the Mediterranean area and throughout the world. In contrast, "borrowing" does not necessarily imply dialogue.

First, because a dialogue must be a two-way interchange. In the cultural domain, borrowings in the Middle Ages went one way only. The Christian North borrowed much from the Muslim South, but the latter knew little or nothing about the North and had little interest in it. The only medieval examples of reciprocal influences are within the Christian North, between Latins and Byzantines. And these are late. It is only in the fifteenth century that the Byzantines set themselves to translating Augustine, Boethius, and Thomas Aquinas.

But also, and more radically, the partners to a dialogue must at least be contemporaries. This is not the case, however. Thomas Aquinas was born twenty-seven years after the death of Averroes, and twenty-one years after that of Maimonides. We have only one example of dialogue in the authentic sense of the word, and its success was somewhat mitigated. I am referring to the treatise in which Ibn Sab'īn of Murcia (1217–1270) responds, between 1237 and 1242, to philosophic questions put to him by Emperor Frederick II. The Spanish mystic scolds the Christian emperor, correcting his questions in pedantic fashion, as if the ruler were a little boy—and incidentally giving him responses that do not shine for their originality.[11]

The Bad Side of History

Marx is quoted as saying that "history advances by its bad side." The authentic statement is somewhat muddier: "The bad side produces the movement which makes history by providing a struggle."[12] Here Marx returns to the Hegelian idea of a ruse of reason. In any event, Marx's statement has a certain plausibility, for in fact wars, and even crusades, have perhaps contributed more to the progress of culture than "dialogue" and other fashionable words.

Cultural influences are often the consequence of invasions. I shall give three examples, in chronological order.

First, the translations from Greek into Arabic made in Baghdad in the ninth century would never have been possible without the Arab conquest of the seventh century and the creation of an empire that included populations of a more advanced culture than the ruling group.

Next, the translations made by the School of Toledo in the twelfth century suppose the conquest of that city by the Castilians in 1085. Not only were the manuscripts a prize of conquest, but also the people who could read them—Jews who had remained in Toledo—were conquered. Two conditions had to be fulfilled for translations: a translator had to be available, and he had to be cultivated. As it happens, the Muslims who remained in the area were not from cultivated circles. In the struggle between Christianity and Islam, the Jews were more or less neutral, a situation that played some nasty tricks on them, with each camp accusing them of cooperating with the other side. In any event, remain they did, and they made translation possible.

And third, the transfer of the Islamic cultural heritage to the Jewish communities of Catalonia and Provence has rightly been emphasized. We have seen the importance of the Ibn Tibbon family and its three generations of translators from Arabic to Hebrew. That would not have occurred, however—or not so soon—if certain Jewish families had not decided to flee the Almohads' arrival in 1148 and settle farther north, on the Christian side of the frontier.

I shall end my list with a pretty but somewhat jarring example of the way in which things really happened. The library of the monastery-palace of El Escorial, not far from Madrid, contains a rich fund of Arabic manuscripts, as everyone knows. Nothing could be more normal, one might say, thinking of Andalusia. In reality, that collection is by no means made up of manuscripts found by the Christian kingdoms in their conquest of Andalusia. It came by ship. Which sends us right back to dreaming about the Mediterranean. The manuscripts are there because a ship owned by a bookseller was *shipwrecked* on the coast of Spain![13] Spain was not even its destination, and its cargo, although it was indeed confiscated, was hardly exploited before the seventeenth century.

Conclusion

All of this may seem very pessimistic. Georges Bernanos tells us that a pessimist is a sad imbecile, while an optimist is a merry imbecile. Given that fact, it is understandable that I would not like to give that impression here.

What it does seem useful to recall is that the dialogue between civilizations, whatever we want to call it, does not belong to the past, but to the future. It is not about memory, but will. We have no models. Admitting that fact might permit us to face today's problems where they lie. That would already be a first step toward resolving them.

14

Was There Any Dialogue between Religions in the Middle Ages?

I cannot give an exhaustive panorama of a question as vast as this and that exceeds my competence. All I hope to do is to pose it as best I can. In order to do this, I will have to present the overall context, describe the space and the orientations of an eventual dialogue, and point out the constraints that prevented it from developing more fully.

The Historical Context

We know—really know—very little about the beginnings of Islam. The oldest historical works written by Muslims were not set down until the ninth century, hence two centuries after the events they are said to narrate. The reports of those who were close to those events are just as slanted as the Muslim historians' accounts; they are more meager and incomplete; and they give us a totally different image of "what really happened." An attempt has been made to write the history of primitive Islam, for methodological reasons systematically ignoring everything that cannot be dated.[1] The writings in a number of languages of non-Muslim chroniclers have been gathered together, translated into English, and subjected to critical examination.[2] Not to mention somewhat risky but highly interesting attempts to see events of the seventh century in new ways that differ strikingly from traditional history.[3]

The earliest event to which we can assign a sure date is the Arab conquest. That historical fact set the stage on which the meeting between Islam and Christianity took place. The oldest document

that we have is a papyrus, a receipt dated to 643, written by an Arab func-
tionary for an Egyptian peasant, showing that he had paid his tax to the
conquerors.[4] That war of conquest seems to have been carried out like all
other wars. The Arabs were neither gentler nor more bloodthirsty than
earlier conquerors from the Assyrians to Alexander the Great.

The conquered areas included the Middle East and Egypt, which was
under Roman—we would say "Byzantine"—domination at the time; Persia, which had its own national dynasty; the southern shores of the Mediterranean basin; and Spain, which was dominated by the Visigoths. Except
for Persia, where Zoroastrianism was the national religion, the majority of the conquered populations (there is no way we can arrive at precise
numbers) were Christian.

The Arab conquerors could neither massacre that many people nor
convert them en masse and at one time. They had no intention of doing
either of these, what is more. That would have been a cruelty that killed
the goose that laid the golden eggs. According to a statement attributed
to ʿAli, the "protected" peoples were "a matter for the Muslims." Similarly,
the caliph ʿUmar is supposed to have written to Abu Obeyda: "If we take
those who are subjected and we share them between us, what would be
left for the Muslims who will come after us? They would not find, by
Heaven, anyone to talk to or from whose labor to profit!"[5]

In this way, a situation arose that contributed in essential ways in determining the possibility and the elaboration of a dialogue between religions. That situation was asymmetrical. There were Christians in the Muslim space. In the Islamic community, they occupied a place defined by law.
In contrast, in Christian lands there were, in theory, only Christians and
Jews. From the Islamic viewpoint, Christians were thus both "inside" and
"outside" their world. For the Christians, on the other hand, the opposite
was true: Muslims were only "outside" their world: only exceptionally and
temporarily did Muslims live on Christian soil.

When that did happen, it was where Christian armies occupied regions
that had been under Muslim domination. This concerned only the lower
strata of the Muslim population, however: peasants or artisans. The "intellectuals" seldom remained under Christian domination: linked with
power, they left with power. We have a number of examples of this sort of
situation. The frontier between Islam and the Roman Empire of the East
was not stable, and in the war between the latter and the caliphs, the front
line in Syria could shift quite quickly. In the tenth century, the Byzantines
once again had the wind in their sails. Towns such as Alep passed back
and forth from Christian to Muslim domination. In Europe, one might cite
certain regions of Spain after the conquest (or *reconquista*) of the Islamic

south by the Christian kingdoms of the north. This was true of Toledo in the reign of Alfonso the Learned, and of Sicily in the second half of the eleventh century, when the Normans took Messina in 1061, then, in 1072, Palermo.

After 1096 the Crusades roused only a weak and belated echo in the Muslim world. Thus the greatest intellectual of medieval Islam (and perhaps of all of Islam), Ghazali (d. 1111), who lived in the region, never alludes to the Crusades and seems not to have noticed them. It was only much later, in the nineteenth century at the earliest, that the Crusades were pinpointed as a symbol of the failed meeting between East and West.

The Social Context

Within these two domains, the context of encounters between religions was also asymmetrical. One particular religion was dominant in each one as what might be called (anachronistically) a "state" religion. Those who governed referred to that religion as one of the principles of their legitimacy. Thus permitting what we would call "freedom of thought" was out of the question. To seek its equivalent in the Middle Ages would be perfectly anachronistic.

The only exception, the one that proves the rule, and the only case of a political power that was neutral toward religions, comes from a situation that sprang up in a part of the Muslim world between 1258 and 1290. The first date is that of the taking of Baghdad by the Mongols. The victors were of several religions: they included Muslims, but also Nestorian Christians, Buddhists, and shamanists. The khans had no specific religion of their own to impose on the vanquished, and they imposed none. This created an atmosphere that encouraged, among others, the work of the Jewish physician Ibn Kammuna, who compared the three religions, showing enormous objectivity for the age.[6] That situation lasted until 1290, when the Great Khan of the moment decided to convert to Islam, the religion that had already been adopted by the majority of his new subjects.

The Islamic system of the *dhimma* consists in tolerating non-Muslim communities, provided that they possessed a holy book. In principle, "pagans" had only the choice between conversion and death. Jews and Christians were subjected to various measures explicitly designed to make them understand, by humiliating them, that it would be in their interest to adopt Islam. They had to pay a special tax and dress in a specific color—blue for Christians; yellow for Jews—and had to ride asses, not horses. Christians could not construct new churches and had to take care not to ring their bells or sing hymns too loudly. As for its social consequences, this system functioned somewhat like a lobster trap, in that it was easy to enter it and impossible to exit. People not only had the right to adopt the religion of the sovereigns, but were even encouraged to do so. On the other hand, it was strictly forbidden—in principle, under pain of death—to leave that religion in favor of another. Medieval Christianity subjected Jews to analogous rules, some of them before Islam arose and others inspired by Islam, such as wearing a round yellow emblem.

Rare exceptions aside, in the Middle Ages conversion came from on high. Leaders took the decisions in questions of religion—which also means in political questions—and the people followed the governing class. In this fashion, entire tribes that were called "barbarians" let themselves be baptized once their leader had declared himself ready to adopt Christianity. This is what happened with Clovis, and later on in the east and the north of Europe, ending with the Lithuanians, the last people to accept baptism, as late as in 1386.

The same model held for later conversions: for example, when Indonesia adopted Islam, the local rajah became a Muslim and his people followed en masse. An awareness of the independent value of the individual was at the time the exception rather than the rule. There is an example of just such an exception in a story related to the Arab conquest: a Muslim general passing a victorious tribe in review realized that its men were Christians. He demanded that the tribe pass over to Islam, the unique religion of the Arabs. All accepted except a certain Layth, who was martyred.[7] Without that act of courage, we would be totally unaware of this episode.

The Intellectual Context

There is an important and observable difference between the situation of Christianity and that of the Islamic world. In Christianity, each religious community has its own language of culture, which was, according to region, Greek or Latin. In Islam, even though the Christian communities long retained their own liturgical language (Coptic or Syriac), Arabic soon became the common language. It has been the language of administration since 685. As for the possibility of a dialogue between religions, the use of Arabic would have both positive and negative consequences. On the positive side, the presence in the Islamic world of a common language permitted easy communication. On the negative side, the non-Muslims could be understood without too much difficulty by their Muslim sovereigns, hence they had to be careful. The use of a different alphabet protected them only up to a certain point. A frontal attack against the dominant religion was just about unthinkable.

Such consequences become clear if we compare the situation of the Jews in Christian and Islamic lands. On Christian soil, both Jews and Christians used the local vernacular in their daily lives. But if we shift to the level of religious knowledge and focus on the social milieu of the clerics of each religion, the conditions of inner dialogue with Judaism become analogous to those determining the external dialogue between Islam and Christianity. The rabbis and the Christian clerics did not write the same language, but rather Hebrew, for the first, and Greek or Latin, for the second. The ulemas wrote in Arabic, whereas their Christian adversaries express themselves in Greek or Latin, resulting in a *dialogue de sourds* (a conversation of the deaf). Moreover, writing in one's own language offers a protection that allows the heterodox to say what they really have on their minds: Jews, for example, can circulate a *Toledot Yeshu*, a tract offering an anti-Christian version of the life of Christ. Things only become tense when converts put their new coreligionists on guard, telling them of the contents of the books in the religion of their fathers.

Even within Christianity, there are differences between East and West. Byzantium was fairly well acquainted with Islam, and this happened relatively soon, even before Islamic dogmatics had crystallized. Thus the polemical writings of John of Damascus, toward the middle of the eighth century, give a picture of the state of disputed questions in Islam at the time.[8] The Qur'an was translated into Greek in the ninth century in the interest of refuting it more efficaciously.

In contrast, Europeans knew Islam rather poorly. For them, Muslims were simple pagans. There were concrete reasons for this view. The first contact with Muslims opened a second front to the south at a time when Europe was already besieged by the Normans in the north. Since Europe believed that it represented Christianity, it considered its enemies, globally, to be pagans. There was little room for more subtle nuances in a tight situation. This explains the caricature still present in the *Song of Roland*: the "Saracin" is an idol-worshipper who adores three divinities, one of which is Muhammad.[9]

It was only in the twelfth century that the naive portrait-as-accusation gave way to a more nuanced view of the adversary. Peter the Venerable, the abbot of Cluny (d. 1156), had the Qur'an translated into Latin, along with other works that gave a more accurate and more detailed picture of Islam. This dossier, produced by the scholars gathered in Toledo, forms what is called the *collectio toletana*, but the manuscript that contains it circulated very little, and its contents were not printed until the sixteenth century.[10]

In the thirteenth century, some began to feel the need for a better acquaintance with Islam. The Franciscan Roger Bacon (d. 1292) included
in the ambitious program for reform that he submitted to the pope the
founding of language schools that would teach Arabic, among other languages. Raymond Martin, a Catalan Dominican, knew enough Arabic and
Hebrew to write his celebrated *Pugio fidei adversus mauros et judaeos* (1278),
the title of which indicates its polemic intent. Ramon Llull (1235–1316), a
Catalan born in Majorca—which had been reconquered not long before
his birth—took the trouble to learn Arabic in order to compose presenta-
tions of Christianity in Arabic for the use of Arabic-speaking people, all of
which have unfortunately been lost.

The Affective Context

What each of the two religions knew about the other is often quite scanty,
but not for the same reasons. It is important to realize what the obstacles
were. They were symmetrical but reversed. In a nutshell: the Christians
knew that they did not know much about Islam; the Muslims thought that
they knew Christianity.

For Christianity, Islam is something that should not have existed. Islam is unforeseen, something new and unexpected, hence paradoxical. As
Christians, they knew (or thought they knew) what Judaism was and what
paganism was, but they could not fit Muslims into any preexistent category. Islam was not pagan—in any event, it was monotheistic—it was not
Jewish, and even less was it Christian. This explains the sense of surprise
easily discernible among the Fathers of the Church who dealt with Islam.
John of Damascus, whom we have already met, considered Islam to be a
Christian heresy.[11]

None of this was true of Islam. For Islam, Christianity was something
well known, an old story. The Qur'an contains information about Christians: along with the One God, they worship other entities such as Jesus
and his mother. Christianity had been surpassed. Christians have refused
to recognize the definitive prophet who should be seen as perfecting their
religion. They missed the boat, so to speak. Moreover, the actual Christians who lived under Muslim domination were divided into sects that
exchanged anathemas, and since they were kept under a common humiliation, they did not seem to have anything interesting to teach Muslims.

These ways of viewing other religions had affective consequences for
each of them. We do not have the same feelings for the unknown that we
do for what is familiar to us. When relations were good between Islam

and Christianity, Christians viewed Muslims as an object of curiosity that could be fascinating, enfants terribles who could be regarded with indulgent tenderness; when relations were less good, they became an object of hatred and fear.

In similar fashion, when things were going well, Islam saw Christianity as an object of sympathy or treated it with the condescending affection that one has for a doddering old uncle who always repeats the same old stories. But it was not by any means an object of curiosity. Curiosity toward the other is, incidentally, a typically European attitude, rare outside of Europe and exceptional in Islam.[12] When things went badly, Islam felt much more scorn for Christianity than hatred.

In the final analysis, that attitude was directly dependent on the place that the two religions occupy in history. To put in flatly: one came before the other. But that order is not only chronological. It was also the object of reflection. Very soon—in fact, as soon as it was constituted as an independent dogmatics—Islam saw itself as a post-Christianity: the oldest texts of Qur'anic style that can be dated are the inscriptions on the Dome of the Rock in Jerusalem (691), which attack the Trinity. Islam sees itself as the final religion, the definitive religion, the religion that picks up from where both Judaism and Christianity leave off, in the sense of Hegel's *Aufhebung*, something that at once abolishes what went before it and takes over from what precedes and prepares it.

The Apologetic Literature

The best I can offer here is a rapid glance, for the most part from secondary sources, at the polemical and apologetic literature.

That literature is, for the most part, addressed to those who share the religion of the work's author. It is for internal use. There is no question of persuading the other to convert by showing him the beauties of one's own religion. Rather, such works are aimed at discouraging one's coreligionists from abandoning their faith in favor of another religion, the absurdities of which must be pointed out. This aim does not encourage objectivity, and even less does it attempt to understand the other's position with any sympathy.

The situation was not the same for Christianity and for Islam. Christianity had to distinguish itself from Judaism, paganism, Gnosticism, and its own heresies; it obviously had no need to define itself as distinct from Islam, which did not yet exist. When Islam entered on to the scene, Christian dogmatics had already been fixed for centuries. Islam, on the other hand, was obliged to define itself as distinct from a Christianity that was already there. The polemic against Christianity (and against Judaism) was not secondary for Islam; it was constitutive. Islam's first work of anti-Christian polemics is none other than its first work in general: the Qur'an.

Later on, polemics were made necessary, not despite conversions to Islam, but—paradoxically—by the very conversion movement itself. To become a Muslim was very easy. All one had to do was pronounce, before witnesses, a short formula of confession of faith (*shahāda*). The catechism to which one had to subscribe is brief and quite plausible, and Muslims were not in the habit of testing the convictions of neophytes. There were obvious advantages to this sort of attitude, but it also contained the danger of syncretism among those who converted as a mere matter of form or without really understanding what they were doing, and who sought to introduce into Islam as much of the content of their former religion as they could. Thus Islam feared it might dissolve into a vague composite religiosity. Polemics served to immunize Muslims against Christianity.

The contents of such polemics are always the same, propelled by the great themes of Christology, the Trinity, and the Bible. (Was it corrupted by those who passed it on or kept it intact? Is Muhammad predicted in it?) From time to time this literature takes on a social tinge, as when Muslims complain that Christians—physicians, for example—have too much influence in society. The theme of a historical corruption of Christianity by St. Paul appears only in the thirteenth century, with Abd al-Jabbār, who may have used some Judeo-Christian texts.[13]

Arguments recur as well. Christians asked: How does a religion come to power, peacefully or by force of arms? How can one recognize the authenticity of the mission of a prophet? Is that mission corroborated by miracles? Is the prophet set apart from other people by a particularly edifying mode of life? These seemingly purely historical questions are biased: the point was to bring out the military character of the expansion of Islam, the absence of miracles by Muhammad, and his active sexual life. In this genre of literature, all arguments are good, provided they strike the adversary. It is understandable that reading these texts does not give a very positive idea of human nature.

The mental attitude that today we consider to be the strict minimum for interreligious dialogue consists in an open mind and an effort to fully understand the interlocutor's position, even to understand it from the inside, in order to "put oneself in his place" by trying to view the other's tradition of origin with his own eyes. That attitude is excessively rare in the Middle Ages. Among the few examples that I know of, there is that of Peter Abelard, in his *Dialogue between a Philosopher, a Jew, and a Christian* (ca. 1140).

In one of his statements, the Jew complains of the humiliating situation in which his people live under Christian domination.[14] What is remarkable is not so much the content of this tirade, but rather the fact that it was written by a Christian. One might also cite a work of Honoré Bouvet, a monk of the late fourteenth century, in which the author places in the mouth of a Jew and a Muslim a cruel satire of the mores of Christians of his time.[15]

Dialogues?

Where dialogues are concerned, what we have is above all literary works presented in dialogue form, as if they reproduced real discussions between representatives of the various religions. They are fictitious, however. This is the case of the dialogue by Abelard, just mentioned, in which the philosopher is a Muslim, but a somewhat unorthodox one, given that he is content to cite only natural law.[16] It is also true of Ramon Llull's *Book of the Gentile and the Three Wise Men* (ca. 1276),[17] and of *De pace fidei*, a work written by Cardinal Nicholas of Cusa after the taking of Constantinople in 1453 that contains a multitude of nationalities as well as a variety of religions.[18] It is also true of the *Colloquium heptaplomeres* written by the French jurist Jean Bodin, probably around 1593, and that, as its title indicates, involves seven persons.[19]

Real dialogues between real people in which each one expresses his genuine convictions in his own words remain an exception. One disputation of this sort, supposed to have taken place in Baghdad in the ninth century, is often cited. In it, representatives of each opinion, even the least admissible ones, are presented as being able to express themselves freely, all having agreed to forgo arguing from a scriptural text, and so on.[20] This is all it takes to inflame the "multi-culti" imagination of our more sensitive souls. In fact, however, the anecdote comes from an author of ultra-strict orthodoxy, who relates it only to express how scandalized he is by such an abominable laxism. It is not impossible that he invented the whole thing, or at the least highly exaggerated it.

Most of the time, the context of such dialogues is polemical. I might signal the *disputatio* held May 30, 1254, at Karakorum in the presence of Möngke, the Great Khan of the Mongols. Several religions coexisted among the Mongols, as we have seen. Those who took part in the debates were the Flemish Franciscan Willem van Ruysbroeck (Rubruquis), the envoy of Louis IX and the pope, Nestorian Christians, Buddhists, and Muslims. Our only source is the Franciscan, who obviously and quite naturally casts himself in the leading role.[21]

Disputations (*wikkuah*) between Jews and Christians were institutionalized. The best known one is the great disputation of Tortosa (1414–16). In these jousts, the Jews were usually forced to participate to respond to the accusations of one of their own coreligionists passed over to Christianity. A certain equity ruled, however. Thus James I of Aragon, the king of Catalonia, although a Christian, declared that the winner of the disputation in Barcelona in 1263 was not the Christian convert Pablo Cristiani, but Nachmanides, the rabbi of Gerona, to whom the king even granted a monetary reward.[22] The fact remains, however, that the atmosphere in such debates was, as a whole, extremely disagreeable, with social pressure being exerted in one direction only. That social pressure increased, taking the form of riots, until the final expulsion of the Jews in 1492.

Public disputations between Christians and Muslims were not institutionalized and were rarer. There is no lack of legends, however: St. Francis of Assisi is a prime example. Ramon Llull made an attempt to arrange something of the sort at Bejaïa (Bougie) and was stoned to death for his pains. There may perhaps have been one case of a disputation of the sort, but our only source about it is a Spanish poem, *La Disputa que fue fecha en la çibdad de Feç delante del Rey e de sus sabios*, supposed to have been written at Nicosia, in Cyprus, in 1469.[23] The disputation reportedly ended with the conversion of the leading doctor of Muslim Law (*faqih*) of Fez. We can see a certain stylization in this story—to say the least. In any event, it is interesting that the dispute could have taken place on the topic of a book on the Trinity and the Incarnation by Ramon Llull, written in Arabic, and entitled *Condus* (perhaps *Qaddūs*, "most holy"). The overall climate of tolerance seems to correspond fairly well with the real situation at the time.

Conclusion: "Preaching to the Converted"

Thus, in the Middle Ages, true dialogues between Islam and Christianity were extremely rare, and, if we mean by that such dialogues as we would think desirable, simply nonexistent. Polemical literature was addressed to people who were already persuaded. The dialogue is more a literary genre than a reality. Attempts to treat the other with equity, and perhaps even to understand him, remained an exception. We have the right to dream, of course, that there will be such dialogues between religions in the future. But nothing authorizes us to project that dream back into the medieval past. Our desire to establish such dialogue may be noble, but it does not owe its nobility to any ancestral predecessors.

15]

Geocentrism as the Humiliation of Man

Everyone knows of the famous passage in Sigmund Freud's *A Difficulty in the Path of Psycho-Analysis* in which he, as the founder of that discipline, explains why some people are reluctant to admit the sexual etiology of neuroses.[1] Freud compares their reticence to negative reactions to two previous major scientific revolutions: the heliocentrism of Copernicus and Darwin's evolution of species by natural selection of the fittest. Those two thinkers, Freud tells us, dealt a blow to human narcissism that was difficult to accept, Copernicus by showing man that he is not the center of the universe, and Darwin by preventing man from considering himself the summit of the animal kingdom. As for Freud himself, he revealed to a proud reason that it is not even mistress in its own domain, but shelters a *folle du logis* much more compromising than imagination had ever been in the classical age.

I shall leave aside any examination of the general validity to be accorded to this sort of "paratheory," which claims to explain resistance to theory itself among those who criticize it. We can imagine arguments such as: You reject the theory of value appreciation because you are unconsciously influenced by bourgeois ideology, and so on.[2] Similarly, I shall barely touch on a difficulty inherent to these criticisms: either the cause of their resistance is feeble, in which case we might wonder why it had such a decisive hold on people's minds and for so long. Or else it was strong, in which case we might wonder how people surmounted it. I shall cast a veil over the narcissistic lack of modesty we note in Freud, who blithely compares himself to the greatest scientists of the past.

Thus I shall only examine Freud's text. And in doing so, I shall leave aside the second and third examples that he cites, which are evolution and psychoanalysis itself, about which I have nothing of special interest to say. I shall concentrate on the first, which is the significance of what has been called the "Copernican revolution."

Just to remind ourselves, in the passage where Freud speaks of the first wound that Copernicus is supposed to have inflicted on the geocentric pride of man, he states:

> In the early stages of his researches, man believed at first that his dwelling-place, the earth, was the stationary centre of the universe, with the sun, moon, and planets circling round it. In this he was naïvely following the dictates of his sense perceptions, for he felt no movement of the earth, and wherever he had an unimpeded view, he found himself in the centre of a circle that enclosed the external world. The central position of the earth, moreover, was a token to him of the dominant part played by it in the universe and appeared to fit in very well with his inclination to regard himself lord of the world. The destruction of this narcissistic illusion is associated in our minds with the name and work of Copernicus in the sixteenth century. . . . When [the heliocentric theory] achieved general recognition, the self-love of mankind suffered its first blow (*Kränkung*), the *cosmological* one.[3]

The Prehistory of an Error

Even if we limit ourselves to a study of this affirmation, we cannot claim to examine and evaluate it exactly unless we study the entire intellectual atmosphere before and after Copernicus, an immense task that I have no intention of taking on, particularly because Freud's statement has already been the object of a number of studies. I am not claiming that the discoveries in astronomy from the sixteenth century on had no effect on the modern mind.[4] I shall limit myself here to an examination of the central idea, which can be summarized thus: Geocentrism placed man at the summit of the perceptible universe; its replacement by another cosmological model dethroned man. This is a quite widespread view.

Freud did not invent the comparison between Copernicus and Darwin. To my knowledge, the first to have proposed it was Ernst Haeckel, an author of "popular philosophy" and champion of positivism at the end of the nineteenth century. Obviously, the founder of "monism" does not mention psychoanalysis. Nonetheless, he traces a parallel between Copernicus and Darwin.[5]

As for the notion that Copernicus dealt a first blow to narcissism, it would be fascinating to write the history of that idea, but to do so would, by any standard, exceed the limits of this essay. Still, without claiming to be exhaustive, I would like to mention two important examples. On the first evening of his *Entretiens sur la pluralité des mondes*, a summary of popular astronomy written in 1687, Fontenelle writes:

> Picture a German [!] named Copernicus. . . . Seized by a noble astronomical fury, he plucks up the Earth and sends her far from the center of the universe, where she was placed, and puts the Sun in the center, to whom the honor rightly belongs. He did well . . . to have put down the vanity of men, who had given themselves the greatest place in the universe, and I'm pleased to see the earth pushed back into the crowd of planets. . . . The same desire which makes a courtier want to have the most honorable place in a ceremony makes a philosopher want to place himself at the center of a world system if he can. He's sure that everything was made for him, and unconsciously accepts that principle which flatters him, and his heart will bend a matter of pure speculation to self interest.[6]

A century and a half later, the Italian poet Giacomo Leopardi expressed the same idea in his dialogue "Il Copernico." He chooses a tone of bitter irony rather than the urbane badinage of Fontenelle. The sun is tired of having to rise every morning to throw its light on a miserable grain of dust. Henceforth, the earth will have to make its own way and do its own work. Copernicus raises several objections regarding the new state of affairs, one of which is psychological:

> Up to now the earth has held first place in the universe, that is to say, the center; and . . . she has been sitting motionless without anything else to do but look around at all the other globes of the universe, the largest as well as the smallest, the shiny as well as the dark, which have kept rolling above and below and by her sides with such a hurry, such a concern, such a vehemence that we are stunned if we just think about it. And, thus, everything proved to be at her services, and the universe looked like a court where the earth sat as if on a throne, and the other globes all around her, like courtiers, guards, and lackeys, tending to one job or another. As a result, the earth has always believed herself to be the empress of the universe. . . . And then what shall I tell you about men? We consider, and shall always consider, ourselves the first and the supremely important among all earthly creatures. Each one of us . . . thinks of himself as an emperor; and not just of Constantinople or Germany or of half the earth—as the Roman emperors were—but as an emperor of the universe, an emperor of the sun, of the planets, of all the stars, visible

and invisible, and the ultimate cause of the stars, of the planets, of your illustrious Excellency, and of all things. But now if we want the earth to abandon that central place, if we make her run, revolve, bustle about continuously, do exactly the same job as has so far been done by the other globes, and, finally, become one of the planets—this will mean that her earthly majesty, and their human majesties, will have to clear the throne and abandon the empire. . . . It will upset all the steps on the ladder of the dignity of things and the order of beings; it will switch the purposes of metaphysics as well.[7]

We see by this that Freud was not alone. To the contrary, he had several precursors. I have preferred to concentrate my remarks on his text for two reasons. First, because Freud expresses his thoughts with great clarity and seriousness of purpose. Second, because his wide reputation contributed to giving his vision of the astronomical revolution a nearly total monopoly, to the point that it is accepted both among the mass of ordinary people and by many scholars, Rudolf Carnap, for example, who claims that the naturalization of psychology adds a fourth blow to human narcissism to the three humiliations already identified.[8]

Two Models of Centrality

However, my claim is that what Freud states in the passage quoted above is false. Even more, it is the contrary of what is true. There is no paradox here, nor do I make any claim to originality. Quite the contrary, all I intend to do (and I beg the reader's indulgence) is, as the French say, to beat down a door that stands wide open, at least for people competent in the field. The better part of the texts that I shall cite will be borrowed from secondary works, which will be identified as appropriate.[9] All I will do is to add a few texts that I have not found cited anywhere else in this connection. These will come, in particular, from authors who wrote in Arabic or in Hebrew, and who are often neglected by those who have considered the question. These texts seem to me to show that in the vision of the pre-Copernican world the earth's central place, far from being a place of honor, as is the case in intra-human relations, was not true where astronomy is concerned. In this context, the center was a modest place, if not the humblest place of all.

We need to take care to draw a distinction between the "common" vision of the world, that of the eternal "man in the street," and the results of philosophical and / or scientific investigation. What Freud claims for the "early stages of man's researches" was in fact the result of a long series of efforts on the part of Greek astronomers. The most ancient vision of the world that has come down to us does not consider the earth as being at the center, but rather as being "below," "here below," "under the sun," and under a sky that was taken to be the sublime sojourn of the divine beings: "*Ihr wandelt droben im Licht.*"[10] The earth is a place of humility and could not possibly be a center. The only conceivable centrality is that of a point in relation to a circle, both of which are situated on a flat plane. The center can be a place of honor when all eyes are turned to it, but that supposes that those gazes are admiring, for a whipping post is also highly visible. When it is the strategic point, the central place permits surveillance of the surrounding space, hence it helps to subject that space to one's power.

That sort of centrality is the practical experience of the man in the street, who (as is true of all of us) feels himself to be on a flat surface and for whom Copernicus's revolution never took place. That sort of centrality can give rise to metaphors: virtue is situated halfway between two extremes, and so on. The temptation is to transpose a notion that possesses an anthropological legitimacy to a consideration of cosmological facts and say that if the earth stands at the center of the world, it must occupy the place of honor. Freud makes precisely this unconscious transposition in the text that I have quoted, thanks to a process that must be called by its name: anthropomorphism.

As it happens, anthropomorphism is not self-evident. Indeed, what is true of a flat plane and its center does not apply to a sphere. The common vision of the world is of the surface: astronomical theory, however, applies to a spherical universe. The question is then to know whether, in the pre-Copernican vision of the world, the center of a sphere is given as high a value as that of a surface—in other terms, if the geometric center is also an axiological center. To respond to that question, we have to turn to the texts. We shall see a much more highly nuanced image emerge from them than has been commonly represented.

The Exceptions

The only ancient text that Hans Blumenberg cites, one in which the central position of man appears as a privilege accorded to him, is drawn from Seneca: "That you may understand how she [nature] wished us, not merely to behold her, but to gaze upon her, see the position in which she has placed us. She has set us in the centre of her creation, and has granted us a view that sweeps the universe (*circumspectus*)."[11] There is no question here of any supremacy of man: nature simply requires an observer in order to deploy all of its riches. The central position of that observer is not a privilege that he can grant himself, but rather a trace of the sovereign power of nature, which puts into his service a disciplined claque seated in the box seats.

To my admittedly limited knowledge, only one medieval author identified the two acceptations of centrality and founded the greatest value he granted to man on the fact that his sojourn, the earth, is at the center of the world. This one author is Saadia Gaon (882–942), a Jewish theologian and apologist (*mutakallim*) who lived in Baghdad in the first half of the tenth century. It is the way in which he sees things, which stands out from the general agreement of the Middle Ages, that makes him interesting for my purposes. The passage given here is from his principal work, the apologetic treatise *The Book of Beliefs and Opinions*:

> Even though we see that the creatures are many in number, nevertheless, we need not be confused in regard to which of them constitutes the goal of creation. For there exists a natural criterion by means of which we can determine which one of all the creatures is the end. When, then, we make our investigation with this criterion [as a guide], we find that the goal is man. We arrive at this conclusion in the following manner: Habit and nature (*binya*) place whatever is most highly prized in the center of things which are themselves not so highly prized. Beginning with the smallest things, therefore, we say that it is noted that the kernel lodges inside of all the leaves. That is due to the fact that the kernel is more precious than the leaves, because the growth of the plant and its very existence depend upon it. Similarly does the seed from which the trees grow, if edible, lodge in the center of the fruit, as happens in the case of the nut. But even if [a tree grows] from an inedible kernel, this kernel is located in the center of the fruit, no attention being paid to the edible portion, which is left on the outside to preserve the kernel. In the same way is the yolk of the egg in the center, because from it springs the young bird and the chicken. Likewise also is the heart of man in the middle of his breast, owing to the fact that it is the seat of the soul and of the natural heat of the body. So, too, is the power of vision located in the center of the eye because it is by means of it that one is able to see. When, therefore, we see that this situation appertains to many things and then find the earth in the center of the heaven with the heavenly spheres surrounding it on all sides, it becomes clear to us that the thing which was the object of creation must be on [*om.*] the earth. Upon further investigation of all its parts we note that the earth and the water are both inanimate, whereas we find that the beasts are irrational. Hence only man is left, which gives us the certainty that he must unquestionably have been the intended purpose of creation.[12]

Thus we have in Saadia—and, to my knowledge, only in him—a clear example of an anthropocentrism based on geocentrism. The text calls for a number of remarks. For one thing, Saadia's position is far from being a naive teleology: the details that he insists on adding about fruits, whose end is the inedible pit at the center and not its edible envelope, shows that he is looking at natural realities from their own viewpoint, not from that of human interest. For another, the force of his reasoning is troubled by a shift in criteria: once we get to the earth, we have to abandon the criterion of centrality to add, first, that of life, which permits him to eliminate the elements, then that of rationality, which excludes the dumb animals. The first criterion leads only to the greater value of the earth itself—which explains the textual variant that I noted in the body of the quotation.

It is also worth noting that later authors criticized Saadia on this point, and severely.[13] The sharpest criticism and also the best known is that of the great traveler and scholar of biblical criticism Abraham Ibn Ezra (1092–1167). The most pertinent passage that I have been able to locate is included in a long digression of the variant (*shittah akheret*) of his *Commentary on the Pentateuch* on the first verse of Genesis. The background context of the passage is a general critique of anthropomorphism, in particular of the idea that man is superior to the angels, a notion to which Ibn Ezra returns elsewhere.[14] He begins by recalling the minuscule size of the earth, almost a geometric point in the universe. Next he subjects Saadia's two examples (the apple seed; the egg yolk) to stinging criticism: "What he alleges, that what is precious in the fruit of the apple tree is the seed, which conserves the species, is not a proof either, because it [the apple] is a composite, whereas this is not the case of the heavens. Moreover, the fruit of the apple tree that passes into action is more precious than what exists in power of being. And what he says, that the chick emerges from the red of the egg—that is, from the yolk—is false, because the yolk is nourishment for the chick."[15] As we can see, and unfortunately for our purposes, Ibn Ezra does not focus his criticism on the supposed connection between the central position and the enhanced value to be attributed to whatever occupies that position.[16]

Geometrical Centrality and Axiological Centrality

Thus Saadia remains an exception. Indeed, the vision of the world that dominated his age and on which his critics founded their remarks is quite different. In the ancient world, several cosmological schemas competed for acceptance with no clear winner.[17] Classical antiquity, on the other hand, agreed on a common model, which it transmitted to the Middle Ages, where it was favorably received by both the clergy and the laity, as far as we can judge.[18] This was Aristotle's vision of the world, corrected by Ptolemy. In his De caelo, Aristotle had explained that the earth, although situated at the geometric center of the universe, does not deserve the dignity that is due to central things in the human domain. In an astronomical context, the center is quite the opposite of a place of honor. In the context of a polemic against the Pythagorean idea that fire, the noblest of the elements, must have the central place, Aristotle draws a careful distinction between the center as a purely geometric notion and the center as the heart or ontological nucleus of a reality.[19]

Thinkers in the Aristotelian tradition followed their master. This was true of the commentators, whom I will cite here rather than copying Aristotle's text itself, which is easily available. In the fourth century, Themistius developed Aristotle's distinction between the center of an animal, strictly speaking, and the geometric center of its body. He gives an example: the geometric center of an animal is its liver, whereas its "substantial middle" (emtsa' 'atsamī), higher in dignity, is its vital force, or its heart.[20] In the early sixth century, Simplicius introduced an analogous example, which he develops in a way that interests our purpose directly. He states: "In the same way in the case of the whole cosmos it turns out that the central point [kentron] is the centre [meson] of the spherical magnitude and body, but it is necessary to seek something else as the most honorable [part] analogous to the heart, namely the centre; and this is not the central point but rather the fixed sphere because it is the starting point of the being of the cosmos and carries around the other spheres [fixed stars?] with it and contains the whole corporeal nature. Here is where one should seek what is most honourable."[21] One thing to notice in this passage is the distinction that Simplicius makes, and which might at first seem surprising, between the "middle" and the "center." The "middle" is not the "center," but rather, and surprisingly, the periphery. This distinction between two types of centrality remained canonical.[22] I shall return to the reversal of center and periphery that it entails, and that seems to us paradoxical.

The Center as "Low"

Among authors who were neither commentators nor disciples of Aristotle, or who were so only quite indirectly, we find a similar view of the center. For them, "at the center" means, above all, "below." This occurs quite clearly in Plotinus: "In every living being the upper parts—head, face—are the most beautiful, the mid and lower members inferior. In the Universe the middle and lower members are human beings; above them, the Heavens and the Gods that dwell there; these Gods with the entire circling expanse of the heavens constitute the greater part of the Cosmos: the earth is but a central point, and may be considered as simply one among the stars."[23]

This passage contains the main themes that I intend to treat in the remainder of this essay. The first of these is equating the center with the "low": if the center is not the center of a two-dimensional figure, but of a sphere, it is also its innermost point. In the case of the cosmic sphere, the interior is by that token inferior, and of an inferiority that is absolute, not relative, because each point on the circumference is "above" the center. Macrobius expresses this notion with perfect clarity: "That which is the center is in the middle, and in a sphere only that which is in the middle can be at the bottom (*In sphaera . . . hoc solum constat imum esse quod medium est*)."[24]

For medieval thinkers, the part of the universe that we spontaneously call its "center" is in reality the low point. For them that notion was the most precise and the most pertinent, both for astronomical information and for the imagination. Many scholars have remarked on this.[25] Equating what is central with what is low occurs in a number of authors, either explicitly or implicitly. What follows are several examples, not in chronological order, but following the idea's logical order of development.

(1) The Stoics: "Under the moon [can be found] the [sphere] of the air which is borne by it [?], next that of the water, and finally that of the earth, situated around the central point (*semeion*) of the universe, which is below (*katō*) everything, while what departs from it is on high up to what is in a circle [around it] in all directions."[26]

(2) Biruni: "At the center of the sphere of the Moon is the earth, and this center is in reality the lowest part."[27]

(3) Pliny the Elder: "The earth is the lowest and central object in the whole."[28] The interest in this passage lies in the way it turns around the relationship of the two notions.

(4) William of Conches (1100–1154): "Earth is the element placed in the middle of the world and for that reason at the lowest point. . . . The configuration of our world resembles that of an egg. As in the middle of the egg is the yolk and on every side of it the white, around the white the skin, around which is the shell, outside of which there is nothing more of the egg, so in the middle of the world there is the earth, all around it from every part water flows, around the water there is air, around which is fire, outside of which there is nothing."[29]

Each time that a thinker of late antiquity or the Middle Ages sketched out his vision of the world, the earth was at the bottom, at the extreme lower limit of being. The earth is the farthest point that can be reached by the divine generosity and on which that generosity could spread its bounty: "All the powers of the gods, taking their origin above (*anōthen*) and proceeding through the appropriate intermediaries, descend even to the last existents and the terrestrial regions."[30] It was not even necessary to recall that the earth stands at the center; it was enough to say that it was below.

The "lowness" of the earth was more important than its central position. Thus when Avicenna wants to present a summary of his vision of the physical universe, the first idea that comes into his head in his hasty notes is not that we are at the center of everything, but that we are "below everything."[31] I am maintaining this literal translation even though it is slightly misleading in its ironic implication. Still, it renders the sentiment of inferiority that an inferior situation in space implies.

Thus I can conclude, with A. H. Armstrong, that "geocentric cosmology did not lead the ancient astronomers and philosophers to a man-centered view of the universe, an exaggerated view of man's importance in the scheme of things. It led them rather to stress his smallness, insignificance, and lowly position in the cosmic order."[32]

From this viewpoint, the center can be thought of in two fashions, which are in no way mutually exclusive. It can appear as a mathematical point without any particular dignity.[33] But it can also seem to be the lowest point, with the result that whatever occupies that point is systematically devalued, beginning with the element that is borne by its weight, which is earth, of which this globe that we call, precisely, "earth" is but the condensation.

The Earth as the Coarsest Element

The devaluation of the element of earth can be seen everywhere. I shall cite only three examples, which come, respectively, from the pagan world, the Islamic world, and the Christian world.

(1) In his commentary to Plato's *Timaeus*, Proclus writes of the All: "The lowest element [the farthest] is the middle (*meson*), encompassed on either side by more divine ones. For the most enmattered (*enulotaton*) and densest (*pakhutaton*) thing reclines in the middle as a result of the creative process (*demiurgia*)."[34]

(2) In their "encyclopedia" (*rasāʾil*) of popular philosophy, the group

known as the "Brethren of Purity" of Basra present a compendium of what the cultivated man of the ninth and tenth centuries was supposed to know. They come back time after time to the structure of the universe, a concentric stacking up of spheres in which the earth occupies the lowest point: "The earth is the center. It has the coarsest substance and [is] the most compact of all the bodies. . . . It is the roughest body and the most obscure, because it is found so far from the sphere that encloses everything."[35]

(3) Thomas Aquinas (1225–1274) states: "And for that reason, in the whole universe, and like the earth, which is contained by all [the spheres], and which is found, as far as place, in the middle, is that of the bodies that is to the highest point material and the most vile (*ignobilissima*), just as the last sphere is to the highest point formal and the most noble and, among the elements, fire is the one that has the most the nature of a container and of a form."[36]

One way to highlight the concrete realization of this devaluation of the earth is to recall that "down" is the direction in which bodies fall. It is thus not surprising that of all the elements, earth, compact and opaque as it is, should be the coarsest, and that it should attract all that is coarse in the universe, like a universal dustbin. This can be seen in a passage from Macrobius: "As a result of the downward rush of matter, there was that vast, impenetrable solid, the dregs and off-scourings (*defaecatis*) of the purified elements, which had settled to the bottom, plunged in continual and oppressing chill, relegated to the last position in the universe, far from the sun. Because this became hardened it received the name *terra*."[37] A metaphor of capital importance is introduced here: that of impurities deposited at the bottom of a bottle or a barrel. It helps us to imagine how a coarse matter must necessarily arrive at the lowest point in reality. The image had a numerous posterity. It even served to express the general law of a vision of the world in which the universe is a system of concentric spheres. This is the case, for example, in a passage of Miskawayh, a Persian historian and man of letters of the early eleventh century: "Each of these spheres is in relation to the sphere that covers it like a dregs (*thufl*) and an impurity (*kadar*) for it."[38]

One could also cite the anonymous neo-Pythagorean author cited by Photius: "Necessarily, evil also is found in the place that surrounds the earth, because the latter occupies the lowest rank in relation to the entire universe and it is appropriate to receive its dregs."[39] Another text that merits being cited is a Jewish work of piety of the early fourteenth century in the genre of *De contemptu mundi*: "They make this earth, placed in the centre, resemble a miserable cavern into which is poured the superfluity of uncleanness, and the filth of nature."[40] Finally, Albertus Magnus, Swabian as he was, does not hesitate to offer an energetic image: "The earth is in fact like an excrement (*faex*) among the simple bodies and, among the elements, the fire is the noblest and has the most form."[41]

The earth's central position, far from being a place of honor for it and for its inhabitants, is instead a place of relegation and scorn. This is expressed magnificently by Maimonides, in a text that has the interest of reflecting the general attitude that I am trying to reconstruct here, in which he reverses the usual analogy between the animals as microcosms and the universe as the macrocosm:

> The heart of every living being possessing a heart is in its middle; thus the other ruled parts surround it so that the utility deriving from them should extend to it wholly in that it is protected and safeguarded by them in such a way that harm coming from outside cannot rapidly reach it. Now in the world as a whole, the position is inverse. Its nobler part surrounds its inferior part, for the former is secure against receiving an influence from what is other than itself. And even if it were capable of receiving such an influence, it would not find outside itself another body that could influence it. Accordingly, this part occasions an overflow into what is inside it, whereas no influence reaches it in any respect nor any force deriving from bodies other than itself. With regard to this point there is also a certain similarity. For in the living being, a part is less noble than other parts to the extent to which it is far off from the ruling part, whereas other parts are nearer to the latter. The position in the world as a whole is the same. For whenever the bodies are near the center, they grow dimmer and their substance coarser, and their motion becomes more difficult, while their light and transparency disappear because of their distance from the noble, luminous, transparent, moving, subtle, and simple body—I mean heaven. On the other hand, whenever bodies are near the latter, they acquire some of these characteristics because of their proximity to it and achieve a certain superiority over what is lower than they.[42]

Alain de Lille expresses the same reversal of perspective in an extremely interesting image: "Man is like an outsider (*alienigena*) inhabiting the suburbs (*suburbium*) of the world." Here the world is compared to a city, the center of which is occupied by the palace of the king, or the heavens above. We live outside the walls, in the suburbs, if not in the shantytowns, like the dispossessed. C. S. Lewis, who discusses this text, concludes: "The medieval model is, if we may use the word, anthropo-peripheral. We are creatures of the Margin."[43] In any event, the image is all the more remarkable because Alain de Lille (as Lewis does not note) continues, offering a parallel with the Platonic three-part division of the soul and its equivalents in the human body, summarized in the *Timaeus*: the head is the "citadel of reason" and shelters wisdom, while the body's midsection contains the heart, the "chamber of the bodyguard," and is the site of "courage and spirit," of magnanimity—and of the angels. The suburbs where the desires are lodged are delicately called "the liver" (*renes*), rather than "the entrails." Thus we are living in the bowels of the universe—an image that we will have occasion to see again.

A passage from Dante is equally eloquent in this context. In it the celestial traveler is contemplating a vision of an order in which God is at the center, a vision that supposedly presents the spiritual world as reflecting the corporeal world. The traveler recalls, as if it were so evident that he is embarrassed to mention it, that normally what is most worthy is found at the periphery:

> but from our world of sense we can observe
> the turning of the spheres are more God's own,
> the further from its center they revolve.[44]

Far from being a place of pride, the earth's place is humble. This is what the Venerable Bede says: "The which [the earth], situated at the center or at the pole of the world / universe, like the heaviest, occupies among the creatures the humblest and most central place (*humillimum . . . ac medium locum . . . tenet*), while water, air and fire precede it toward the high by the lightness of their nature as by their position."[45]

Man in the Deepest Dungeon

Where the earth is situated has disagreeable consequences for those who inhabit it. To quote Cicero: "Do we not also understand that everything in a higher position is of greater value, and that the earth is the lowest thing, and is enveloped by a layer of the densest kind of air? Hence for the same reason what we observe to be the case with certain districts and cities, I mean that their inhabitants are duller-witted than the average owing to the more compressed quality of the atmosphere, has also befallen the human race as a whole owing to its being located on the earth, that is, in the densest region of the world."[46] Cicero is alluding here to the theory of climates: the subtle air of Attica produces brighter people, the thicker air of Thebes explains the proverbial dullness of the Thebans. Men in general, however, because they have been placed on the earth, are the Boeotians of the universe.

Ibn Tufayl (d. 1185) expresses the same idea more brutally: "The whole was like an animal. The light-giving stars were its senses. The spheres, articulated one to the next, were its limbs. And the world of generation and decay within it was like the juices and wastes in the beast's belly, where smaller animals often breed, as in the macrocosm."[47] In other words, man at the center of the universe is like a dung beetle on a cow pie.

That situation is humiliating, we would all agree. This was also the opinion of a philosopher of an earlier generation, Ibn Bājja (d. ca. 1138), who quotes an otherwise unknown poet by the name of Ibn al-Jallāb: *"Muhit as-samawāti awlā binā / fa-madhā al-khulūd ilā 'l-markaz."* The Spanish scholar who edited this text, Miguel Asin Palacios, follows his usual custom of paraphrasing more than translating, but he expresses the idea perfectly: "The celestial sphere that surrounds the cosmos is the worthiest place for us, but what will it be like to live eternally at the center of the sphere?"[48]

From Humiliation to Humility

Humiliation can be suffered passively. It can also be accepted and taken on as a means for acquiring the virtue of humility. In a general way, cosmological themes are not rare in the context of exhortations to humility: man is invited to reflect on his smallness and the lowness of his position in the universe. This theme did not wait for the enlargement of the known world that occurred with the discovery of astronomical instruments or the terror inspired by "the eternal silence of infinite space." To the contrary, it moved seamlessly out of the Middle Ages into the modern age. One case in point, to pick an example, is the *Duties of the Heart* of Bahya ibn Paquda, doubtless the most famous and the most broadly read work of Jewish spirituality of all time. Although man is for Bahya, as for the majority of medieval thinkers, the goal of creation, he never offers man's place in the physical universe as an argument that would speak in support of his value in the eyes of God. To the contrary, man is almost nothing when compared to the celestial spheres.[49]

This idea is rendered forcefully by Abraham, the son of the great Moses Maimonides: "Furthermore one must regard His statement [God is taken here to be the author of the Bible], exalted be He, at the end of the verse: 'That I am the LORD who exercise mercy, justice and righteousness in the earth' (Jeremiah 9:23). For that is something the consideration of which conduces necessarily to extreme humility, because the earth and what is in it are the least and smallest creatures in comparison with the heavenly world [li-anna 'l-arda wa-mā fihā aqallu 'l-mawjūdāt, wa-asgharu-hā bi-'l-nisbati li-'l-'ālami 'l-'alawiyyi], wherefore His solicitude for its denizens is surprizing."[50]

When St. Bonaventure proposes to show how Christ is in seven ways the middle (medium) of all things, his third point involves the middle as distance. This is the earth, "clearly the center . . . the lowest, and of modest size," which receives the full influence of all the celestial bodies. Similarly, the Son of God did not only come to the surface of the earth, but descended to its center (to Hell), thus making possible salvation by the humility of the cross, which symbolizes that centrality.[51]

Meister Eckhart introduces a cosmological element into the structure of his spiritual doctrine, but he transposes the paradox of the Incarnation to the level of the birth of God in the soul. He integrates this paradox into a dialectical game that reverses values, in the spirit of the Magnificat: "He hath put down the mighty from their seat, and hath exalted the humble and meek." In a sermon in German, Eckhart illustrates this point with a strange image: "The earth is the farthest of all from the sky and has crept into a corner, being ashamed. She would like to flee the beautiful heavens from one corner to the other, but what would her refuge be? If she were to flee downwards, she would come to the sky. If she flees upwards, she cannot escape either. It [the sky] chases her into a corner and presses his power into her, making her bear fruit. Why? The highest flows into the lowest."[52] One might prefer to this description of a cosmic ravishment the more peaceful tone of another of his sermons: "This star [the one star that is above the sun] not only flows into the sun; rather, it flows through the sun, through all the stars to the earth, making her fruitful."[53] The position of the earth at the bottom of the world is the reason for the presence of its most remarkable gifts, the precious metals. Similarly, the man who humbles himself attracts divine grace in such an irresistible way that it cannot be prevented from flowing into him.

All of these texts explicitly stress the idea of humility: the fact that we live on the earth, far from urging us to sentiments of pride, ought, to the contrary, to lead us to humility and gratitude toward God. God has raised up man by tearing him away from his indignity, for Jews and Muslims, by giving him His Law; for Christians, by incarnating himself. The grace that God grants to man in this fashion is all the more extraordinary because man has no special reason to attract the attention of God and should, in fact, normally arouse divine scorn. This attitude is not exclusive to the Middle Ages: we can find a trace of it as late as in Schelling: "What scandalizes many people [is] that the sojourn of man is not those proud children of heaven who might in some fashion esteem themselves superior to human things, but rather the earth, well below. It is about this that it is written: 'To the humble he gives his grace.' God has thought so much of man that he has contented himself with a purely terrestrial man."[54]

Such a view of the earth persisted even after Copernicus had proposed his hypothesis, for example in Montaigne (1533–1592), who knew of the Copernican thesis. For Montaigne, the creature man "feels and sees himself lodged here, amid the mire and dung of the world, nailed and riveted to the worst, the deadest, and the most stagnant part of the universe, on the lowest story of the house and farthest from the vault of heaven, with the animals of the worst condition of the three [those that walk, fly, or swim]; and in his imagination he goes planting himself above the circle of the moon, and bringing the sky down beneath his feet."[55]

Heliocentrism as a Promotion

The heliocentric hypothesis, proposed in 1540, was thus received in various ways. I shall permit myself to say only very little about it, for a large number of historians have already studied the reception of the Copernican theory.[56] We need to remember that it remained a hypothesis without physical verification until the mid-eighteenth century. One might wonder whether the most widespread reaction to it might not have been, quite simply, no reaction at all. I am not speaking here of uncultivated people, who would not even have gotten word of the new theory. I am thinking of those who reacted with a more or less ironic indifference. I shall offer only one example of this here, quite simply because I cannot remember having seen it cited anywhere. Thomas Browne concludes his *Religio medici* (ca. 1635) by saying that there is no happiness under the sun, citing in support of his statement the familiar passage from Ecclesiastes. But he adds a revealing parenthesis: "There is no happiness under (or, as *Copernicus* will have it, above) the Sunne."[57] Where have anguish, humiliation, woundedness gone? Everything is turned into a witticism. Do we laugh at what anguishes us?

The Copernican hypothesis, far from being considered a wound, was felt as a flattering promotion: instead of crouching in a dungeon, man was henceforth the inhabitant of a neighborhood as chic as the sun's.

Heliocentrism was felt as a promotion accorded to the earth, even before Copernicus, by Nicholas of Cusa, for whom the heliocentric theory was simply one possibility. In a chapter on the rehabilitation of the earth, we read: "It is not true that the earth is the lowliest and lowest. For although [the earth] seems more central with respect to the world, it is also for this same reason nearer to the pole. . . . Therefore, the earth is a noble star which has a light and a heat and an influence (*influentia*) that are distinct and different from each other star. . . . Furthermore, the influence which [it] receives is not evidence establishing its imperfection. For being a star, perhaps the earth, too, influences the sun and the solar region. . . . And since we do not experience ourselves in any other way than as being at the center where influences converge, we experience nothing of this counter-influence (*refluentia*)."[58] It is worth noting that, in relation to knowledge, our central place on the earth is more a handicap than an advantage here.

After Copernicus's work had been published, some wondered whether the earth merited a place of honor that put it on the same plane as all the other celestial bodies, and even the sun. Drawing this consequence of the heliocentric idea was not to speak in favor of Copernicus, but rather to raise an objection to him. This is implicit in the statement of the Reformation figure Philip Melanchthon: "*Terram etiam inter sidera collocant.*"[59] Others were clearer about their objections. Thus the Italian Francesco Ingoli brandished an entire arsenal of arguments against Galileo. One of these was drawn from "theological science" (*doctrina theologorum*): the earth has to be at the center of the world, because Hell, the sojourn of the Devil and the damned, is situated at its center.[60] The argument is quite explicit in John Wilkins, who invokes an argument deduced "from the vileness of our earth, because it consists of more sordid and base matter than any other part of the world; and therefore must be situated at the centre, which is the worst place, and at the greatest distance from those purer incorruptible bodies, the heavens."[61]

We find the same argument, and even Melanchthon's expression, but this time used in a positive sense, in the writings of a decided partisan of Copernicus, Galileo, who has his spokesman, Salviati, say: "As for the earth, we seek rather to ennoble and perfect it when we strive to make it like the celestial bodies, and, as it were, place it in heaven, from which your philosophers have banished it."[62]

Conclusion

The Italian historian of science Paolo Rossi, whom I have already cited, quotes these texts, adding a disillusioned remark:

It is often useless to cite the texts, and many true statements seem destined to fall into the void when they contrast with the more diffused *idola theatri*. To read the digressions of novelists, essayists, journalists and intellectuals of various kinds after the space projects and the landing on the moon, and to read the pages of many historians and philosophers, it would seem that geocentrism and anthropocentrism have always been indissolubly welded together. The acceptance of the astronomical doctrines of Copernicus' hereby seems to have implied the renunciation of an anthropocentric world-view as such. Lovejoy unsuccessfully devoted many pages of his major historical work to demonstrating the falsity of these associations.[63]

I have done nothing but pick up on what Arthur Lovejoy, Paolo Rossi, and many others set out to do. Why should I hope to have more success than they?

16

Was Averroes a "Good Guy"?

Averroes has not been lucky. He is not the only Arab philosopher to be in the same fix. Farabi, who was perhaps greater than Averroes, was only rarely translated in the Middle Ages, hence was not widely known in Europe. Averroes was not well received in the Arab world, which almost totally forgot him after his death. In contrast, he was translated and commented upon, and quite quickly, by both Christians and Jews of the northern Mediterranean. What is most curious, however, and what makes him unique is the paradox that in Europe Averroes was unlucky even when he was lucky.

The Good Arab

In appearance, in fact, fortune smiled on him. All the more so because he narrowly escaped death. For a long time he was a personage of legend, and of black legend at that. Was he guilty, as Thomas Aquinas stated, of being more the corruptor of Aristotelian philosophy than its interpreter?[1] He was accused of impious declarations: "May my soul die a philosopher's death" (*mouriatur anima mea morte* [or *mortem*] *philosophorum*).[2] Was he not the damned author of the terrible treatise "On the Three Impostors," in which humanity was duped by a shepherd, a physician, and a camel driver, immediately recognizable as the founders of the three monotheistic religions?[3] The book was as famous as it was elusive—that is, until people tired of looking for it and decided to write it (in several versions, what is more) in the seventeenth century.

The negative view of Averroes changed with Ernest Renan's monograph and changed even more after the publication of Léon Gauthier's works about him.[4] Averroes became a good sort of Muslim, a nice man, in the Hollywood sense of a "good guy." There was a genuine Averromania. Even recently he has been the hero of a film, and now that the French Republic, one and indivisible, has cast him in the role of the good Arab, he stands ready to serve. After having created moderate Islamists and called them representative, the Republic now offers us their intellectual equivalent, projecting back to the Middle Ages the academic version of the yes-man.

A patent sign of that consecration is that Averroes has just made his official entry into the French university. He has of course long been included among the authors about whose works candidates for the *agrégation* in philosophy who offer Arabic as a foreign language could be interrogated in their oral examination. This has enabled me to have had the pleasure of teaching him. From now on, however, Averroes is on the list of authors whose works may be presented at the philosophy oral exams for the *baccalauréat*.[5]

I greet this news with *mixed* joy. What work could students offer? Common sense requires a text translated in French, commercially available, of a reasonable length, and of a level of difficulty accessible to college-age youngsters. Only one work responds to these requirements, and it is the *Decisive Discourse*. A good translation by Léon Gauthier was republished not too long ago, but it is now out of print.[6] The more recent translation by Marc Geoffroy, with a long essay by Alain de Libera, has now appeared in paperback.[7] Both of these men, who are incidentally scholars of an irreproachable competence, are thus assured a lifetime income.

A Marginal Work

Thus, more by the force of things than as a result of careful thought, Averroes has been brought down to one text alone.

We need to pause for a bird's-eye view of Averroes' entire output. The sage of Cordova commented on all the available works of Aristotle at least once, and on occasion three times. For each of these nineteen works, he wrote a summary or "epitome" (*jawāmiʿ*). He wrote a paraphrase (*talkhīs*) of sixteen of them. Five works (*Posterior Analytics, Physics, De caelo, De anima*—546 pages of Latin in the Crawford edition–and *Metaphysics*—1,736 pages of Arabic in the Bouyges edition) were treated to a "great" commentary (*tafsīr*). The latter dealt with Aristotle as Tabarī and others had done for the Qur'an: the passage to be commented on is first reproduced as a whole, then given again, phrase by phrase, and explicated. These works have come down to us only partially in the original Arabic, but thanks to Hebrew and Latin translations that fill in the blanks of the Arabic text, we possess them all. Their explications are profound and precise.

Averroes also wrote a voluminous refutation of Ghazali (588 pages of Arabic in the Bouyges edition), and some philosophic monographs: *On the Substance of the Sphere, On the Conjunction, On the Beatitude of the Soul,* and so on. Finally, outside the philosophical field, he composed a voluminous work on the law (two volumes of some 500 pages each in the English translation) and some medical works (270 pages in Spanish).

This means that we have before us a thinker of imposing stature and universal genius. The problem is that with the *Decisive Discourse,* the Averroes of the candidates for bachelor's degrees is reduced to a portion of his entire work that can be estimated as being something between one-hundredth and one-five-hundredth of his entire oeuvre.

Moreover, the *Decisive Discourse* is the first panel of a diptych whose second half, the *Unveiling of Methods of Demonstration Regarding the Principles of Religion,* which has long awaited an integral translation into French, is some four times its length.[8] In the edition in Arabic, the *Decisive Discourse* runs to twenty-six pages, and the *Unveiling* to just under one hundred.

The *Decisive Discourse* had very little influence in the European Middle Ages. It never had the honor of a translation into Latin, with the exception of a brief appendix translated into Latin as "Epistula ad amicum" in the *Pugio fidei* of the Dominican Raymond Martin.[9] The hypothesis of the Spanish Arabist Miguel Asin Palacios that Thomas Aquinas knew of the theological thought of Averroes through his fellow Dominican Raymond Martin, first put out in 1904, is still cited by Marc Geoffroy, who neglects to mention that the idea was refuted as soon as the book appeared.[10] Be that as it may, the *Pugio fidei* dates from 1278, four years after the death of Thomas Aquinas.

In contrast, the *Decisive Discourse* was translated into Hebrew—fairly late, in the fifteenth century—and it exerted a certain influence on Jews such as Shem Tov Falaquera or Elijah Delmedigo.[11]

Any discernible echo of this work in the pre-modern Arab world was extremely limited. It was printed for the first time in the West by the German Orientalist Marcus Joseph Müller in 1859, who translated it in 1875. Editions subsequently published in the Arab world during the "Awakening" (*Nahda*) of the late nineteenth century pirate that edition.

Truth and Originality

One might argue that where quantity is concerned, the *Decisive Discourse* is admittedly only a very small part of Averroes' production, but quantity is only a secondary consideration if the work expresses his thought. Moreover, the majority of Averroes' texts are commentaries, which bear less weight than original works.

But it that true? For us, an original work expresses the thoughts of the author, speaking in his or her own name. A commentary is instead a historical work in which the author can show proof of much talent in the art of interpretation, but remains silent (and is even morally bound to keep silent) concerning his own personal positions. We will have to rid ourselves of that way of seeing things if we want to understand Averroes. Like all medieval authors, he had not adopted the historical point of view that for several centuries has seemed natural to us. For him, Aristotle was the absolute summit of humanity—with the exception, of course, of the prophets. Aristotle's intellect ceded only to the men to whom God had dictated the rules of the just community. Dante's statement about Aristotle—"the master sage of those who know" (*il maestro di color che sanno*) is often repeated.[12] But that compliment pales beside the hyperbolic eulogies with which Averroes covers Aristotle. These were to serve as an example to Malebranche to illustrate what he called the "preoccupation of commentators."[13] Averroes sees Aristotle as the summit of human possibilities and God's gift to humankind.[14]

That attitude continued after Averroes: his commentator and Jewish disciple Moses of Narbonne went even further, saying that if Aristotle has said something, there is no reason to seek elsewhere.[15] It even preceded Moses, for whether he knew it or not, he was quoting an earlier philosopher, Farabi, who writes calmly that after Aristotle philosophy is no longer a search, but the content of a teaching: there is no longer any need to seek out knowledge, but only to transmit it.[16]

For Averroes, what Aristotle had said was thus quite simply *true*: the truth and nothing but the truth. It was also the *complete* truth. This explains why he does not hesitate to add to his commentaries theories that were developed long after Aristotle. One example of this is the role of the nerves in perception, something that Aristotle knew nothing about and that was established by Galen.[17]

We are familiar with this way of thinking in the religious domain and with the syncretism that sees the Qur'an or the Upanishads as containing mentions of atoms, microbes, the theory of evolution, and so on, according to the current state of Western science. Where Aristotle is concerned, that mental habit persisted for some time. In Galileo's day, the Padua Aristotelian Cesare Cremonini recognized the invention of the telescope in a passage of the *Generation of Animals*.[18]

Thus from the point of view of Averroes himself, truth and originality were not only two different things, but were diametrically opposed. It is possible that he regarded his own original works as little more than works of circumstance, aimed at defending philosophy against its adversaries, but by no means as establishing a truth that he believed he already possessed.

This does not mean that Averroes was not an original thinker. All I am saying is that he did not *strive* to be one. It often happens that a sort of malicious law applies to thinkers as it does to writers and artists: those who seek originality at all costs and trumpet their success in uprooting all that came before them are often merely warming up and serving with their own insipid sauce some old notions that are new only because they had been forgotten. In contrast, those who have no other conscious (or at least stated) ambition than to take their place in a great tradition, bringing to it a few minimal adaptations or updatings, often turn out to be, in retrospect, powerful innovators, if not revolutionaries. Many medieval thinkers fit this mold, and Averroes is not the least among them.

The *Decisive Discourse*

The *Decisive Discourse* is a juridical consultation, a sort of *fatwa*, a word familiar to the West since it was launched against Salman Rushdie. Let me recall that it does not necessarily designate a condemnation, and even less a condemnation to death, but simply the response of a jurist (*muftī*) to a question put to him regarding the legitimacy of a certain practice. In this work, Averroes describes the philosophical activity that took place before the tribunal of the *sharia*. This is the contrary to what happened in Christianity when Thomas Aquinas, at the beginning of his *Summa theologica*, poses the question of the legitimacy of theology before the tribunal of philosophy by asking, "Is another teaching required apart from philosophical studies?"[19]

Averroes' campaign plan was to replace the Malachite jurists and the theologians of the Ash'arite Kalām as advisers to the prince. Averroes' text ends with an allusion to the victorious regime (*al-amr al-ghālib*) under which he lives.[20] He appeals to the secular arm to assure the triumph of his reading of Islamic Law.

His strategy is to show that philosophical investigation is obligatory for those who have the means—that is, the elite among the philosophers—

and forbidden to others—that is, the mass of the good people. As with Pascal, those who most "trouble the world, and are bad judges of everything" are half-baked scholars,[21] in Averroes' case, those of the Kalām.

Was the work intended to show the *agreement* of philosophy and religion? This is what is suggested by the titles chosen by some translators, such as "harmony," "concord," and so on. Other, more recent translators, are more circumspect. Thus Marc Geoffroy translates the title more literally: "The book of the decisive discourse in which is established the connection (*ittisāl*) existing between revelation (*sharia*) and philosophy (*hikma*)."[22] The translation of the three words I have given in parentheses seems to me problematic, and, personally, I prefer the even more literal translation of Charles Butterworth: "The Book of the Decisive Treatise determining the connection between the Law and wisdom," or, even more exact, a rendering that Butterworth himself declares unusable: "Book of decisively judging the statement and determining the connection between the Law and wisdom."[23] In his introduction to Marc Geoffroy's translation, Alain de Libera attacks, several times and with great eloquence, the interpretation that sees conciliation in that "connection."[24] Perhaps. The fact remains that when Averroes himself refers to his work in the work that follows it, he uses the title "Decisive discourse on the correspondence (*mutābaqa*)" or "on the accord (*muwāfaqa*) of wisdom and the Law."[25]

A Tough Guy

In general, Averroes is not a tender heart. And not only in his juridical works, or in those in which one might think that he is deliberately putting his readers on a false scent, but even when he writes as a philosopher. Thus in his *Commentary on Plato's Republic*, he raises no objection to the elimination of handicapped children.[26] Nor does he react when Plato's Socrates, reaching over the centuries to Pol Pot, suggests the expulsion of adults from the ideal city to be founded. Averroes' only reservation is technical: another method for achieving the end recommended by the Socrates of the *Republic* might prove more effective.[27]

We find the same attitude in a work in which Averroes defends philosophy against its detractors. In the famous *Incoherence of the Incoherence*, his aim is to counter the attacks of Ghazali. He twice justifies putting the heterodox to death.

One of these passages, which comes at the very end of the work, is available in both French and English translation. Averroes states: "Those who are in doubt about this and object to it and try to explain it are those who seek to destroy the religious prescriptions [Laws] and to undo the virtues. They are, as everyone knows, the heretics (*zindiqs*) and those who believe that the end of man consists only in sensual enjoyment. When such people have really the power to destroy religious belief *both theologians and philosophers will no doubt kill them*" (emphasis mine).[28] On another occasion in the same work, he states:

> As to the objection which Ghazali ascribes to the philosophers over the miracle of Abraham, such things are only asserted by heretical (*zanādiqa*) Muslims. The learned among the philosophers do not permit discussion or disputation about the principles of religion, and he who does such a thing needs, according to them, a severe lesson. For whereas every science has its principles and because every student of this science must concede its principles and may not interfere with them by denying them, this is still more obligatory in the practical science of religion that pertains to the Law (*sharʿiyya*), for to walk on the path of the religious virtues is necessary for man's existence, according to them, not in so far as he is a man, but in so far as he has knowledge; and therefore it is necessary for every man to concede the principles of religion [the Law] and invest with authority the man who lays them down. The denial and discussion of these principles denies human existence, *and therefore heretics must be killed*. [emphasis mine][29]

In the first text that I have quoted, Averroes relates what the founders of religions and the philosophers—in unanimity for once—would have done. He does not explicitly take a position in favor of their attitude. In the second text, he sides with them and pronounces the sentence in his own name. The question thus arises: Is he speaking here as a pious Muslim, as a doctor of the Law, or as a philosopher?

I am afraid that he is speaking *also* as a philosopher. For in the final analysis, whoever said that philosophers were tender hearts? Who can still turn a blind eye to what might be called their weakness for power? We might recall Heidegger's flirtation with Nazism, and we have seen many intellectuals of our own times, some of whom have never apologized, display a penchant for the most criminal ideological regimes—the Soviet Union, China, Cambodia, Iran, and others. I might also cite the servility of self-proclaimed "philosophers" of the French eighteenth century before "enlightened" despots seen, for example, in Voltaire's glorification of the invasion of Silesia, without a declaration of war, by Prussia under Frederick II. Nor have we forgotten, to go back to an earlier age, Plato's collusion with the tyrant of Syracuse. All of this should lead the philosophers' corporation to an examination of conscience, and it would be all too easy to spare ourselves by seeing these cases as simple exceptions. In any event, it is hard to see why men of the Middle Ages should be expected to do any better than their predecessors and their successors.

To end on a more "progressive" note, however: Averroes took advantage of the passage of the *Republic* in which Socrates defends the equality of the guardians of the city, men and women, to make a few remarks that may in fact refer to the condition of women in Islamic lands.[30] He notes that the women of his time had no other function than caring for children and making money by spinning and weaving, which relegated them to the level of plants. That said, Averroes says nothing more about the wrong done to women in this manner, accentuating instead the burden that they represent for their husbands.

An Organic Intellectual

Why are French students going to study the *Decisive Discourse*? It is a good bet that it will be in order to show that Islam is compatible with our own fads, call them what you will: reason, modernity, progress, secularity, et cetera. This risks ascribing to Averroes problematics that were by no means his, but at the same time it blocks off any more straightforward access to the literal meaning of what he wrote. That literal meaning is clarified by its context, by a specific historical situation, and by specific, presupposed dogmas—all topics that defy full investigation in a senior-year philosophy class. At the most, the professor would be well advised to call on the help of a good book that reconstructs the background to Averroes' work. I am thinking, in particular, of the modest but precise biography by Dominique Urvoy.[31]

We know of Gramsci's concept of the "organic intellectual," who stands opposed to the "critical intellectual." Averroes is being turned into the very type of the critical intellectual. He was also an "organic intellectual," however, and there is every indication that he saw himself as such.[32] He saw himself primarily as pursuing a profession that put him in the service of Islam. That profession is not that of a philosopher. Moreover, philosophic activity, in the Middle Ages, was institutionalized only within Christianity. In Islamic lands and in the Jewish communities, it remained a hobby, a passion indulged in apart from one's true occupation. Averroes' true occupation was religious law. He was in fact the chief Qādi (religious judge) of Cordova. That position within the Muslim city brought with it obligations. In the long term, he had to apply Islamic Law. More precisely, he had to preach the "holy war" when his sovereign decided to wage it. As a philosopher, he also had to provide a rational basis for that war.[33]

Averroes can be understood more accurately as in the service of the Almohads. He praises the regime he serves, criticizing that of the Almoravids, whom his masters had overthrown.[34] He gives a philosophical version of the official doctrine of Ibn Tūmart, the Mahdi of the Almohads. This is a theme on which Dominique Urvoy has strongly insisted, for a long time alone.[35] His intuition has recently been confirmed by Marc Geoffroy, who discovered a version of the *Unveiling* in which Averroes, probably in response to remarks made by a theologian, adapts his work to orthodox Almohad doctrine.[36]

As for knowing whether Averroes was sincere in all of these activities or whether he simply felt coerced into giving the power structure what it wanted to hear—who can decide?

Conclusion

Averroes was without any doubt a great philosopher and a great scholar, and, in particular, a great commentator of Aristotle. But he was a man of his time. He felt himself an integral part of the Muslim city of his epoch. Did he share that society's convictions at the bottom of his heart? Who can judge? The fact remains that he defended those convictions in his written works, which are the only documents that we possess. To make Averroes the precursor of anything, to make him the totem of some sort of progressivism or some sort of reform is perhaps working for a noble cause. But it goes against historical truth.

Appendix]&..

Original Texts

As I have indicated in my preface, all of the texts that appear in this volume have been revised in some way. Nevertheless, this list indicates the first publication or the first oral presentation of each text.

Interview:
"La religion et la philosophie," interview with Christophe Cervellon and Kristell Trego. *Le Philosophoire* 22 (2004): 25–44.

Chapter 1:
"La philosophie médiévale, example pour l'Europe d'aujourd'hui." In *Actes del simposi internacional de filosofia de l'edat mitjana: El pensament antropològic medieval en els àmbits islàmic, hebreu i cristià, Vic-Girona, 11–16 d'abril de 1993*, ed. Paloma Llorente et al. Patronat d'Etudis Osonencs, Series "Actes," no. 1, Vic, 1996, pp. 3–9.

Chapter 2:
"Sens et valeur de la philosophie dans les trois cultures médiévales." In *Was ist Philosophie im Mittelalter?. . .* , ed. Jan Aertsen and Andreas Speer. Miscellanea Mediaevalia, 26, pp. 229–44. Berlin: de Gruyter, 1998.

Chapter 3:
"En quoi la philosophie islamique est-elle islamique?" In *L'Orient chrétien dans l'Empire musulman: Hommage au Professeur Gérard Troupeau*, ed. Geneviève Gobillot, pp. 119–41. Versailles: Éditions de Paris, 2005. Translated into German as "Wie islamisch ist die islamische Philosophie?" In *Wissen über Grenzen: Arabisches Wissen*

und lateinisches Mittelalter, ed. Andreas Speer and Lydia Wegener. Miscellanea Mediaevalia, 33, pp. 165–78. Berlin: de Gruyter, 2006.

Chapter 4:
"Le déni d'humanité: Sur le jugement: 'ces gens ne sont pas des hommes' dans quelques textes antiques et médiévaux." *Lignes* 12 (December 1990), "Penser le racisme," pp. 217–32.

Chapter 5:
"Un modèle médiéval de la subjectivité: La chair." In *Ibn Rochd, Maïmonide, saint Thomas, ou la filiation entre foi et raison: Le Colloque de Cordoue,* pp. 36–62. Castelnau-les-Lez: Climats; Paris: Association freudienne internationale, 1994. Translated into English as "A Medieval Model of Subjectivity: Towards a Rediscovery of Fleshliness." In *The Ancients and the Moderns,* ed. Reginald Lilly, pp. 230–47. Bloomington: Indiana University Press, 1996.

Chapter 6:
"Is Physics Interesting? Some Late Ancient and Medieval Answers." *Graduate Faculty Philosophy Journal* 23, no. 2 (2002): 183–201. Presented as the seventh Shlomo Pines Memorial Lecture before the Israeli Academy of Sciences and the Humanities (Jerusalem), January 8, 1997. Repeated at the University of Pennsylvania, February 2, 1997, and at Notre Dame University, Jacques Maritain Center, November 2, 1998. Unpublished in French.

Chapter 7:
"Inclusion et digestion: Deux modèles d'appropriation culturelle." In *Le Souci du passage: Hommage à Jean Greisch,* ed. Philippe Capelle, G. Hébert, and Marie-Dominique Popelard, pp. 77–96. Paris: Cerf, 2003. Translated into German as "Inklusion und Verdauung: Zwei Modelle kultureller Aneignun." In *Hermeneutische Wege: Hans-Georg Gadamer zum Hundertsten,* ed. Günter Figal, Jean Grondin, and Dennis J. Schmidt, pp. 295–308. Tübingen: Mohr, 2000.

Chapter 8:
"Trois regards musulmans sur la cité chrétienne." *Le trimestre psychanalytique* 3 (1996), "Le théologico-politique," pp. 17–28.

Chapter 9:
"Le Jihād des philosophes." Translated by E. Patard. In *Enquêtes sur l'Islam: En hommage à Antoine Moussali,* ed. Joseph Bosshard and Anne-Marie Del-

cambre, pp. 242–61. Paris: Desclée de Brouwer, 2004. Originally published as "Der Dschihad der Philosophen." In *Krieg im Mittelalter*, ed. Hans-Henning Kortüm, pp. 77–91. Berlin: Akademie Verlag, 2001.

Chapter 10:
"Le truchement ou les traductions arables." Traductions et identité: Romains, Arabes et Juifs face à la culture greque, Annual seminar, *La Question de l'identité* (Claude Moatti). École doctorale, "Pratiques et théorie du sens," Université de Paris VIII, Saint-Denis, June 3, 2002. Unpublished.

Chapter 11:
"L'entrée d'Aristote en Europe: L'intermédiaire arabe." In *Aristote, l'école de Chartres et la Cathédrale: Actes du colloque européen des 5 et 6 juillet 1997*, ed. Roger Faloci, pp. 73–79. Chartres: Association des Amis du Centre Médiéval Européen de Chartres, 1998.

Chapter 12:
"Les sources extra-européennes de l'Europe philosophique." In *Existe-t-il une Europe philosophique? 16ᵉ forum Le Monde Le Mans, 22 au 24 octobre 2004*, ed. Nicolas Weill, pp. 189–95. Rennes: Presses Universitaires de Rennes, 2005.

Chapter 13:
"Quelques mythes méditerranéens." *Latinité et héritage islamique*, 3ᵉ Colloque international, Académie de la Latinité, Paris, March 23, 2003. Unpublished in French. Translated into Italian, abridged and without notes, as "Mediterraneo spazio di dialogo: È una leggenda." *Vita e Pensiero* 88 (2005–2006): 31–37.

Chapter 14:
"Y a-t-il eu au Moyen Âge un dialogue entre l'islam et le christianisme?" In *Les relations culturelles entre chrétiens et musulmans au moyen âge: Quelles leçons en tirer de nos jours?*, ed. Max Lejbowicz. Rencontres médiévales européennes, 5, pp. 15–27. Turnhut: Brepols, 2005.

Chapter 15:
"Le géocentrisme comme humiliation de l'homme." In *Herméneutique et ontologie: Mélanges en hommage à Pierre Aubenque*, ed. Rémi Brague and Jean-François Courtine, pp. 203–23. Paris: Presses Universitaires de France, 1990. Augmented version in German: "Geozentrismus als Demütigung des Menschen." *Internationale Zeitschrift für Philosophie* 1 (1994): 1–24. Augmented

version in English: "Geocentrism as a Humiliation for Man." *Medieval Encounters* 3 (1997): 187–210.

Chapter 16:
"Averroès était-il un gentil?" Institut Universitaire de Formation des Maîtres, Aix-en-Provence, March 10, 2004. Mosaiksteine, Kulturen des Islam, Münchener Zentrum für Islamische Studien, University of Munich, May 11, 2004. Unpublished.

Notes

Interview

1. The review that originally published this interview unfortunately omitted the name of Kristell Trego. I am restoring it here in homage to that young philosopher, who prepared, under my direction, and defended a remarkable thesis on St. Anselm and Greek philosophy. I much look forward to its publication.

2. Avicenna, *The Life of Ibn Sina: A Critical Edition and Annotated Translation*, ed. and trans. William E. Gohlman (Albany, NY: SUNY Press, 1974), 78–79.

3. I am thinking, for example, of the Church of Jesus Christ of Latter-Day Saints and *The Book of Mormon*.

4. The term "forgotten heritage" came into fashion thanks to Maria Rosa Menocal, *The Arabic Role in Medieval Literary History: A Forgotten Heritage* (Philadelphia: University of Pennsylvania Press, 1987). See also Alain de Libera, *Penser au Moyen Âge* (Paris: Seuil, 1991), chap. 4, esp. pp. 98–104.

5. Étienne Bonnot de Condillac, *Cours d'étude*, vol. 6, chap. 1, "Comment les Arabes ont cultivé les sciences," in *Oeuvres philosophiques*, ed. Georges Le Roy, 3 vols. (Paris: Presses Universitaires de France, 1948), 2:131a; Jean-Antoine-Nicolas de Caritat, marquis de Condorcet, *Esquisse d'un tableau historique des progrès de l'esprit humain*, ed. Alain Pons (Paris: Flammarion, 1988), chap. 6, p. 173; quoted from *Sketch for a Historical Picture of the Progress of the Human Mind*, trans. June Barraclough (London: Weidenfeld and Nicolson, 1955), 87. See also *Esquisse*, chap. 7, p. 184 (on chivalry).

6. Duns Scotus, *Ordinatio*, Prologue, 1, par. 3; translated into French by Gérard Sondag as *Prologue de l'Ordinatio* (Paris: Presses Universitaires de France, 1999), 58. I shall return to this passage below, p. 48.

7. *Le Livre de l'échelle de Mahomet (Liber scale Machometi; He skala tou Moameth)*; translated into French by Gisèle Besson and Michèle Brossard-Dandré, Lettres Gothiques (Paris: Livre de Poche, 1991).

8. See Dominik Perler and Ulrich Rudolph, *Occasionalismos: Theorien der Kausalität im arabisch-islamischen und im europäischen Denken* (Göttingen: Vandenhoeck & Ruprecht, 2000).

9. Simon ben Zemah Duran, *Qeshet u-Magen* (1423; Livorno, 1785), 19ff.; Elijah ben Moses Abba Delmedigo, *Sefer Behinat ha-dat* (An examination of religion)

(in Hebrew), ed. Jacob Joshua Ross (Tel Aviv: Tel Aviv University, 1984), "Introduction," 44–48.

10. Harold J. Berman, *Law and Revolution: The Formation of the Western Legal Tradition* (Cambridge, MA: Harvard University Press, 1983).

11. Justin Martyr, *Dialogue avec Tryphon*, 135, ed. Georges Archambault, 2 vols. (Paris: Picard, 1909), 286; quoted from *The Dialogue with Trypho*, trans. A. Lukyn Williams (New York: Macmillan, 1930), 278.

12. See Biruni, *Chronologie orientalischer Völker von Albērūnī* (in Arabic), ed. Eduard Sachau (Leipzig: Brockhaus, 1923; Frankfurt: Unveränderter Nachdruck, 1969), 207; translated into English by Eduard Sachau as *The Chronology of Ancient Nations* (London, 1879; Frankfurt: Minerva, 1969); and Guy G. Stroumsa, "'Le sceau des prophètes': Nature d'une métaphore manichéenne," in *Savoir et Salut* (Paris: Cerf, 1992), 275–88.

13. On Luxenberg, see Rémi Brague, "Le Coran: Sortir du cercle?" *Critique* 671 (April 2003): 232–51. See also Christoph Luxenberg, *Die syro-aramäische Lesart des Koran: Ein Beitrag zur Entschlüsselung der Koransprache* (Berlin: Das Arabische Buch, 2004); translated into English as *The Syro-Aramaic Reading of the Koran: A Contribution to the Decoding of the Language of the Koran* (Berlin: Schiler, 2007).

14. For a recent summary of this question, see Hava Lazarus-Yafeh, *Intertwined Worlds: Medieval Islam and Bible Criticism* (Princeton, NJ: Princeton University Press, 1992).

15. The ideas expressed in this paragraph are developed further below: see pp. 222–29.

16. John Philoponus, *De opificio mundi libri VII*, 1.1, ed. Walther Reichardt (Leipzig, 1897), p. 3; Giordano Bruno, *La cena de le ceneri*, beginning of IV; translated into English by Edward A. Gosselin and Lawrence S. Lerner as *The Ash Wednesday Supper* (Hamden, CT: Archon, 1977).

17. I am borrowing this notion from the works of Jan Assmann, in particular, *Moses der Ägypter: Entzifferung einer Gedächtnisspur* (Munich: Hanser, 1998), 208–9; translated into English as *Moses the Egyptian: The Memory of Egypt in Western Monotheism* (Cambridge, MA: Harvard University Press, 1997).

18. Friedrich Nietzsche, *Die fröhliche Wissenschaft*, 4, par. 285, in *Sämliche Werke: Kritische Studienausgabe*, ed. Giorgio Colli and Mazzino Montinari, 15 vols. (Munich: Deutscher Taschenbuch Verlag; New York: de Gruyter, 1988), 3:528; quoted from *The Gay Science* in *The Portable Nietzsche*, trans. Walter Kaufmann (1952; New York: Viking Penguin, 1974), 93–102, esp. 98.

19. Thomas Aquinas, *Summa contra Gentiles* (Rome: Editio Leonina Manualis, 1934), 3.69, then 122; quoted from *The Summa contra Gentiles of Saint Thomas Aquinas*; translated into English by the English Dominican Fathers, 4 vols. (London: Burns & Washbourne, 1923), 3:168, 122.

20. Immanuel Kant, *Der Streit*, in *Werke in sechs Bänden*, ed. Wilhelm Weischedel, 6 vols. (Darmstadt: Wissenschaftliche Buchgesellschaft, 1983), 6:340ff.; translated into English by Mary J. Gregor and Robert Anchor as *The Conflict of the Faculties*, in Kant, *Religion and Rational Theology*, trans. and ed. Allen W. Wood and George di Giovanni (Cambridge: Cambridge University Press, 1996), 233–328.

21. A. M. Ramsay, *An Essay upon Civil Government . . . Translated from the French* (London, 1722), chap. 2, "Of the Law of Nature," 11, after Fénelon, *Essai philosophique sur le gouvernement civil*, in *Oeuvres*, 3 vols. (Paris: Didot, 1985), 3:353b.

22. Francesco Petrarca, *De vita solitaria*, 2.9.1–4. For a modern edition, see *De vita solitaria*, ed. Marco Noce (Milan: Mondadori, 1992); translated into English by Jacob Zeitlin as *The Life of Solitude* (Urbana: University of Illinois Press, 1924; Westport, CT: Hyperion, 1948).

23. John Locke, *A Letter Concerning Toleration*, quoted from *Two Treatises of Government and A Letter Concerning Toleration*, ed. Ian Shapiro (New Haven, CT: Yale University Press, 2003), 246.

24. Nietzsche, *Die fröhliche Wissenschaft*, 3, par. 125; in his *Kritische Studienausgabe*, 3:480, quoted from *The Gay Science*, trans. Kaufmann, 95.

25. Jean-Jacques Rousseau, "La profession de foi du vicaire savoyard," in *Émile*, 1, in *Oeuvres complètes*, ed. Bernard Gagnebin and Marcel Raymond, 5 vols. (Paris: Gallimard, 1959–95), vol. 4 (1969), pp. 632–33; quoted from *Emile; or, On Education*, trans. Allan Bloom (New York: Basic Books, 1979), 312, emphasis mine.

26. Ernest Renan, *Souvenirs d'enfance et de jeunesse*, final sentence, in *Oeuvres complètes*, ed. Henriette Psichari, 7 vols. (Paris: Calmann-Lévy, 1947–), vol. 2 (1948), p. 909; quoted from *Recollections of My Youth*, trans. C. B. Pitman (New York: G. P. Putnam's Sons, 1883), 321.

27. Jeannine Quillet, *Les Clefs du pouvoir au Moyen Âge* (Paris: Flammarion, 1972), 44.

28. See Rémi Brague, "The Angst of Reason," in *Faith and Reason: The Notre Dame Symposium 1999*, ed. Timothy L. Smith (South Bend, IN: St. Augustine's Press, 2001), 235–44; translated into French by Irène Fernandez as "L'angoisse de la raison," *Communio* 25, no. 6 (November–December 2000): 13–24.

29. See E. R. Dodds, introduction to Proclus, *Stoicheiōsis theologikē: The Elements of Theology*, a revised text, trans. E. R. Dodds (Oxford: Oxford University Press, 1963), xxii–xxiii.

30. Nietzsche, *Die fröhliche Wissenschaft*, 5, par. 344, in *Kritische Studienausgabe*, 3:574–77.

31. Gilbert K. Chesterton, *The Blue Cross*, in *The Father Brown Omnibus* (New York: Dodd, Mead, 1935), 3–23, esp. 18–19.

32. See Rémi Brague, "L'impuissance du Verbe: Le Dieu qui a *tout* dit," *Diogène* 170 (April–June 1995): 49–74.

33. Rémi Brague, *Europe, la voie romaine*, 3rd ed. (Paris: Gallimard, 1999); translated into English by Samuel Lester as *Eccentric Culture: A Theory of Western Civilization* (South Bend, IN: St. Augustine's Press, 2002).

34. Joseph H. Weiler, *Un'Europa cristiana: Un saggio esplorativo* (Milan: BUR, 2003); translated into German as *Ein christliches Europa: Erkundungsgänge* (Salzburg: Puster, 2005).

35. Gustave Flaubert, *Salammbô*, chap. 13; translated into English by A. J. Krailsheimer (Harmondsworth, UK: Penguin, 1977).

36. Ignaz Goldziher, *Sur l'islam: Origines de la théologie musulmane* (Paris: Desclée de Brouwer, 2003). See my introduction to this work, 7–35, esp. 19–20.

37. Benedetto Croce, "Perché non possiamo non dirci 'cristiani,'" in *Discorsi di varia filosofia*, Saggi filosofici, 11 (Bari: Laterza, 1945), 1:11–23.

Chapter 1

1. Plato *Menexenus* 235d. See also Rémi Brague, *Introduction au monde grec: Études d'histoire de la philosophie* (Chatou: La Transparence, 2005), 9.

2. See my projected program, by now out-of-date and only partially realized: Rémi Brague, "Élargir le passé, approfondir le passé," *Le Débat* 72 (November–December 1992): 29–39.

3. I am referring to Gérard Sondag, *maître de conférences* at the Université Blaise-Pascal, Clermont-Ferrand.

4. See G. L. Burr, "How the Middle Ages Got Their Name," *American Historical Review* 20 (1914/1915): 813–15; and Nathan Edelman, "The Early Uses of Medium Aevum, Moyen-Âge, Middle Ages," *Romanic Review* 29 (1938): 3–25.

5. See Rémi Brague, "L'eurocentrisme est-il européen?" in *La Latinité en question* (Paris: Institut des Hautes Études de l'Amérique Latine et Union Latine, 2004), 249–59, esp. 251–52.

6. See Alain Besançon, *Histoire et expérience du moi* (Paris: Flammarion, 1971), 190.

7. See Lucie Varga, *Das Schlagwort vom "finisteren Mittelalter"* (Baden bei Wien: Rohrer, 1932).

8. See Theodor E. Mommsen, "Petrarch's Conception of the Dark Ages," *Speculum* 17 (1942): 226–42; and Hugo Friedrich, *Epochen der italienischen Lyrik* (Frankfurt: Klostermann, 1964), 173.

9. See Herbert Weisinger, "The Renaissance Theory of the Reaction against the Middle Ages as a Cause of the Renaissance," *Speculum* 20 (1945): 461–67, esp. 462.

10. François Rabelais, *Pantagruel*, chap. 8, in *Oeuvres complètes*, ed. Jacques Boulenger, revised and completed by Lucian Scheler (Paris: Gallimard, 1955), 204; quoted from *The Complete Works of François Rabelais*, trans. Donald M. Frame (Berkeley: University of California Press, 1991), 160.

11. See the passage from John Foxe cited in Weisinger, "The Renaissance Theory," 465.

12. See Werner Krauss, "Das Mittelalter in der Aufklärung," in *Medium aevum romanicum: Festschrift Hans Rheinfelder*, ed. Heinrich Bihler and Alfred Noyer-Weidner (Munich: Hueber, 1963), 223–31.

13. See Edward Gibbon, *The History of the Decline and Fall of the Roman Empire* (1788), ed. J. B. Bury, 3 vols. (New York: Heritage Press, 1946), 3:2441, 2431.

14. Jean-Antoine-Nicolas de Caritat, marquis de Condorcet, *Esquisse d'un tableau historique des progrès de l'esprit humain*, ed. Alain Pons (Paris: Flammarion, 1988), chap. 1, p. 94; chap. 2, p. 100; chap. 3, p. 115.

15. See Alain de Libera, *Penser au Moyen Âge* (Paris: Seuil, 1991), 33, 36, 38, etc.

16. Novalis, *Die Christenheit oder Europa*, in *Schriften*, vol. 2, *Das philosophisch-theoretische Werk*, ed. Hans-Joachim Mähl (Stuttgart: Kohlhammer, 1999), 732–50.

17. Henry Adams, *Mont Saint Michel and Chartres*, ed. Raymond Carney (London: Penguin, 1986). It is a mystery to me that neither this work nor Adams's autobiographical *The Education of Henry Adams* (1907)—available in a recent edition, ed. Ira B. Nadel (Oxford: Oxford University Press, 1999)—has been translated into French.

18. See Adams, *The Education*, 25, pp. 317–26.

19. Adams, *Mont Saint Michel and Chartres*, 3, p. 46.

20. Ibid., 1, p. 7; 8, p. 132; 9, p. 168; 10, p. 186.

21. Ibid., 5, p. 78; 6, p. 99; 8, p. 138; 13, pp. 247, 260.

22. Ibid., 7, p. 105; 8, p. 139.

23. Ibid., 9, p. 157; 10, 183.

24. Thomas Aquinas, *Summa theologica*, 5 vols. (Paris: Lethielleux, 1939), 1a, q. 1, a. 1: *"Videtur quod non sit necessarium, praeter philosophicas disciplinas aliam doctrinam haberi"* (Any other teaching beyond that of science and philosophy seems needless), quoted from English translation (New York: Blackfriars / McGraw-Hill), p. 4 (Latin), p. 5 (English).

25. See, for example, Kurt Flasch, *Das philosophische Denken im Mittelalter: Von Augustin zu Machiavelli* (Stuttgart: Reclam, 1986).

26. Moses of Narbonne, *Der Commentar des Rabbi Moses Narbonensis Philosophen aus dem XIV: Jahrhundert zu dem Werke More Nebuchim des Maimonides*, ed. Jacob Goldenthal (Vienna, 1952), 2.19, p. 32a.

27. See Georges Vajda, *Isaac Albalag, averroïste juif, traducteur et annotateur d'al-Ghazali* (Paris: Vrin, 1960), 38.

28. Al-Khatabi, MS, in Farabi, *Deux ouvrages inédits sur la rhéthorique (Kitāb al-Hatāba)*, ed. J. Langhade and M. Grignaschi (Beirut: Dar el-Mashreq, 1971), 136n2 (p. 137).

29. Ibn Sab'īn, *Correspondance philosophique avec l'Empereur Frédéric II de Hohenstaufen*, ed. Serefettin Yaltkaya (Paris: de Boccard, 1943).

30. See Maimonides, *Guide for the Perplexed*, 1.71. For the Christian influence on the Jewish Kalām, see *Dāwīd ibn Marwān al-Muqammis's Twenty Chapters ('Ishrūn Maqāla)*, ed. and trans. Sarah Stroumsa (Leiden: Brill, 1989).

31. See Alexander Altmann, "Problems of Research in Jewish Neoplatonism" (in Hebrew), *Tarbiz* 27, no. 4 (July 1958): 501–7.

32. Shlomo Pines, "Scholasticism after Thomas Aquinas and the Teachings of Hasdai Crescas and His Predecessors," trans. Alfred L. Ivry (1967), in *The Collected Works of Shlomo Pines*, 5 vols. (Jerusalem: Magnes; Leiden: Brill, 1979–96), 5:489–589.

33. My thanks for this idea to Professor Warren Z. Harvey, Hebrew University of Jerusalem.

34. See Stylianos G. Papadopulos, "Thomas in Byzanz: Thomas-Rezeption und Thomas-Kritik in Byzanz zwischen 1354 und 1453," *Theologie und Philosophie* 48 (1974): 274–304.

35. Samuel Ibn Tibbon, *Ma'amar Yiqqawu ham-main*, ed. M. L. Bisseliches (Pressburg, 1837), 175.

36. *The Monks of Kūblai Khān Emperor of China or the History of the Life and Travels of Rabban Sāwmā, Envoy and Plenipotentiary of the Mongol Khāns to the Kings of Europe, and Markōs who as Mär Yabkh-Allāhā III Became Patriarch of the Nestorian Church in Asia*, translated from the Syriac by Sir E. A. Wallis Budge (London: Religious Tract Society, 1928), chap. 8, pp. 183–84. There is a French translation of this work: "Histoire du Patriarch Mar Jabalaha III et du moine Rabban Çawma," translated from the Syriac by Jean-Baptiste Chabot, *Revue de l'Orient latin* 2 (1894): 107ff. I attempted to consult this translation in a library that holds this rare review, but I was unable to get around the vigilance of the functionaries charged with preventing readers from having access to it. My attention was drawn to this text by Johannes Fried, *Die Aktualität des Mittelalters: Gegen und Überheblichkeit unserer Wissensgesellschaft* (Stuttgart: Thorbecke, 2002), 43–44.

37. Ibn Khaldūn, *[Muqaddima] Les Prolégomènes d'Ibn-Khaldoun, texte arabe publié d'après les manuscrits de la Bibliothèque impériale*, ed. Étienne Quatremère, 3 vols. (Paris: Institut de France, 1858; repr., Beirut: Librairie du Liban, 1996), 6.18, vol. 3, p. 93; quoted from *The Muqaddimah: An Introduction to History*, trans. Franz Rosenthal, 3 vols. (New York: Pantheon, 1958), 6.18, vol. 3, pp. 17–18. See also Ibn Khaldūn, *Livre des examples*, trans. Abdesselam Cheddadi (Paris: Gallimard, 2002), 946.

38. I owe the term "inferiority complex" to Charles Touati, "La controverse de 1303 autour des études philosophiques et scientifiques," in *Prophètes, talmudistes, philosophes* (Paris: Cerf, 1990), 215; see also 208. For several other references, see Aviezer Ravitzky, "Samuel ibn Tibbon and the Esoteric Character of the *Guide of the Perplexed*," *Association of Jewish Studies Review* 6 (1981): 116n113.

39. See the passages from Cydones, Scholarios, and others cited in Friedrich Fuchs, *Die höheren Schulen von Konstantinopel im Mittelalter*, Byzantinisches Archiv, Heft 8 (Leipzig: Teubner, 1926), 66–67.

40. Isaac Abravanel, *Commentary on Joshua*, 10, 12 (repr., Jerusalem: Torah ve-Da'at, 1976), 53b.

41. Maimonides, *Guide for the Perplexed* (in Arabic), ed. Issachar Joël (Jerusalem: Junovitch, 1929), 3.48, p. 439, 15–18; translated into French by Salomon Munk as *Guide des égarés*,

3 vols. (Paris, 1856–66; repr., Paris: Maisonneuve, 1970), 1:396; quoted from *The Guide of the Perplexed*, trans. Shlomo Pines (Chicago: University of Chicago Press, 1963), 598.

42. *Rasā'il Ikhwān al-safā'*, ed. Butrus al-Bustanī, 4 vols. (Beirut: Dar Sadir, 1983); translated into German by Alma Giese as *Mensch und Tier vor dem Könoig der Dschinnen* (Hamburg: Meiner, 1990), 103.

43. Virgil *Aeneid* 6.847–53.

44. Bernard of Chartres, cited by John of Salisbury, *Metalogicon*, 3.4, *Patrologiae cursus completus . . . Series Latina*, ed. Jacques-Paul Migne and Adalberto Hamman (Paris, 1844–64), 199, p. 900c.

Chapter 2

1. Ferdinand de Saussure, *Cours de linguistique générale*, ed. Charles Bally et al. (Paris: Payot, 1964), part 2, chap. 4, pp. 155–69; for the example, see p. 160. This work is available in English translation by Roy Harris as *Course in General Linguistics*, ed. Charles Bally et al. (Lasalle, IL: Open Court, 1986).

2. I am borrowing this term as it is used in Michel Foucault, *Les mots et les choses: Une archéologie des sciences humaines* (Paris: Gallimard, 1966), 13; translated into English as *The Order of Things: An Archaeology of the Human Sciences* (1971; repr., New York: Vintage, 1994).

3. Marie-Dominique Chenu, "Les 'Philosophes' dans la philosophie chrétienne médiévale," *Revue des Sciences philosophiques et théologiques* 26 (1937): 27–40.

4. See Isidore of Seville, *Etymologies*, 2.24.3 and 8.6.1–2.

5. Al-Kindī, *Epistle on Definitions*, no. 73, ed. M. A. Abū Rida; vol. 1 of *Rasā'il al-Kindi al-falsafiyah*, 2nd ed. (Cairo: Dar al-Fikr al-'Arabī, 1978), p. 172, 8–9; al-Kindī, *Sur la philosophie première*, chap. 1, in *Métaphysique et cosmologie*, ed. Roshdi Rashed and Jean Jolivet, vol. 2 of al-Kindī, *Oeuvres philosophiques et scientifiques d'Al-Kindi*, 2 vols. (Leiden: Brill, 1998), 7–100, esp. p. 9, 9 and p. 13, 15–16.

6. Farabi, in Ibn Abū Usaybi'ah, *'Uyūn al-anba' fi tabaqāt al-atibbā'*, ed. N. Rida (Beirut: Dar Maktabat al-Hayat, n.d.), p. 604, 9–13.

7. Shahrastani, *Kitāb al-Milal wa-n-Nihal*, ed. William Cureton (London, 1842–46; Leipzig: Harrasowitz, 1923), 251.

8. Ibn Khaldūn, *[Muqaddima] Les Prolégomènes d'Ibn Khaldoun, texte arabe publié d'après les manuscrits de la Bibliothèque impériale*, ed. Étienne Quatremère, 3 vols. (Paris: Institut de France, 1858; Beirut: Librairie du Liban, 1996), 6.30, vol. 3, p. 210, 7–8; translated into English by Franz Rosenthal as *The Muqaddimah: An Introduction to History*, 3 vols. (New York: Pantheon, 1958); Ibn Khaldūn, *Livre des exemples*, trans. Abdesselam Cheddadi (Paris: Gallimard, 2002), 1034.

9. See Al-Amiri, *Kitāb al-I'lam bi-manāqib al-Islām* (On the merits of Islam), ed. Ahmad 'Abd al-Hamīd Ghurāb (Cairo: Dar al-Katib al-'Arabi, 1967), vol. 2, 40, 360. Since I have been unable to consult this edition, I have used the translation in Franz Rosenthal, *The Classical Heritage in Islam*, trans. Emile and Jenny Marmorstein (Berkeley: University of California Press, 1975), 74.

10. See, for example, Farabi, *Kitāb Tahsīl as-Sa'āda*, in *A'mal al-Falsafiyya*, ed. Ja'far Al Yasin (Beirut: Dar al-Manahil, 1992), 119–97, par. 65, p. 196.

11. See al-Muqammas, *Ishrūn Maqālat*, in *Dāwūd ibn Marwān al-Muqammis's Twenty Chapters ('Ishrūn Maqāla)*, ed. and trans. Sarah Stroumsa (Leiden: Brill, 1989), 9; and Saadia Gaon, *Kitāb al-Amānāt wa-'l-I'tiqādāt*, ed. Yosef Kafah (Jerusalem: Sura, 1970), introduction, 26; translated into English by Samuel Rosenblatt as *The Book of Beliefs and Opinions* (1948; repr., New Haven, CT: Yale University Press, 1976).

12. Moses ben Ezra, *Kitāb al-Muhādara wal-Mudhākara / Liber Discussionis et Commemorationis (Poetica hebraica)*, ed. Abraham Solomon Halkin (Jerusalem: Mekize Nirdamim, 1975), 40. The editor's Hebrew translation states: "The names of philosophy are Greek names" (41).

13. Jehuda Halevi, *The Book of Refutation and Proof of the Despised Faith: The Book of the Khazars (Known as the Kuzari)* (in Hebrew), ed. David H. Baneth and Haggai Ben-Shammai (Jerusalem: Magnes, 1977), 1, par. 63, p. 17, 8–11; translated into French by Charles Touati as *Le Kuzari, apologie de la religion méprisée* (Louvain: Peeters, 1994), 16; quoted from the English translation by Hartwig Hirschfeld as *The Kuzari (Kitab al Khazari): An Argument for the Faith of Israel* (1905; repr., New York: Schocken, 1964), 53.

14. Johann Gottlieb Fichte, *Reden an die deutsche Nation* (1807 / 1808), fifth discourse, in *Ausgewählte Werke in sechs Bänden*, ed. Fritz Medicus (1910; repr., Darmstadt: Wissenschlaftliche Buchgesellschaft, 1962), 5:440; translated into English by R. F. Jones and G. H. Turnbull as *Addresses to the German Nation* (Chicago: Open Court, 1922).

15. See, among other works, Jean Leclerq, *L'amour des lettres et le désir de Dieu: Initiation aux auteurs monastiques du Moyen Âge* (1957; repr., Paris: Cerf, 1990), 99–100.

16. See Pierre Hadot, *Exercices spirituels et philosophie antique* (Paris: Études Augustiniennes, 1981; 3rd ed. 1993; repr., Paris: Michel, 2002); translated into English by Michael Chase as *Philosophy as a Way of Life: Spiritual Exercises from Socrates to Foucault*, ed. Arnold Davidson (Oxford: Blackwell, 1995).

17. See Ihor Ševčenko, "The Definition of Philosophy in the Life of Saint Constantine," in *For Roman Jakobson: Essays on the Occasion of His Sixtieth Birthday*, ed. Morris Halle (The Hague: Mouton, 1956), 449–57.

18. See Franz Dölger, "Zur Bedeutung von *philosophos* und *philosophia* in Byzantinischer Zeit," in *Byzanz und die europäische Staatenwelt* (Etal: Buch-Kunstverlag, 1953; repr., Darmstadt: Wissenschaftliche Buchgesellschaft, 1964), 197–208.

19. Michel Psellus, *Chronographie ou histoire d'un siècle de Byzance, 976–1077*, ed. Emile Renauld, 2 vols. (Paris: Belles Lettres, 1926–28); chap. 3, 1:73; quoted in Dölger, "Zur Bedeutung," 199.

20. Dölger, "Zur Bedeutung," 203–4.

21. Bernard of Clairvaux, *De consideratione*, 3.4 (15), in *Opera*, ed. Jean Le Clercq et al., 9 vols. (Rome: Editiones Cistercienses, 1957–77), 3:442, 22–25; also in *Patrologiae cursus completus Series Latina*, ed. Jacques-Paul Migne and Adalberto Hamman (Paris, 1844–64), 182, p. 767a; quoted from *Five Books on Consideration: Advice to a Pope*, trans. John D. Anderson and Elizabeth T. Kennan (Kalamazoo, MI: Cistercian Publications, 1976), 98.

22. *Perush ham-millot haz-zarot*, in *Doctor Perplexorum (Guide for the Perplexed)* by R. Moses ben Maimon (Rambam), Hebrew version of R. Samuel Ibn Tibbon, revised by Yehuda Even-Shemuel (Jerusalem: Mosad ha-Rav Kuk, 1987), 75.

23. See Maimonides, *Guide for the Perplexed* (in Arabic), ed. Issachar Joël (Jerusalem: Junovitch, 1929), 1.71 (at the beginning), p. 121, 9–26; translated into French by Salomon Munk as *Guide des égarés*, 3 vols. (Paris, 1865–66; Paris: Maisonneuve, 1970), 1:4; translated into English by Shlomo Pines as *The Guide of the Perplexed* (Chicago: University of Chicago Press, 1963).

24. See Maimonides, *Guide for the Perplexed*, 2.11, p. 192; 3, preface, p. 297, 17-1; Munk trans., pp. 9, 4.

25. See *Midrash Bereshit Rabba*, 1.1, ed. Julius Theodor and Chanoch Albeck (Jerusalem: Wahrmann, 1965), 8.

26. Marcus Jastrow, *Dictionary of the Targumim, the Talmud Babli and Yerushalmi, and the Midrashic Literature* (1886–1903; repr., New York: Judaica Press, 1985), s.v. "philosopher," 1164a.

27. See Annemarie Schimmel, *Mystische Dimensionen des Islam: Geschichte des Sufismus* (Cologne: Diedrichs, 1985), 71; translated into English as *Mystical Dimensions of Islam* (1975; repr., Chapel Hill: University of North Carolina Press, 1990).

28. In particular, I am basing my remarks on the summary in Henry Corbin, *Histoire de la philosophie islamique* (Paris: Gallimard, 1986); translated into English by Liadain Sherrard with Philip Sherrard as *History of Islamic Philosophy* (London: Kegan Paul International, 1993).

29. Corbin, *Histoire*, 57.

30. Ibid., 51, 55, 121.

31. Ibid., 492; Corbin, *History*, 365–66.

32. Corbin, *Histoire*, 391, 418.

33. Henry Corbin, *La philosophie iranienne islamique aux XVIIe et XVIIIe siècles* (Paris: Buchet-Chastel, 1981), 18.

34. Corbin, *Histoire*, 24.

35. John Duns Scotus, *Prologue de l'Ordinatio*, French translation by Gérard Sondag (Paris: Presses Universitaires de France, 1999), 1, par. 3.

36. Maimonides, *Guide for the Perplexed*, 1.31, pp. 44–45; Munk trans., 107–8.

37. Farabi, *Kitāb al-Burhān*, chap. 5, in *Al-Mantiq ʿinda al-Farabi*, ed. Majid Fakhry (Beirut: Dar al-Machreq, 1987), 4:85, 11–17; also available in *Al-Mantiqiyyat li-ʾl-Farabi*, ed. Muhammad Taqī Dānishʿpazhwūh (Qum, 1408 h / 1987–89), 2:336; quoted and translated into French in Rémi Brague, "*Eorum praeclara ingenia*: Conscience de la nouveauté et prétention à la continuité chez Fārābī et Maïmonide," in *Études de Philosophie Arabe*, ed. Dominique Mallet, Actes du Colloque (Bordeaux, June 17–19, 1994), *Bulletin d'Études orientales* 48 (1996): 87–102, esp. 95.

38. Thomas Aquinas, *Summa contra Gentiles*, 3.48 (Rome: Editio Leonina Manualis, 1934), 279a. Compare this with Hasdai Crescas, *The Light of the Lord (Sefer Or Adonai)* (in Hebrew), ed. Shelomoh Fisher (Jerusalem: Ramot, 1990), 2.5.5, p. 222: "The Philosopher, from the fact that his eyes had not been rendered seeing by the lamp of the Torah, and that, from another viewpoint, he was oppressed (*nilhas*) by strong presumptions (*horaʾot*) that teach the survival of the human soul, knew specious arguments to consolidate those presumptions, even if the latter are far indeed from the intellect and, for even greater reason, from the Torah."

39. Gersonides, *Milhamot ha-Shem* (in Hebrew) (Riva di Trento, 1560; Leipzig, 1866); translated into French by Charles Touati as *Les guerres du Seigneur, Livres III et IV* (Paris: Mouton, 1968), 67; quoted from *The Wars of the Lord*, trans. Seymour Feldman, 3 vols. (Philadelphia: Jewish Publication Society of America, 1984–89), 2:107.

40. See Leo Strauss, *Persecution and the Art of Writing* (New York: Free Press, 1952; repr., Chicago: University of Chicago Press, 1988), 9.

41. Warren Z. Harvey, "On Averroes, Maimonides, and the Excellent City" (in Hebrew), in *ʿIyunim be-sugyot filosofiyot: Devarim she-neemru be-ʿerev li-khevod Shelomoh Pines be-hagiʿo li-gevurot* (Jerusalem: Israeli Academy of Sciences and Humanities, 1992), 19–31, esp. 21.

42. Hergé, *L'Oreille cassée* (Tournai: Casterman, 1945), 24.

43. Strauss, *Persecution and the Art of Writing*, 19, 21. See also Strauss, "How to Begin to Study Medieval Philosophy" (1944), in *The Rebirth of Classical Political Rationalism: An In-*

troduction to the Thought of Leo Strauss, Essays and Lectures, ed. Thomas L. Pangle (Chicago: University of Chicago Press, 1989), 223.

44. I am pursuing here a line of thought sketched out in Rémi Brague, *Europe, la voie romaine*, 3rd ed. (Paris: Gallimard, 1999); translated into English by Samuel Lester as *Eccentric Culture: A Theory of Western Civilization* (South Bend, IN: St. Augustine's Press, 2002). My thoughts on text and commentary are developed further in chapter 9, below, pp. 147–58.

45. Corbin, *Histoire de la philosophie islamique*, 219; quoted from *History of Islamic Philosophy*, 153.

46. What appears here is a more extensive statement of reflections sketched in Rémi Brague, "Athènes, Jérusalem, La Mecque: L'interprétation 'musulmane' de la philosophie grecque chez Leo Strauss," *Revue de Métaphysique et de Morale* 3 (July–September 1989): 309–36. For a version of this article in English translation, see "Athens, Jerusalem, Mecca: Leo Strauss' 'Muslim' Understanding of Greek Philosophy," in "Hellenism and Hebraism Reconsidered: The Poetics of Cultural Influence and Exchange," *Poetics Today* 1, no. 19 (1998): 235–59.

47. See A. I. Sabra, "The Appropriation and Subsequent Naturalization of Greek Science in Medieval Islam: A Preliminary Statement," *History of Science* 25 (1987): 223–43, esp. 240.

48. Corbin, *Histoire de la philosophie islamique*, 285; see also 346.

49. See Jean Jolivet, *Aspects de la pensée médiévale* (Paris: Vrin, 1987), 53–61.

Chapter 3

1. Lawrence V. Berman, "The Ethical Views of Maimonides within the Context of the Islamicate Civilization," in *Perspectives on Maimonides: Philosophical and Historical Studies*, ed. Joel L. Kraemer (Oxford: Oxford University Press, 1991), 13–32.

2. Alexandre Kojève, *Essai d'une histoire raisonnée de la philosophie païenne*, 3 vols. (Paris: Gallimard, 1968–73), vol. 1, *Les Présocratiques* (1968); vol. 2, *Platon, Aristote* (1972); vol. 3, *La philosophie hellénistique, les néo-platoniciens* (1973). See also Kojève, *Kant* (Paris: Gallimard, 1973).

3. Friedrich Nietzsche, *Der Antichrist*, par. 10, in *Sämliche Werke: Kritische Studienausgabe*, ed. Giorgio Colli and Mazzino Montinari, 15 vols. (Munich: Deutscher Taschenbuch Verlag; New York: de Gruyter, 1988), 6:176.

4. See Emerich Coreth et al., eds., *Christliche Philosophie im katholischen Denken des 19. und 20. Jahrhunderts*, 3 vols. (Graz: Styria, 1987).

5. See Rémi Brague, "Sens et valeur de la philosophie dans les trois cultures médiévales," in *Was ist Philosophie im Mittelalter?*, ed. Jan Aertsen and Andreas Speer, Miscellanea Mediaevalia, 26 (Berlin: de Gruyter, 1998), 229–44; translated into English as chap. 2, above.

6. See Warren Z. Harvey, "Shlomo Pinès et son approache de la pensée juive," in Shlomo Pines, *La liberté de philosopher: De Maïmonide à Spinoza*; French translation from Hebrew and English by Rémi Brague with Renée Bouveresse-Quillot and Gérard Haddad (Paris: Desclée de Brouwer, 1997), 25–44.

7. René Descartes, letters to Père Mesland, February 9, 1645, and 1646, in *Oeuvres*, ed. Charles Adam and Paul Tannery, 13 vols. (Paris: Cerf, 1897–1913), vol. 4 (1901), 163–70, 346–48.

8. For examples of this attitude, see Dimitri Gutas, *Greek Thought, Arabic Culture: The Graeco-Arabic Translation Movement in Baghdad and Early 'Abbasid Society (2nd–4th / 8th–10th Centuries)* (London: Routledge, 1998), 83–90.

9. Farabi, in Ibn Abī Usaybiʿah, ʿUyūn al-anbaʾ fi tabaqāt al-atibbāʾ, ed. N. Rida (Beirut: Dar Maktabat al-Hayat, n.d.), 60; see Sarah Stroumsa, "Al-Farabi and Maimonides on the Christian Philosophical Tradition: A Re-evaluation," Der Islam 68 (1991): 263–87.

10. Avicenna, "Letter to Kiyā," in Mubāhathāt, ed. Muhsin Bidārfar (Qum: Intishārāt Baydār, 1413 / 1992), par. 1159, p. 372. I am using the French translation of Shlomo Pines, "La 'Philosophie orientale' d'Avicenne et sa polémique contre les Bagdadiens" (1952), in The Collected Works of Shlomo Pinès, 5 vols. (Jerusalem: Magnes; Leiden: Brill, 1979–96), 3:301–33, esp. 302.

11. Farabi, Against John the Grammarian, 4.8, in Muhsin Mahdi, "Alfarabi against Philoponus," Journal of Near Eastern Studies 26 (1967): 233–60, esp. 257; Avicenna, correspondence with Biruni, response to the 2nd question, par. 16, in Avicenna, Rasāʾil, ed. Bidār (Qum, n.d.), 416.

12. Maimonides, Guide for the Perplexed (in Arabic), ed. Issachar Joël (Jerusalem: Junovitch, 1929), 1.71, p. 122; translated into French by Salomon Munk as Guide des égarés, 3 vols. (Paris, 1856–66; repr., Paris: Maisonneuve, 1970), 1:341–42.

13. Maimonides, letter to Samuel Ibn Tibbon, in Alexander Marx, "Texts by and about Maimonides" (in Hebrew), Jewish Quarterly Review, n.s. 25, no. 4 (1935): 371–81, esp. 378–80. See Pines, La liberté de philosopher, 93–94. On the reception of this text, see Steven Harvey, "Did Maimonides' Letter to Samuel Ibn Tibbon Determine Which Philosophers Would Be Studied by Later Jewish Thinkers?" Jewish Quarterly Review 83 (1992): 51–70.

14. See Sarah Stroumsa, "Note on Maimonides' Attitude towards Joseph Ibn Saddiq" (in Hebrew), in Shlomo Pines: Jubilee Volume on the Occasion of His Eightieth Birthday, Jerusalem Studies in Jewish Thought, 9, 2 vols. (Jerusalem: Hebrew University, 1988–90), 1:33–38.

15. There are several examples of this in Albertus Magnus, De unitate intellectus, 1.

16. Thomas Aquinas, Summa theologica, 1a, q. 50, a. 3c.

17. See, for example, Thomas Aquinas, Summa contra Gentiles, 1.6; and John Duns Scotus, Prologue de l'Ordinatio, French translation by Gérard Sondag (Paris: Presses Universitaires de France, 1999), 150.

18. See Jean Jolivet, Aspects de la pensée médiévale (Paris: Vrin, 1987), 55–61.

19. Albertus Magnus, De anima, 3.2, col. 1, lines 59–60, in his Opera omnia, vol. 7, pt. 1, ed. Clemens Stroick (Münster: Aschendorff, 1968), 177b.

20. Thomas Aquinas, Summa contra Gentiles, 3.65, etc.

21. Meister Eckhart, Sermon 44, in Die Deutschen Werke (hereafter abbreviated DW), ed. Josef Quint, vols. 3–5 of Die deutschen und lateinischen Werke (Stuttgart: Kohlhammer, 1936–), 2:349, 6; Sermon 61, in DW, 3:44, 1; Sermon 75, in DW, 3:296, 9 (lêraere).

22. Eckhart, Sermon 45, in DW, 2:362, 1; Das buoch der götlichen troestunge, in DW, 5:20, 16.

23. Eckhart, Von dem edelm Menschen, in DW, 5:115, 13.

24. Eckhart, Sermon 47, in DW, 2:396, 2.

25. Eckhart, Sermon 80, in DW, 3:380, 2; 3:384, 2; Sermon 83, in DW, 3:441, 2.

26. Eckhart, Sermons 26 and 37, in DW, 2:30, 1; 2:218, 3; 2:220, 2.

27. Eckhart, Sermon 31, in DW, 2:121, 4.

28. Eckhart, Sermon 61, in DW, 3:44, 1.

29. Duns Scotus, Prologue de l'Ordinatio, 1, par. 3, p. 58.

30. See Averroes, Tahafot al-tahafot: Incohérence de l'incohérence, ed. Maurice Bouyges (1930; repr., Beirut: Dar el-Machreq, 1987), 4, par. 27, p. 276.

31. Farabi, Alfarabi's Book of Letters (Kitāb al-Hurūf): Commentary on Aristotle's Metaphysics (in Arabic), ed. and trans. Muhsin Mahdi (Beirut: Dar el-Machreq, 1969), 2, pars. 108–58, pp. 131–61; par. 106, p. 157.

32. Averroes, *Tahafot al-tahafot*, 3, par. 68, p. 179.

33. Ibid., par. 56, p. 173; 8, par. 4, p. 393; Averroes, *Talkīs mā baʿda al-tabīʿah: Averroes' Epitome of Aristotle's Metaphysics*, ed. ʿUthmān Amīn (Cairo: al-Halabī, 1958), 4, par. 60, p. 153n8.

34. Averroes, *Talkīs / Epitome of Aristotle's Metaphysics*, 2, par. 19, p. 47n5.

35. Averroes, *Tahafot al-tahafot*, Questions of Physics, 3, par. 7, pp. 407, 579.

36. Averroes, *Talkīs / Epitome of Aristotle's Metaphysics*, respectively, 2, par. 23, p. 51, and par. 46, p. 73n15; 3, par. 43, p. 106; introduction, par. 13, p. 6; 2, par. 1, p. 33.

37. Averroes, *Tahafot al-tahafot*, 6, par. 29, p. 325; par. 84, p. 353.

38. Averroes, *Epitome in physicorum libros*, ed. Josep Puig (in Arabic) (Madrid: Consejo Superior de Investigaciones Cientificas, 1983), 8, pp. 134–35.

39. Nasīr ad-Dīn Tūsī, *The Nasirean Ethics*, trans. from the Persian by G. M. Wickens (London: Allen Unwin, 1964), 1.9, p. 121; p. 292n1210.

40. Ibid., 3.1, p. 187; 2.1, p. 155.

41. Ibid., pp. 25–26, 59, 66, 105, 116.

42. Massimo Campanini, *Introduzione alla filosofia islamica* (Bari: GFL editori Laterza, 2004).

43. Ibid., 73–74.

44. Qurʾan 112:3. Here and elsewhere, the Qurʾan is quoted from *The Qurʾan: Translation*, trans. Abdullah Yusuf Ali, 13th ed. (Elmhurst, NY: Tahrike Tarsile Qurʾan, 2004). For earlier texts, see Macrobius, *Commentarii in Somnium Scipionis*, in *Macrobius*, ed. James Willis, 2 vols. (Leipzig: Teubner, 1963), 1.5.1, p. 17; and Candidus the Arian, *Letter to Marius Victorinus on Divine Generation*, in Marius Victorinus, *Traités théologiques sur la Trinité*, ed. Paul Hadot, 2 vols. (Paris: Cerf, 1960), 1:10. For later texts, see Fourth Lateran Council (1215), in Heinrich Denzinger, *Enchiridion symbolorum* (Fribourg: Herder, 1911), par. 432, p. 191; translated into English by Roy J. Deferrari as *The Sources of Catholic Dogma* (St. Louis, MO: Herder, 1957). For the pre-Socratic era, see Philolaos, in Hermann Diels and Walther Kranz, *Die Fragmente der Vorsokratiker* (in Greek and German), 11th ed., 3 vols. (Zurich: Weidmann, 1964), 44B 20, 1:416; selections in English translation by Kathleen Freeman as *Ancilla to the Pre-Socratic Philosophers* (1948; repr., Cambridge, MA: Harvard University Press, 1957).

45. Plotinus *Enneads* 6.7 [38], 37, 1–16.

46. Farabi, *Al-Farabi on the Perfect State: Abū Nasr al-Farābī's Mabādiʾ Ārāʾ al-madinah al fādilah*, trans. Richard Walzer (Oxford: Clarendon Press, 1985), 4.14, par. 9, pp. 222–24.

47. Averroes, *Fasl al-maqāl*, par. 2; translated into French by Marc Geoffroy as *Le Livre du discours décisif* (Paris: GF-Flammarion, 1996), 102; translated into English by George F. Hourani as *On the Harmony of Religions and Philosophy* (London: Luzac, 1961).

48. Avicenna, in Hassan ʿAsī, *Qurʾanic Exegesis and Sufi Terms in the Philosophy of Avicenna* (in Arabic) (Beirut: MJ, 1983), 86–88; Ghazali, *The Niche of Lights (Mishkat al-anwar)* (in English and Arabic), trans. David Buchman (Provo, UT: Brigham Young University Press, 1998).

49. Campanini, *Introduzione alla filosofia islamica*, 121–34.

50. See Averroes, *Tahafot al-tahafot*, translated into English by Simon van den Bergh as *Tahafut al-tahafut (The Incoherence of the Incoherence)*, 2 vols. (London: Luzac, 1961), 2:212b. The term *liberum arbitrium* (in Latin) does appear in the index, however: see 2:213a.

51. See Wolfgang Wieland, "Der Ewigkeit der Welt (Der Streit zwischen Johannes Philoponos und Simplicius)," in *Die Gegenwart der Griechen im neuren Denken, Festschrift für H. G. Gadamer zum 60. Geburtstag* (Tübingen: Mohr, 1960), 291–316.

52. See Muhsin Mahdi, "Alfarabi against Philoponus."

53. See Richard Bodéüs, *Le Philosophe et la cité: Recherches sur les rapports entre morale et politique dans la pensée d'Aristote* (Paris: Belles Lettres, 1982).

54. See Jean-Claude Vadet, *Les idées morales dans l'islam* (Paris: Presses Universitaires de France, 1995).

55. Averroes, *Commentary on Plato's "Republic,"* ed. and trans. E. I. J. Rosenthal (Cambridge: Cambridge University Press, 1969), 2.1.7, p. 61. See also Shlomo Pines, *Ben mahashevet Yisrael le-mahashevet ha-ʿamim: Mehkarim be-toldot ha-filosofyah ha-yehudit*. Studies in the History of Jewish Philosophy: The Transmission of Texts and Ideas (in Hebrew) (Jerusalem: Mosad Bialik, 1977), 86.

56. Avicenna, *Al-Shifa Al-llahiyyat (1) (La Métaphysique)*, ed. Georges C. Anawati and Saʾid Zayed (Cairo: Organisation générale des imprimeries gouvernementales, 1960), 10.4–5.

Chapter 4

1. See, for example, Aristotle *Metaphysics* E / 1, in English translation as *The Metaphysics*, ed. Hugh Tredennick, Loeb Classical Library, 2 vols. (Cambridge, MA: Harvard University Press, London: William Heinemann, 1957); and Maimonides, *Traité de logique*, translated from the Arabic by Rémi Brague (Paris: Desclée de Brouwer, 1996), 97; translated into English by Israel Efros as *Milot ha-higayon: Maimonides' Treatise on Logic* (New York: American Academy for Jewish Research, 1938).

2. See, for example, Farabi, *Catalogue of Sciences (De scientiis)*, chap. 3.

3. See, for example, Ludwig Edelstein, "Motives and Incentives for Science in Antiquity," in *Scientific Change: Historical Studies in the Intellectual, Social and Technical Conditions for Scientific Discovery and Technical Invention, from Antiquity to the Present*, ed. A. C. Crombie (New York: Basic Books, 1963), 15–41.

4. Ibn Khaldūn, [*Muqaddima*] *Les Prolégomènes d'Ibn Khaldoun, texte arabe publié d'après les manuscrits de la Bibliothèque impériale*, ed. Étienne Quatremère, 3 vols. (Paris: Institut de France, 1858; repr., Beirut: Librairie du Liban, 1996), 6.30, vol. 3, p. 214, 15–17; quoted from the English translation by Franz Rosenthal, *The Muqaddimah: An Introduction to History*, 3 vols. (New York: Pantheon, 1958), 3:251–52. See also Ibn Khaldūn, *Livre des exemples*, trans. Abdesselam Cheddadi (Paris: Gallimard, 2002), 1038.

5. René Descartes, "Lettre de l'auteur à celui qui a traduit le livre," *Principes de la Philosophie*, in *Oeuvres*, ed. Charles Adam and Paul Tannery, 13 vols. (1897–1913), vol. 9, pt. 2, pp. 14, 23–31.

6. Xenophon *Memorabilia* 1.1.11; translated into English by Amy L. Bonnette (Ithaca, NY: Cornell University Press, 1994).

7. Diogenese of Oinoanda, in *Supplement to Diogenese of Oinoanda: The Epicurean Inscription*, ed. Martin Ferguson Smith (Naples: Bibliopolis, 1993), fragment 3, p. 4; commentary, pp. 38–39.

8. Epicurus *Sentences vaticanes* 27, ed. Sedley-Long, 156; quoted from Epicurus, *Letters, Principal Doctrines and Vatican Sayings*, trans. Russel M. Geer (New York: Macmillan, 1964), 67.

9. Epicurus, Epicurus to Pythocles, par. 85, in *Epicurus: The Extant Remains*, trans. Cyril Baily (Oxford: Clarendon Press, 1926; repr., Westport, CT: Hyperion, 1979), 57.

10. Karl Marx, "Differenz der demokritischen und epikuräischen Naturphilosophie," in *Karl Marx Werke: Artikel, Literarische Versuche bis März 1843*, vol. 1 of Karl Marx and Friedrich Engels, *Gesamtausgabe* (Berlin: Dietz, 1975), 21–87.

11. Epicurus, "The Principal Doctrines," 11, in *The Epicurus Reader: Selected Writings and Testimonia*, trans. and ed. Brad Inwood and L. P. Gerson (Indianapolis: Hackett, 1994), 33. It is not certain that Epicurus is putting heavenly phenomena and death on the same plane here.

12. Porphyry, *De abstinentia*, ed. and trans. Jean Bouffartigue (Paris: Belles Lettres, 1977–), 1.8.4, p. 47; quoted from the English translation by Gillian Clark, *On Abstinence from Killing Animals* (Ithaca, NY: Cornell University Press, 2000), 33.

13. Lucretius *De rerum natura* 5.5.1204ff.

14. Simplicius, in *Commentaria in Aristotelem Graeca*, ed. Hermann Diels, 23 vols. (Berlin: Reimer, 1882–1907; repr., Berlin: de Gruyter, 2002), vol. 9, *Simplicii in Aristoteles Physicorum libros quattuor priores commentaria*, 4, 17-5, 21, my translation.

15. See Steven Harvey, "The Hebrew Translation of Averroes' Prooemium to His *Long Commentary on Aristotle's Physics*," *Proceedings of the American Academy of Jewish Research* 52 (1985): 55–84.

16. See Edelstein, "Motives and Incentives for Science," 22ff.

17. Albertus Magnus, *Alberti Magni ex ordine praedicatorum de Vegetabilibus libri VII*, ed. Karl Friedrich Wilhelm Jessen and Ernest H. F. Meyer (Berlin, 1867), 7.1.1, p. 591n1; quoted from the version given in Albertus Magnus, *Ausgewählte Texte: Lateinisch-Deutsch*, ed. Albert Fries (Darmstadt: Wissenschaftliche Buchgesellschaft, 1981), 8.

18. Albertus Magnus, *De bono* (On the Good), 4, q. 1, a. 2, sol. (4), in *Opera omnia* (Münster: Aschendorff, 1968), vol. 28 (1951), 224, 91-225, 4.

19. Aristotle *Nicomachean Ethics* 6.7, ed. H. Rackham, Loeb Classical Library (Cambridge, MA: Harvard University Press; London: William Heinemann, 1975), 340–47.

20. Anaxoras, in Hermann Diels and Walther Kranz, *Die Fragmente der Vorsokratiker* (in Greek and German), 11th ed., 3 vols. (Zurich: Weidmann, 1964), 59B 21, vol. 2, p. 43.

21. Isaiah 40:26; Psalms 19:2; Romans 1:19.

22. Galen *De usu partium corporis humani* 3.1; translated into English by Margaret Tallmadge May as *Galen on the Usefulness of the Parts of the Body*, 2 vols. (Ithaca, NY: Cornell University Press, 1968).

23. See Warren Z. Harvey, "Averroes and Maimonides on the Philosophical Duty to Contemplate (iʿtibār)" (in Hebrew), *Tarbiz* 58, no. 1 (1988): 75–83.

24. Bahya ibn Paquda, *Kitāb al-hidāya ilā farāʾid al-qulūb* (Duties of the heart), ed. and trans. A. S. Yahuda (Leiden: Brill, 1912), 2, par. 1, p. 97, 10–15, and par. 3, p. 100, 5–8; quoted from the English translation by Menahem Mansoor, with Sara Arenson and Shoshana Dannhauser, *The Book of Direction to the Duties of the Heart* (London: Routledge & Kegan Paul, 1973), 153, 155–56.

25. Bonaventure, *Collationes in Hexaëmeron*, 12, in *Opera omnia*, ed. A. C. Peletier, 15 vols. (Paris: Vivés, 1864) vol. 9 (1867), pp. 87b–88a; quoted from the English translation by José de Vinck, *The Collations on the Six Days*, vol. 5 of *The Works of Bonaventure: Cardinal, Seraphic Doctor, and Saint* (Paterson, NJ: St. Anthony Guild Press, 1970), 179–80. On the intellectual kinship between Bahya and Bonaventure, see Ermenegildo Bertola, "Platonismo escolastico-cristiano y arabe-judio: s. Buenaventura y R. Bahya ben Pacuda," *Sefarad* 10 (1950): 385–400.

26. Maimonides, *Guide for the Perplexed* (in Arabic), ed. Issachar Joël (Jerusalem: Junovitch, 1929), 1.5, p. 84, 13ff; translated into French by Salomon Munk as *Guide des égarés*, 3 vols. (Paris, 1856–66; repr., Paris: Maisonneuve, 1970), 1:217–19; quoted from the English translation by Shlomo Pines, *The Guide of the Perplexed* (Chicago: University of Chicago Press, 1963), 123.

27. Al-Kindī, *Sur la philosophie première*, chap. 1, in *Métaphysique et cosmologie*, ed. Roshdi Rashed and Jean Jolivet, vol. 2 of *Oeuvres philosophiques et scientifiques d'Al-Kindi*, 2 vols. (Leiden: Brill, 1998), p. 15, 11–14.

28. Qur'an 2:164, etc.

29. Al-Amiri, *Kitāb al-Iʿlam bi-manāqib al-Islām*. Since I have been unable to locate the edition by Ahmad Abd al-Hamīd Ghurāb (Cairo: Dar al-Katib al-ʿArabi, 1967), I am quoting from the edition by Franz Rosenthal, *The Classical Heritage in Islam*, trans. Emile and Jenny Marmorstein (Berkeley: University of California Press, 1975), 65–66.

30. Averroes, *Le Livre du discours décisif*, ed. and trans. Marc Geoffroy (Paris: GF-Flammarion, 1996); quoted from Averroes, *On the Harmony of Religions and Philosophy*, trans. George F. Hourani (London: Luzac, 1967), 44.

31. Steven Harvey, *Falaquera's Epistle of the Debate: An Introduction to Jewish Philosophy* (Cambridge, MA: Harvard University Press, 1987), p. 73 (in Hebrew). See also Elijah ben Moses Abba Delmedigo, *Sefer Behinat ha-dat* (An examination of religion) (in Hebrew), ed. Jacob Joshua Ross (Tel Aviv: Tel Aviv University, 1984), p. 77, 3–4.

32. Maimonides, *Guide for the Perplexed*, 1.3, p. 50, 8–12; Munk trans., pp. 120–22; quoted from *The Guide of the Perplexed*, trans. Pines, 74–75. See also ibid., 1.55, p. 88, 4; Munk trans., p. 226.

33. Plato *Timaeus* 28c. For citations of this passage, see, for example, Ibn Khaldīn, *Muqaddima*, 30, vol. 3, p. 215; Ibn Khaldīn, *Livre des examples*, 1038. Further references are given in note 1029 of the Franz Rosenthal translation of *Muqaddima*, 3:252–53n1029.

34. Plato *Timaeus* 47b; translated into French by L. Brisson (Paris: Garnier-Flammarion, 1999), 144; quoted from the English translation by R. G. Bury, Loeb Classical Library, *Plato*, vol. 9 (Cambridge, MA: Harvard University Press; London: William Heinemann, 1981), 107–9. See also ibid., 90d.

35. See Rémi Brague, *La Sagesse du monde: Histoire de l'expérience humaine de l'Univers* (Paris: Fayard, 1999), new rev. ed. (Paris: LGF, 2002); translated into English by Teresa Lavender Fagan as *The Wisdom of the World: The Human Experience of the Universe in Western Thought* (Chicago: University of Chicago Press, 2003).

36. Paul Edward Dutton, ed., *The Glosae super Platonem of Bernard of Chartres* (Toronto: Pontifical Institute of Mediaeval Studies, 1991), p. 140, 32ff. (text in Latin).

37. Averroes, *Aristotle's Middle Commentary on Physics*, preface (in Latin), Juntine ed. (Venice, 1552), vol. 4, p. 2c. See Harvey, "The Hebrew Translation of Averroes' Prooemium," p. 66, 22–23.

38. Seneca, *Naturales Quaestiones*, preface, par. 12, trans. Thomas H. Corcoran, Loeb Classical Library (Cambridge, MA: Harvard University Press; London: William Heinemann, 1971), 9–11.

39. See, for example, Plato *Laws* 7.804b.

40. Thomas Aquinas, *Summa contra Gentiles*, 2.3 (Rome: Editio Leonina Manualis, 1934), 95a; quoted from *The Summa contra Gentiles of Saint Thomas Aquinas*, translated into English by the English Dominican Fathers (London: Burns & Washbourne, 1923), 2:2, 4, 6.

41. Thomas Aquinas, *In Symbolum Apostolorum Expositio*, chap. 1, pars. 879–86, in his *Opuscula Theologica*, ed. Raimondo M. Spiazzi, 2 vols. (Turin: Marietti, 1954), 196b–198a.

42. Maimonides *Guide for the Perplexed* 2.1. See Thomas Aquinas, *Commentary on the Sentences*, 2, d. 1, q. 1, a. 5c, in *S. Thomae Aquinatis Opera Omnia*, ed. Roberto Busa, 7 vols. (Stuttgart: Frommann-Holzboog, 1980), 1:126a; and Thomas Aquinas, *De articulis fidei et de Ecclesiae sacramentis*, 3. See Jacob Guttmann, "Der Einfluss der maimonideschen Philosophie auf das christliche Abendland," in Wilhelm Bacher et al., *Moses ben Maimon: Sein Leben, seine Werke und sein Einfluss*, 2 vols. (Leipzig: Fock, 1908), 1:135–230, esp. 193–94.

43. Augustine, *Soliloquies*, 1.2.7, in Bibliothèque Augustinienne, *Oeuvres de saint Augustin* (Paris: Desclée de Brouwer, 1936–), 5:16.

44. Hasdai Crescas, *The Light of the Lord (Sefer Or Adonai)* (in Hebrew), ed. Shelomoh Fisher (Jerusalem: Ramot, 1990), 2.6.1, pp. 233ff.

45. Averroes, *Epitome De anima*, ed. Salvator Gómez Nogales (Madrid: Consejo Superior de Investigaciones Cientificas; Instituto Hispano Arabe de Cultura, 1985), par. 99, pp. 95–96.

46. Gersonides, *Milhamot ha-Shem* (in Hebrew) (Riva di Trento, 1560; repr., Leipzig, 1866), 1.4, p. 6a–b; p. 26; quoted from *The Wars of the Lord*, trans. Seymour Feldman, 3 vols. (Philadelphia: Jewish Publication Society of America, 5745 / 1984), 1:131.

47. Gersonides, *Milhamot ha-Shem*, introduction, p. 2c; p. 5; Feldman trans., 1:96.

48. Ibid., 5.1.1, p. 31c; Feldman trans., 1:189.

49. See Blaise Pascal, *Pensées*, no. 139, ed. Léon Brunschvicg (Paris: Hachette, 1925), 56; and Gotthold Ephraim Lessing, *Eine Duplik*, 1, in his *Werke*, ed. Helmut Göbel et al. (Darmstadt: Wissenschaftliche Buchgesellschaft, 1996), 8:33.

50. Gersonides, *Commentary on the Song of Songs*, cited in Gad Freudenthal, "Sauver son âme ou sauver les phénomènes: Sotériologie, épistémologie et astronomie chez Gersonide," in *Studies on Gersonides: A Fourteenth-Century Jewish Philosopher-Scientist*, ed. Gad Feudenthal (Leiden: Brill, 1992), 325.

51. Gersonides, *Milhamot ha-Shem*, 5.2.4, p. 42d; p. 257. For Themistius, see my translation: Themistius, *Paraphrase de la Métaphysique d'Aristote (livre Lambda)*, trans. Rémi Brague (Paris: Vrin, 1999), 86, 94.

52. Gersonides, *Milhamot ha-Shem*, 1.12, p. 16a–b; pp. 85–88.

53. Ibid., 2.2, p. 17a; p. 95; 5.1.1, p. 31a; p. 189.

54. Gersonides, *Commentary on the Torah*, p. 210a, point 9; quoted in Charles Touati, *La pensée philosophique et théologique de Gersonide* (Paris: Minuit, 1973; repr., Paris: Gallimard, 1992), 440n24.

55. Rainer Maria Rilke, letter of November 13, 1925, in his *Briefe aus Muzot: 1921 bis 1926*, ed. Ruth Sieber-Rilke and Carl Sieber (Leipzig: Insel, 1935), 335.

56. Gersonides, *Milhamot ha-Shem*, 1.1, p. 17a, p. 90.

Chapter 5

1. Walter Benjamin, *Thesen zur Philosophie der Geschichte*, par. 7, at the end.

2. Edmund Husserl, *Die Krisis der europäischen Wissenschaften und die transzendentale Phänomenologie*, ed. Walter Biemel, Husserliana, vol. 6, 2nd ed. (The Hague: Nijhoff, 1962), par. 2, p. 4; translated into English by David Carr as *The Crisis of European Sciences and Transcendental Phenomenology: An Introduction to Phenomenological Philosophy* (Evanston, IL: Northwestern University Press, 1970).

3. Martin Heidegger, *Nietzsche*, 2 vols. (Pfullingen: Neske, 1961), 2:141; see also 2:167, 182; translated into English by David Farrel Krell, 4 vols. (San Francisco: Harper & Row, 1979–87).

4. Martin Heidegger, *Holzwege*, 4th ed. (Frankfurt: Klostermann, 1963), 100; translated into English by Julian Young and Kenneth Haynes as *Off the Beaten Track* (New York: Cambridge University Press, 2002); Immanuel Kant, *Critique of Pure Reason*, trans. and ed. Paul Guyer and Allen N. Wood (Cambridge: Cambridge University Press, 1998), 246.

5. Heidegger, *Nietzsche*, 2:154–55; quoted from *Nietzsche*, vol. 4, *Nihilism*, trans. Frank A. Capuzzi, ed. David Farrell Krell (San Francisco: Harper & Row, 1982), 107.

6. See Alain Renaut, *L'Ère de l'individu: Contribution à une histoire de la subjectivité* (Paris: Gallimard, 1989), 40ff.; translated into English by M. B. DeBevoise and Franklin Philip as *The Era of the Individual: A Contribution to a History of Subjectivity* (Princeton, NJ: Princeton University Press, 1997).

7. It is possible, however, that Heidegger had the impression that the promise had never been fulfilled when he took part in the Thor Seminar in 1966; see Heidegger, *Questions IV*, trans. Jean Beaufret (Paris: Gallimard, 1976), 222.

8. Heidegger, *Holzwege*, 103; Heidegger, *Die Frage nach dem Ding: Zu Kants Lehre von den tranzendentalen Grundsätzen* (Tübingen: Niemeyer, 1962), 77; translated into English by W. B. Barton Jr. and Vera Deutsch as *What Is a Thing?* (Chicago: Regnery, 1968); Heidegger, *Nietzsche*, 2:135, 146.

9. See Guy G. Stroumsa, "Caro salutis cardo: Formation de la personne chrétienne," in *Savoir et salut* (Paris: Cerf, 1992), 199–223.

10. Aristotle *Politics* 1.2.1253a 9–10, 7.13.1332b 5. For the context, see Rémi Brague, *Aristote et la question du monde: Essai sur le contexte cosmologique et anthropologique de l'ontologie* (Paris: Presses Universitaires de France, 1988), 261–63.

11. See, for example, Augustine, *De Trinitate*, 7.4.7, in Bibliothèque Augustinienne, *Oeuvres de saint Augustin* (Paris: Desclée de Brouwer, 1936–), 15:528; translated into English by Arthur West Haddan as *On the Trinity: De Trinitate Libri XV* (New York: n.p., 1887); John Scotus Erigena, *De divisione naturae*, 4.7, in *Patrologiae cursus completus . . . Series Latina* (hereafter *PL*), ed. Jacques-Paul Migne and Adalberto Hamman (Paris, 1844–64), 122:768b–c; Bernard of Clairvaux, *In dedicatione ecclesiae*, 5.7, in *Opera*, ed. Jean Le Clercq et al., 9 vols. (Rome: Editiones Cistercienses, 1957–77), 5:393; and Bernard of Clairvaux, *De consideratione*, 4.7, in *Opera*, 3:415; translated into English by John D. Anderson and Elizabeth T. Kennan as *Five Books on Consideration: Advice to a Pope* (Kalamazoo, MI: Cistercian Publications, 1976).

12. See, for example, Augustine, *De moribus ecclesiae catholicae*, 1.27.52, in his *Oeuvres*, 1:212; and Augustine, *Commentary on the Gospel of John / Tractatus in epistolam Ioannis I*, 19.15, in Corpus Christianorum, Series Latina (Tournai: Brepols, 1953–), 36:415.

13. See Étienne Gilson, *Introduction à l'étude de saint Augustin* (1943), 4th ed. (Paris: Vrin, 1969), 58; translated into English by L. E. M. Lynch as *The Christian Philosophy of Saint Augustine* (1960; repr., New York: Octagon, 1988).

14. Plato *Symposium* 203a.2.

15. See, for example, Plotinus *Enneads* 4.8 [6].4.32; (for *amphibios*), 3.2 [47].8.9–10; and Hierocles, *Commentary on the Golden Verses (Hieroclis Commentarium in Aureum Carmen)*, in *Fragmenta Philosophorum Graecorum*, ed. Friedrich Wilhelm August Mullach (Paris, 1860), 462b. Hierocles is translated into English from the French of André Dadier by N. Rowe as *Commentary of Hierocles on the Golden Verses of Pythagoras* (Wheaton, IL: Theosophical Publishing, 1971).

16. Augustine, *Der Gottesstaat (De civitate Dei)*, trans. into German by Carl Johann Perl, 2 vols. (Paderborn: Schöningh, 1979), 9.13.3, vol. 1, p. 588; quoted from *The City of God against the Pagans*, ed. and trans. R. W. Dyson (Cambridge: Cambridge University Press, 1988), 376.

17. Farabi, "Responses to Questions Put to Him," no. 4, in *Risalatan falsafiyatan* (in Arabic), ed. Ja'far Al Yasin (Beirut: Dar al-Manahil, 1987), 80–81.

18. Dionysius the Areopagite, *The Divine Names (De divini nominibus)*, 4.1, 6.2, in *Patrologiae cursus completus . . . Series graeca* (hereafter *PG*), ed. Jacques-Paul Migne and Ferdinand Cavallera (Paris, 1866), 3:693c, 856c; *The Celestial Hierarchy (De coelesti hierarchia)*,

1.3, (*PG* 3:121c); 2.4 (*PG* 3:144b); *The Hierarchy of the Church* (*De ecclesiastica hierarchia*), 1.2 (*PG*, 3:373a).

19. On Muslim angelology as a whole, see Fahmi Jadʾān, "La place des anges dans la théologie musulmane," *Studia Islamica* 41 (1975): 23–61; on the philosophers, see 33–42. See also *Al-Farabi on the Perfect State: Abu Nasr al-Farabi's Mabadi ara ahi al madina al-fadila,* trans. Richard Walzer (Oxford: Clarendon Press, 1985), 2.3, pars. 1–10, pp. 100–104; and Avicenna, *Al-Shifa Al-llahiyyat (1) (La Métaphysique),* ed. Georges C. Anawati and Saʾid Zayed (Cairo: Organisation générale des imprimeries gouvernementales, 1960), 9.4, p. 404; translated into English by Parviz Morewedge as *The Metaphysica of Avicenna (Ibn Sīnā)* (London: Routledge & Kegan Paul, 1973).

20. See Maimonides, *Guide for the Perplexed* (in Arabic), ed. Issachar Joël (Jerusalem: Junovitch, 1929), 1.49, p. 73; translated into French by Salomon Munk as *Guide des égarés,* 3 vols. (Paris, 1856–66; repr., Paris: Maisonneuve, 1970), 1:175.

21. Thomas Aquinas, *De substantiis separatis,* pars. 42–172, in *Opuscula Philosophica,* ed. Raimondo M. Spiazzi (Turin: Marietti, 1954), pp. 21–58; translated into English by Francis J. Lescoe as *Tractatus de substantiis separatis* (West Hartford CT: St. Joseph College, 1962); Dante *Convivio* 2.5; translated into English by Richard H. Lansing as *Dante's Il convivio (The Banquet)* (New York: Garland, 1990).

22. Augustine, *Der Gottesstaat (De civitate Dei),* 19.9, vol. 2, p. 462.

23. Immanuel Kant, *Die Religion innerhalb der Grenzen der blossen Vernunft,* 2, in *Werke in sechs Bänden,* ed. Wilhelm Weischedel, 6 vols. (Darmstadt: Wissenschaftliche Buchgesellschaft, 1983), 4:743; translated into English by George di Giovanni as *Religion within the Boundaries of Mere Reason,* in *Religion and Rational Theology,* trans. Allen N. Wood and George di Giovanni (Cambridge: Cambridge University Press, 1996), 39–216. See also Alexis de Tocqueville, letter to Eugène Stoffels, January 3, 1843, in *Oeuvres et correspondances inédites,* ed. Gustave de Beaumont, 2 vols. (Paris, 1861), 1:449.

24. Augustine, Sermon 362, 15.17, in *PL,* 39:1622; quoted from *The Works of Saint Augustine: A Translation for the 21st Century, Sermons 111/10 (341–400) on Various Subjects,* trans. Edmund Hill, ed. John E. Rotelle (Hyde Park, NY: New City Press, 1995), 253.

25. See Caroline Walker Bynum, "Material Continuity, Personal Survival and the Resurrection of the Body: A Scholastic Discussion in Its Medical and Modern Contexts," *History of Religions* 30 (1990): 51–85, esp. 70.

26. Augustine, *Der Gottesstaat (De civitate Dei),* 14.3, vol. 1, p. 316.

27. Bernard of Clairvaux, *Sermons on the Song of Songs* (Sermones super *Cantica canticorum*), 26.6.9, in *Opera,* 1:177 (*PL,* 183, 909c–d); quoted from *On the Song of Songs,* trans. Kilian Walsh, 4 vols. (Spencer, MA: Cistercian Publications, 1971–80), 2:69. The importance of this passage for the new conception of carnality was clearly seen by Colin Morris, *The Discovery of the Individual (1050–1200)* (New York: Harper & Row, 1973), 67.

28. See Bernard of Clairvaux, *On the Love of God (De diligendo Deo),* 8.23–24, in *Opera,* 3:138–39. The same idea appears in William of Saint-Thierry, *Commentaire sur le Cantique des cantiques (Expositio super Cantica canticorum),* ed. M. M. Davy (Paris: Vrin, 1958), par. 20, p. 50; translated into English by Mother Columba Hart as *Exposition on the Song of Songs* (Spencer, MA: Cistercian Publications, 1970).

29. Bernard of Clairvaux, *Sermon on the Vigil of the Nativity (In Vigilia Nativitatis Domini Sermo),* 4.7, in *Opera,* 4:225. Anna Maiorino Tuozzi, *La conoscenza de sè nella scuola cisterciense* (Naples: Istituto Italiano per gli Studi Storici, 1976), 29, gives a clear summary of the implications of this image.

30. See the references to the controversy over whether men or angels (usually conceived as the intellects of the celestial spheres) are the ultimate goal of creation in Saadia

Gaon, Ibn Ezra, and others in a tightly packed note in Henry Malter, *Saadia Gaon: His Life and Works* (Philadelphia: Jewish Publication Society of America, 1921), 212–13n485.

31. Qur'an 2:31–33.

32. See, for example, William of Saint-Thierry, *On the Nature of the Body and the Soul* (*De natura corporis et animae*), 2, in *PL*, 180:721d; Thomas Aquinas *Summa theologica* 1a, q. 93, a. 3; and Dante *Convivio* 4.19.6.

33. See, for example, Thomas Aquinas, *Summa contra Gentiles* (Rome: Editio Leonina Manualis, 1934), 1.12, p. 10b.

34. Bernard of Clairvaux, *On the Song of Songs* (*Sermones in Cantica*), 5.1, 1–4, in *Opera*, 1:21–23, in *PL*, 183:799a–800b.

35. Ulrich von Wilamowitz-Moellendorff, *Der Glaube der Hellenen*, 2 vols. (Berlin: Weidmann, 1931–32), 1:45.

36. Aristotle *De anima* 3.12.434b 10–18.

37. Thomas Aquinas *Summa contra Gentiles* 4.84, p. 555b.

38. Aristotle *De anima* 3.13.435a 12–13.

39. See Brague, *Aristote et la question du monde*, 372.

40. Aristotle *Metaphysics* Λ.9.1074b 36; Aristotle *De anima* 3.4.429b 9.

41. See Aristotle, *On the Motion of Animals*, 3.699a 25; translated into English by Anthony Preus as *On the Movement and Progression of Animals* (Hildesheim: Olms, 1981).

42. Edmund Husserl, *Grundlegende Untersuchungen zum phänomenologischen Ursprung der Räumlichkeit der Natur* (or *Umsturz der Kopernikanischen Lehre . . . die Ur-Arche Erde bewegt sich nicht*), in *Philosophical Essays in Memory of Edmund Husserl*, ed. Marvin Farber (Cambridge, MA: Harvard University Press, 1940), 307–25, esp. 323; see also 311, 318.

43. See Shlomo Pines, "La conception de la conscience de soi chez Avicenne et chez Abu'l Barakāt al-Baghdādī," in *The Collected Works of Shlomo Pinès*, 5 vols. (Jerusalem: Magnes; Leiden: Brill, 1979–96), 1:181–258, esp. (on Avicenna) 181–216. The first to have compared Avicenna and Descartes was perhaps Giuseppe Furlani, "Avicenna e il *Cogito ergo sum* di Cartesio," *Islamica* (1927): 53–72.

44. *Avicenna's De Anima: Being the Psychological part of Kitāb al-shifāʾ* (in Arabic), ed. Fazlur Rahman (London: Oxford University Press, 1959), 1.1, p. 16; in Latin translation as *Liber de anima, seu Sextus de Naturalibus*, ed. Simone van Riet, 2 vols. (Louvain: Peeters; Leiden: Brill, 1972), 1:36. There is an analogous parable in ibid., 5.7, p. 255 (Latin version, p. 262), that refers to the passage cited. See also Avicenna, *Livre des théorèmes et des avertissements*, ed. J. Forget (Leiden: Brill, 1892), 119; and Avicenna, *Livre des directives et des remarques* (*Kitab al-Isarāt wa l-tanbihāt*), trans. Amélie-Marie Goichon (Paris: Vrin, 1951), 303–4.

45. See Rémi Brague, "L'anthropologie de l'humilité," in *Saint Bernard et la Philosophie*, ed. Rémi Brague (Paris: Presses Universitaires de France, 1993), 129–52.

46. Isidore of Seville, *Etymologies*, 10.116, in *PL*, 82, p. 379b; Papias, *Vocabularium*, p. 148a.

47. This etymology is cited by Quintilian, but with disapproval: see *The Orator's Education*, 1.6.34, ed. and trans. Donald A. Russell, Loeb Classical Library (Cambridge, MA: Harvard University Press, 2001). See also Isidore of Seville, *Etymologies*, 7.6.4, s.v. "Adam," in *PL*, 82, p. 379b: "*humus hominis faciendi materia fuit*"; Papias, *Vocabularium*, p. 147a.

48. Cited in Charles-Henri de Fouchécour, *Moralia: Les notions morales dans la littérature persane du 3ᵉ/9ᵉ au 7ᵉ/13ᵉ siècle* (Paris: Recherches sur les Civilisations, 1986), 341.

49. Bernard of Clairvaux, *Sermon for the Sunday of 1 November* (*Pro Dominica 1 Novembris*), 2.2, in *PL*, 183, p. 347a.

50. Bernard of Clairvaux, *Sermon for All Saints' Day* (*In Festo Omnium Sanctorum Sermo I*), 1.9, in *PL*, 183, p. 457c.

51. Arnaldus of Bonneval, *De operibus sex dierum*, in *PL*, 189, p. 1529b.

52. See Rémi Brague, "Le géocentrisme comme humiliation de l'homme," in *Hermé-neutique et ontologie: Hommage à Pierre Aubenque* (Paris: Presses Universitaires de France, 1990) and below, chap. 15, "Geocentrism as the Humiliation of Man."

53. See the references in Brague, "L'anthropologie de l'humilité," 133n123.

54. 2 Corinthians 4:7. For Bernard of Clairvaux, see Bernard of Clairvaux, *On the Psalm Qui habitat* (*In Psalmum XC, Qui Habitat*), 7.14, 17.3, in *Opera*, 4:423, 488 (*PL*, 183, pp. 208b, 251d); translated into English by Marie-Bernard Saïd as *Sermons on Conversion: On Conversion, A Sermon to Clerics and Lenten Sermons on the Psalm "He Who Dwells"* (Kalamazoo, MI: Cistercian Publications, 1981); Bernard of Clairvaux, *On the Nativity of the Blessed Virgin Mary* (*In Navitate B. Mariae Virginis Sermo*), 17, in *Opera*, 5:287 (*PL*, 183, p. 447a); Bernard of Clairvaux, *De diversis* (*Sermones De Diversis*), 18.5, in *Opera*, vol. 6, pt. 1, p. 160 (*PL*, 183, p. 589b).

55. Bernard of Clairvaux, *Sermon on Missus est* (*Super* Missus Est Homillae), 3.9, in *Opera*, 4:42 (*PL*, 183, p. 75d).

56. See, for example, *Mystic Treatises of Isaac of Nineveh*, English translation from Bedjan's Syriac text by A. J. Wensinck, Verhandelingen der Koninklijke Akademie van Wetenschappen to Amsterdam, Afdeeling letterkunde. Nieuwe reeks.d. 23, no. 1 (Amsterdam, 1923), 65, p. 298 [444].

57. Bernard of Clairvaux, *De gradibus humilitatis et superbiae*, 1.2, in *Opera*, 3:17 (*PL*, 182, p. 942b); quoted from *The Steps of Humility*, trans. George Bosworth Burch (Cambridge, MA: Harvard University Press, 1942), 125.

58. See Bruno Michel, "La considération et l' 'unitas spiritus,'" in *Saint Bernard et la Philosophie*, ed. Brague, 109–27.

59. See above, p. 95.

60. Arthur Schopenhauer, *Preisschrift über die Grundlage der Moral*, in *Sämtliche Werke*, ed. Wolfgang von Löhneysen, 5 vols. (Darmstadt: Wissenschaftliche Buchgesellschaft, 1980), 3:658.

61. See below, chap. 6, "The Denial of Humanity."

62. Maurice Merleau-Ponty, *Le visible et l'invisible: Suivi de notes de travail*, ed. Claude Lefort (Paris: Gallimard, 1964); translated into English by Alphonse Lingis as *The Visible and the Invisible: Followed by Working Notes*, ed. Claude Lefort (Evanston, IL: Northwestern University Press, 1968). On *"chair"* equated with *Leib*, see *Le visible*, 309; on the claimed radical novelty of the concept, see ibid., 183, 193.

63. See, for example, Didier Franck, *Chair et corps: Sur la phénoménologie de Husserl* (Paris: Minuit, 1981).

64. Pierre Jean Olivi, *Quaestiones in secundum librum Sententiarum*, ed. Bernardus Jansen, 3 vols. (Ad Claras Aquas [Quaracchi] prope Florentiam: Collegii S. Bonaventurae, 1922–26), q. 57, 2:338.

65. See, for example, Jean Grondin, *Einfürung in die philosophische Hermeneutik* (Darmstadt: Wissenschaftliche Buchgesellschaft, 1991), 51–52.

66. Gorgias, *On Non-Being*, fragment, in *Die Fragmente der Vorsokratiker* (in Greek and German), 3 vols. ed. Hermann Diels and Walther Kranz (Berlin: Weidmann, 1956), 82b 3, vol. 2, pp. 279ff.; in Sextus Empiricus, *Adversus Mathematicos*, 7, pars. 65 and 83–86. See also Plato *Gorgias* 481c 5–d 1.

67. See Plato *Parmenides* 135c 2; Aristotle *Metaphysics* Γ.4.1006b 8; and Themistius, *Commentary on the Treatise of the Soul* (*Themistii in Libros De anima paraphrasis*), chap. 6, in

Commentaria in Aristotelem Graeca, ed. Richard Heinze (Berlin: Reimer, 1882–1907), vol. 5, pt. 3 (1899), p. 104, 2–3.

68. Thomas Aquinas, *De unitate intellectus*, chap. 3, par. 216, in *Opuscula Philosophica*, ed. Spiazzi, p. 76n; quoted from the English translation by Beatrice H. Zedler, *On the Unity of the Intellect against the Averroists* (Milwaukee: Marquette University Press, 1968), 51. See also Plotinus *Enneads* 4.3 [27].3.25–26.

69. Thomas Aquinas, *De unitate intellectus*, chap. 1, par. 180, in *Opuscula Philosophica*, ed. Spiazzi, p. 65b.

70. Johann Wolfgang von Goethe to Lavater, September 20, 1780.

71. See Thomas Aquinas, who admits a direct, but unsounded *locutio*: *Summa theologica*, 1a, q. 107, a. 1, ad. 1 m. See also Dante, *De vulgari eloquentia*, ed. Aristide Marigo (Florence: Le Monnier, 1948), 1.3.1, p. 18; translated into English by Steven Botterill (Cambridge: Cambridge University Press, 1996). On Dante, see Karl-Otto Apel, *Die Idee der Sprache in der Tradition des Humanismus von Dante bis Vico*, 2nd ed. (Bonn: Bouvier, 1975).

72. See Aristotle *Nicomachean Ethics* 9.9.1169b 33–34; and Thomas Aquinas's commentary on the passage in *Commentary on Aristotle's Nicomachean Ethics*, trans. C. I. Litzinger, O.P. (1964; repr., Notre Dame, IN: Dumb Ox Books, 1993), 9.9.1169b 33–34, 9.10, par. 1896, p. 496a.

73. Thomas Aquinas, *De unitate intellectus*, chap. 4, par. 239, in *Opuscula Philosophica*, ed. Spiazzi, p. 83a.

Chapter 6

1. Aristotle *Politics* 7.7.1327b 29–33.

2. See Friedrich Nietzsche, *Morgenröte*, 3, par. 205, and 4, par. 241, in *Sämliche Werke: Kritische Studienausgabe*, ed. Giorgio Colli and Mazzino Montinari, 15 vols. (Munich: Deutscher Taschenbuch Verlag; New York: de Gruyter, 1988), 3:180–83, 202.

3. See Bernard Pautrat, preface to his translation of Spinoza, *Éthique* (Paris: Seuil, 1988), 11 (on Charles Appuhn). On Boulainvilliers, see (among others) Hannah Arendt, *The Origins of Totalitarianism* (1951; repr., New York: Schocken, 2004); translated into French by Martine Leirus as *L'impérialisme* (Paris: Fayard, 1982), 75–76.

4. See Hugo Ott, *Martin Heidegger: Unterwegs zuer seiner Biographie* (Frankfurt: Campus, 1988), 183, 315; on Husserl's letter to Mahnke, see ibid., p. 178; translated into English by Allan Blunden as *Martin Heidegger: A Political Life* (New York: HarperCollins, 1993).

5. To cite just one work, there are dozens of other examples that Henri de Lubac has gathered together, with dazzling erudition, to illuminate the context of the theme of Proteus in the Italian Renaissance in his *Pic de la Mirandole: Études et discussions* (Paris: Aubier Montaigne, 1974), 184–217.

6. Aristotle *Politics* 1.2.1253a 29; quoted from *Politics*, ed. H. Rackham, Loeb Classical Library (London: William Heinemann; Cambridge, MA: Harvard University Press, 1959), 11–13.

7. See Rémi Brague, "Note sur la traduction arabe de la *Politique* d'Aristote: Derechef, qu'elle n'existe pas," in *Aristote politique: Études sur la Politique d'Aristote*, ed. Pierre Aubenque (Paris: Presses Universitaires de France, 1993), 423–33.

8. Thomas Aquinas, *Commentarii in octo libros politicorum Aristotelis expositio*, 1, par. 39, ed. Raimondo M. Spiazzi (Turin: Marietti, 1966), p. 12a; quoted from Thomas Aquinas, *Commentary on Aristotle's Politics*, trans. Ronald J. Regan (Indianapolis: Hackett, 2007), 18.

9. Aristotle *Politics* 3.2.1281b 19–20; Rackham trans., 223.

10. Thomas Aquinas, *Commentarii in octo libros politicorum Aristotelis expositio*, 8, par. 426, ed. Spiazzi, p. 149a.

11. Cicero, *De officiis*, 1.30.105, ed. Karl Atzert (Leipzig: Teubner, 1963), p. 36; translated into French by Émile Bréher in *Les Stoïciens*, ed. Pierre-Maxime Schuhl (Paris: Gallimard, 1962), 531; quoted from *De officiis*, trans. Walter Miller, Loeb Classical Library (Cambridge, MA: Harvard University Press; London: William Heinemann, 1968), 107–9.

12. Seneca, *De vita beata*, par. 5, in *Les Stoïciens*, 727–28; quoted from Seneca, "De vita beata; On the Happy Life," in *Moral Essays*, trans. John W. Basore, Loeb Classical Library (London: William Heinemann; New York: G. P. Putnam's Sons, 1932), 111–13.

13. Epictetus, *Entretiens*, 2.22.27–28, in *Les Stoïciens*, 947; quoted from Epictetus, *The Discourses as Reported by Arrian*, trans. W. A. Oldfather, Loeb Classical Library, 2 vols. (Cambridge, MA: Harvard University Press, 2000), 1:391.

14. Epictetus *Entretiens* 4.5.19, in *Les Stoïciens*, 1071; quoted from Epictetus, *Discourses*, Oldfather trans., 2:339.

15. See the texts cited by Charles Touati in his notes to Levi ben Gershom (Gersonides), *Les Guerres du Seigneur, Livres III et IV*, trans. Charles Touati (Paris: Mouton, 1968), 133–34n14; Bahya ibn Paquda, *Kitāb al-hidāya ilā farā'id al-qulūb* (Duties of the heart), ed. and trans. A. S. Yahuda (Leiden: Brill, 1912), 3.6, p. 156; translated into French by André Chouraqui as *Les devoir des coeurs*, 2nd ed. (Paris: Desclée de Brouwer, 1972), 213; translated into English by Menahem Mansoor, with Sara Arenson and Shoshana Dannhauser, as *The Book of Direction to the Duties of the Heart* (London: Routledge & Kegan Paul, 1973); Joseph ben Jacob ibn Zaddik, *ha-ʿOlam ha-Katan*, ed. Saul Horovitz (Breslau: Schatzky, 1903; reproduction, Jerusalem: n.p., 1967), 43; Abraham Ibn Daoud, *The Exalted Faith (Emunah ha-ramah)* (in Hebrew and English), ed. and trans. Norbert M. Samuelson, translation edited by Gershon Weiss (Rutherford: Fairleigh Dickinson University Press, 1986), 24; and Maimonides, *Guide for the Perplexed* (in Arabic), ed. Issachar Joël (Jerusalem: Junovitch, 1929), 1.7; translated into French by Salomon Munk as *Guide des égarés*, 3 vols. (Paris, 1856–66; repr., Paris: Maisonneuve, 1970), 1:51.

16. Hermes Trismegistus, "La Clef (Traité X)," in *Corpus Hermeticorum*, ed. A. D. Nock and A.-J. Festugière, 2 vols. (Paris: Les Belles Lettres, 1960), par. 24, 1:125.

17. *Hebrew-English Edition of the Babylonian Talmud*, ed. Rabbi Dr. I. Epstein, 40 vols. (London: Soncino Press, 1960–90), *Bava Mezi'a*, 21:651, and *Yebamoth*, 13:404–5; quoted from *The Talmud of Babylonia: An American Translation*, trans. Jacob Neusner (Chico, CA: Scholars Press, 1984–93), *Tractate Bava Mesia Chapters 7–10*, 180.

18. *Le Zohar*, French trans. by Charles Mopsik (Lagrasse: Verdier, 1981–), 1:117.

19. *Hebrew-English Edition of the Babylonian Talmud*, ed. Epstein, 405n2.

20. Moritz Lazarus, *Die Ethik des Judentums* (Frankfurt, 1898), appendix 10, pp. 378–79, citing *Yebamoth* 63a; quoted from the English translation by Henrietta Szold, *The Ethics of Judaism*, 4 vols. (Philadelphia: Jewish Publications Society of America, 1900), 1:264–65.

21. See Johann Andreas Eisenmenger, *Entdecktes Judentum*, 2 vols. (1700), 2:2–3. This text does not refer to the Talmud, but to later texts that contain the same idea.

22. Boethius, *De consolatione philosophiae*, 4, prosa 3; quoted from Boethius, *The Theological Tractates and The Consolation of Philosophy*, ed. S. J. Tester, Loeb Classical Library, rev. ed. (London: Heinemann, 1973), 334–35.

23. Pseudo-Aristotle *Physionomica* 1.805a 22–23.

24. Qur'an 8:20–22. See the French translation by Régis Blachère, *Le Coran*, 3 vols. (Paris: Maisonneuve, 1947) no. 97, p. 831. See also Rudi Paret, *Der Koran: Kommentar und Konkordanz* (Stuttgart: Kohlhammer, 1989), 127.

25. Rémi Brague, *La Loi de Dieu* (Paris: Gallimard, 2005), 328n106; translated into English by Lydia G. Cochrane as *The Law of God: The Philosophical History of an Idea* (Chicago: University of Chicago Press, 2007), 279n106.

26. Ibn Bājja, *Conduct of the Solitary*, chap. 2, in *Rasāʾil ibn Bājjah al-llāhīyah (Opera metaphysica)* (in Arabic), ed. and trans. Majid Fakhry (Beirut: Dar an-Nahar, 1968), 48; translated into Spanish by Miguel Asín Palacios as *El régime del solitario* (Madrid: Consejo Superior de Investigaciones Cientificas, 1946), 48; translated into French by Salomon Munk in "Des principaux philosophes arabes et leurs doctrines," in *Mélanges de philosophie juive et arabe* (Paris: Vrin, 1955), 392.

27. Quoted from *The Kuzari (Kitab al Kuzari): An Argument for the Faith of Israel*, trans. Hartwig Hirschfeld (1905; repr., New York: Schocken, 1964), 37.

28. This notion appears in Maimonides, letter to Samuel Ibn Tibbon, in Alexander Marx, "Texts by and about Maimonides" (in Hebrew), *Jewish Quarterly Review*, n.s. 25, no. 4 (1935): 371–81, 380a. There are also Averroes' hyperboles, lampooned in Nicolas de Malebranche, *Recherche de la Vérité*, bk. 2, part 2, chap. 6, in *Oeuvres*, ed. Geneviève Rodis-Lewis, 2 vols. (Paris: Gallimard, 1979), 1:224–25.

29. Jehuda Halevi, *The Book of Refutation and Proof of the Despised Faith: The Book of the Khazars (Known as the Kuzari)* (in Hebrew), ed. David Baneth and Haggai Ben-Shammai (Jerusalem: Magnes, 1977), 1, par. 1, p. 4, 8–9; translated into French by Charles Touati as *Le Kuzari, apologie de la religion méprisée* (Louvain: Peeters, 1994), 2.

30. Ibn Khaldūn, *[Muqaddima] Les Prolégomènes d'Ibn Khaldoun, texte arabe publié d'après les manuscrits de la Bibliothèque impériale*, ed. Étienne Quatremère, 3 vols. (Paris: Institut de France, 1858; repr., Beirut: Librairie du Liban, 1996), 2.24, vol. 1, p. 269; quoted from the English translation by Franz Rosenthal, *The Muqaddimah: An Introduction to History*, 3 vols. (New York: Pantheon, 1958), 1:301. See also Ibn Khaldūn, *Livre des exemples*, trans. Abdesselam Cheddadi (Paris: Gallimard, 2002), 410; *Muqaddima*, 1.3, vol. 1, p. 150; *Livre des exemples*, 314. See also Bernard Lewis, *Race and Color in Islam* (New York: Harper & Row, 1971), 38; translated into French by André Iteanu and Françoise Briand as *Race et couleur en pays d'Islam* (Paris: Payot, 1982), 59–62.

31. My thanks to Mme. J. Hansel for bringing this text to my attention.

32. Marginal commentary to the *Kuzari*, ed. Isaac Goldman (Warsaw, 1885; repr., n.p.: Hadaran, 1959), pp. 31b–32c. On the malediction of Ham and its "racist" interpretation, see Lewis, *Race and Color*, 66–67; *Race et couleur*, 67n90.

33. Halevi, *Book of Refutation*, 1, par. 62, p. 17, 4; translated into English by Hartwig Hirschfeld as *The Kuzari (Kitab al Khazari): An Argument for the Faith of Israel* (1905; repr., New York: Schocken, 1964), 52; Jehudah Halevi, *Sefer ha-Kuzari*, trans. Ibn Tibbon, ed. Isaac Goldmann (Warsaw, 1872), 1:76; Halevi, *Le Kuzari*, trans. Touati, 16.

34. Maimonides, *Commentary on the Mishnah* (in Arabic), introduction, 6, in *Haqdamot ha-RaMBaM la-Mishnah*, ed. I. Shaylat (Jerusalem: Birkat Moshe, 1992), 353; quoted from Maimonides, *Introduction to the Talmud*, trans. Zvi L. Lampel (New York: Judaica Press, 1975), 159.

35. Maimonides, *Commentary on the Mishnah*, *Baba Qamma*, 4.3 (37b), in the Eliyahu Vilna edition of the Talmud, p. 284 / 142b, col. 2 (in Hebrew). *Mishnah ʿim perush Rabenu Mosheh Ben Maïmon*, Seder Neziqin, ed. Yosef Kafah, 3 vols. (Jerusalem: Mosad Rav Kook, 1964–68), vol. 2, Nashim, Nezikin, pp. 15b–16a.

36. Maimonides, *Guide for the Perplexed*, 3.51, p. 455, 6–12; Munk trans., p. 431; quoted from *The Guide of the Perplexed*, trans. Shlomo Pines (Chicago: University of Chicago Press, 1963), 618–19.

37. See, for example, Avicenna, *Al-Shifa Al-llahiyyat (1) (La Métaphysique)*, ed. Georges C. Anawati and Saʾid Zayed (Cairo: Organisation générale des imprimeries gouvernementales, 1960), 10.5, p. 453; translated into English by Parviz Morewedge as *The Metaphysica*

of *Avicenna (Ibn Sīnā)* (London: Routledge & Kegan Paul, 1973). See also Lewis, *Race and Color*, 29, 34; *Race et couleur*, 53, 60.

38. Meister Eckhart, "About Disinterest," in *Die Deutschen Werke*, ed. Josef Quint, vols. 3–5 of *Die deutschen und lateinischen Werke* (Stuttgart: Kohlhammer, 1936–), 1:420, 451–52n; quoted from *Meister Eckhart: A Modern Translation*, trans. Raymond Bernard Blakney (New York: Harper and Bros., 1941), 87.

39. See, for example, Plato *Phaedra* 249e 5–6. See also Farabi, *Al-Farabi on the Perfect State: Abu Nasr al-Farabi's Mabadi ara ahi al madina al-fadila*, trans. Richard Walzer (Oxford: Clarendon Press, 1985), 5.16, par. 7, pp. 270–72.

40. See the astonishing passage in Plato *Philebus* 28c 7, and an unexpected parallel in Friedrich Nietzsche, fragment, Autumn 1887, 10 [90], in *Sämliche Werke: Kritische Studienausgabe*, 12:507; also in *The Will to Power*, par. 677.

41. See, for example, Ulysses' exhortations to his companions in Dante, *Divine Comedy*, *Inferno*, canto 26, lines 118–20; on which, see Hugo Freidrich, "Odysseus in der Hölle," in his *Romanische Literaturen*, Aufsätze II, *Italien und Spanien*, 2 vols. (Frankfurt: Klostermann, 1972), 1:71–118, esp. 91–115.

Chapter 7

1. Biruni, *Chronologie orientalischer Völker von Albērūnī*, ed. Eduard Sachau (Leipzig, 1878), chap. 15, p. 129, 19–20; quoted from the English translation by Eduard Sachau, *The Chronology of the Ancient Nations* (London, 1879; repr., Frankfurt: Unveränderter Nachdruck, 1969), 287.

2. Al-Bīrūnī, *Tahqīq mā li-'l-Hind min maqūla maqbūla la 'l-'aql wa mardūla*; translated into German as *In den Gärten der Wissenschaft*, ed. Gotthard Strohmaier, 2nd ed. (Leipzig: Reclam, 1991), no. 58, p. 163. Also worthy of consideration, but to be read with prudence, is al-Biruni, *Le livre de l'Inde*, trans. Vincent-Mansour Monteil (Arles: Acted Sud [Sinbad], 1996), 284; translated into English by Eduard Sachau as *Alberuni's India: An Account of the Religion, Philosophy, Literature, Geography, Chronology, Astronomy, Customs, Laws and Astrology of India about AD 1030*, 2 vols. (London: K. Paul Trench, Trübner, 1888), 2:161.

3. See, for example, Thomas Aquinas, *Summa theologica*, 5 vols. (Paris: Lethielleux, 1939), 2a, 2ae, q. 43, a. 8.

4. Aristotle *Rhetoric* 1.8.

5. See Rémi Brague, "Note sur la traduction arabe de la *Politique* d'Aristote: Derechef, qu'elle n'existe pas," in *Aristote politique: Études sur la Politique d'Aristote*, ed. Pierre Aubenque (Paris: Presses Universitaires de France, 1993), 423–33.

6. Averroes, *Commentaire moyen à la Rhétorique d'Aristote*, 1.8.8, in a critical edition of the Arabic text and French translation by Maroun Aouad, 3 vols. (Paris: Vrin, 2002), 2:70. On the context of this passage, see Rémi Brague, "Islam," in *Dictionnaire de Philosophie politique*, ed. Philippe Raynaud and Stéphane Rials (Paris: Presses Universitaires de France, 1996), 296–302, esp. 300.

7. Averroes, *Tahafot al-tahafot: Incohérence de l'incohérence*, ed. Maurice Bouyges (1930; repr., Beirut: Dar el-Machreq, 1987), 20, par. 6, p. 583, 10; translated into English by Simon van den Bergh as *Tahafut al-tahafut (The Incoherence of the Incoherence)* (London: Luzac, 1961).

8. Averroes, *Grand Commentaire de la Métaphysique (Tafsir Ma ba'd at-tabi'at)*, ed. Maurice Bouyges, 3 vols. in 4 pts. (Beirut: Dar el-Machreq, 1973), vol. 1, Grand Alpha, C 5, p. 63, 14.

9. Averroes, *Commentaire moyen à la Rhétorique*, 1.8.6, ed. Aouad, 2:69.

10. Muhsin Mahdi, "Al-Farabi," in *Dictionary of Scientific Biography*, ed. C. C. Gillispie (New York: Charles Scribner's Sons, 1970–90), 4:523a–26b.

11. For a trace within the Jewish domain, see the critique of Plato's *Republic* implicit in Gersonides, *Milhamot ha-Shem* (in Hebrew), (Riva di Trento, 1560; Leipzig, 1866), 2.2, 17b, 97; translated into English by Seymour Feldman as *The Wars of the Lord*, 3 vols. (Philadelphia: Jewish Publication Society of America, 1984–89).

12. I have drawn heavily on Muhsin Mahdi, *Ibn Khaldūn's Philosophy of History: A Study in the Philosophic Foundation of the Science of Culture* (Chicago: University of Chicago Press, 1964), 245–46.

13. Ibn Khaldūn, *[Muqaddima] Les Prolégomènes d'Ibn Khaldoun, texte arabe publié d'après les manuscrits de la Bibliothèque impériale*, ed. Étienne Quatremère, 3 vols. (Paris: Institut de France, 1858; repr., Beirut: Librairie du Liban, 1996), 2.12, vol. 1, p. 244, 18–20; translated into English by Franz Rosenthal as *The Muqaddimah: An Introduction to History*, 3 vols. (New York: Pantheon, 1958); Ibn Khaldūn, *Livre des exemples*, trans. Abdesselam Cheddadi (Paris: Gallimard, 2002), 390. The passage from Averroes mentioned is *Commentaire moyen à la Rhétorique*, 1.5.6, ed. Aouad, 2:40.

14. Ibn Khaldūn, *Muqaddima*, 1, supplement, vol. 1, p. 131; Ibn Khaldūn, *Livre des exemples*, 302.

15. Ibn Khaldūn, *Muqaddima*, 3.31, vol. 1, p. 415, 3–18; quoted from Rosenthal trans., *The Muqaddimah*, 1:472–73.

16. Ibn Khaldūn, *Muqaddima*, 3.31, vol. 1, p. 415, 18–419, 4, and p. 418, 5–422, 16; Ibn Khaldūn, *Livre des exemples*, pp. 533–34 and pp. 534–38.

17. Ibn Khaldūn, *Muqaddima*, 1, supplement, vol. 1, p. 110; esp. 2.18, p. 256, 2–257; *Livre des exemples*, pp. 288, 399–400. See Shlomo Pines, "Ibn Khaldūn et Maïmonide: Comparaison entre deux textes," in *La liberté de philosopher: De Maïmonide à Spinoza*, French translation from Hebrew and English by Rémi Brague (Paris: Desclée de Brouwer, 1997), 289–99.

18. Ibn Khaldūn, *Muqaddima*, 3.9, vol. 1, p. 297; *Livre des exemples*, p. 432.

19. Ibn Khaldūn, *Muqaddima*, 2.12, vol. 1, p. 244, 6–16; *Livre des exemples*, p. 389.

20. Ibn Khaldūn, *Muqaddima*, 3.23, vol. 1, p. 343, 11–12; *Livre des exemples*, p. 470.

21. Ibn Khaldūn, *Muqaddima*, 2.16, vol. 1, pp. 252–53; *Livre des exemples*, pp. 396–97.

22. Ibn Khaldūn, *Muqaddima*, 3.29, vol. 1, p. 394, 5–7; *Livre des exemples*, p. 515.

23. Alfred Morabia, *Le Gihād dans l'islam médiéval: Le "combat sacré" des origines au XIIᵉ siècle* (Paris: Albin Michel, 1993).

24. Maulana Muhammad Ali, *A Manual of Hadith*, 3rd ed. (London: Curzon Press, 1978), chap. 19, pp. 252–65.

25. Ibn Khaldūn, *Muqaddima*, 3.35, vol. 2, pp. 65–66; *Livre des exemples*, p. 589.

26. Ibn Khaldūn, *Muqaddima*, 3.29, vol. 1, p. 408, 3; *Livre des exemples*, p. 526.

27. Ibn Khaldūn, *Muqaddima*, 3.35, vol. 2, p. 72, 6; *Livre des exemples*, pp. 594–95.

28. Qur'an 3:83. See the French translation by Régis Blachère, *Le Coran*, 3 vols. (Paris: Maisonneuve, 1947), no. 99, p. 878. On this passage, see also Rudi Paret, *Der Koran: Kommentar und Konkordanz* (Stuttgart: Kohlhammer, 1989), 74. See also *Le Coran*, Blachère trans., 13:15, no. 92, p. 709; 41:11, no. 72, p. 361.

29. Ibn Khaldūn, *Muqaddima*, 3.31, vol. 1, p. 422, quoted from Rosenthal trans., 1:480; see also *Livre des exemples*, p. 537.

30. Ibn Khaldūn, *Muqqaddima*, 3.32, vol. 2, pp. 36–37, and 4.6, vol. 2, pp. 226–27; *Livre des exemples*, pp. 566, 722–23.

31. See Alain Ducellier, *Les Byzantins: Histoire et culture* (Paris: Seuil, 1988), 124, 130.

32. Ibn Khaldūn, *Muqaddima*, 3.24, vol. 1, p. 354, 8, where he says that the convocation of Islam is "general" (ʿāmma); *Livre des exemples*, p. 480, which uses "universal."

33. Ibn Khaldūn, *Muqaddima*, 1.1, vol. 1, p. 72, 17–19; *Livre des exemples*, p. 246. In a contrary sense, see Jehuda Halevi, *The Book of Refutation and Proof of the Despised Faith: The Book of the Khazars (Known as the Kuzari)* (in Hebrew), ed. David Hartwig Baneth and Haggai Ben-Shammai (Jerusalem: Magnes, 1977), 1, par. 97, p. 32, 2; translated into French by Charles Touati as *Le Kuzari, apologie de la religion méprisée* (Louvain: Peeters, 1994), 30; translated into English by Hartwig Hirschfeld as *The Kuzari (Kitab al Khazari): An Argument for the Faith of Israel* (1905; repr., New York: Schocken, 1964). See also Maimonides, *Guide for the Perplexed* (in Arabic), ed. Issachar Joël (Jerusalem: Junovitch, 1929), 3.29, p. 375, 20–21; translated into French by Salomon Munk as *Guide des égarés*, 3 vols. (Paris, 1856–66; repr., Paris: Maisonneuve, 1970), 1:221.

34. See *An Arab Philosophy of History: Selections from the Prolegomena of Ibn Khaldūn of Tunis (1332–1406)*, trans. and arranged by Charles Issawi (1950; repr., London: John Murray, 1969), 136n1.

35. See *Urdū Encyclopaedia of Islām*, s.v. "al-ʿamma wa-ʾl-khassah," 4:1098a–1100a (Muhammad Abdul Jabbar Beg).

36. See Fred McGraw Donner, *The Early Islamic Conquests* (Princeton, NJ: Princeton University Press, 1981), 267–71.

37. Ibn Khaldūn, *Muqaddima*, 3.31, vol. 1, p. 419, 2–4, quoted from Rosenthal trans., 1:477; *Livre des exemples*, p. 535.

38. Annemarie Schimmel, *Und Muhammad is sein Prophet: Die Verehrung des Propheten in der islamischen Prömmigkeit* (Munich: Diederichs, 1989), 55; quoted from Schimmel, *And Muhammad Is His Messenger: The Veneration of the Prophet in Islamic Piety* (Chapel Hill: University of North Carolina Press, 1985), 72.

39. Ibn Khaldūn, *Muqaddima*, 6.33, vol. 3, p. 245, 3; *Livre des exemples*, p. 1062.

40. See the references to a Syriac code in Patricia Crone and Michael Cook, *Hagarism: The Making of the Islamic World* (Cambridge: Cambridge University Press, 1977), 180n18.

41. Did Ibn Khaldūn have direct knowledge of the text of the Gospels? Or was he relying on an intermediary text? Direct knowledge is not to be excluded absolutely, but it does not seem likely.

42. For references, see Sarah Stroumsa, "Avicenna's Philosophical Stories: Aristotle's Poetics Reinterpreted," *Arabica* 39 (1992): 183–206, esp. 198–99.

Chapter 8

1. Alfred Morabia, *Le Gihâd dans l'islam médiéval: Le "combat sacré" des origines au XIIᵉ siècle* (Paris: Albin Michel, 1993), 106, 321 (on Farabi), 312 (on the Brethren of Purity).

2. Joel L. Kraemer, "The Jihâd of the Falāsifa," *Jerusalem Studies in Arabic and Islam* 10 (1987): 288–324.

3. Jehuda Halevi, *The Book of Refutation and Proof of the Despised Faith: The Book of the Khazars (Known as the Kuzari)* (in Hebrew), ed. David Hartwig Baneth and Haggai Ben-Shammai (Jerusalem: Magnes, 1977), 1, par. 3, p. 6, 9–10; translated into French by Charles Touati as *Le Kuzari, apologie de la religion méprisée* (Louvain: Peeters, 1994), 5; quoted from the English translation by Hartwig Hirschfeld, *The Kuzari (Kitab al Khazari): An Argument for the Faith of Israel* (1905; repr., New York: Schocken, 1964), 39. For the classic commentaries in Hebrew (Moscato, Zamocz), see, ad loc, *Sefer ha-Kuzari*, trans. Ibn Tibbon, ed. Isaac Goldman (Warsaw, 1872), 1:43.

4. Averroes, *Tahafot al-tahafot: Incohérence de l'incohérence*, 17.17, ed. Maurice Bouyges (1930; repr., Beirut: Dar el-Machreq, 1987), p. 527, 11; translated into English by Simon van den Bergh as *Tahafut al-tahafut (The Incoherence of the Incoherence)*, 2 vols. (London: Luzac, 1961), 322.

5. See Dominique Urvoy, *Averroès: Les ambitions d'un intellectuel musulman* (Paris: Flammarion, 1998), 146.

6. Karl Popper, *The Open Society and Its Enemies*, 2 vols. (1945; repr., Princeton, NJ: Princeton University Press, 1971); translated into French by Jacqueline Bernard and Philippe Monod as *La société ouverte et ses ennemis* (Paris: Seuil, 1979).

7. On Farabi's conception of war, see Charles E. Butterworth, "Al Farabi's Statecraft: War and the Well-Ordered Regime," in *Cross, Crescent, and Sword: The Justification and Limitation of War in Western and Islamic Tradition*, ed. James Turner Johnson and John Kelsay (New York: Greenwood Press, 1990), 79–100.

8. Farabi, *Fusūl muntaz͑ah*, ed. Fawzi Mitri Najjar (Beirut: Dar el-Machreq, 1971), par. 59, p. 66; par. 79, p. 85.

9. Farabi, *Kitāb al-Milla wa nasus ujrā*, ed. Muhsin Mahdi (Beirut: Dar el-Machreq, 1971), par. 7, p. 48, 10.

10. Farabi, *Fusūl muntaz͑ah*, par. 67, pp. 76–77.

11. Farabi, *Al-Farabi on the Perfect State: Abu Nasr al-Farabi's Mabadi ara ahi al-madina al-fadila*, trans. Richard Walzer (Oxford: Clarendon Press, 1985), 6.18, pars. 1–3, pp. 286–90.

12. Thérèse-Anne Druart, "Le sommaire du livre des 'Lois' de Platon . . . par Abu Nasr al-Farabi: Édition critique et introduction," *Bulletin d'Études orientales* 50 (1998): 109–55, esp. 126.

13. Farabi, *Kitāb Tahsīl as-Sa͑āda*, in *A͑mal al-Falsafiyya*, par. 47, p. 168, 3–5, ed. Ja͑far Al Yasin (Beirut: Dar al-Manahil, 1992), 1:119–97; translated into English by Muhsin Mahdi as *The Attainment of Happiness*, in Mahdi, *Alfarabi's Philosophy of Plato and Aristotle*, rev. ed. (Ithaca, NY: Cornell University Press, 1969), 13–50, esp. 36.

14. Farabi, *Kitāb Tahsīl as-Sa͑āda*, p. 168, 7–8; Mahdi trans., 36. The idea recalls to mind Plato's *Republic*, but it also prefigures the concept of "priest" (*prêtre*) in Condorcet, *Esquisse d'un tableau historique des progrès de l'esprit humain* (1794).

15. Farabi, *Kitāb Tahsīl as-Sa͑āda*, par. 48, p. 170, 2; for Mahdi's reading, see his translation, 37.

16. Ibid., p. 170, 45; Mahdi trans., 37.

17. Ibid., par. 52, pp. 176–77; Mahdi trans., 40–41. Kraemer uses the adjective "totalitarian": "The Jihād of the Falāsifa," 304.

18. Qur'an 2:256. On the interpretation of this passage, see Rudi Paret, "Sure 2, 256: lā ikrāha fī d-dīni: Toleranz oder Resignation?" *Der Islam* 45 (1969): 299–300.

19. Avicenna, *Al-Shifa Al-llahiyyat (1) (La Métaphysique)*, 10.5, ed. Georges C. Anawati and Sa'id Zayed (Cairo: Organisation générale des imprimeries gouvernementales, 1960), p. 453, 2–454, 1; translated into English by Nichael E. Marmura as "Healing: Metaphysics X," in *Medieval Political Philosophy: A Sourcebook*, ed. Ralph Lerner and Muhsin Mahdi, 2nd ed. (Ithaca, NY: Cornell University Press, 1972), 108–9; the French translation by Georges C. Anawati, *La métaphysique du Shifā Avicenne* (Paris: Vrin, 1985), is difficult to understand.

20. Avicenna, *Al-Shifa*, 10.5, p. 453, 2–5.

21. Ibid., p. 453, 6–9.

22. Ibid., p. 453, 10–14.

23. Ibid., p. 453, 17, 19.

24. Ibid., 10.4, p. 450, 16; p. 447, 5.

25. Bahmanyār ibn al-Marzubān, *Al-Tahsīl*, 3.11.4, par. 12, ed. Murtaza Mutahhari (Tehran: Dāneshgah, 1975), 817; quoted in James W. Morris, "The Philosopher-Prophet in Avicenna's Political Philosophy," in *The Political Aspects of Islamic Philosophy: Essays in*

Honor of Muhsin S. Mahdi, ed. Charles E. Butterworth (Cambridge, MA: Harvard University Press, 1992), 152–98, esp. 185–86.

26. See Morabia, *Le Gihād dans l'islam*, 237–38; for Ibn Taymiyya, see ibid., 246. For a similar position on the problem, see, for example, Thomas Aquinas, *Summa theologica*, 2a, 2ae, q. 10.

27. Ibn Rushd (Averroes), *The Distinguished Jurist's Primer*, vol. 1, *Bidāyat al-Mujtahid wa Nihāyat al-Muqtasid*, trans. Imran Ahsan Khan Nyazee, translation reviewed by Muhammad Abdul Rauf (Reading, UK: Garnet, 1994), chap. 10, "The Book of Jihād," 454–87. See also *Jihād in Medieval and Modern Islam: The Chapter on Jihād from Averroes' Legal Handbook Bidāyat al-Mujtahid . . .* , ed. Rudolph Peter (Leiden: Brill: 1977), 9–25.

28. See Morabia, *Le Gihād dans l'islam*, 297.

29. See Josep Puig, "Material on Averroes' Circle," *Journal of Near Eastern Studies* 51 (1992): 257.

30. See Henri Bergson, *Mélanges*, ed. André Robinet (Paris: Presses Universitaires de France, 1972), esp. 1246–48, 1259–61, 1288–90.

31. Averroes, *Aristotelis Stagyritae Ethicor[um] lib. X . . .* , 5 (10, 1137b), Juntine edition (Venice, 1552), vol. 3, fol. 39b; in Hebrew in *Averroes' Middle Commentary on Aristotle's Nicomachean Ethics in the Hebrew Version of Samuel ben Judah*, critical edition by Lawrence V. Berman (Jerusalem: ha-Akademyah ha-leʾumit ha-Yisreʾelit le-madaʾim, 1999), book 5, 527–32, pp. 199–200.

32. Aristotle, *Nicomachean Ethics*, 5.10 (14), 1137b 27–29; in Arabic as Aristū, *al-Akhlaq*, ed. ʿAbd al-Rahman Badawi (Kuwait: Wakalat al-Matbuʿat, 1979), p. 203, 16–18. The Greek word *psephisma* is rendered quite exactly by the Arabic *isdār marsūmin khāssin*, "promulgation of a particular regulation."

33. Averroes, *On Plato's Republic*, ed. and trans. Ralph Lerner (Ithaca, NY: Cornell University Press, 1974).

34. Averroes, *Commentary on Plato's "Republic,"* 1.7–8, ed. and trans. E. I. J. Rosenthal (Cambridge: Cambridge University Press, 1969), pp. 25–27 / 118.

35. Ibid., 1.7.11, p. 26, 14–18; quotation, p. 118.

36. Qurʾan 2:154; 3:146, 167, 169, etc.

37. See Averroes, *Commentary on Plato's "Republic,"* 1.7.9, Rosenthal trans., p. 26, 9; 2.3.1, p. 63, 1. On the same topic, see Shlomo Pines, "On the Political Theories of Averroes" (in Hebrew), in *Ben mahashevet Yisrael le-mahashevet ha-ʿamim: Mehkarim be-toldot ha-filosofyah ha-yehudit*, Studies in the History of Jewish Philosophy: The Transmission of Texts and Ideas (Jerusalem: Mosad Bialik, 1977), 91–92.

38. Averroes, *Commentary on Plato's "Republic,"* 1.7.10, Rosenthal trans., p. 26, 14–15.

39. Ibid., 1.28.3–29.3, p. 60 / 173–75.

40. See Morabia, *Le Gihād dans l'islam*, 18–19.

41. See Maxime Rodinson, *Mahomet* (1961; repr., Paris: Seuil, 1994), 226; translated into English by Anne Carter as *Mohammed* (New York: Penguin, 1983).

42. See Maimonides, *Guide for the Perplexed* (in Arabic), ed. Issachar Joël (Jerusalem: Junovitch, 1929), 1.31, p. 44, 29–45, 16; translated into French by Salomon Munk as *Guide des égarés*, 3 vols. (Paris, 1856–66; repr., Paris: Maisonneuve, 1970), 1:107–9. On this topic, see Rémi Brague, *"Eorum praeclara ingenia:* Conscience de la nouveauté et prétention à la continuité chez Farabi et Maïmonide," in *Études de philosophie arabe*, Acts of a Colloquy, Bordeaux, June 17–19, 1994, *Bulletin d'études orientales* 48 (1996): 87–102, esp. 97–98.

43. Aristotle *Politics* 7.14.1333b 38–1334a 2. In his commentary on this passage, Thomas Aquinas raises no objections: see Thomas Aquinas, *Commentarii in octo libros Politicorum Aristotelis expositio*, 7.11, par. 1214, ed. Raimondo M. Spiazzi (Turin: Marietti, 1966), 393a.

44. See Rémi Brague, "Note sur la traduction arabe de la *Politique* d'Aristote: Derechef, qu'elle n'existe pas," in *Aristote politique: Études sur la Politique d'Aristote*, ed. Pierre Aubenque (Paris: Presses Universitaires de France, 1993), 423–33.

45. Butterworth, "Al-Farabi's Statecraft," 84, 92ff., 100n47.

46. Morabia, *Le Gihād dans l'islam*, 175.

47. Averroes, *Grand Commentaire de la Métaphysique (Tafsir Ma ba'd at-tabi'at)*, 3.C 3, e, ed. Maurice Bouyges, 2nd ed., 3 vols. in 4 pts. (Beirut: Dar el-Machreq, 1973), 1:313.

48. See Morabia, *Le Gihād dans l'islam*, 297.

49. See, for example, Farabi, *Kitab al-siyasah al-madaniyah*, ed. Fawzi Mitri Najjar (Beirut: Dar el-Machreq, 1964), 87.

50. Avicenna, *Al-Shifa*, 1.8, p. 53, 13–15. See ad loc, R. E. Houser, "Let Them Suffer into the Truth: Avicenna's Remedy for Those Denying the Axioms of Thought," *Journal of the American Catholic Philosophical Association* 73 (1999): 107–33. The passage is quoted in Duns Scotus, *Lectura* 1, d. 39, q. 1–15, n. 40, in his *Opera Omnia*, 20 vols. (Vatican City: Typis Polyglottis Vaticanis, 1950), 17:49. See also John Duns Scotus, *Ordinatio*, appendix A, 1, in *Opera*, 6:415. My thanks to Professor Rolf Schönberger for this reference.

51. Averroes, *Commentary on Plato's "Republic,"* 1.17.8, 2.17.3; Rosenthal trans., p. 38, 16–17; p. 78, 26.

52. See Leo Strauss, "The Law of Reason in the *Kuzari*" (1943), in *Persecution and the Art of Writing* (1952; repr., Chicago: University of Chicago Press, 1988), 117.

Chapter 9

1. I am returning here to ideas in Rémi Brague, *Europe, la voie romaine*, 3rd ed. (Paris: Gallimard, 1999), 138–41; translated into English by Samuel Lester as *Eccentric Culture: A Theory of Western Civilization* (South Bend, IN: St. Augustine's Press, 2002).

2. Aristotle *De anima* 2.7.418b 6–7.

3. See Bernard of Clairvaux, "De Adventu Domini Sermo III" (Sermon on Advent, 3), in his *Opera*, ed. Jean Le Clercq et al., 9 vols. (Rome: Editiones Cistercienses, 1957–77), 4:179; *Patrologiae cursus completus . . . Series Latina* (hereafter *PL*), ed. Jacques-Paul Migne and Adalberto Hamman (Paris, 1844–64), 183:46b–c; and Rémi Brague, ed., *Saint Bernard et la Philosophie* (Paris: Presses Universitaires de France, 1993), 147–48.

4. Günter Grass, *Der Butt: Roman* (Darmstadt: Luchterhand, 1985), 510; quoted from *The Flounder*, trans. Ralph Manheim (New York: Harcourt Brace Jovanovich, 1978), 503.

5. See "The Instruction of Amen-em-Opet," 1, in *Ancient Near Eastern Texts Relating to the Old Testament*, ed. James B. Pritchard, 2nd ed., corr. (Princeton, NJ: Princeton University Press, 1955), 421b. On the Bible, see Maimonides, *Guide for the Perplexed* (in Arabic), ed. Issachar Joël (Jerusalem: Junovitch, 1929), 1.30, p. 43, 3–8; translated into French by Salomon Munk as *Guide des égarés*, 3 vols. (Paris, 1856–66; repr., Paris: Maisonneuve, 1970), 1:101.

6. Michel de Montaigne, "Du pédantisme," in his *Essais*, 1.25, ed. Pierre Villey, 3 vols. (Paris: Alcan, 1930–31), 1:266. The image of digestion is on 261. Montaigne is quoted here from *Complete Essays*, trans. Donald M. Frame (Stanford, CA: Stanford University Press, 1958), 103.

7. Friedrich Nietzsche, *Vom Nutzen und Nachteil der Historie für das Leben*, in *Sämliche Werke: Kritische Studienausgabe*, ed. Giorgio Colli and Mazzino Montinari, 15 vols. (Munich: Deutscher Taschenbuch Verlag; New York: de Gruyter, 1988), 1:251.

8. Friedrich Nietzsche, fragment, Spring–Autumn 1881, 11 [141], in *Sämliche Werke*, 9:494. Unfortunately, there is no article on "Einverleibung" in the *Historisches Wörterbuch der Philosophie*, 12 vols. (Basel: Schwabe, 1971–). On Nietzsche, see Martin Heidegger,

Nietzsche, 2 vols. (Pfullingen: Neske, 1961), 1:331–32; and Didier Franck, *Nietzsche et l'ombre de Dieu* (Paris: Presses Universitaires de France, 1998).

9. Friedrich Nietzsche, *Jenseits von Gut und Böse*, 1, par. 23, in *Sämliche Werke*, 5:168; translated into English by Walter Kaufmann as *Beyond Good and Evil: Prelude to a Philosophy of the Future* (1966; repr., New York: Vintage, 1989).

10. Augustine *De Trinitate* 12.14.23; in Bibliothèque Augustinienne, *Oeuvres de saint Augustin* (Paris: Desclée de Brouwer, 1936–), 16:256. See *On the Trinity: De Trinitate Libri XV*, trans. Arthur West Haddan, rev. and annotated by William G. T. Shedd (New York, 1887).

11. Paul Valéry, "Littérature," in his *Tel Quel, II: Autres rhumbs*, in *Oeuvres*, ed. Jean Hytier, 2 vols. (Paris: Gallimard, 1960), 2:677.

12. Kurt Flasch, *Einfürung in die Philosophie des Mittelalters* (Darmstadt: Wissenschftliche Buchgesellschaft, 1987), 2–3.

13. See, for example, *Sefer Moreh Nevukhim le-ha-rav ha-elohi rabbeynu Mosheh ben Maymōn ha-sefardī . . . be haʿataqat ha-rav R. Shmuel Ibn Tibbōn ʿim sheloshah peyrūshim ha-nōdaʿim u-mefūrsamin: Efōdī, Shem Tov, N. Crescas* (Warsaw, 1872), rev. ed. by Yehuda ibn Shmuel (Jerusalem: Mossad Harav Kook, 1981).

14. Pseudo-Dionysius the Areopagite, "Paraphrasis Pachymerae," Greek paraphrase of Georgios Pachymeres, in *Patrologiae cursus completus . . . Series graeca*, ed. Jacques-Paul Migne and Ferdinand Cavallera (Paris, 1866), 3:747–906.

15. See Edward William Lane, *An Arabic-English Lexicon* (Beirut: Librairie du Liban, 1968), 538b. This meaning is not listed in Reinhart Dozy, *Supplément aux dictionnaires arabes* (in Arabic), 2 vols. (Leiden, 1881; repr., Beirut: Librairie du Liban, 1968), 1:264a, which does note the meaning of the corresponding verb in a "literary" context: 262a. Moustafa Chouémi and Charles Pellat, *Dictionnaire arabe-français-anglais*, 4:2494b, give "mise au point, révision définitive (d'un brouillon), établissement (d'un texte), rédaction (d'un livre, d'un journal, etc.), formulation (d'une ordonnance, etc.)" but offer no dated example.

16. See Helmut Gätje, "Averroes als Aristoteleskommentator," *Zeitschrift der Deutschen Morgenländlischen Gesellschaft* 114 (1965): 59–65, esp. 62.

17. See Themistius, *Paraphrase de la* Métaphysique *d'Aristote (livre Lambda)*, trans. Rémi Brague (Paris: Vrin, 1999), 9–10 and n. 1.

18. See Gérard Troupeau, "Le rôle des Syriaques dans la transmission et l'exploitation du patrimoine philosophique et scientifique grec," *Arabica* 38 (1991): 1–10.

19. These texts are accessible in the convenient but unsatisfactory editions of Majid Fakhry and R. Al-ʿAjam, *Al-Mantiq ʿinda al-Farabi*, 4 vols. (Beirut: Dar el-Machreq, 1985–87). See also *Alfarabi's Commentary on Aristotle's Peri Hermeneias [De interpretatione]*, ed. William Kutsch and Stanley Marrow (Beirut: Imprimerie Catholique, 1960); translated into English by F. W. Zimmerman as *Al-Farabi's Commentary and Short Treatise on Aristotle's De Interpretatione* (London: Oxford University Press, 1981).

20. Avicenna, "Notes sur la 'Théologie d'Aristote,'" in Abd al-Rahmān Badawi, *Aristoteles apud Arabes* (in Arabic), 3rd ed. (Kuwait: Wakālat al-Marbūʾāt, 1977), 37–74; translated into French by Georges Vajda as "Les notes d'Avicenne sur la 'Théologie d'Aristote,'" *Revue Thomiste* 51 (1951): 346–406.

21. The *Commentary on the Theology of Aristotle* and the *Book of Pure Good* (*Liber de causis*) are the longest and the best known of these works.

22. I am borrowing the term "Avicennism" from Dimitri Gutas, *Avicenna and the Aristotelian Tradition: Introduction to Reading Avicenna's Philosophical Works* (Leiden: Brill, 1988), 261.

23. See the list of authors in Avicenna, *Livre des directives et des remarques (Kitab al-Isarāt wa l-tanbihāt)*, trans. Amélie-Marie Goichon (Paris: Vrin, 1951), 73ff.

24. See Henry Corbin, *La philosophie iranienne islamique aux XVIIe et XVIIIe siècles* (Paris: Buchet / Chastel, 1981), 247–50.

25. Rolf Schönberger, *Was ist Scholastik?* (Hildesheim: Bernward, 1991), 87.

26. Petri Fonsecae, *Commentariorum . . . in libros Metaphysicorum Aristotelis Stagirita*, 4 vols. (Cologne, 1615; repr., Hildesheim: Olms, 1964). The first edition of this work was published in Rome in 1577–89.

27. Silvestro Mauro, *Aristotelis opera omnia quae extant brevi paraphrase et litterae perpetuo inhaerente expositione illustrata*, ed. Franz Ehrle et al., 4 vols. (Paris: Lethielleux, 1885–86). This work was first published in Rome in 1668.

28. See Shlomo Pines, "La 'Philosophie orientale' d'Avicenne et sa polémique contre les bagdadiens" (1952), in *The Collected Works of Shlomo Pinès*, 5 vols. (Jerusalem: Magnes; Leiden: Brill, 1979–96), 3:301–33.

29. See Mauro Zonta, *La filosofia antica nel Medioevo ebraico: Le traduzioni ebraiche medievali dei testi filosofici antichi* (Brescia: Paideia, 1996), 152 and passim. See my critical review in *Bulletin de philosophie médiévale*, 2, Archives de philosophie 61 (1998): 25–27.

30. Friedrich Schlegel, fragments from *Athenäum*, par. 229, in *Kritische Ausgabe seine Werke*, ed. Ernst Benler et al., 3 vols. (Munich: Schöningh / Thomas Verlag, 1967), vol. 2, *Charakteristiken und Kritiken I (1796–1801)*, ed. Hans Eichner, 202.

31. Ibn Khaldūn, *[Muqaddima] Les Prolégomènes d'Ibn Khaldoun, texte arabe publié d'après les manucrits de la Bibliothèque impériale*, ed. Étienne Quatremère, 3 vols. (Paris: Institut de France, 1858; repr., Beirut: Librairie du Liban, 1996), 6.4, vol. 3, p. 27; quoted from the English translation by Franz Rosenthal, *The Muqaddimah: An Introduction to History*, 3 vols. (New York: Pantheon Books, 1958), 3:317–18. See also Ibn Khaldūn, *Livre des examples*, trans. Abdesselam Cheddadi (Paris: Gallimard, 2002), 1088.

32. A fundamental work in this connection is Joseph Schacht, *The Origins of Muhammadan Jurisprudence* (1950; repr., Oxford: Clarendon Press, 1975). For some highly pertinent remarks, see Patricia Crone and Michael Cook, *Hagarism: The Making of the Islamic World* (Cambridge: Cambridge University Press, 1977), 97–101.

33. On the example of Andalusia, see Dominique Urvoy, *Averroès: Les ambitions d'un intellectuel musulman* (Paris: Flammarion, 1998), 80–82; translated into English by Olivia Stewart as *Ibn Rushd, Averroes* (London: Routledge, 1991).

34. See Brague, *Europe, la voie romaine*.

35. See Harold J. Berman, *Law and Revolution: The Formation of the Western Legal Tradition* (Cambridge, MA: Harvard University Press, 1983), esp. 122.

36. See Jan Assmann, *Das kulturelle Gedächtnis: Schrift, Erinnerung und politische Identität in frühen Hochkulturen* (Munich: Beck, 1997), 289–90.

37. See A. I. Sabra, "The Andalusian Revolt against Ptolemaic Astronomy: Averroes and al-Bitrujī," in *Transformation and Tradition in the Sciences: Essays in Honor of I. Bernard Cohen*, ed. Everett Mendelsohn (Cambridge: Cambridge University Press, 1984), 133–53.

38. See Nietzsche, *Vom Nutzen und Nachteil der Historie für das Leben*, 1:251.

39. See Michel Henry, *La Barbarie* (Paris: Grasset, 1987), 58–70.

40. I owe my knowledge of this technique to Mme. Cristina Flitner (Graz), who in June 1997 presented her work to me at Eggenberg Castle.

41. See, among other works, Friedrich Nietzsche, *Zur Genealogie der Moral*, 2, par. 1, in *Sämliche Werke*, 5:291–92; translated into English by Douglas Smith as *On the Genealogy of Morals: A Polemic* (Oxford: Oxford University Press, 1996).

Chapter 10

1. See Claude Moatti, *La Raison de Rome: Naissance de l'esprit critique à la fin de la République* (Paris: Seuil, 1997), 57–95.

2. Dimitri Gutas, *Greek Thought, Arabic Culture: The Graeco-Arabic Translation Movement in Baghdad and Early ʿAbbasid Society (2nd–4th / 8th–10th Centuries)* (London: Routledge, 1998); and Cristina D'Ancona Costa, *La casa della sapienza: La trasmissione della metafisica greca e la formazione della filosofia araba* (Milan: Guerini, 1996).

3. See Gutas, *Greek Thought, Arabic Culture*, 151ff.

4. Among a good many other works, see the summary in Maurice Lombard, *L'Islam dans sa première grandeur (VIIIᵉ–XIᵉ siècle)* (Paris: Flammarion, 1971); translated into English by Joan Spencer as *The Golden Age of Islam* (New York: American Elsevier, 1975).

5. Gutas, *Greek Thought, Arabic Culture*, 36–45.

6. See ibid., 61ff. For an overall view of the controversy, see Ida Zilio-Grandi, "Le opere di controversia islamo-cristiana nella formazione della letteratura filosofica araba," in *Storia della filosofia nell'islam medievale*, ed. Cristina D'Ancona Costa, 2 vols. (Turin: Einaudi, 2005), 1:101–36.

7. See Hava Lazarus-Yafeh, *Intertwined Worlds: Medieval Islam and Bible Criticism* (Princeton, NJ: Princeton University Press, 1992).

8. See Anton Baumstark, "Das Problem eines vorislamischen christlich-kirchlichen Schrifttums in arabisher Sprache," *Islamica* 4 (1931): 562–75.

9. For an overview, see Ahmed Djebbar, *Une histoire de la science arabe: Introduction à la connaissance du patrimoine scientifique des pays d'islam*, Entretiens avec Jean Rosmorduc (Paris: Seuil, 2001). For an overall presentation in greater depth, see Roshdi Rashed, ed., *Histoire des sciences arabes*, 3 vols. (Paris: Seuil, 1997).

10. This hadith is cited in Franz Rosenthal, *Knowledge Triumphant: The Concept of Knowledge in Medieval Islam* (Leiden: Brill, 1970), 89n4; Louis Massignon, *Essai sur le lexique technique de la mystique musulmane*, 2nd ed. (Paris: Vrin, 1958), 127; translated into English by Benjamin Clark as *Essay on the Origins of the Technical Language of Islamic Mysticism* (Notre Dame, IN: Notre Dame Press, 1997). Bayhaqī says about it: "Its content (*matn*) is widespread (*mashhūr*), but its chains of transmission (*asānid*) are weak (*daʾif*)"; quoted in Ghazali, *Ihyāʾ ʿulūm al-Dīn* (Revival of the religious sciences) (in Arabic), 5 vols. (Beirut: Dar al-Kutub al-Ilmiyya, 1996), 1:15.

11. See Ignaz Goldziher, *Études sur la tradition islamique: Extraites du tome II des Muhammadanische Studien*, trans. Léon Bercher (Paris: Maisonneuve, 1952), 218.

12. *Ahbār as-Sīn wa l-Hind: Relation de la Chine et de l'Inde rédigée en 851*, ed. Jean Sauvaget (Paris: Belles Lettres, 1948), par. 72, p. 26, 4.

13. See Christoph Luxenberg, *Die syro-aramäische Lesart des Koran: Ein Beitrag zur Entschlüsselung der Koransprache* (Berlin: Das Arabische Buch, 2004); translated into English as *The Syro-Aramaic Reading of the Koran: A Contribution to the Decoding of the Language of the Koran* (Berlin: Schiler, 2007).

14. See Michel Tardieu, "Sabiens coraniques et sabiens de Harran," *Journal Asiatique* 274 (1986): 1–44.

15. Gutas, *Greek Thought, Arabic Culture*, 139.

16. See Marie-Geneviève Balty-Guesdon, "Le Bayt al-hikmah de Baghdad," *Arabica* 29 (1992): 131–50; and Gutas, *Greek Thought, Arabic Culture*, 53–60. For a presentation of this controversy, see Cecilia Martini Bonadeo, in *Storia della filosofia nell'islam medievale*, ed. D'Ancona Costa, 1:263–70.

17. Götz Schregle, *Deutsch-Arabisches Wörterbuch* (Wiesbaden: Harrasowitz, 1977), 1245a.

18. Maimonides, *Traité de logique*, translated from the Arabic by Rémi Brague (Paris: Desclée de Brouwer, 1996), 102 and note; Maimonides, *Guide for the Perplexed* (in Arabic), ed. Issachar Joël (Jerusalem: Junovitch, 1929), 3.29, p. 380, 16; translated into French by Salomon Munk as *Guide des égarés*, 3 vols. (Paris, 1856–66; repr., Paris: Maisonneuve, 1970), 1:242.

19. See D'Ancona Costa, *La casa della sapienza*, 13–31.

20. Rémi Brague, *Europe, la voie romaine*, 3rd ed. (Paris: Gallimard, 1999), 136; translated into English by Samuel Lester as *Eccentric Culture: A Theory of Western Civilization* (South Bend, IN: St. Augustine's Press, 2002).

21. Brague, *Europe, la voie romaine*, 127.

22. In Gustav von Grunebaum, *Studien zum Kulturbild und Selbstverständnis des Islams*, translated into French by Roger Stuvéras as *L'Identité culturelle de l'islam* (Paris: Gallimard, 1973), 162.

23. Razi, *Spiritual Medicine*, chap. 5, p. 42, 15–56, in *Opera philosophica*, ed. Paul Kraus (Cairo, 1939); translated into French by Rémi Brague as *La médecine spirituelle* (Paris: Garnier-Flammarion, 2003), p. 99 and n. 99.

24. Maimonides, *Guide for the Perplexed*, 2.39, p. 270, 1; Munk trans., 306. See also Maimonides, *Masekhet ʿAvodah Zarah': Im perush Mosheh ben Maimon (Maimonides' Commentar zum Tractat ʿAboda Zara)*, 4.7 (in Arabic), ed. Joseph Wiener (Berlin, 1895), 28.

25. Gutas, *Greek Thought, Arabic Culture*, 85ff.

26. Brague, *Europe, la voie romaine*, 113.

27. Bernard Lewis, *The Muslim Discovery of Europe* (1982; repr., New York: Norton, 2001); translated into French by Annick Pélissier as *Comment l'islam a découvert l'Europe* (Paris: Gallimard, 1990).

28. Jean Chardin, *Voyages de Monsieur le chevalier Chardin, en Perse, et autres lieux de l'Orient . . .* , new ed. (Amsterdam: Aux dépens de la Compagnie, 1755), vol. 3, *Description générale de la Perse*, chap. 11, p. 53.

29. Herodotus *Histories* 2.53; Plato *Critias* 113a. See Jan Assmann, *Maʾat: Gerechtigkeit und Unsterblichkeit im Alten Ägypten* (Munich: Beck, 1990), 22–23.

30. See, for example, "Theology of Aristotle" 6.53, in ʿAbd al-Rahmān Badawi, *Plotinus apud arabes: Theologia Aristotelis et fragmenta quae supersunt* (Cairo, 1955), 80.

31. See the Arabic translation of Aristotle *Poetics* 1.1447a 13 in Jaroslaus Tkatsch, *Die arabische Übersetzung der Poetik des Aristoteles und die Grundlage der Kritik des griechischen Textes* (Arabic and Latin), 2 vols. (Vienna: Holder-Pichler-Tempsky, 1928–32), 1:220; *Averroes' Middle Commentary on Aristotle's Poetics*, trans. Charles Butterworth, 2nd ed. (South Bend, IN: St. Augustine's Press, 2000), 59; and Jorge Luis Borges, "La busca de Averroes," *Sur* 17, no. 152 (June 1947): 36–45; reprinted in Borges, *El Aleph* (Buenos Aires: Losada, 1949), 93–104.

32. Gutas, *Greek Thought, Arabic Culture*, 125.

33. Farabi, *Alfarabi's Book of Letters (Kitāb al-Hurūf): Commentary on Aristotle's Metaphysics* (in Arabic), ed. and trans. Muhsin Mahdi (Beirut: Dar el-Machreq, 1969), 1.1; 36; 82; etc., pp. 61, 82, 111, etc.; "The Philosophy of Plato . . ." in Muhsin Mahdi, *Alfarabi's Philosophy of Plato and Aristotle*, rev. ed. (Ithaca, NY: Cornell University Press, 1969), 53–67.

Chapter 11

1. Among recent syntheses, see B. G. Dod, "Aristoteles Latinus," in *The Cambridge History of Later Medieval Philosophy: From the Rediscovery of Aristotle to the Disintegration of Scholasticism*, ed. Norman Kretzmann et al. (Cambridge: Cambridge University Press, 1982), 45–79; and Jean Jolivet, "The Arabic Inheritance," in *A History of Twelfth-Century Western*

Philosophy, ed. Peter Dronke (Cambridge: Cambridge University Press, 1988), 113–48. I might also note two collective works: *Traductions et traducteurs au Moyen Âge: Actes du colloque international du CNRS* . . . (Paris: Centre National de la Recherche Scientifique, 1989); and Jacqueline Hamesse and Marta Fattori, eds., *Rencontres de cultures dans la philosophie médiévale: Traductions et traducteurs de l'antiquité tardive au XVIᵉ siècle* (Louvain-la-Neuve: Cassino, 1990). See also Cristina D'Ancona Costa, ed., *Storia della filosofia nell'Islam medievale*, 2 vols. (Turin: Einaudi, 2005), 783–843.

2. See Hanna-Barbara Gerl, *Philosophie und Philologie: Leonardo Brunis Übertragung der Nikomachischen Ethik in ihren philosophischen Prämissen* (Munich: Fink, 1981).

3. See Dod, "Aristoteles Latinus," 46.

4. For this hypothesis, see J. W. Thompson, "Introduction of Arabic Science into Lorraine in the Tenth Century," *Isis* 12 (1929): 184–91, esp. 188–90. For the source, see *Monumenta Germaniae Historica, Scriptores*, ed. Georg Heinrich Pertz (Hannover: Hahn, 1826–), vol. 4 (1841), no. 33, pp. 337–77. For the legend, see Kurt Flasch, *Das philosophische Denken im Mittelalter: Von Augustin zu Machiavelli* (Stuttgart: Reclam, 1986) 165. For the facts, see Mary Catherine Welborn, "Lotharingia as a Center of Arabic and Scientific Influence in the Eleventh Century," *Isis* 156 (1931): 188–99.

5. See Pierre Riché, *Gerbert d'Aurillac, pape de l'an Mil* (Paris: Fayard, 1987), 23–27.

6. See Marie-Thérèse d'Alverny, "Avendauth?" (1954), in her *Avicenne en Occident: Recueil d'articles* . . . (Paris: Vrin, 1993), no. 8, pp. 19–43.

7. See Marie-Thérèse d'Alverny, "Les traductions à deux interprètes, d'arabe en langue vernaculaire et de langue vernaculaire en latin," in *Traductions et traducteurs au Moyen Âge*, 193–201.

8. See Dod, "Aristoteles Latinus," 52; and Jolivet, "The Arabic Inheritance," 115n9.

9. See Gad Freudenthal, "Les sciences dans les communautés juives médiévales de Provence: Leur appropriation, leur rôle," *Revue des Études Juives* 152 (1993): 29–136.

10. See Mario Zonta, *La filosofia antica nel Medioevo ebraico: Le traduzioni ebraiche medievali dei testi filosofici antichi* (Brescia: Paideia, 1996), 83–84, 114.

11. See Aristotle *Physics* 2.3.

12. Saʿid al-Andalusī, *Kitāb Tabaqāt al-Umam*, ed. H. Boualouane (Beirut: Dar al-Talīʾa li-l-tabāʿat wa-l-nashr, 1985); translated into French by Régis Blachère as *Livre des Catégories des nations* (Paris: Larose, 1935); translated into English by Semaʿan I. Salem and Alok Kumar as *Science in the Medieval World: Book of the Categories of Nations* (Austin: University of Texas Press, 1991).

13. See Shlomo Pines, "Shiʾite Terms and Conceptions in Judah Halevi's Kuzari," in *The Collected Works of Shlomo Pinès*, 5 vols. (Jerusalem: Magnes; Leiden: Brill, 1979–96), 5:265–70.

14. See Shlomo Pines, *La Liberté de philosopher: De Maïmonide à Spinoza*, French translation from Hebrew and English by Rémi Brague with the collaboration of Renée Bouveresse-Quilliot and Gérard Haddad (Paris: Desclée de Brouwer, 1997), 94.

15. Peter Abelard, *Dialogo tra un filosofo, un giudeo e un cristiano*, Italian translation by Cristina Trovò, Latin text on facing pages (Milan: Rizzoli, 1992), 730–32, p. 94.

16. See Alain de Libera, *Penser au Moyen Âge* (Paris: Seuil, 1991), 193–94.

Chapter 12

1. For a summary, see Mario Zonta, *La filosofia antica nel Medioevo ebraico: Le traduzioni ebraiche medievali dei testi filosofici antichi* (Brescia: Paideia, 1996).

2. See above, chap. 3, "Just How Is Islamic Philosophy Islamic?"

3. See Kurt Flasch, *Das philosophische Denken im Mittelalter: Von Augustin zu Machiavelli* (Stuttgart: Reclam, 1986), 202, 266.

4. See James Kritzeck, *Peter the Venerable and Islam* (Princeton, NJ: Princeton University Press, 1964).

5. Also called the "ladder of ascension" or the "golden ladder." See above, p. 5, and *Le Livre de l'échelle de Mahomet (Liber scale Machometi; He skala tou Moameth)*, trans. Gisèle Besson and Michèle Brossard-Dandré, Lettres Gothiques (Paris: Livre de Poche, 1991).

6. See Augustine, *Der Gottesstaat (De civitate Dei)*, German translation by Carl Johann Perl, 2 vols. (Paderborn: Schöningh, 1979), 8.23–26, 1:540–58; translated into English by Henry Bettenson as *Concerning the City of God against the Pagans* (London: Penguin, 2003).

7. See Flasch, *Das philosophische Denken*, 219 (on Abelard), 322 (on Albertus Magnus), 462 (on Bradwardine).

8. See ibid., 262–63, 527.

9. See ibid., 180–87.

10. Harold J. Berman, *Law and Revolution: The Formation of the Western Legal Tradition* (Cambridge, MA: Harvard University Press, 1983), 14; translated into French by Raoul Audouin as *Droit et révolution* (Aix-en-Provence: Librairie de l'Université d'Aix-en-Provence, 2002). See also Rémi Brague, *La Loi de Dieu* (Paris: Gallimard, 2005), 167–68; translated into English by Lydia G. Cochrane as *The Law of God: The Philosophical History of an Idea* (Chicago: University of Chicago Press, 2007).

11. See Rémi Brague, *Europe, la voie romaine*, 3rd ed. (Paris: Gallimard, 1999); translated into English by Samuel Lester as *Eccentric Culture: A Theory of Western Civilization* (South Bend, IN: St. Augustine's Press, 2002).

Chapter 13

1. Albert Camus, *L'Homme révolté*, in *Essais*, ed. Roger Quillot and Louis Faucon (Paris: Gallimard, 1965), 702; translated into English by Anthony Brower as *The Rebel: An Essay on Man in Revolt* (New York: Knopf, 1956). See also Camus, "La culture indigène: La nouvelle culture méditerranéenne" (1937), in *Essais*, 1321–27.

2. Flavius Josephus, *Contre Apion*, ed. Théodore Reinach, trans. Léon Blum (1930; repr., Paris: Belles Lettres, 2003).

3. See Salo Wittmayer Baron, *A Social and Religious History of the Jews*, 3 vols. (New York: Columbia University Press, 1937); translated into French by Valentin Nikiprowetzsky as *Histoire d'Israël: Vie sociale et religieuse* (Paris: Presses Universitaires de France, 1956), vol. 1, *Des origines au début de l'ère chrétienne*, 255–57.

4. See Dominique Urvoy, *Averroès: Les ambitions d'un intellectuel musulman* (Paris: Flammarion, 1998), 176–88.

5. Ibn Khaldūn, [*Muqaddima*] *Les Prolégomènes d'Ibn Khaldoun, texte arabe publié d'après les manuscrits de la Bibliothèque impériale*, ed. Étienne Quatremère, 3 vols. (Paris: Institut de France, 1858; repr., Beirut: Librairie du Liban, 1996), 6.39, vol. 3, p. 26; translated into English by Franz Rosenthal as *The Muqaddimah: An Introduction to History*, 3 vols. (New York: Pantheon Books, 1958); Ibn Khaldūn, *Livre des exemples*, trans. Abdesselam Cheddadi (Paris: Gallimard, 2002), 1079.

6. Henri Pirenne, *Mahomet et Charlemagne* (1922), in *Histoire économique de l'Occident médiéval* (Bruges: Desclée de Brouwer, 1951), 62–70; translated into English by I. E. Clegg as *Economic and Social History of Medieval Europe* (New York: Harcourt, Brace, 1956). For a dossier on the reception of Pirenne's ideas, see Paul Egon Hübinger, ed., *Bedeutung und Rolle des Islam beim Übergang vom Altertum zum Mittelalter* (Darmstadt: Wissenschaftliche Buchgesellschaft,).

7. See Maurice Lombard, *L'Islam dans sa première grandeur (VIII–XIe siècle)* (Paris: Flammarion, 1971); translated into English by Joan Spencer as *The Golden Age of Islam* (New York: American Elsevier, 1975).

8. Marcel Proust, *Le Temps retrouvé*, in *À la recherche du temps perdu*, ed. Pierre Clarac and André Ferré, 3 vols. (Paris: Gallimard, 1954), 3:870; translated into English by C. K. Scott Moncrieff as *Remembrance of Things Past*, 2 vols. (1927; repr., New York: Random House, 1934), *The Past Recaptured*, 994.

9. See Ignaz Goldziher, *Sur l'islam: Origines de la théologie musulmane* (Paris: Desclée de Brouwer, 2003), and my introduction to this work, esp. 13.

10. See Rémi Brague, *Europe, la voie romaine*, 3rd ed. (Paris: Gallimard, 1999), chaps. 4–6; translated into English by Samuel Lester as *Eccentric Culture: A Theory of Western Civilization* (South Bend, IN: St. Augustine's Press, 2002).

11. Ibn Sabʿin, *Correspondance philosophique avec l'Empereur Frédéric II de Hohenstaufen*, ed. Serefettin Yaltkaya (Paris: de Boccard, 1943), p. 45, 19ff.; p. 48, 9ff.; p. 62, 19ff.; p. 64, 7ff.; p. 71, 1ff.

12. Karl Marx, *Misère de la philosophie*, 2.1, in *Oeuvres*, ed. Maximilien Rubel (Paris: Gallimard, 1965), vol. 1, *Économie*, 89; quoted from *The Poverty of Philosophy: A Reply to M. Proudhon's Philosophy of Poverty* (1847), in *Writings of the Young Marx on Philosophy and Society*, trans. and ed. Loyd D. Eaton and Kurt H. Guddat (Garden City, NY: Doubleday, 1967), 298.

13. Braulio Justel Calabozo, *La Real Biblioteca de El Escorial y sus manuscritos arabes: Sinopsis histórico-descriptiva* (Madrid: Instituto Hispano-arabe de Cultura, 1978), *non vidi*.

Chapter 14

1. Patricia Crone and Michael Cook, *Hagarism: The Making of the Islamic World* (Cambridge: Cambridge University Press, 1977).

2. See Robert G. Hoyland, *Seeing Islam as Others Saw It: A Survey and Evaluation of Christian, Jewish and Zoroastrian Writings on Early Islam* (Princeton, NJ: Darwin Press, 1999).

3. See, for example, Yehuda D. Nevo and Judith Koren, *Crossroads to Islam: The Origin of the Arab Religion and the Arab State* (Amherst, NY: Prometheus, 2003); Edouard-Marie Gallez, *Le messie et son prophète: Aux origines de l'Islam*, 2 vols. (Versailles: Éditions de Paris, 2005); and Karl-Heinz Ohlig and Gerd R. Puin, eds., *Die dunklen Anfänge: Neue Forschungen zur Entsehung und frühen Geschichte des Islam* (Berlin: Schiler, 2006).

4. *Papyrus Erzherzog Rainer: Führer durch die Ausstellung* (Vienna, 1894), no. 558, p. 130, or Adolf Grohmann, *From the World of Arabic Papyri* (Cairo, 1952), 113–15.

5. ʿAli, quoted in Alfred Morabia, *Le Gihād dans l'islam médiéval: Le "combat sacré" des origines au XIIe siècle* (Paris: Albin Michel, 1993), 270. See also the letter of ʿUmar to Abu Obeyda, quoted in Abū Yūsuf Yaʿkub, *Livre de l'impôt foncier (Kitāb el-Kharādj)*, trans. Edmond Fagnan (Paris: Geuthner, 1921), 218; and in the texts given in Antoine Fattal, *Le statut légal des non-musulmans en pays d'Islam* (Beirut: Dar el-Machreq, 1958), 91.

6. Saʿd ibn Mansūr Ibn Kammūnah, *Ibn Kammūna's Examination of the Three Faiths: A Thirteenth-Century Essay in the Comparative Study of Religion*, ed., Moshe Perlmann (1967; repr., Berkeley: University of California Press, 1971).

7. See Hoyland, *Seeing Islam as Others Saw It*, 352–54.

8. John of Damascus, *Controverse entre un musulman et un chrétien*, in *Écrits sur l'islam*, ed. Raymond Le Coz (Paris: Cerf, 1992), 228–51.

9. On this point, see, for example, Stephan Hotz, *Mohammed und seine Lehre in der Darstellung abendländischer Autoren vom späten 11. Bis zur Mitte des 12. Jahrhunderts: Aspekte, Quellen und Tendenzen in Kontinuität und Wandel* (Frankfurt: Lang, 2002).

10. See James Kritzeck, *Peter the Venerable and Islam* (Princeton, NJ: Princeton University Press, 1964).

11. John of Damascus, *Islam*, in *Écrits sur l'islam*, 210–27.

12. See Rémi Brague, "L'eurocentrisme est-il européen?" in *La Latinité en question* (Paris: Institut des Hautes Études de l'Amérique Latine et Union Latine, 2004), 249–59, esp. 252–53. On Muslims' lack of curiosity about Europe, see Bernard Lewis, *The Muslim Discovery of Europe* (1982; repr., New York: Norton, 2001); translated into French by Annick Pélissier as *Comment l'islam a découvert l'Europe* (Paris: Gallimard, 1990).

13. See the articles of Shlomo Pines in *The Collected Works of Shlomo Pinès*, 5 vols. (Jerusalem: Magnes; Leiden: Brill, 1979–96), 4:211–486.

14. Peter Abelard, *Dialogo tra un filosofo, un giudeo e un cristiano*, Italian translation by Cristina Trovò, Latin text on facing pages (Milan: Rizzoli, 1992), 254–94, pp. 58–62; translated into English in *Peter Abelard, Collatones*, ed. and trans. John Marenbon and Giovanni Orlandi (Oxford: Clarendon Press, 2001).

15. See Brague, "L'eurocentrisme est-il européen?" 256–58.

16. Abelard, *Dialogo*, 81, p. 4; see also Jean Jolivet, *Aspects de la pensée médiévale* (Paris: Vrin, 1987), 53–61.

17. Ramon Llull, *Le Livre du gentil et des trois sages*, translated from the Catalan by Armand Llinarès (Paris: Cerf, 1993); translated into English by Anthony Bonner as *The Book of the Gentile and the Three Wise Men*, in *Selected Works of Ramon Lull*, ed. Anthony Bonner, 2 vols. (Princeton, NJ: Princeton University Press, 1985), 1:91–304.

18. Nicholas of Cusa, *De pace fidei*, in his *Philosophisch-theologische Schriften*, ed. Leo Gabriel, trans. Dietlind and Wilhelm Dupré, 3 vols. (Vienna: Herder, 1967), 3:705–97; translated into English by Jasper Hopkins as *Nicholas of Cusa's De pace fidei and Cribratio Alkorani* (Minneapolis: A. J. Banning, 1994).

19. Jean Bodin, *Colloquium heptaplomeres de rerum sublimium arcanis abditis*, ed. Ludwig Noack (Schwerin, 1857; repr., Stuttgart: Frommann, 1966); translated into English by Marion Leathers Daniels Kuntz, as *Colloquium of the Seven about Secrets of the Sublime* (Princeton, NJ: Princeton University Press, 1975).

20. Abu ʿUmar ibn Saʿdī, in the biographical dictionary of al-Jumaydī (Cairo, 1953) (*non vidi*). This discussion is cited in Lenn E. Goodman, *Jewish and Islamic Philosophy: Crosspollinations in the Classic Age* (New Brunswick, NJ: Rutgers University Press, 1999), vii.

21. Willem van Ruysbroeck, *Voyage dans l'empire mongol, 1253–1255*, trans. Claude and René Kappler (Paris: Payot, 1993), chap. 33, pp. 182-86; translated into English by Peter Jackson as *The Mission of Friar William of Rubruck: His Journey to the Court of the Great Khan Möngke, 1253–1255*, ed. Peter Jackson and David Morgan (London: Hakluyt Society, 1990).

22. See "Wikkuah Ha-RaMBaN," in *Kol Kitvey RaMBaN*, ed. Hayim Dov Shevel (Jerusalem: Mosad Rav Kook, 1963), 1:302–20; on the king's gift, see ibid., 1:320. See also Nahmanides, *La Dispute de Barcelone*, trans. Eric Smilévitch, 4th ed. (Lagrasse: Verdier, 2000), 62; translated into English by Charles B. Chavel as *The Disputation at Barcelona / Ramban* (New York: Shilo, 1983); and F. I. Baer, "Contribution to a Critical Study of the Disputations of R. Yehiel of Paris and R. Moses Nahmanides" (in Hebrew), *Tarbiz* 2, no. 2 (1931): 10.

23. See Francisa Vendrell de Millás, "La tradición de la apologetica Iuliana en el reino de Fez," *Estudios Lulianos* 1, no. 2 (1957): 371–76.

Chapter 15

1. Writing this text was much facilitated by the rich holdings and the convenience of the libraries of the University of Cologne (Thomas-Institut, Martin-Buber Institute, Seminar on Orientalism), which I was able to exploit during a sojourn there made possible by the Alexander von Humboldt Foundation, to which I express my thanks.

2. I am borrowing this example from Hans Blumenberg, *Die Genesis der kopernikanischen Welt* (1975; repr., Frankfurt: Suhrkamp, 1981), 316, 762. Blumenberg clearly perceives that the Copernican revolution was made tolerable because a renascent anthropocentrism was transposed onto an ideal base (which, incidentally, made it much more radical and demanding than the supposed medieval anthropocentrism in which man shared his central position with the other inhabitants of the earth), thus rendering its physical dimension superfluous (47, 91, 244, 325, 565). That revolution was only a particular case of the inability to reach beyond anthropocentrism under other guises (egocentrism, "we-centeredness," privileging the present over the past, etc.) (97–98, 108, 201, 272). Blumenberg also sees clearly what humbles the earth in the medieval model: the center, far from being a place of honor, is the domain of the devil (40, 312); the earth is lowly and unworthy because it is central (162, 215; see also 518), exposed to all sorts of influence (166–67); and a dregs at the bottom of the world (793). However, at times Blumenberg uses expressions that connect with the theory of the "wound to narcissism" such as "sheltered in the middle of the world" (374). See also 99 (corrected on 106). Blumenberg is available in English translation by Robert M. Wallace, *The Genesis of the Copernican World* (Cambridge, MA: MIT Press, 1987).

3. Sigmund Freud, *Eine Schwierigkeit der Psychoanalyse*, first published in *Imago* 5 (1917), in Freud, *Gesammelte Werke* (1947), 18 vols. (Frankfurt: Fischer, 1961–68), vol. 12 (1966), 1–12, esp. 7. For an analogous attempt to find precedents for the humiliation of man, see Rudolf Carnap, "Psychologie in physikalischer Sprache," *Erkenntnis* 3 (1932–33): 110; quoted in Blumenberg, *Die Genesis der kopernikanischen Welt*, 710. Freud is quoted here from *A Difficulty in the Path of Psycho-Analysis* (1917), in *The Standard Edition of the Complete Psychological Works of Sigmund Freud*, ed. James Strachey vol. 17, *An Infantile Neurosis and Other Works* (1955; repr., London: Hogarth Press, 1995), 135–44, esp. 139–40.

4. Although the work itself is somewhat disappointing, there is useful bibliography in Fernand Hallyn, *La structure poétique du monde: Copernic, Kepler* (Paris: Seuil, 1987); translated into English by Donald M. Leslie as *The Poetic Structure of the World: Copernicus and Kepler* (New York: Zone, 1990). According to Marjorie Hope Nicolson, "The Copernican hypothesis disturbed man little, indeed disturbed the layman not at all," and the real novelty was not heliocentrism but the discovery of new stars: see Nicolson, *The Breaking of the Circle: Studies in the Effect of the "New Science" upon Seventeenth-Century Poetry*, rev. ed. (New York: Columbia University Press, 1960), 115. Chapter 3 of this work, "The Death of a World" (115–22), develops the thesis quoted.

5. Ernst Haeckel, *Natürliche Schöpfungsgeschichte: Gemeinverständliche wissenschaftliche Vorträge über die Entwickelungslehre* . . . (Berlin: Reimer, 1868), 5th ed. (1974), 35; translated into English by E. Ray Lankester as *The History of Creation* . . . , 2 vols. in 4 pts. (New York: Appleton, 1876). For proof of Freud's dependence on Haeckel, see Paul-Laurent Assouin, *Introduction à l'épistémologie freudienne* (Paris: Payot, 1981), 197ff. I owe this reference to Assouin to the kindness of Professor Yvon Brès.

6. Bernard le Bovier de Fontenelle, *Entretiens sur la pluralité des mondes*, critical ed., ed. Alexandre Calame (Paris: Didier, 1966), "Première soirée," 28–30; quoted from Fontenelle, *Conversations on the Plurality of Worlds*, trans. H. A. Hargreaves (Berkeley: University of California Press, 1990), 15–17.

7. Giacomo Leopardi, *Operette morali*, ed. Paolo Ruffilli, 6th ed. (Milan: Garzanti, 1992), 284; quoted from *Operette morali: Essays and Dialogues*, trans. Giovanni Cecchetti (Berkeley: University of California Press, 1982), 433–35.

8. Carnap, "Psychologie in physikalischer Sprache," 110.

9. These are, in chronological order: Arthur O. Lovejoy, *The Great Chain of Being: A Study of the History of an Idea* (1933; repr., Cambridge, MA: Harvard University Press, 1950), 101–8, 344–45n4–14; E. M. W. Tillyard, *The Elizabethan World Picture* (1943; repr., London: Penguin, 1972); C. S. Lewis, *English Literature in the Sixteenth Century Excluding Drama* (Oxford: Clarendon Press, 1954), esp. 2–3; Nicolson, *Breaking of the Circle*; C. S. Lewis, *The Discarded Image: An Introduction to Medieval and Renaissance Literature* (Cambridge: Cambridge University Press, 1964), esp. 55, 58, 62–63; Paolo Rossi, "Nobility of Man and Plurality of Worlds," in *Science, Medicine and Society in the Renaissance: Essays to Honor Walter Pagel*, ed. Allen G. Debus, 4 vols. (New York: Science History Publications, 1972), 2:131–62, an essay that owes much to Lovejoy.

10. Friedrich Hölderlin, *Hyperions Schicksalslied*, in his *Sämtliche Werke*, ed. Friedrich Beissner, 6 vols. (Stuttgart: Cotta, 1946), 1:265.

11. Seneca, *De otio*, 5.4, ed. René Waltz (Paris: Hachette, 1909), 117, quoted from "De otio" in Seneca, *Moral Essays*, trans. John W. Basore, Loeb Classical Library, 3 vols. (London: William Heinemann; New York: G. P. Putnam's Sons, 1932), 2:191. It seems to me that Blumenberg gives this text an exaggerated importance as a representative of Stoicism in general: see Blumenberg, *Die Genesis der kopernikanischen Welt*, quotation p. 27, allusions pp. 106, 208, 234, 433, 647, 728. See also Hans Blumenberg, *Die Legitimität der Neuzeit* (Frankfurt am Main: Suhrkamp, 1988), 300, 324; in English translation by Robert M. Wallace as *The Legitimacy of the Modern Age* (Cambridge, MA: MIT Press, 1983). Germaine Aujac, "Stoïcisme et hypothèse géocentrique," *Aufstieg und Niedergang der römanischen Welt* 2, 36-1 (1989): 1430—53, presents an overall summary of Stoic doctrine. Aujac shows how important it was for the Stoics that cosmology be founded on a rational order rather than chance. She says little about the importance (or lack of it) of the central position of the earth.

12. Rabbénu Saʿadia ben Yoseph Fayyumī, *Sefer ha-nibkhar be-emunot ve-deʿot*, Arabic original and Hebrew translation by Joseph Qāfih (Jerusalem: Sura, n.d.), 4th treatise, introduction, 150–51; quoted from Saadia Gaon, *The Book of Beliefs and Opinions*, trans. Samuel Rosenblatt (New Haven, CT: Yale University Press, 1948), 180–81.

13. See the references given in Henry Malter, *Saadia Gaon: His Life and Works* (Philadelphia: Jewish Publication Society of America, 1921), 212–13n485. This rich note, however, refers in particular to the question of whether man is the summit and aim of creation, rather than the angels or the celestial bodies, hence the argument of the centrality of the earth is marginal to it.

14. Ibn Ezra, *Perushey Hatorah*, ed. Arthur Weiser, 3 vols. (Jerusalem: Mosad Rav Kook, 1976), preface to Genesis, vol. 1, pp. 7–8; on Genesis 1:1, vol. 1, p. 12; on Exodus 23:25, vol. 2, p. 164; translated into English by H. Norman Strickman and Arthur M. Silver as *Ibn Ezra's Commentary on the Pentateuch* (New York: Menorah, 1968–).

15. Ibn Ezra, *Perushey Hatorah*, p. 156, 27–30; p. 156, 11–157, 27; citation 157, 11–15.

16. The principle on which Saadia bases his argument, according to which the content is of greater value than the container, is diametrically opposed to another and more widespread principle that grants greater value to what surrounds than to what is surrounded. See Aristotle *De caelo* 2.13.293b 13–14; and Servius, *Commentary on the Aeneid*, 1.381, in *Stoicorum Veterum Fragmenta*, ed. Hans von Arnim, 4 vols. (Leipzig: Teubner, 1903–24), vol. 2, p. 559; henceforth abbreviated as *SVF*.

17. See G. E. R. Lloyd, "Greek Cosmologies," in *Ancient Cosmologies*, ed. Carmen Blacker and Michael Loewe (London: Allen and Unwin, 1975), 198–224, esp. 205.

18. See Charles-Victor Langlois, *La Connaissance de la nature et du monde au Moyen Âge d'après quelques écrits français à l'usage des laïcs* (Paris: Hachette, 1911), esp. 78, 155, 349.

19. Aristotle *De caelo* 2.13.293a–b.

20. Themistius, *Themistii in libros Aristotelis De Caelo paraphrasis* (in Hebrew) 2.13.293b 6, in *Commentaria in Aristotelem Graeca* (Berlin: Reimer, 1882–1907), vol. 5, pt. 4 (1902), p. 83, 11–13 (for the Hebrew), p. 124, 23–26 (for the Latin).

21. Simplicius, in *Commentaria in Aristotelem Graeca*, vol. 7 (1894), p. 514, 13–18; quoted from Simplicius, *On Aristotle's "On the Heavens 2.1–9,"* trans. Ian Mueller (Ithaca, NY: Cornell University Press, 2004), 54.

22. See, for example, *Rasā'il Ikhwān al-Safā'*, ed. Butrus al-Bustanī, 4 vols. (Beirut: Dar Sadir, 1983), 2.2 (16), vol. 2, p. 30; Averroes, *Commentary on the De caelo*, 2.41, C 74, p. 148 A–G, Justine edition (1564); and Albertus Magnus, *De caelo et mundo*, 2.41, ed. Paul Hassfeld, in Albertus Magnus, *Opera Omnia* (Münster: Aschendorff, 1971), vol. 5, 1, pp. 179–81. The distinction can be found in Calcidius, *Commentary on the Timaeus*, par. C, pp. 151–52, in Jan Hendrik Waszink, *Timaeus: A Calcidio translatus commentarioque instrustus* (London: Warburg Institute, 1962), who borrows from Theon of Smyrna: *Theonis Smyrnaei philosophi platonici, Expositio rerum mathematicarum et legendum Platonem utilium*, ed. Eduard Hiller (Leipzig: Teubner, 1878), 187–88.

23. Plotinus, *Enneads*, 3.2 [47], 8, 2–7, in *Plotini Opera*, ed. Paul Henry and Hans-Rudolf Schwyzer, 3 vols. (Paris: Desclée de Brouwer, 1951–73), p. 279; quoted from *The Enneads*, trans. Stephen MacKenna, 4th ed. rev. (London: Faber, 1967), 167.

24. Macrobius, *Commentarii in Somnium Scipionis*, 1.22.4, in *Macrobius*, ed. James Willis, 2 vols. (Leipzig: Teubner, 1965), 91; quoted from *Commentary on the Dream of Scipio*, trans. William Harris Stahl (New York: Columbia University Press, 1990), 181–82. The same idea can be found in Abraham bar Hiyya Savasorda, *Hegyon han-nefesh ha-'atsumah*, ed. Geoffrey Wigoder (Jerusalem: Mosad Byalik, 1971), 3, pp. 101–2. The passage is interesting, among other reasons, because it contains the first occurrence of the Hebrew word for "center": *merkaz*.

25. Blumenberg, *Die Genesis der kopernikanischen Welt*, 40. See also Lewis, *Discarded Image*, 98–99; and Hallyn, *Structure poétique du monde*, 146.

26. Arius Didymus, in *Doxographi Graeci*, ed. Hermann Diels (Berlin: de Gruyter, 1965), 466, 14–17; also in *SVF*, vol. 2, par. 527, p. 169. The same idea can be found in *SVF*, vol. 2, par. 557 (Cleomedes).

27. Al-Biruni, *Elements of Astrology*, trans. R. Ramsay Wright (London: Luzac, 1934), 34 (*non vidi*); quoted in Seyyed Hossein Nast, *An Introduction to Islamic Cosmological Doctrines: Conceptions of Nature and Methods Used for Its Study by the Ikhwan al-Safā', al-Biruni and Ibn Sinā* (Cambridge, MA: Belknap Press of Harvard University Press, 1964), 139.

28. Pliny the Elder, *Natural History*, 2.4.5, par. 11; Rackham trans., 177.

29. William of Conches, *Elementa philosophiae*, 3; in *Patrologiae cursus completus . . . Series Latina*, ed. Jacques-Paul Migne and Adalberto Hamman (Paris, 1844–64), 90:1167 (hereafter cited as *PL*); cited in Klaus Bernath, "Thomas von Aquin und die Erde," in *Thomas von Aquin: Werke und Wirkung im Licht neurer Forschung*, ed. Albert Zimmermann and Clemens Kopp, Miscellanea Mediaevalia, 19 (Berlin: de Gruyter, 1988), 175–91; quoted from *A Dialogue on Natural Philosophy (Dragmaticon Philosophiae)*, trans. Italo Ronca and Matthew Curr (Notre Dame, IN: University of Notre Dame Press, 1997), 120, 25.

30. Proclus, *Elementatio theologica*, par. 140; quoted from *The Elements of Theology*, trans. E. R. Dodds (1933; repr., New York: Oxford University Press, 1992), 125. See also

Maximus of Tyre, *Dissertationes*, ed. Friedrich Dübner translated as *Theophrasti characteres*
. . . *Maximi Tyrii dissertationes* . . . (Paris: Firmin-Didot, 1877), 17.12, p. 70; translated into
English by Thomas Taylor as *The Dissertations of Maximus Tyrius*, 2 vols. (London, 1804).

31. Avicenna, *Notes on Aristotle, Metaphysics, Lambda*, in ʿAbd al-Rahman Badawi, *Aristu
ʿinda al-ʿArab* (in Arabic), 3rd ed. (Kuwait: Wakalat al-Matbuʿat, 1978), p. 33, 14.

32. A. M. Armstrong, in *Plotinus*, trans. A. H. Armstrong, Loeb Classical Library, 7 vols.
(Cambridge, MA: Harvard University Press, 1966–88), 3:68–69n. See also Marcus Aurelius,
The Meditations of the Emperor Marcus Aurelius, ed. and trans. A. S. L. Farquharson, 2 vols.
(Oxford: Clarendon Press, 1968), 2:595, and the texts to which the editor refers there.

33. See, for example, Calcidius, *Commentary on the Timaeus*, in Lewis, *Discarded Image*,
pp. 49–59, esp. p. 55, and par. C, p. 151, 12ff.; cited in Stephan Gersh, *Middle Platonism and
Neoplatonism: The Latin Tradition*, 2 vols. (Notre Dame, IN: University of Notre Dame
Press, 1985), 480.

34. Proclus Diadochus, in *Procli Diadochi in Platonis Timaeum Commentaria*, ed. Ernst
Diehl, 3 vols. (Leipzig: Teubner, 1903–6), par. 155, 10–12; quoted from Proclus, *Commentary
on Plato's Timaeus*, trans. Harold Tarrant (Cambridge: Cambridge University Press, 2007),
252.

35. *Rasāʾil Ikhwān al-Safāʾ*, 3.1 (32), vol. 3, pp. 187, 197; translated into German by
S. Diward as *Arabische Philosophie und Wissenschaft in der Enzyklopädie Kitāb Ihwān as-Safāʾ*,
vol. 3, *Die Lehre von Seele und Intellekt* (Wiesbaden: Harrasowitz, 1975), 65, 99.

36. Thomas Aquinas, *Commentaria in libros Aristotelis De caelo et mundo* (ca. 1272), 2.13.20,
no. 7, ed. Raimondo M. Spiazzi (Turin: Marietti, 1952), 202b.

37. Macrobius *Commentarii in Somnium Scipionis* 1.22.6, p. 92; quoted from *Commentary
on the Dream of Scipio*, 182; mentioned in Lewis, *Discarded Image*, 62–63.

38. Miskawayh, *al-Fawz al-asghar (Le Petit Livre du Salut)*, ed. S. ʿUdeymah, French
translation by Roger Arnaldez (Tunis: Maison Arabe du Livre, 1987), 100–101 (Arabic), 61
(French).

39. *Anonymous Photii*, cod. 249, in *The Pythagorean Texts of the Hellenistic Period*, ed.
Holger Thesleff (Åbo: Åbo Akademi, 1965), p. 239, pars. 11–13. The image is an ancient
one, given that it is already present in the Stoics, who speak of the earth as the "deposit"
(in the sense of "dregs") (*hypostathme*) of humidity: see *SVF*, vol. 1, par. 105. In the passage
of Diogenes Laertius in which the idea figures (7.137) the term is erroneously translated
as "base"; *Les Stoïciens*, trans. Émile Bréhier, ed. Pierre-Mazime Schuhl (Paris: Gallimard,
1962), 60. It can also be found as late as the fifteenth century, in the writings of the Spanish
Jewish philosopher Joseph Albo, *Sefer ha-ʿikarim (Book of Principles)*, 4.23, ed. Isaac Husik
(Philadelphia: Jewish Publication Society of America, 1946), 208.

40. Jedaiah b. Abraham Bedersi (1270–1340), *Behinat ha-ʿOlam*, 4.12.10, ed. Mosheh
David Frank-Kamenientsky (Vilna, 1879), 46; quoted from Bedersi, *An Investigation of
Causes Arising from the Organization of the World*, trans. Rabbi Tobias Goodman (Brooklyn:
n.p., 1951), 24.

41. Albertus Magnus *De caelo et mundo* 1.4.6, p. 16, 27–29, ed. Hassfield. Such passages
form the background of a text of Immanuel Kant's: *Das Ende alle Dinge*, in *Werke in sechs
Bänden*, ed. Wilhelm Weischedel, 6 vols. (Darmstadt: Wissenschaftliche Buchgesellschaft,
1983), 6:180n, where it is given as the theory of a "Persian wit" (unfortunately not identified by the editors), according to whom the earth provides the latrines for the entire universe. See Kant, "The End of All Things," in *Religion and Rational Theology*, trans. and ed.
Allen W. Wood and George di Giovanni (Cambridge: Cambridge University Press, 1996),
217–32, esp. 224n. There is an analogous tale in Voltaire's "Sottisier," s.v. "Mahométisme,"
in Voltaire, *Supplément aux oeuvres en prose*, in *Oeuvres complètes* (Paris), vol. 32 (1880), 515.

42. Maimonides, *Guide for the Perplexed* (in Arabic), ed. Issachar Joël (Jerusalem: Junovitch, 1929), 1.72, p. 133, 15–26; translated into French by Salomon Munk as *Guide des égarés*, 3 vols. (Paris, 1856–66; repr., Paris: Maisonneuve, 1970), 1:372; quoted from the English translation by Shlomo Pines, *The Guide of the Perplexed* (Chicago: University of Chicago Press, 1963), 192. This text was probably written in response to Saadia Gaon (on whom, see above), but whom Maimonides does not mention by name.

43. Alain de Lille, *De planctu naturae*, Prosa, 3, 108–9, in *PL*, 210:444a–b; Lewis, *Discarded Image*, 58, who also gives references.

44. Dante, *Divine Comedy, Paradiso*, canto 28, lines 49–51; quoted from *The Divine Comedy*, trans. Mark Musa, vol. 3, *Paradise*, 332. There is a similar image in Teresa of Avila, cited in Hallyn, *Structure poétique du monde*, 149.

45. The Venerable Bede, *De natura rerum*, ed. Charles W. Jones and F. Lipp, Corpus Christianorum, Series Latina, vol. 123 A (1975) (Tournai: Brepols, 1953–), par. 45, p. 228, 6–9.

46. Cicero *De natura deorum* 2.6.17; quoted from *De natura deorum*, trans. H. Rackham, Loeb Classical Library (London: William Heinemann; New York: G. P. Putnam's Sons, 1933), 141. See also Lovejoy, *Great Chain of Being*, 344n6, and the parallel texts in Cicero, *De natura deorum*, ed. Arthur Stanley Pease, 2 vols. (Cambridge, MA: Harvard University Press, 1955–58), 2:592–93.

47. Ibn Tufayl, *Hayy ben Yaqdhān*, ed. Léon Gauthier (Beirut: Imprimerie Catholique, 1936), 61; quoted from *Ibn Tufayl's Hayy ibn Yaqzān: A Philosophical Tale*, trans. Lenn Evan Goodman (New York: Twayne, 1972), 130.

48. Ibn Bājja, *Farewell Letter*, in his *Rasā'il ibn Bājjah al-llāhīyah (Opera metaphysica)* (in Arabic), ed. Majid Fakhry (Beirut: Dar an-Nahar, 1968), 121; translated by Miguel Asin Palacios, in *Al-Andalus* 8 (1943): 21ff. (text) and 53ff. (translation).

49. Bahya ibn Paquda, *Kitāb al-hidāya ilā farā'id al-qulūb* (Duties of the heart), ed. and trans. A. S. Yahuda (Leiden: Brill, 1912). See 2.6, p. 122, 20–123, 21, esp. p. 123, 17; on humility, see 6.5, no. 2, p. 266, 9; no. 5, p. 268, 1–4; 8.3, no. 18, p. 332, 8–10; translated into English by Menahem Mansoor, with Sara Arenson and Shoshana Dannhauser, as *The Book of Direction to the Duties of the Heart* (London: Routledge & Kegan Paul, 1973).

50. Abraham Maimonides, *The High Ways to Perfection*, ed. Samuel Rosenblatt, 2 vols. in 1 (New York: Columbia University Press, 1927–38), 2:63–65.

51. Bonaventure, *Collationes in Hexaëmeron*, 1.22, in his *Opera omnia* (Quaracchi: Collegii S. Bonaventurae, 1882–1902), vol. 5 (1891), p. 333a; quoted from *The Works of Bonaventure: Cardinal, Seraphic Doctor, and Saint*, trans. José de Vinck, vol. 5, *Collations on the Six Days* (Paterson, NJ: St. Anthony Guild Press, 1970), 12.

52. Meister Eckhart, Sermon 14, "Surge, illuminare Iherusalem," in his *Deutschen Werke*, ed. Josef Quint, vols. 3–5 of *Die deutschen und lateinischen Werke* (Stuttgart: Kohlhammer, 1936–), 1:233–34; quoted from "Surge illuminare Ierusalem (Is. 60:1)," trans. Frank Tobin, in *Meister Eckart Teacher and Preacher*, ed. Bernard McGinn (New York: Paulist Press, 1986), 272. See also the French translation by Alain de Libera in Eckhart, *Traités et sermons*, ed. Alain de Libera (Paris: Garnier-Flammarion, 1993), 370.

53. Eckhart, Sermon 54, in *Deutschen Werke*, 2:551–52; quoted from *Meister Eckart Teacher and Preacher*, ed. McGinn; and Sermon 14, "Surge, illuminare Ierusalem (Is. 60:1)," trans. Tobin, 272.

54. Friedrich Wilhelm Joseph von Schelling, *Philosophie der Mythologie* (1857), 2 vols. (Darmstadt: Wissenschaftliche Buchgesellschaft, 1957), 1:494; cited in Blumemberg, *Die Genesis der kopernikanischen Welt*, 95. I regret finding in an otherwise remarkable work, Kurt Flasch, *Das philosophische Denken im Mittelalter: Von Augustin zu Machiavelli* (Stutt-

gart: Reclam, 1986), 301, the idea that man's central place in the universe makes divine solicitude in his regard more plausible.

55. Michel de Montaigne, *Essais*, ed. Pierre Villey, 3 vols. (Paris: Alcan, 1930–31), 2.12, p. 239; quoted from *Complete Essays*, trans. Donald M. Frame (Stanford, CA: Stanford University Press, 1958), 330–31. The passage is discussed in Lovejoy, *Great Chain of Being*, 102; and in Lewis, *English Literature*, 3. In this connection, Montaigne does not differ from earlier authors such as Boaistuau, cited in Tillyard, *Elizabethan World Picture*, 47, 120.

56. See, for example, Heiko A. Oberman, "Reformation and Revolution: Copernicus' Discovery in an Era of Change," in *The Cultural Context of Mediaeval Learning*, ed. John Emery Murdoch and Edith Dudley Sylla (Dordrecht: Reidel, 1975), 397–435.

57. Thomas Browne, *Religio medici*, ed. W. A. Greenhill (1881; repr., London: Macmillan, 1950), 2.15, p. 123; quoted from Browne, *Religio Medici and Other Works*, ed. L. C. Martin (Oxford: Clarendon Press, 1964), 75. Browne did not believe that the earth moves: see ibid., 2.13, p. 120.

58. Nicholas of Cusa, *De docta ignorantia*, ed. Ernest Hoffmann and Raymond Klibansky (Leipzig: Meiner, 1932), 2.12; quoted from *Nicholas of Cusa On Learned Ignorance*, trans. Jasper Hopkins (Minneapolis: Banning, 1981), 117–19. See also Blumemberg, *Die Genesis der kopernikanischen Welt*, 293; and Lewis, *English Literature*, 3.

59. Philip Melanchthon, *Initia doctrinae physicae* (1549), chap. 20, "Quis est motus mundi," in *Corpus Reformatorum*, vol. 13 (1846), 216; quoted in Blumemberg, *Die Genesis der kopernikanischen Welt*, 379, 384n99.

60. Francesco Ingoli, *De situ et quiete terrae disputatio*, in Galileo Galilei, *Opere*, Edizione nationale, 20 vols. in 21 pts. (Florence: Barbèra, 1890–1909), 5:408. Ingoli may have been influenced by Cardinal Bellarmine: see Roberto Francesco Romolo, Cardinal Bellarmino, *Controversia generalis de Christo*, book 5, chap. 10, in his *Opera omnia*, ed. Justin Fèvre, 12 vols. (Paris: Vivès, 1870–74), vol. 1 (1870), 418; and Bellarmino, *Controversia generalis de purgatorio*, 2.6, in his *Opera omnia*, 3:109–12. I thank Professor William R. Shea, currently the title-holder of Galileo's chair at the University of Padua, for these references to Ingoli and Bellarmine.

61. John Wilkins, *The Discovery of a New World; or, A Discourse Tending to Prove that it is Probable There may be Another Habitable World in the Moon* (1638), in *Philosophical and Mathematical Works*, 2 vols. (1708; repr., London, 1802), 1:190; quoted from Rossi, "Nobility of Man," 137, who cites Wilkins's "To the Reader" (unnumbered pages) in the first edition (London, 1638). See also Lovejoy, *Great Chain of Being*, 102.

62. Galileo Galilei, *Dialogo dei due massimi sistemi del mondo*, quoted from *Dialogue Concerning the Two Chief World Systems—Ptolemaic and Copernican*, trans. Stillman Drake (1953; repr., Berkeley: University of California Press, 1962), 37. See also Rossi, "Nobility of Man," 137.

63. Rossi, "Nobility of Man," 137.

Chapter 16

1. Thomas Aquinas, *De unitate intellectus contra Averroistas*, 2, par. 214.

2. Louis Moréri, *Grand dictionnaire historique*; Pierre Bayle, *Dictionnaire historique*, *s.v.* Averroès, etc.

3. See Friedrich Niewöhner, *Veritas sive varietas: Lessings Toleranzparabel und das Buch von den drei Betrügern* (Heidelberg: Schneider, 1988).

4. Ernest Renan, *Averroès et l'averroïsme: Essai historique* (1852), in his *Oeuvres complètes*, ed. Henriette Psicheri, 10 vols. (Paris: Calmann-Lévy, 1947–61), vol. 3 (1949), pp. 10–365;

Léon Gauthier, *La théorie d'Ibn Roshd (Averroès) sur les rapports de la religion et de la philosophie* (Paris: Leroux, 1909; repr., Paris: Vrin, 1982).

5. Law of July 4, 2001, on the Programme d'enseignement de la philosophie en classe terminale des séries générales, *Bulletin officiel de l'Éducation nationale*, no. 28, July 12, 2001.

6. Ibn Rochd (Averroes), *Traité décisif (Façl el-maqāl) sur l'accord de la religion et de la philosophie*, ed. and trans. Léon Gauthier (Algiers, 1948; repr., Paris: Vrin, 1983); translated into English by George F. Hourani as *On the Harmony of Religions and Philosophy* (London: Luzac, 1961).

7. Averroes, *Le Livre du discours décisif*, ed. and trans. Marc Geoffroy, preface by Alain de Libera (Paris: GF-Flammarion, 1996).

8. I have high expectations for the thesis on this topic being prepared under my direction by Barbara Canova-Geoffroy.

9. The "Epistula ad amicum" is easily accessible in Manuel Alonso Alonso, *Teologia de Averroes: Estudios y documentos* (Madrid: Consejo Superior de Investigaciones Cientificas, 1947; repr., Cordova: Universidad de Córdoba, 1998), 357–65.

10. Averroes, *Livre du discours décisif*, 190n49. See Laureano Robles Carcedo, "En turno a una vieja polémica: El 'Pugio Fidei' y Tomás de Aquino," *Revista Española de Teologia* 34 (1974): 321–50; 35 (1975): 21–41 (*non vidi*).

11. Steven Harvey, *Falaquera's Epistle of the Debate: An Introduction to Jewish Philosophy* (Cambridge, MA: Harvard University Press, 1987); Elijah ben Moses Abba Delmedigo, *Sefer Behinat ha-hat* (An examination of religion) (in Hebrew), ed. Jacob Joshua Ross (Tel Aviv: Tel Aviv University, 1984).

12. Dante, *Divine Comedy*, *Inferno*, canto 4, line 131, trans. Mark Musa (Harmondsworth, UK: Penguin, 1986), 101.

13. Nicolas de Malebranche, *Recherche de la Verité*, 2.1.5, in *Oeuvres*, ed. Geneviève Rodis-Lewis, 2 vols. (Paris: Gallimard, 1979), 1:224–25.

14. See the stupefying texts cited in Étienne Gilson, *History of Christian Philosophy in the Middle Ages* (New York: Random House, 1955), 642n17. (The notes do not appear in the French edition of this work.)

15. Moses of Narbonne, *Commentary on the* De substantia orbis *of Averroes*, reprinted in the critical edition of Averroes, *De substantia orbis*, ed. Arthur Hyman (Cambridge, MA: Medieval Academy of America; Jerusalem: Israel Academy of Sciences and Humanities, 1986), 44n15.

16. Farabi, *Alfarabi's Book of Letters (Kitāb al-Hurūf): Commentary on Aristotle's Metaphysics* (in Arabic), ed. and trans. Muhsin Mahdi (Beirut: Dar el-Machreq, 1969), 2, par. 143, p. 152.

17. *Averrois Cordubensis Commentarium magnum in Aristotelis De anima libros*, 2, par. 107, ed. F. Stuart Crawford, trans. Michael Scot (Cambridge, MA: Medieval Academy of America, 1953), 298.

18. Aristotle, *De generatione animalium* (On the generation of animals), 5.1.780b 18–22. I am ashamed to admit that I cannot trace where I read the anecdote about Cremonini.

19. Thomas Aquinas *Summa theologica* 1a, q. 1, a 1; quoted from the Blackfriars translation, 1:5.

20. Averroes, *Livre du discours décisif*, par. 72, p. 170.

21. Pascal, *Pensées*, ed. Léon Brunschvicg (Paris: Hachette, 1925), no. 327, quoted from *Pascal's Pensées* (New York: E. P. Dutton, 1955), 94.

22. Averroes, *Livre du discours décisif*, 103.

23. Averroes, *Decisive Treatise and Epistle Dedicatory*, trans. Charles E. Butterworth (Provo, UT: Brigham Young University Press, 2001), xix.

24. Averroes, *Livre du discours décisif*, 65–67, 81–82.

25. Averroes, *Kashf an manāhij al-adilla fī qawāʾid al-milla*, in *Falsafat Ibn Rushd* (1910) (Beirut: Dar al-Afāq al-Jadīda, 1982), 45, 90.

26. Averroes, *On Plato's Republic*, ed. and trans. Ralph Lerner (Ithaca, NY: Cornell University Press, 1974), 1.17.8, p. 38, 16ff.

27. Ibid., 2.17, p. 78, 26–79, 1.

28. Averroes, *Tahafot*, 20, "Questions of Physics," 4, par. 2, pp. 585–86; translated into French by Marc Geoffroy as *Tahafot al-tahafot: L'incohérence de l'incohérence* in *Islam et la raison: Anthologie de textes juridiques, théologiques et polémiques*, preface by Alain de Libera, "Pour Averroès" (Paris: Garnier-Flammarion, 2000), 204, with Geoffroy's additions; quoted from the English translation by Simon van den Bergh, *Tahafut al-tahafut (The Incoherence of the Incoherence)*, 2 vols. (London: Luzac, 1961), 1:362.

29. Averroes, *Tahafot al-tahafot*, 17, "Questions of Physics," 1, par. 17, p. 527; van den Bergh translation, 1:322.

30. Averroes, *On Plato's Republic*, 1.25.9–10, p. 54, 6–13.

31. Dominique Urvoy, *Averroès: Les ambitions d'un intellectuel musulman* (Paris: Flammarion, 1998).

32. Massimo Campanini uses Gramsci's expression in his introduction to his edition of Averroes, *Il trattato decisivo: Sull'accordo della religione con la filosofia* (Milan: Rizzoli, 1994), 9.

33. See above, pp. 138–41.

34. Averroes, *On Plato's Republic*, 3.11.5, p. 92, 4–8.

35. See Urvoy, *Averroès*, 57–60.

36. Marc Geoffroy, "Ibn Rushd et la théologie almodahiste: Une version inconnue du *Kitāb al-Kasf ʿan manāhig al-adilla* dans deux manuscrits d'Islanbul," *Medioevo* 26 (2001): 327–51.

Index